ALSO BY LESLIE SAVAN

The Sponsored Life: Ads, TV, and American Culture

Slam Dunks
and
No-Brainers

Slam Dunks
and
No-Brainers

LANGUAGE IN YOUR LIFE,
THE MEDIA, BUSINESS, POLITICS,
AND, LIKE, WHATEVER

LESLIE SAVAN

ALFRED A. KNOPF   NEW YORK   2005

THIS IS A BORZOI BOOK
PUBLISHED BY ALFRED A. KNOPF

Copyright © 2005 by Leslie Savan

Portions of this book previously appeared, sometimes in
slightly different form, in *The Village Voice, Time,
New York, ArtByte, Seed,* and on the Web site *Salon.*

Owing to limitations of space, permission to reprint previously
published material may be found following the index.

www.aaknopf.com

Knopf, Borzoi Books, and the colophon are
registered trademarks of Random House, Inc.

Library of Congress Cataloging-in-Publication Data
Savan, Leslie.
Slam Dunks and No-Brainers : language in your life, the media, business,
politics, and, like, whatever / Leslie Savan.—1st ed.
p.   cm.
Includes bibliographical references and index.
ISBN 0-375-40247-0 (hard.)
1. Mass media and language—United States.   2. Mass media and
culture—United States.   3. Language and culture—United States.
4. Intercultural communication—United States.   5. Popular culture—
United States.   6. English language—Rhetoric.   7. United
States—Civilization—20th century.   I. Title.
P96.L342U557   2005
302.23'0973—dc22   2005045142

Manufactured in the United States of America
First Edition

To the guys in my life:
Sid, Dan, Boone,
and
Glenn

CONTENTS

Slam Dunks
and
No-Brainers

PROLOGUE

Are We Having Fun Yet?

A little girl, maybe five years old, approaches me in a doctor's waiting room while her mother is seeing the doctor. The girl is playing Fortune Teller, a kids' game that predicts the future with a piece of paper folded like an origami flower. Numbers are written on each petal. She asks me to choose a number, and, using her thumb and fingers, she opens and shuts the folded paper that number of times. I make more choices, until eventually she pulls back one corner, under which my fortune is written. "You're going to be a movie star," the girl tells me with certainty.

"Ah, well, if I do I'll come back and give you my autograph," I say with a chuckle, thinking that's a good-natured response to something that, however silly, I should play along with. So I'm taken aback when, instead of skipping off happily, the girl says, with steel in her voice, "Oh, I don't *think* so."

"What don't you think—that I'll be a movie star, or that I'll come back and give you my autograph?" I ask.

"You won't give me your autograph," she says.

Here was this child, wide-eyed enough to believe I'd become

a movie star, but cynical enough to be sure that once I made it big I'd forget the little people who put me there.

And this junior jadedness was expressed in a catchphrase that popped out of her mouth almost *Exorcist*-like. It's the same phrase that, many times a day for years, a tough drill sergeant in Metamucil's Marine Corps uttered confidentially to the camera, between bouts of yelling orders at his men: "When I'm out here, am I supposed to say, 'Slow down, I'm constipated'?" Pause. "I don't *think* so."

Nobody thinks so, regardless of the topic. "I'm right up there with the big dogs, girls," Elastigirl says in the opening moments of *The Incredibles*. "Leave saving the world to men? I don't *think* so."

I started to connect the dots and notice that expressions like these—not clichés exactly, but snappy turns of phrase with a tele-visual sheen—were everywhere. Whether watching TV, surfing the Web, or just eavesdropping, you could hear "I don't *think* so," "connect the dots," and dozens of other punchy locutions coming from the mouths of babes and the lips of the vice president, from train conductors and copywriters, from domestic terrorists and their potential victims.

"What was he *thinking*?" an Oklahoma City resident asked when the verdict came down in the bombing trial of Timothy McVeigh. Maybe he was thinking about what his convicted co-conspirator, Terry Nichols, had advised him in a letter before the explosion: "Go for it!"

On *The Simple Life Reunion*, Paris Hilton and Nicole Richie recounted the highs and lows of life on the farm, like the time Nicole had to shove her arm up a cow's butt to check if the animal was pregnant. Paris ran away screaming, but Nicole was reso-lute. As she explained, "You just had to, like, go for it."

Albert Einstein, after much theorizing, finally decides that Pepsi tastes better than Coke. "Duh!" responds the commercial's seven-year-old actress. Realizing how clueless he has been, Einstein smacks his forehead and says, "It's a no-brainer!"

"Duh. Do I feel stupid, or what?" said a teenage girl in New Jersey on learning that the moans from the high school bathroom stall on prom night came not from a couple having sex, as she had assumed, but from another girl giving birth (and then dumping the baby).

Elsewhere in New Jersey, a gift shop in a mall featured an ecology motif. "You think these people care about the environment?" a twenty-eight-year-old advertising copywriter shopping there snorted to a *New York Times* reporter. "Yeah, right. It's about the money, dude. Hel-lo?"

"WE FLY THE NEWEST JET FLEET. BLING-BLING," Continental Airlines bragged in a print ad. (The bling, it said, came from jets "loaded with the latest in technology, comfort and dependability.")

Sitting in a train waiting to depart New Haven for New York, I saw a conductor try to oust a homeless man sleeping on a seat. They talk, the conductor pulls at the guy's arm, but the man doesn't actually leave the train until the conductor shouts, "You're history, man!"

"You think I'm dissing you 24/7!" a young woman screamed into a pay phone on a downtown street in Manhattan.

"Everyone is working 24/7," Tom Ridge said in a press conference to introduce the new homeland security agency he was then heading up.

As Enron was beginning to implode, Ken Lay told a company gathering that there wouldn't be layoffs and that Enron would survive the storm. An employee asked the CEO, "I would like to know if you are on crack."

"No way, José," said Jesse Helms, back when he was chairman of the Senate Foreign Relations Committee, on the likelihood that he'd allow GOP moderate William Weld to become ambassador to Mexico. As usual, José didn't get his way.

But others do. As sheriff's deputies cornered ex-con Roy Ratliff in a remote California area where they believed he was going to kill the two teenage girls he had kidnapped, Ratliff waved his gun and shouted, "No way!" The deputies fired seventeen shots and killed him. Is it possible that any of the shooters could resist saying, at least to himself, "Way!"?

Tom Mauser, whose son Daniel was killed with an assault weapon at Columbine High School, tried to enter an NRA convention to persuade the speaker, Vice President Dick Cheney, to extend the federal assault weapons ban. But when Mauser reached the convention hall, security guards forced him out as some conventioneers applauded and yelled, "Get a life!"

Upon such popular catchphrases, wars are launched. According to the Bob Woodward book *Plan of Attack,* Cheney told the Saudi ambassador, Bandar bin Sultan, before the invasion of Iraq, "Prince Bandar, once we start, Saddam is toast," and the CIA director, George Tenet, assured President Bush that finding Saddam's weapons of mass destruction would be a "slam dunk."

And with such pop, people are laid to rest. A videotape from the gun camera of a fighter jet over Fallujah in April 2004 showed about twenty people, tiny and indistinct, crossing a street. The pilot asks his ground spotter, "I got numerous individuals on the road. Do you want me to take those out?"

SPOTTER: "Take 'em out."
PILOT: "Ten seconds."
SPOTTER: "Roger."
For ten seconds, we hear the pilot breathing.
PILOT: "Impact!"
The people disappear under the plume of an enormous explosion.
PILOT: "Oh, dude!"

As someone posted on the right-wing Freerepublic.com, which linked to the video, "These USAF guys, may allah be pleased with them, added the PERFECT American touch to the explosion . . . 'Ohh Duuude' . . . freakin CLASSIC!"

So many perfect American touches, though often they're less about bombs than what's da bomb.

"Mac OS X. Suddenly, other operating systems seem so 20th century," sniffed a 2002 magazine ad.

"How many times can one radio station play the same fucking Alanis Morissette song?? I mean, she isn't even popular right now," Racheloni posted on her blog in 2003. "What is the dilio yo?"

"Having fun yet?" the TV asked. "Get to the Wiz!"

"I was, like, Yesss!" a girl whooped somewhere else on TV.

"Yesss!" my babysitter would say. Though she grew up in Finland, she'd also say "momento," "crunch time," and "go for it."

"If I ever want to have an affair with a married man again, especially if he's the president," Monica said on the Linda Tripp tapes, "please shoot me."

On *Just Shoot Me!,* an NBC sitcom in perpetual reruns, David Spade wore a T-shirt that read "Whassup?!," the once wildly popular line in Budweiser ads.

"Don't go there, girlfriend!" said Dr. Evil in *Austin Powers: The Spy Who Shagged Me,* gleefully baffling 1960s government officials with his late 1990s lingo. (Dr. Evil had traveled back in time to blow up Washington, D.C.) The line got one of the movie's biggest laughs.

Star Jones, co-host of the ABC show *The View,* exhorted the first woman ever to land a space shuttle, "You go there, Colonel Eileen Collins!" Big applause.

I said to my son when he was starting to crawl, "Don't go there"—meaning the garbage can, the toilet, the oven, anywhere that was dangerous or troublesome—and I don't know anymore whether I was saying it as a simple command or saying it with attitude and a sense that I was connected to everyone else who is saying and hearing these phrases; and that maybe at the end of *Don't go there,* I too will hear, if only faintly, the sound of applause, because . . .

It's showtime!

Yo! It's the buzzphrases, stupid.

Is this a no-brainer, or what? What we need is an in-your-face, wake-up-and-smell-the-java look at why literally gazillions of us talkmeisters are talkin' the talk—big-time.

I mean, get real. These words and phrases and attitudes are eating us for breakfast. We're toast. And we're eating their dust. Or is it their shorts? Bottom line, we need to ask, What's wrong with this picture?

It's, like, you know? We're not thinking outside the box. We're on cruise control with this stuff: Interactive, proactive.

The F-word, the L-word, the other L-word. Face time, phone tag, on the same page. That's not appropriate. That's not acceptable. He's not available. Omigod!: This is your brain.

I hate when that happens.

Don't get me started. These phrases from hell are history. They are so busted. I got their number. I'll be their worst nightmare. I'll shout, "Who's your daddy?" Why? Because I can. I'm pumped! I'm amped! I'm smokin'! I'm cookin'! Yesss!

Yeah, right. As if. Puh-leeze. Ex*cuse* me? Hel-*lo*?!

Ouch. I'm not having this conversation. I'm outta here.

Hey, lighten up. Chill. Find your comfort zone. Get your groove on. The lifestyle community is about options: merch, tudes, toons. TGIF, TCBY. WMD, WWJD?

Whatever. I'm talkin' a book that, best-case scenario, takes no prisoners as it puts its ass on the line, kicks some butt, walks the walk, produces some roadkill, and gives 110 percent to explain that even though pop words rock, they, like, really suck. Oh, they sound smart, but, trust me, I'm going to step up, break 'em down, and show you they ain't called no-brainers for nothing.

You don't have to be a brain surgeon to see that too much pop is totally lame-o. But what if a rocket scientist just doesn't get it and refuses to opt out? What if he hollers, "Pop words rule!"?

No prob: I'll grab him by the lapels, jerk him around, yank his chain, bust his chops, rattle his cage, push his buttons, hang him out to dry, and let him twist slowly, slowly in the wind. Oh, he'll be one sick puppy, and he won't be a happy camper. He might even throw a hissy fit. But here's the beauty part: He'll get with the program.

"Are we having fun yet?" I'll tease him. "What part of 'no' don't you understand?" I'll taunt him. "Having a bad hair day?" I'll torment him.

And if he so much as asks for more wiggle room, I won't mince words when I tell this guy (whoever the hell he is), Here's the dilio.

CHAPTER 1

Here's the Deal

From the tough-guy *kick ass* to the airless *opt*, from the high-strung *Hel-lo?!* to the laidback *hey*, from the withering *whatever* to the triumphant *Yesss!*, an army of brave new words is occupying our social life with coast-to-coast attitude. The catchwords, phrases, inflections, and quickie concepts that Americans seem unable to communicate without have grown into a verbal kudzu, overlaying regional differences with a national (even an international) pop accent that tells us more about how we think than we think.

What makes a word a pop word? First of all, we're not talking mere clichés. Most pop phrases are indeed clichés—that is, hackneyed or trite. But a pop phrase packs more rhetorical oomph and social punch than a conventional cliché. It's the difference, say, between *It's as plain as the nose on your face* and *Duh*, between *old hat* and *so five minutes ago*. Pop is the elite corps of clichés.

Nor is the pop vocabulary simply a collection of slang. Some pop phrases, like *bling bling* or *fashionista*, may technically be slang, or "nonstandard" and probably transient English. But most pop speech today is made up of perfectly ordinary and permanent words, like *don't go there* and *hello*. It's how our tongues twist them that changes everything.

Here's my definition: Pop language is, most obviously, verbal expression that is widely popular and is part of popular culture. Beyond that, it's language that pops out of its surround; conveys more attitude than literal meaning; pulses with a sense of an invisible chorus speaking it, too; and, when properly inflected, pulls attention, and probably consensus, its way. (And if it does most of the above, it gives you a reward: a satisfying "pop.")

There have always been popular catchphrases, of course, and in the everyday jungle of small talk, they've always been used as verbal machetes, proven tools for cutting through confusion—as well as for showing off, fitting in, dishing dirt, shutting someone up, flirting, and fighting. But today, as the media repeat and glamorize buzzphrases constantly, the ability to spout a catchy word or two has become a more highly valued skill—a social equalizer, a sign that you, too, share the up-to-date American personality.

Or, to put that in pop: These phrases are our go-to guys—whether flashing bling or singing "Ka-ching!," they get the job done.

And everybody has them working. Coming off a spate of fund-raisers in 2003, George W. Bush appeared on *The Tonight Show* and joked to Leno about the audience: "These folks didn't pay five grand apiece to get in here? I'm outta here!" As John Kerry took the controls of a helicopter on a campaign hop in Iowa, he shouted, "Rock 'n' roll!" And, of course, both men said (Bush of Iraqi insurgents, Kerry of Bush's attacks on his record), "Bring 'em on!" As it turns out, AARP-eligible presidential candidates are not so far removed, ideal-American-personality-wise, from babelicious Gen X actresses, like Cameron Diaz, who told Demi Moore in *Charlie's Angels: Full Throttle*, "Bring it on, bitch!"

Light, self-conscious, and theatrical, chockful of put-downs and exaggerated inflections, today's pop talk projects a personality that has mastered the simulation of conversation. It's a sort of air guitar for the lips, seeking not so much communication as a confirmation that . . . hey, we're cool.

Human communication may seem to hold greater possibilities than that, but the first obligation of pop language is not to help us plumb life's mysteries but to establish that you recognize and can characterize any pre-characterized thing or situation. A famous person not looking up to par? Someone somewhere will say, "Bad hair day." A familiar name escapes you? "I'm having a senior moment." Did you do something dumb? "What was I *thinking*?" Producing the right phrase at the right time reassures us: I'm awake, it says. I connect.

The pop response can be punched in from Seattle to Waco, from the Laundromat to the New York Stock Exchange. Each modular phrase is part of a franchise deal, whose terms are the same everywhere. When I say "No way" and you say "Way," we may be exchanging a nod of appreciation for our mutual acquaintance with Wayne and Garth or Bill and Ted (assuming we're old enough to remember those characters), but we are also reducing each other to interchangeable parts, minor guest stars in that moment's passing sitcom.

Though pop ripples with such ironic attitude, irony is not the only attitude the language conveys. The desirable mass personality is not so one-dimensional: Sometimes it's a baseball-capped, down-to-earth regular guy, trading in *roadkill, goin' south,* and *I owe you*. At other times it's socially earnest, talking up *community, giving back, empowerment,* and, in general, its *issues*. Or its voice might suddenly turn all corporate cubicle with *bottom lines, agendas,* and *win-wins,* asking people it meets, "And *you* are?" The same person who forms an "L" with his hand and places it on his forehead to call someone "Loser" can probably, when necessary, switch-hit to a morally upright *It's the right thing to do*. These catchphrases (and occasional gestures) may play on different teams, but they all have one thing in common: the ability to be neatly snapped into place, thereby releasing a little waft of *some* attitude.

And the attitude—or, more precisely, the platitude as attitude—is emboldened by the knowledge that, if properly phrased, it will resonate with millions. Whether biting or benign, what all pop phrases have in common is the roar of a phantom crowd: They always speak of other people having spoken them. It's as if the words came with built-in applause signs and laugh tracks. And keeping us on track, they provoke in us click responses, the sort of electronic-entertainment tic we twitch and jerk with more often lately. We hear *too much information, your worst nightmare,* or (my worst nightmare) *Duh,* and we immediately sense the power structure of the moment. In fact, we may subconsciously applaud such speakers because they've hypertexted our little lives right into *Desperate Housewives, American Idol,* or whatever piece of media currently holds life's sparkle.

BRAVE NEW WORDS

Hey, lady, lighten up. It just feels good to grab the mot juste; there's a rush, a ride, and a whirl. And, OK, some pop talk is on the predictable side, but what's so wrong with knowing how someone will finish a sentence? At least it makes us feel that we know what's going on in the world.

It's true, pop can be just plain fun, and it's always supremely useful. Coinages like *yuppie, glitterati,* and *red state/blue state* help organize the world, setting up reassuring stepping stones through the raging currents of affairs. These stones may amount to little more than hardened stereotypes, but without them, how could we navigate postmodern life? The very term *road rage,* for instance, has made us more aware of the phenomenon, probably saved a few lives: Do *you* want to be a red-faced, veins-popping-out-of-your-skull road-rage warrior who kills children in order to get one car ahead on the highway? Now that road rage has a handy label, we may believe that violence on the road occurs more often than it actually does, as one study has suggested. However, *workplace rage, air rage* (angry airline passengers), *sideline rage* (uncontrollable parents or coaches at children's sports games), and *roid rage* (steroid-induced aggression) apparently really have increased. Whether a trend is smaller or larger than the coinage that describes it, it's the words themselves that are all the rage.

Pop speech is a form of entertainment that almost anyone can perform. It connects people instantly. It can keep conversations bobbing with humor and work against our taking ourselves too seriously. It's nothing if not accessible.

But while pop language is fun, useful, and free, it is so in the same way that advertising-supported media is fun, useful, and "free": It requires subtle social and political trade-offs. And so I come not to praise pop, but to ask, What do we lose and gain in the deal?

A friend of mine who rewrites movie scripts is often told to add certain phrases to "punch them up," he says. "It's like McDonald's discovered that people have three basic tastes—sweet, salty, and fat—and therefore it never has to create foods for more subtle tastes." *Yesss!* (the spoonful of sugar in so many movies) takes care of positive, overcoming-the-odds feelings, while *Hel*-lo?! covers dealing with idiots, *I don't* think *so* can stop a fool in his tracks, and so on.

This is the main trade-off: Pop's prefab repartee can serve as thought replacement. *Get over it. Not ready for prime time. It's a no-brainer.* Repeated and mentally applauded over years, pop language carves tunnels that ideas expressed otherwise are too fat to fit through. Whatever point a speaker is making, it gains acceptance not on its merits, but on how familiarly it's presented and how efficiently tongue snaps into groove. It's as if each of these phrases were itself a no-brainer.

Which leads to the questions: Does a buzz-loaded repertoire displace thinking with a pleasant buzz? Are we, in fact, talking about some kind of syllabic soma?

As the late Neil Postman wrote in his book *Amusing Ourselves to Death,* Aldous Huxley painted a more probable future in *Brave New World* than George Orwell did in *1984,* because, over the long run, pleasure is more likely than fear to produce compliant citizens. In "Huxley's vision, no Big Brother is required to deprive people of their autonomy, maturity and history," Postman wrote. "As he saw it, people will come to love their oppression, to adore the technologies that undo their capacities to think. . . . Orwell feared those who would deprive us of information. Huxley feared those who would give us so much that we would be reduced to passivity and egoism. Orwell feared that the truth would be concealed from us. Huxley feared the truth would be drowned in a sea of irrelevance."

Today, there are clearly attempts by the government and corporations to conceal truth and to insist, as Newspeak did, that War Is Peace and Ignorance Is Strength—but rarely in so many words. Such harsh notes don't jibe with our vernacular. Much more effective is the let-me-entertain-you language of the mass media; it bubbles and bops, tickles and cajoles until we come to adore it. I'm not saying that pop language is a tranquilizing drug with totalitarian side effects, like Huxley's soma. In its ability to break through obfuscation, which it does every day, pop can be a powerful force for truth. But in its ability to divert thought and numb our imaginations with commercial confetti, pop can also be a force that drowns the truth in "a sea of irrelevance."

WAY/NO WAY

The pleasure of pop derives from our intimate, id-ridden relationship with media and marketing. The continual flow between the way "real people" talk and a mass media that mines their speech in order to better sell things (products, arguments, "personalities") creates commercial-flavored norms that real people then absorb. Pop language both reflects and shapes those norms, with all their unspoken values and expectations.

That's what this book is about. What it's not about is collecting gaffes or other evidence for the grammar police (there's an overworked phrase). And while I will occasionally cover word origins and first-recorded uses, this book is not really about them either.

And jargon? Get outta here. Unlike the jargon that binds relatively small groups (be they skateboarders or day traders, instant-message junkies or ink-stained wretches), true pop pops for everyone, regardless of age, race, class, region, or occupation.

Pop lingo is usually stereotyped as the domain of media-savvy adolescents, Gen Xers, and Boomers, but pop permeates us all. Militia men, gangsta rappers, soccer moms, and all of their children traffic in *Yeah, right, Not even close,* and *You just don't get it.* Even a low hipness level is no longer a barrier. In spots for the U.S. Mint, a very downtown George Washington was out hawking the golden dollars with the refrain that "It's so money." *Suck* has global reach. *Cool* is simply galactic.

By definition, jargon doesn't have such demographic reach, though some jargon may eventually move on to broader status. And so, while I will discuss "mini-pop" lingoes from which mass-pop may derive (such as hip-hop slang or the corporate patois), this book isn't a compendium of various group jargons. The focus here is on words that have already reached general circulation; that float, perhaps for years, in the mainstream; and that function as verbal viruses, spreading through the media and flying off our tongues before we even know it.

VOX-OFFICE HITS

But a viral quality only partly describes pop language. After all, as William Burroughs said, *all* language is a virus. Perhaps the better metaphor is that these are celebrity words, the stars of our sentences. Amid the fractured, fuzzy notions and mumbled grunts of everyday verbal intercourse, a snappy catchphrase practically steps out of the limo and onto the red carpet, a confident grin gracing its flash-lit face.

Skillfully applied, the celebrity word can temporarily stun us—much the way seeing a famous person does—and make us more likely to buy whatever it's saying or selling.

Take George Tenet's now infamous remark that finding weapons of mass destruction in Iraq would be a "slam dunk," as Bob Woodward reported in *Plan of Attack.* On December 21, 2002, Tenet and his top deputy at the CIA, John McLaughlin, went to the Oval Office, where McLaughlin gave a detailed intelligence briefing to Bush, Dick Cheney, National Security Adviser Condoleezza Rice, and White House Chief of Staff Andrew Card.

It's not clear whether all the charts, photos, and intercepts convinced anyone in the room that Iraqi WMD actually existed. But apparently more to the point, the presentation failed to persuade anyone that the evidence would persuade the public. "In terms of marketing," Woodward wrote, the briefing was "a flop." Bush complained that "Joe Public" wouldn't understand it, and asked, "[T]his is the best we've got?" "From the end of one of the couches in the Oval Office," Woodward continued, "Tenet rose up, threw his arms in the air. 'It's a slam dunk case!' " he said. Bush asked how confident he was, and the director of the CIA, a Georgetown basketball fan, repeated the arms gesture, saying, "Don't worry, it's a slam dunk!" Bush later told Woodward that "McLaughlin's presentation 'wouldn't have stood the test of time,' but Tenet's reassurance, 'That was very imporant.' "

Just three weeks later, another pop phrase helped the White House make its case for war in Iraq. Woodward described the scene in the vice president's West Wing office on January 11, 2003. Cheney had gathered Secretary of Defense Donald Rumsfeld and Joint Chiefs of Staff chairman General Richard Myers to meet with Bandar bin Sultan, chief representative of the Saudi monarchy in the U.S. and a longtime friend of the Bush family. Bandar was reluctant to use his influence to win the support of Saudi Arabia for the invasion of Iraq without assurances that the U.S. would definitely get rid of Saddam after having failed to do so in 1991.

> "What is the chance of Saddam surviving this?" Bandar asked. He believed Hussein was intent on killing everyone involved at a high level with the 1991 Persian Gulf War, including himself.
>
> Rumsfeld and Myers didn't answer.
>
> "Saddam, this time, will be out, period?" Bandar asked skeptically. "What will happen to him?"
>
> Cheney, who had been quiet as usual, replied, "Prince Bandar, once we start, Saddam is toast."
>
> . . . "I am convinced now that this is something I can take to my Prince Abdullah," Bandar said, "and think I can convince him."

. . . [After Bandar left] Rumsfeld voiced some concern about the vice president's "toast" remark. "Jesus
Christ, what was that all about, Dick?"

"I didn't want to leave any doubt in his mind what
we're planning to do," Cheney said.

As the interchanges show, Cheney not only can wield a pop
phrase, but he is fully aware of the language's power and deliberately uses it. All the other props in the scene—the West Wing
office, the military brass, even a map of the attack plans marked
TOP SECRET NOFORN (meaning no foreigners were supposed to
see them)—failed to persuade the prince. But when the Vice
President of the United States reached for the same swaggering
phrase used by Bill Murray in *Ghostbusters* to signal an attack
on the evil Sumerian goddess Gozer—Murray shouted, "This
chick is toast!"—well, that was the kind of talk the Arabian prince
could understand.

The impressive thing about international celebrity words
is that, while they can create consensus for war, they are just
as useful for the little guy on the homefront. By tossing off *It's
show time!*, or *Who's your daddy?*, or declaring this or that dic-
tator is toast, we can all assert power and attitude. A vocabulary
studded with high-profile words allows people to feel special, individualistic, above the crowd—and, simultaneously, very
much part of the crowd, drawing power from the knowledge that
they're speaking the same language as millions of other clued-in
individuals.

Not all celebrity words are equal, of course. Some famous
phrases are Frank Sinatra, resonant and long-lasting; some are
Beck, experimental fusion rockers that at one point seemed to
sum up the moment; more than a few are Norma Desmond, has-
beens that nevertheless have a hold on our imaginations. The
popularity and potency of a word—its vox office, you might
say—exist on a spectrum.

And let's not forget that the pop tongue is made up of more
than individual phrases. Much of it is structural and damn near
indestructible, coming in forms like Top 10 lists, Befores and
Afters, quickie quizzes ending in "All of the above," hyphenated

suffixes *(-friendly, -driven, -based, -free, -proof, -challenged, -ready, -gate)*, or (a favorite of mine) hyphenated adjectives, like "veins-popping-out-of-your-skull road rage." Pop appears in clever deviations from common constructions, as in this late-nineties headline promoting the pistol-packing-chick TV series *La Femme Nikita:* "36-24-.45." Or in extremely concise plays on words, like the line that reportedly sold a movie script about a genetically engineered dog running amuck: "Jaws with paws." And pop arrives purely in rhythms, such as saving the punchiest word or image for the end of a sentence, unlike this one.

In spoken pop, the inflection is often crucial. Sometimes it's as obvious as a drawn-out syllable and an interrogative note *(Hel-lo?!)* or a flat affect *(Yeah, right)*. But it may be more complex. A housewife to a "smart" dishwasher in a GE spot: "If you're so smart, how come you're doing the dishes?" Dishwasher (with Jack Benny timing): "I *hate* when she says that."

And speaking of spoken, whether pop words appear primarily in speech or primarily in writing, they tend to start spoken, like *dilio* (or *dillio* or *dilly*). A kind of ironic, goateed Latino for *deal* (and as such, on the esoteric side of the pop spectrum), *dilio* started as spoken, moved to Hollywood ("Jessica, you are the real dilio!" a producer of the Fox show *Dark Angel* told its star, Jessica Alba, in accepting a People's Choice Award), but now resides mostly in blogdom.

But even if most pop begins as speech, it eventually swings both ways—we write what we say. *Duh* and *I don't* think *so*, such big oral sluggers, appear in writing because they long ago reached the level of household phrases. When a word has truly arrived, a reader has only to silently supply the right inflection, something you'll frequently be called upon to do in this book.

GOTCHA!

Call me crazy, but I anticipate a few gotchas! from readers.

One is that you'll catch me discussing phrases that seem passé. And you will, because, along with everything else this book isn't about, it isn't about the latest buzzwords or those that are (to use a passé but still pop phrase) on the cutting edge. Even if I were trying to be up to the moment, I couldn't, since of course I'm writing all this long before it will be published.

But more important, I think that people love to declare a little too much that some catchphrase is hot or not. No one can really know what's the very latest except within one's own relatively small circles. When the map is larger, national, what's so last millennium and what's the next big thing become a blur. Trends overlap, shrink, bulge, and shrink again.

Even people who make a living tracking word usage don't agree. *Yadda, yadda, yadda* made it into the 1996 *Random House Webster's College Dictionary* because the editor then in charge of new words there, Jesse Sheidlower, was convinced of its staying power, according to *The New York Times*. But the editor in chief of *Webster's New World College Dictionary*, Michael Agnes, found *yadda*'s usage declining and blocked it. Furthermore, wrote the *Times*, "when the editors of four dictionaries provided their unabridged new word lists for comparison, there was no overlap."

Not only is it impossible to always keep up-to-date, but the compulsion to do so can make you look like a fool. In 1992 *The New York Times*'s Style section published a glossary of what was supposed to be grunge slang. The newest term for a loser, for instance, was "cob nobbler." "Swingin' on the flippity flop" meant hanging out. "Tom-Tom Club" was code for uncool outsiders. It was a hoax, the words fabricated by a young record company sales rep in Seattle. When word of the joke got out, the *Times* editors must have felt like real "lame-stains" (uncool people).

Always riding the cutting edge not only can produce some nasty burns, it's much less interesting than understanding the long-lasting stuff. Many of our favorite words don't go out of style so much as, their fifteen minutes of fame past, they become our mental default system—which is exactly what I find intriguing about language that's pop, whether or not it also happens to be "hot."

It's not a word's freshness date that makes it pop but its degree of persuasive power. Senior pop phrases—like *fifteen min-*

utes of fame—may well be clichés, but they still discharge more jolt than nonpop clichés. Whether a phrase is two months old or two hundred years old, whether it's zesty or mild, it counts as pop in my book as long as most of us and most media rely on its audience-drawing power to sell and persuade.

After all, formerly hot terms like *chill, dis,* and *bottom line* are still going strong after a generation or two. *Gimme a break* was no spring chicken when the sitcom *Gimme a Break!* first aired, in 1981. But in a pinch, it's still a phrase of choice. Regarding Abu Ghraib, a *Newsweek* letter to the editor read, "The media are screaming bloody murder after seeing a few prisoners in naked poses? Give me a break."

No way/Way sounds so 1989 slacker, but its call-and-response rings to this day. In an episode of *Queer Eye for the Straight Guy,* a woman sees her guy transformed and exclaims, "No way!" The Fab Five, watching her on video, cry in unison, "Way!"

In order to reach such Mick Jaggeresque longevity, pop words may have to endure several phrase phases. If a phrase makes it big, like, for instance, *Go for it,* it might be followed by a period of soft ridicule for overuse. If it survives that, it wins the right to be repeated, but only with irony (for a while, many of us couldn't say *Go for it* any other way). If it survives that, it gets stronger, like a Raid-resistant roach—and it sheds the irony and begins to seem as indispensable as, say, *Do the math* or *24/7.* That is, the phrase becomes a thought, or more accurately, a stand-in for a thought. Given the right circumstances, we almost cannot not say it.

The thrill is gone; been there, done that; same old, same old. But that's neither here nor there, because if a phrase has the right stuff, it doesn't merely express an idea, it *owns* the motha'.

Meanwhile, an entire class of pop phrases exists solely to separate the au courant from the passé. Among the still reasonably vogue phrases that help indicate whether a phrase or a fashion continues to be in vogue are the *so's*—*so over, so five minutes ago,* and so on. I can swear I saw a fashion headline years ago that read, "So Over Is So Over"—but that's so not true. Half in, half out among the vogue-on-vogue phrases are *in/out; That was then, this is now; Same old, same old.*

"I'll write people off if they use a slang expression whose shelf life has expired," writer Merrill Markoe said in the preface of the 1997 book *Buzzwords*. "One little 'been there, done that' or 'I give good phone' and I tune out everything else that person says." Yet, seven years later, *been there* was, if not flying off the shelves, still being stocked. "A lot of people feel like, 'I've been there, done that. I've met everybody there is to meet. I'll take a break,' " an advertising consultant said about online dating when the trend began to plateau.

On *I give good phone,* Markoe is right: it's history. Thousands of phrases, pop or otherwise, serve their purpose and simply die. But I can't agree with others who declare that *it's history* is toast. *Toast* has more burn and conveys total destruction (which is probably why Cheney chose it to predict Saddam's fate). But *history* expresses a finality of its own. Journalism and advertising have found that no one pays attention if you say something is different or changed—the old thing should at least get badly bruised. In a story about changes on the PBS show *NOW, The Washington Times* wrote, as David Brancacci replaced Bill Moyers, "Then there's the show's handsome blue-and-green hued set: It's history." Likewise, if we are to believe a spot for the satellite TV company DirecTV, "Cable is history." Maybe our fixation on "What's Next" and "Who's Next" (as publications love to title technology and people stories) prevents us from seeing that *history,* along with other aging pop, repeats itself, as history does.

The second gotcha! I anticipate is that readers will assume that I assume that we talk this way all the time, when obviously we don't. Unlike the characters in the movie *Clueless,* where the comedy turned largely on an overdeveloped fluency in buzz-speak, most of us are not talking pop 24/7. These phrases occur with widely varying frequency, tending to surface when our own individual personality needs a charge from the group one. For many of us that is when we're trying to impress someone or during an argument: When logic is weak weaponry or is just too difficult to grasp, phrase-fighting busts out. For others, *suck* or *whatever* emerges most freely during small talk, or perhaps when speaking with someone you are afraid won't be stimulated by more pedestrian patter. "Gimme five!" dozens of (white) grandfathers say to young children, though they probably wouldn't say it to a peer. A good, I don't know, 93 to 97 percent of the time we *don't* talk pop—but looking at why we do when we do and how it affects communication is my focus.

Lastly, readers will see me using many of the buzzwords, inflections, structures, and writers' tricks of the trade that are this book's very target, and you might think I'm a hypocrite or just blind to my own dependency on pop language (not to mention more conventional clichés or turns of speech).

Sure, I could claim I sprinkle on the pop in order to illustrate what I'm criticizing. And I do, but that's only part of it. I'm clearly using some pop as a joke or as an elbow in the ribs. The reasons for the rest of it may not be so clear because I may not be aware of it myself—it has slipped under my radar. Some phrases, like *slipped under my radar,* are just so ingrained and right to the point that I figure, Why fight them?

It is difficult to speak without some pop in the voice. I can no more completely avoid it than I can avoid the phrases and rhythms that most every parent uses with a baby ("Are you my boy?" "Who's the silly willy?"), a language that is nearly universal because the impulses are.

But it is also true that I'm just as determined to entertain you as most writers are. We try to hide the premeditation of it all with the breezy tone that's encoded in the pop vocabulary. After all, if we don't immediately connect, if we don't use words that *push your buttons,* we fear we will bore you and not get assignments.

In fact, noticing my own strong temptation to use these phrases, in writing and speech, is what made me want to write about them in the first place. What is their pull on me, and why do I resist? (My resistance, at least, probably has something to do with where I grew up as a teenager: a spanking new subdivision in suburban St. Louis that was named—because the developers didn't bulldoze every sapling in sight—Nottingham Among the Trees.)

And while we're on the subject of me, I should lay out my prejudices: There are some pop locutions that I like and others I bristle at every time. As you might by now suspect, I like *road rage* but hate *I don't think so.* (Maybe because I believe a lot of road rage is caused by people who say *I don't* think *so.*) There are phrases I wish I could stop using, but can't, like *like, you know,* while others I feel ridiculous saying, like *cool. Blah, blah, blah*— can't think without it; I find it funny and oddly cozy. *Yadda, yadda, yadda,* however, won't leave my lips. I have a soft spot for, and a dependency on, pop words that describe aspects of pop culture (and that seem to come in couplets): *sound bite, shelf life, shrink-wrapped, industrial-strength, freeze-dried, freeze-frame,* and *flash-freeze.* Essential to writing this book is *dumb down*—it is a box outside of which I cannot think. But other words of this ilk, such as *phone tag* and *wiggle room,* are just too cute for moi. *The culture* is one that I, like many writers, am embarrassingly addicted to.

And so it is definitely a self-conscious challenge to write about overused locutions while using some myself. I'm torn between wanting to write in lively, accessible language and cringing at the possibility that I'm digging those thought grooves a little deeper.

There's no completely avoiding pop language, because it goes beyond the words themselves. It evolves from the way the world works—in any era, the popular language is the most powerful means of persuasion we can collectively dream up, and I will use it to try to persuade you that I shouldn't always use it to persuade you.

This dilemma should lead, throughout the book, to a look at the very nature of language: Is everything we say a semi-programmed turn of speech? Are new combinations of old idioms the only original forms of speech left to us? How does one communicate without resorting to the words and rhythms of the moment?

But first, the biggest gotcha!: Wasn't it always thus?

CHAPTER 2

Pop Talk Is History

lthough it might be hard for the self-referential among us to
believe, neither the TV generation nor the cyber generation
invented pop language. Every era had, or so we must sur-
mise, its own punchy expressions: words that could, in effect,
replace a punch, project a better image, or at least throw a
speaker a rhetorical life jacket.

There are important differences between yesterday's and
today's pop, both in the forces that shape the language and in
the way the language influences us (and I'll get to those differences shortly). But pop phrases—in one form or another—run
throughout history.

During the early nineteenth century, as Charles Mackay
recorded in his 1841 book, *Memoirs of Extraordinary Popular Delusions and the Madness of Crowds,* London was gaga over phrases
like *Has your mother sold her mangle?, There he goes with his eye out!,
What a shocking bad hat!,* and (most charmingly) *Quoz,* expressions that were the cat's meow for months or years and then
vanished.

The king of catchphrases, Mackay wrote, was *flare up!* It began meaning largely what it has always meant ("any sudden outburst either of fire, disturbance, or ill-nature," as he said). But during the Reform Riots of 1831, when Bristol, England, went up in flames, *flare up!* leapt to the heights of an all-purpose exclamation. "It answered all questions, settled all disputes, was applied to all persons, all things, and all circumstances, and became suddenly the most comprehensive phrase in the English language," Mackay wrote.

> A lover's quarrel was a *flare up;* so was a boxing-match between two blackguards in the streets; and the preachers of sedition and revolution recommended the English nation to *flare up* like the French. So great a favourite was the word, that people loved to repeat it for its very sound. They delighted apparently in hearing their own organs articulate it. . . . Even in the dead hours of the night, the ears of those who watched late, or who could not sleep, were saluted with the same sound. The drunkard reeling home showed that he was still a man and a citizen by calling *"flare up!"* in the pauses of the hiccough. Drink had deprived him of the power of arranging all other ideas; his intellect was sunk to the level of the brute's: but he clung to humanity by the one last link of the popular cry. While he could vociferate that sound, he had rights as an Englishman, and would not sleep in a gutter, like a dog!

Mackay's description of the pop word's potential is timeless. Whether drunk or sober, whether dazed by work, entertainment, or family dysfunction, most of us at times are routinely deprived of the power of arranging all other ideas, our intellect sinking to the level of the brute's. But as long as we can vociferate certain sounds, we still have rights as an Englishman, an American, or an acceptable person wherever we may live.

And there have always been words that prevented gutter sleep. The word *phrasemonger* arose around 1805, according to the *Random House Webster's Unabridged Dictionary,* though obviously there were mongers before. The further back you go, however, the more difficult it is to understand the role that catchphrases played, much less what those phrases actually were.

You might assume, for instance, that the Greeks and the Romans were bursting with vox populi pop, but we just don't know for sure. Only a relatively small amount of written material from the ancient world has survived, and that was usually written in an elevated style that eschewed commonly spoken Greek or Latin. "We have formal speeches that are preserved, of course, like Cicero's and Demosthenes', but anything like 'Duh' is not going to be in speeches of theirs," says Jo-Ann Shelton, a professor of classics at the University of California, Santa Barbara, and author of *As the Romans Did*. In the comedies, though, the characters are supposed to be speaking colloquially. "There is no doubt," she says, "that all sorts of phrases popular at the time, including references to current events and celebrities, were embedded in the comedies, especially in the plays of Aristophanes and Plautus. Something like 'Make my day.' But we don't have other preserved materials to which we can compare the comedies, to learn if the characters were repeating everyday expressions, or if the audience picked up on expressions coined by the playwrights."

The most extensive collection of colloquial Latin that has been preserved, the graffiti on the walls of Pompeii, is of limited help in recognizing popular phrases, because "there aren't enough examples to see patterns of repetition," Shelton says. So we don't know if "I don't want to sell my husband," "I have screwed many girls here," "Epaphra is not a ballplayer," and "When you are dead, you are nothing" were one-liners cracking them up at the Forum, or just one-shots of gossip, complaints, brags, and would-be wisdom. (Probably the latter, for as one Pompeiian wrote, "I am amazed, o wall, that you have not collapsed and fallen, since you must bear the tedious stupidities of so many scrawlers.") "We just don't have enough that was written," says Shelton, "and not enough that was written and was not formal."

BETHUMPED WITH WORDS

In other words, until relatively recently, there wasn't the right kind of media to record the pop of the time. For nearly a thousand years after the fall of Rome, Latin continued to be the language of the elite class, and the common people spoke (unwritten) local dialects. If there were catchphrases in medieval French, for instance, they would have had to be translated into Latin for us to read them, and wit rarely survives such a translation.

But then, in the Renaissance, came the flowering of the vulgate. The Bible was translated into all the tongues of Europe, and Protestant reformers began to insist on translating religious ceremonies so that everyone could take in the Word of God. Add the printing press and the beginnings of mass literacy, and for the first time we can glimpse pop speech peeking over the horizon of history.

The absolute greatest source of English words and phrases ever, of course, was Shakespeare. Cited some 33,000 times in the *Oxford English Dictionary*, more than any other single source, Shakespeare either coined or popularized hundreds of phrases that we're still spouting (*flesh and blood, laughing stock, one fell swoop, sea change, more in sorrow than in anger, not slept one wink, too much of a good thing*, and *brave new world*, to mention a few). But back then, did audiences walk out of *Hamlet* and start joking about their every little decision, asking, "To eat or not to eat?" That is, was Shakespeare the Seinfeld or Bart Simpson of his day?

The short and long of it (that's from *The Merry Wives of Windsor*) is, Maybe. What interplay there was between Shakespeare's written verse and the speech patterns of everyday Elizabethans is not easy to discern. But as a kind of Renaissance medium unto himself, Shakespeare processed nonpop into pop much like the media do today: He borrowed the people's argot and—though we'll never know to what extent—reflected some of it back to them with a new sheen.

Shakespeare even wrote about the fascination street talk

could have for upper-class types in *1 Henry IV,* in a scene where Prince Hal discusses what he has learned about life from Falstaff. As Stephen Greenblatt writes in his book *Will in the World: How Shakespeare Became Shakespeare,* "In Falstaff's seedy haunts . . . Prince Hal gains access to an urban cast of characters far removed from anything he has known before, and he takes particular delight in having learned their language: 'They call drinking deep "dyeing scarlet," and when you breathe in your watering they cry "Hem!" and bid you "Play it off!" ' " It seems, Greenblatt says, "a thinly disguised depiction of Shakespeare's own linguistic apprenticeship in taverns."

"Shakespeare was a vacuum, sucking in words from everywhere," adds Kenneth Gross, author of *Shakespeare's Noise,* which explores the Bard's use of insults, curses, and gossip. "He's grabbing stuff from the spoken language, including popular songs and slang, but also from the Bible, poems and romances, courtesy manuals, books of magic, pamphlets about witchcraft and discoveries in the new world, English translations of French translations of Plutarch's *Lives.*" *Play fast and loose* (from *King John*), for instance, originated from a sixteenth-century game called fast and loose that was every bit as honest as today's three-card monty. That is, Gross says, Shakespeare's works are replete with words and phrases that "he didn't invent but that he used in a strikingly new, more figurative way."

We may never know whether a particular phrase in Shakespeare (or any phrase now famously Shakespearean, like *To be or not to be*) became pop in his time. But there's some reason to believe that in general a phrase could indeed, after a stint on the stage, return to Elizabethans with more dazzle in its voice. "There's a famous case in a pamphlet by Thomas Lodge, published in 1596, five years before Shakespeare's *Hamlet* was written," says Gross. "In lampooning a certain melancholy character, Lodge mentions a popular stage version of an earlier *Hamlet,* perhaps written by Thomas Kyd or even the young Shakespeare himself, in which the ghost cries 'like an oyster-wife, "Hamlet revenge!" ' You get a sense that 'Hamlet, revenge!' was in circulation, or in common memory, because otherwise a popular pamphleteer wouldn't have used the phrase to appeal to his audience. It certainly wouldn't surprise me that some of Shakespeare's own phrases got into the public ear and that the public was invited to take great pleasure in them."

How much in the ear was, as always, limited by the media of the day; if Shakespeare and his contemporary dramatists functioned as media, they were micro, not mass, media. "Newspapers hadn't been invented at this point," Gross reminds us. "Spoken language—in the street, the church, and the theater—was undoubtedly a powerful means of spreading ideas, and people would have shared many words, proverbs, biblical phrases, etc. But there was no medium with the distinct power of radio, movies, or television to give almost instant currency to colloquial verbal formulas or particular intonations. In the past, the process of diffusion was slower and more uncertain."

The closest things to newspapers back then were those aforementioned pamphlets. They dealt in everything from the Bible and politics to crime and social scandals. Among the most famous were the coney-catching pamphlets. Ostensibly published to warn the public, they often included long lists of "cant"— the jargon of con men, or "coney catchers" (*coney,* meaning a swindler's dupe, probably comes from the Latin *cuniculus* for rabbit). Beginning to appear in the mid-sixteenth century, these compilations of cant are among the earliest and richest records of language that came not from writers or orators but from "the street." Rather, much of it did—the pamphlets were so popular that publishers cranked them out for more than two hundred years, sometimes inventing entries just to keep up.

Most cant faded long ago, but in his book *Our Marvelous Native Tongue,* Robert Claiborne cites a 1698 publication, *A New Dictionary of the Terms Ancient and Modern of the Canting Crew,* that included some still perfectly current words, like *crony, duds, fence* (to sell stolen property), *sock* (to hit), and *clap* (for venereal disease). While bits and pieces of various group jargons have always drifted into the mainstream to become entrenched expressions, Claiborne points out, "Of all the trades and professions, easily the champion, both at coining words and in its contributions to the general vocabulary, is crime. Like aviation and show business [two jargons that have also fed the broader language], it has glamour."

Glamour, even the littlest dab, is key to pop. And that, too, has pretty much always been the case.

According to the "uniformitarian principle" in linguistics, "the things that are typical of speech today are typical of speech in the past, at least in societies similar to ours," John McWhorter, a historical linguist and associate professor of linguistics at the University of California, Berkeley, told me. "It's typical for groups in society not only to have their own in-group argot, but also to use a vigorous slang to convey what we now call attitude. That has always been around."

GEOPOP

So not only is pop not the exclusive province of the TV and cyber generations, no way is it exclusive to English. English does have the largest vocabulary of any language (having been fed by both German and, through the Norman invasion, French and its Latin base); therefore it might be expected to have the largest pop vocabulary. And the U.S is the place with the most, and the most exported, pop culture. But pop language would exist even if English, or America, didn't.

For example, wasn't Yiddish the pop of the Diaspora? With Jews dispersed across so many different language groups, Yiddish (along with religion and tradition, of course) was one of the forces holding Jews together and providing identity (not unlike the brand names, sitcom comebacks, and other media lingua franca that hold together and provide identity to fragmented, distracted Americans). And Yiddish words themselves—*shtick, shlep, shmooze, shmuck, shlump, shlock, oy vay, kvetch, meshugge, cockamamy, zaftig*—are attitudinally charged. They jump out, warm you up, and predictably help persuade you of a speaker's point. That is, Yiddish has most of the key components of pop.

In addition, a lot of our current pop—*Don't get me started, Don't ask, Get outta here, To die for, Enough already*—is Yiddish-influenced English, or, as the late Leo Rosten called it, Yinglish. Is Yiddish inherently comical (and thus pop), or did it only acquire a sense of humor over the decades? Did native Yiddish speakers from the old country also find their language always good for a laugh? I don't think my grandparents did—they fought plenty in Yiddish. But my father, speaking the occasional Yiddish or Yinglish phrase now, rarely says it without humor.

The answer bears out my experience, but is still a little disappointing: "There is nothing inherently funny about Yiddish," said linguist Paul Glasser, research associate at YIVO Institute for Jewish Research. "For native Yiddish speakers, it was simply their everyday language. However, among those in the next generation who could speak the language only with difficulty but who could maybe say a joke or a punchline in Yiddish—they became fluent in Yiddish jokes as opposed to Yiddish itself. This is pretty natural. When a language makes the transition from being a full-throated language to more of a spice, the words that survive the shift tend to be the more affective, emotional words."

So by association, Yiddish began to practically *shvitz* with humor, a tendency augmented by the fact that so many comedy writers were either Yiddish speakers or their children. And not only in America. "Jews in Germany and in Israel also think of Yiddish as a language meant for jokes," Glasser said. (The showbiz connection brings even Yiddish a glamour.) He admits, though, "there's a missing link" in explaining why, even if you know all this, you still can't say, say, *farblondzhet* (lost your way) without it sounding funny. Go figure.

And you don't have to be Jewish, English, or American to love pop talk.

It's there in French. "*Faut pas exagerer*—one must not exaggerate. You say that and you are French," David (the Slangman) Burke, author of many books on foreign slang, assured me. "A woman walks by with tons of make-up on, and you say, *'Faut pas exagerer.'*" Also big, he said, is reverse talk. "A woman is a *femme;* you reverse it, and you get *meuf.* They spell it how they would pronounce it. Slang for man is *mec;* they reverse it and it becomes *queme.*"

It's there in Spanish. In Cuba, they're saying *"Desmaya eso,"* reports the writer and Spanish speaker Marc Cooper, who has frequently visited the island. "You hear it constantly. People were straining to find an excuse to say it. It literally means 'make that pass out.' But what it really means is 'Forget about it,' 'That's too far out,' 'That's too much': 'Elian [Gonzalez] should live in Miami with Marisleysis.' *'Desmaya eso!'* But it can also mean the best, cool; it can be negative or affirmative. That's why I cringe when I hear it. It's overly generic."

In Chile, added Cooper (who worked as a translator for the slain president Salvador Allende), "*Super* is used the same way we use it, but it's as big there now as it was here in the seventies." This pop *super* bears little relationship to the straighter *super* that's been a Spanish word for eons to mean *extra* or *big*. "This newer one, which is pronounced just the way an American pronounces it, comes from watching American shows on TV. It's as if their own *super* didn't exist."

Of course, foreign-word borrowing works in both directions and always has, but the process isn't a simple reversal. When other languages borrow from English, the words tend to become pop. But when Americans dapple their conversations with foreign phrases (other than cooking or other specialty terms), the words, while also pop, tend to be used as some sort of joke. We witty Americans occasionally season our speech with an ironic *Moi?*, a relaxed *No problemo*, or a reveling-in-its-fakeness *correcto-mundo*. Arnold Schwarzenegger's *Hasta la vista, baby!* is no longer *caliente* (though his *girlie men* is), but the kind of situation that demands that phrase and nothing else is now bred in our bones, even if most Americans have no idea what *hasta* or *la vista* means.

Whether authentic or faux, the foreign phrases dotting our English often come in costume. For an American, the purpose of pulling out a foreign word is to tap a stereotype, positive or negative: Yiddish steps in for a quick jig of menshiness. French is supposed to sound sexy, sophisticated, or, more likely these days, "elitist." Spanish, especially in the last twenty or so years, is used for some multiculti cool with a dash of Hawaiian-shirt irony.

However, when non-English-speaking countries use American pop, the stereotype drawn upon is less focused and less jocular. Even though, since our invasion of Iraq, we are the most hated nation on earth, our pop phrases, like our (nonboycotted) commercial products, are still used to signal an established kind of cool and power. "Non-stop" is the name of a twenty-four-hour convenience store in Prague. In Germany, *flirt, happy ending, clever, power,* and *administration* are everyday words. Japan is well known for using English in product labels, ads, and store signs ("Used Shop—since 1990" reads a sign in Nagasaki, while another store offers "selfish fashion"). Japlish is also taking over common conversation among teenagers, as the name for this tendency indicates: *ko-gyaru-go,* or "high school gal-talk" *(gyaru* is the Japanese pronunciation of *gal). Ko-gyaru-go* includes such global pop as *chekaraccho* ("Check it out, Joe"), *disu* (to diss), and *deniru* (to go to a Denny's restaurant).

WHO NEEDS ESPERANTO WHEN YOU'VE GOT COCA-COLA?

The word trade deficit most definitely runs in America's favor. You could almost produce a de facto pop dictionary simply by alphabetizing the Americanese that other countries over the years have tried to ban or discourage. In 1997, *Newsweek* wrote about "a list of 3,500 foreign words that can't be used in schools, bureaucracies or companies. . . . Herewith, some of the silliest examples: Turkey: *hit, hot, cool.* Iran: *intellectual, police, fax, computer, secular.* France: *cheeseburger, stress, bulldozer, brainstorming, air bag, log on.*" This is not to mention France's futile firewall against *le weekend, le sandwich, e-mail,* and *money.*

American words of pure attitude have even more latitude. *OK* and *cool* are among the most-recognized words in the world. As is *Coke*—which rather cleverly contains *OK.* (This is more than just my little joke. In the mid-nineties, Coca-Cola, disguising its multinational corporate parentage, launched an "indie" soda named OK. Though targeted to what must have seemed a lucrative market—resentful, depressed twelve-year-old males—OK sold poorly and was quickly KOed.)

Coca-Cola is so ubiquitous that it's not always considered American. The Stanford University linguist Arnold Zwicky recalled how, about thirty years ago, his wife, Ann Daingerfield

Zwicky, "was teaching an ESL [English as a Second Language] class at Ohio State and used one of her ice-breaker topics: words borrowed into English from your native language. Alas, this time the first word offered was 'Coca-Cola,' by (I believe) a speaker of Hindi. An Arabic speaker . . . denied this with scorn; 'everybody' knows 'Coca-Cola' is an Arabic word. Pandemonium ensued. Even a female student from Japan, normally silent in class, was moved to dispute the others' absurd claims. The only thing they were agreed on was the idea that the headquarters of the Coca-Cola Company could possibly be in 'Atlanta'—or anywhere in the U.S.—was preposterous (or evidence that America just grabbed everything away from the rest of the world)."

I doubt that ESL students still believe that a generation later. But take any number of attitudinal English phrases and they begin to form an all-terrain Esperanto. When a Spanish-language newspaper interviewed a Mexican soccer player, he spoke, of course, in Spanish—until he asked himself a rhetorical question, and then he slammed in an English *I don't* think *so*.

American lexical hegemony is obviously due to the global spread of all other forms of American pop—television, movies, music, fashion, advertising, and products—and by a U.S.-dominated Internet. That is, it's due to the media, which sow our words farther, faster, and more ferociously. But pop-pushing media didn't start with the movies, or even with newspapers. The original media were people moving around. Mass migration to and within America created a prolific slang.

In his book *Roughing It,* Mark Twain wrote in 1872 about the slang used in Virginia City, Nevada, in the 1860s:

> As all the peoples of the earth had representative adventurers in the Silverland, and as each adventurer had brought the slang of his nation or his locality with him, the combination made the slang of Nevada the richest and the most infinitely varied and copious that had ever existed anywhere in the world, perhaps, except in the mines of California in the "early days." Slang was the language of Nevada. It was hard to preach a sermon without it, and be understood. Such phrases as "You bet!" "Oh,

no, I reckon not!" "No Irish need apply," and a hundred others, became so common as to fall from the lips of a speaker unconsciously. . . .

BEEN THERE, SAID THAT

So, we're not the first generation to sling slang, and, despite our dominance of the word market, ours is hardly the only spot on earth that slings it. But, worse for our collective ego, many of the phrases that we think of as so current were actually born in decades that we think of as so over. What follows comes from Tom Dalzell and his excellent book *Flappers 2 Rappers: American Youth Slang.*

Babe (meaning a pretty girl), *foxy* (well-dressed), *freak* ("someone who is exceptionally proficient in a given area"), *killer* ("one who does things easily"), and *tacky* ("shoddy") were all said by college students—circa 1900.

The 1920s flappers gave us many phrases that we now consider ridiculously peppy *(cat's meow, cat's pajamas, hot diggity dog!, hotsy-totsy, all wet, heebie-jeebies).* But some of that effusive talk is still with us: *bozo, unreal, lounge lizard, a hoot,* and *Oh, yeah* (equivalent to our *Yeah, right*).

While some of us might throw a thirties phrase (like *swell* or *doll up*) into our repertoire to sound humorously retro, as if we're referencing a James Cagney movie, quite a few of today's pop phrases derive straight from that decade, their meanings unaltered: *cheesy, cramp your style, large* ("active and exciting"), *hot, juicy, slick, slam* ("an insult" or "to criticize harshly").

Groovy is not just a sixties word in revival. It arose in the forties (with roots even earlier), as did the no-longer-cool but Boomer-basic *neat. Super* (along with *super-duper, supersolid, super-colossal*) also had its first heyday in the forties, as did the curious *Abercrombie,* meaning then "a know-it-all" and derived from equipment and apparel seller Abercrombie & Fitch. Today Abercrombie & Fitch is known more for its snob appeal and sexed-up catalogues.

Even the self-conscious cherishing of one's own slanguage is not solely a Boomer/Gen X, Y, or Z phenomenon. "The Flapper movement was the first youth movement to generate its own slang dictionaries," writes Dalzell (who is also the coeditor of *The New Partridge Dictionary of Slang and Unconventional English*). And before flappers, Dalzell says, the media were full of "the nation's first true pop phrase"—*23 skidoo.* "Everywhere you turned, you heard or read it—in comics, songs, conversation, on the stage. It meant everything and nothing and anything. When the young man said it, he summoned the laugh of the crowd."

WHAT'S THE DIFF?

But while some pop language and many current pop phrases themselves go way back, the role of pop language in our lives is not the same as it ever was. What we have today is pop of a different order. Over recent generations, pop language has more completely absorbed the values and serviced the needs of those triumphant twin social forces: marketing and mass media.

It was marketing, in fact, that brought us *media* as we know it. Until the twenties, write David Barnhart and Allan Metcalf in their book *America in So Many Words, media* had been "just an obscure Latin plural of medium" and a medium was a person who conjured the spirits of the dead. "Then came modern advertising and . . . [s]uddenly in the advertising world it was smart to speak of placing ads in different *media,* or in one particular *media,* the word being used as a singular as well as a plural."

Society's march to a more commercialized beat took place gradually over the last century, as media began to conjure the consuming spirit. But the beat greatly accelerated during the second half. So while Boomers and Xers (both were also marketing terms before becoming fundamental pop concepts) didn't invent pop talk, the media and marketing environments that they grew up in and that they, in turn, ramped up have seriously tweaked the nature of pop language, making it more indispensable to everyone's thinking. (Business pop like *ramp up* and *tweak* have infected my thinking, too.)

There's no single turning point when mass media and

marketing began to change the tune of pop language. But the first televised presidential debate—which Kennedy won largely because he looked relaxed while Nixon looked too "hot," literally from sweat and figuratively for the "cool medium" (as McLuhan dubbed television)—did set a standard of media-savviness that any player, left, right, or apolitical, would from then on need to reach in order to succeed.

As has often been pointed out, Kennedy's debate victory seemed to signal the rise of images over words (people who had only heard the candidates on radio thought Nixon had won). But as the importance of image grew with television, so, too, grew the importance of words' being more like images—able not just to evoke images, as words have always done, but to actually approach the immediate burn-into-your-brain zap of a picture. Just when we thought that words would wilt in a blast of visuals, this "word-as-image" began to ascend, verbally and typographically. Throughout the 1980s and 1990s, more and more television commercials, despite the vast visual and acoustical resources at their disposal, were relying on simple, boldly drawn words, usually as superimposed titles or as white titles on a black screen. To take but a few: "This Is What Dry Is" (Michelob Dry), "The Pitch" (Apple Macintosh), "Surprised?" (Goodyear), and, most famously, "Real Life, Real Answers" (John Hancock). "There was more time spent on titles than pictures," Don Easdon, a co-creator of the Hancock campaign, said at the time. "It was a very anti-slick way of giving information. It's not in your face."

If one picture is worth a thousand words, some words (or phrases, like *in your face*) are lowering the ratio. For ad agencies, the trend of using words, spoken or printed, that have the wallop of pictures continues today as one way to "cut through the clutter" of other, increasingly ubiquitous ads. And, perhaps less obviously, it's one way that we regular, non-ad-industry people use to cut through the clutter of everyone else's increasing number of ads for themselves.

A correctly delivered *Stick a fork in him—he's done* or *That's gotta hurt* can position us in ways we hope to be seen. Those moments when we speak mass words operate like mini-commercials, some of the dozens of ads we run daily on our not entirely privately owned channels. The growing tendency to treat oneself as a brand to be sold (whether to potential employers, investors, or lovers, or to oneself) is quite dependent on the ability to produce the right utterances at the right time. A Web site called Personal Branding even gave its lookees a hot tip: "Develop a catch phrase."

Today, you can get paid to wrap your car, novel, or forehead in an ad (with categories like "Head Advertising" and "Chest Advertising," a Web site called Bodybillboardz lists people selling ad space on various parts of their bodies). Schools have more corporate communiqués than cliques. "Viral marketing"—buzz manufactured by a company, usually without disclosing the source—can create a movie or product hit: Some liquor brands hire actors to rave about them at crowded bars; teenagers gushing about products may have been enlisted to do so. The heavens themselves are sponsored, as rocket-riding Pizza Hut logos streak outer space. Even the public toilet isn't sacred. Among the advertisers who have placed ads in restrooms is ABC TV: Men at urinals would suddenly hear the digitalized voice of Norm Macdonald (promoting his sitcom *Norm* in 2000) saying, "Look at the size of that thing!" and "Hey, watch your shoes!" When everything in the universe is available as an ad space, the need for clutter-cutting, forceful formulae increases—and more words and phrases go on the payroll.

Professional communicators have long known the power of the shiny word. That's why marketers (marketing includes every activity involved in selling, from consumer research and package design to public relations and advertising) so eagerly borrow our most catchy phrases and beam them back at us, hoping we'll identify with their clients. "Coolhunters" and other market researchers scout the urban youth scene, trading CDs and T-shirts for lingo and fashion tips that they can then inject into the creation of their image, like collagen into lips.

As we, too, feel the need to sell ourselves, we begin to perform more and therefore require more crowd-pleasing language. We, too, need test-marketed words. And so we repeat the words that marketing has already mined from us and then offers back through the media.

Only now, the words return to us with some (as marketers like to say) added value. When catchphrases have been through the media and marketing mill, not only do they acquire a celebrity cachet but they're more consumer-ready, as if each phrase carried a chic little shopping bag waiting to be filled.

But wait, there's more. In an Everyman's version of Warhol's Campbell's Soup cans, people, inside or outside of media, create instant pop simply by citing a brand-name product outside of its usual context. Uttering "Mmm, mmm, good," "McJob," "Tagamet moments" (as *Time* once referred to Senator John McCain's displays of anger), or "a healthy alternative to Halcion" (as *Newsweek*, the same week, characterized former senator Bill Bradley's speaking style) can give the slog of communication some cartoony bounce. "I Googled *Wal-Mart Republicans*" is more fun to say than "I found *Wal-Mart Republicans* on a search engine."

Some of marketing's and media's influence on language, however, is more basic: It's, like, just do the math. Over the last few decades there have simply been more media outlets to fill. As the number of cable TV channels and Web sites has soared, so has the demand for language, imagery, gimmicks (e.g., giving away millions of dollars on iWON.com, initially backed by CBS), or any trope that grabs you. Why must a medium so desperately clutch you to its bosom? To expose you to the advertisements running on it. The amount of money a media outlet can charge for an ad depends on how many eyes or ears, or "impressions," it can deliver to an advertiser. As has often been said about advertising, it's you, the audience, that is the real product being sold—to the advertisers who pay for all the "free" media. Television, radio, and Web sites generate little or no income but that from advertising (the relative handful of subscription-only enterprises excepted). So more media outlets mean more motivation to use, and to actively promote, the language with the strongest hooks around.

Another reason for the higher pitch of pop is that the forces of media and marketing are in constant interplay with a third, and increasingly splenetic, force: politics. This process certainly didn't begin with JFK and the sixties, but, again, that's when it got a big bump, as the great "culture wars" got under way. The feuding flavors of identity politics and the more general us-versus-them conflicts—right vs. left, fundamentalist vs. secular, white vs. black, straight vs. gay, traditional vs. alternative— have increased the opportunities for phrases to swell to pop status. *Politically correct, red states/blue states, moral values, culture of life, Get used to it, Get over it, They just don't get it, elites, flip-flop, spin:* We cultural warriors and lifestyle soldiers need more killer language to pulverize the enemy, or at least to define ourselves against those not us.

As often happens in cultural skirmishes, there's a whole lotta role-switching going on. When one side snatches a phrase from the other side, the phrase's currency may rise even higher. *Politically correct,* usually hurled by the right at anything to its left, was what some newish lefties once called the more rigid of the Old Left. Before that, it was a Communist term, used unironically. Later, of course, there was a TV show named after it. (Its host, Bill Maher, was fired for not being PC enough for the right's taste. But that didn't stop the phrase from almost exclusively stinging the left.) Feminists used to sic Neanderthal white men with *They just don't get it;* now those same men aim the phrase back at the libbers and their kind. The Sinclair Broadcasting spokesman Mark Hyman, in his nightly commentary aired on the conglomerate's sixty-two TV stations, ridiculed Democrats who believed that millions of people voted against their own interests by voting for Bush in 2004. And he did it with a pop threefer: "Hello? Earth to liberals. You just don't get it."

The sixties also saw cultural enemies swipe broader media lessons from one another. The word *yippie,* for instance, was based on the insight of Abbie Hoffman, Paul Krassner, and the Youth International Party that you couldn't change the world by shouting tirades at it—you had to entertain it. *Yippie,* playing off *hippie* and the childhood whoop, propagandized by stealing some of that mainstream TV magic power. Dress, music, language: Much of Yip politics was based on the clever use of symbolism to persuade an audience—that is, it was one of the left's few successful forays into advertising.

During the same decade (as Thomas Frank has detailed in his book *The Conquest of Cool*), a reverse but much grander larceny was taking place. Corporate advertising started to mimic counterculture and rock 'n' roll style, trying to make "consumers" believe that, by buying a particular product, they were nonconforming individualists kicking Establishment butt. Gaining steam ever since (and later, rolling hip-hop into the franchise), the bogus rebel stance has become *the* Establishment way of pushing products: Burger King's "Sometimes you gotta break the rules"; Audi's "RULES FOR PEOPLE WHO NEVER FOLLOW RULES"; Apple's "Think Different"; Reebok's "Defy Convention" campaign ("Defy the Man," "Defy authority," it agitated as a "suit" got a pie smashed into his face); the American Express headline, "Question Authority (Get 500 Membership Rewards)"; the Estée Lauder mascara called "Individualist"; the press release titled "Dr Pepper and Nintendo Promote Individuality" (part of the soft drink's self-described "celebrity-based 'Be You' campaign," an oxymoron that pretty much sums up the entire phenomenon).

When corporations pitch rebellious, anticorporate attitude and when the public accepts it, without a blink, as cool, then the pressure is on language to likewise hold corporate and anticorporate values simultaneously. Mainstream talk and the kind of talk that gives you a little twist that makes you different become one and the same. This paradox barely existed a century ago, which is another reason pop language is so different today. Never before has the language of marketing tried so hard to impersonate the language of the street, the hood, the rave club, or wherever "edge" and "authenticity" are believed to breed. (Not only was street talk not a marketing tool back when, it rarely made it to print. "One hundred years ago it wasn't respectable to put a lot of colloquial language and slang words into print," said Edmund Weiner, the principal philologist of the *Oxford English Dictionary*. "It's only been in the last century that the gap between written and spoken language has narrowed.")

Clearly, the conflict-hungry mass media benefit from exaggerating the culture wars. But the mass media also benefit from a more casual frisson every time they sponge from cultures that are even remotely alternative, as phrases like the Valley Girlish *whatever* or the probably black-drag-queen-created *Don't go there*—phrases that were once a few degrees off center—pop up in TV-anchor chitchat. During the 2004 Summer Olympics, an anchor of CNN's *In the Money* told his co-anchor, "You rock! You rock!" when she was able to identify the Finnish flag.

When a word travels from one side to the other, whether the sides are based on age, sensibility, or politics, the friction makes it shoot off a few sparks, lending it a cometlike aura, however briefly. That friction also eventually wears down a word's edges. But edgeless words, rather than losing their popitude, can actually gain some, because they've now satisfied another criterion for big-time pop: safety. (By the time *That sucks* became the mantra of *Beavis and Butt-Head*, hardly anyone still associated it with fellatio.) Though the crossover pop word may allude to a wilder, bolder past, it's now just boldly bland. And that's exactly the quality a word needs to reach wide circulation and to serve as a better salesman.

POP EATS SLANG FOR BREAKFAST

The difference between today's and yesteryear's pop language to some extent parallels the difference between pop and slang: Pop is infused with media and marketing; slang usually isn't. Since pop and slang are so intertwined, it might help to compare them more closely.

A major difference is that speaking slang is universal, but speaking pop depends on certain social conditions. "Slang is used everywhere around the world. To be human is to use language expressively and to have words that come and go," says the linguist John McWhorter. "Around the world, teenage males in particular do what is generally considered fucking up the language. In some villages in Senegal where they speak a very obscure language, an older man told me that he could barely understand what the teenage boys in his village were saying. The same tendency appears in Kenya, in Germany, in Manchester, England: Males dwell more on the rule-breaking kinds of speech.

"But the sort of post–*National Lampoon,* cocktail-party pop attitude is not quite as universal as more general slang is," he says. "It's spoken primarily in Western culture and in Japan, in 'tall-building cultures,' as I call them." Tall-building cultures (aka First World cultures) are the places most pervaded by the systems of media and marketing.

Within such a culture, like our own, slang and pop not only coexist but overlap. Whether a phrase is one or the other, or both, may depend on when in its life cycle you catch it. Something that's slang but not (yet) pop probably sounds more "authentic," because slang is closer in spirit to the moment of its coinage.

Tight and *sweet,* for instance, are two youth slang words that essentially mean the same thing, but only one is pop. *"Tight* is major contemporary slang for *good,"* says slang pro Dalzell, "but because of its sexual overtones, it's not embraced as pop. *Tight*'s littermate, *sweet,* on the other hand, went from slang to pop very quickly." *Sweet* graduated from playing *dude*'s sidekick in the 2000 culty hit *Dude, Where's My Car?* (one dude said, "Duuude," to which the other never failed to reply, "Sweeet") to becoming the temperate punch line in a 2004 Morgan Stanley ad (a financial adviser tells a middle-aged couple that if they juggle their portfolio, they can finally build their dream summer home. "Sweeet," the man exhales).

Dalzell compares slang and pop this way: "With slang, a situation creates a need for a word or expression, which then gets coined and spread and used again. It's bottom up." Pop, even if it begins as slang, "is more top down." The vocabularies of pop and slang also differ in size, he says. "One reason is that slang includes jargon, which is huge and constantly being coined. But the number of pop words and phrases can probably actually be counted. Pop's vocabulary is smaller in number, but repeated more often by more people."

Like pop music, pop language is always evolving in order to

appeal to as large an audience as possible, and therefore pop may bear little relationship to its more specific, colorful, slangy roots. It has been bleached, made one-size-fits-all. When a word ceases to reflect any particular place, opinion, history, or group of people, it sheds some meaning. But because it means less, we can use it more frequently.

Still, slang is not disappearing because of pop. The two are not in a zero-sum game. Far from it. Pop eats slang for breakfast—and every day it must have its breakfast. Slang will keep bubbling up as long as people create it and will keep supplying food for pop's expanding stomach. "Slang won't disappear," says Dalzell, "because the need for slang—to define and support tribe identity—will not disappear."

In a word, the difference between slang and pop is the difference between the deep, comically elongated *Whassup?!* that the independent filmmaker Charles Stone III and his pals in Philadelphia started playing with twenty years ago and the overnight celebrity *Whassup?!* mimicked by millions after the Stone crew first let it rip in a Budweiser commercial in the winter of 1999–2000. *Whassup?!* had become so pop that only days into its peak some people couldn't bring themselves to say even a mild "What's up?" for fear of sounding too trendy.

Which brings us to the foundation for so much of our current pop language—and to another reason why today's pop ain't your pop's pop—and that is the defining contributions of black Americans.

CHAPTER 3

What's Black, Then White, and Said All Over?

African-American vernacular, black English, black talk, Ebonics, hip-hop slang—whatever you want to call it, black-inspired language is all over mainstream pop talk like white on rice.

The talk may be everywhere, but, oddly enough, even during the rabid debate over Ebonics in the late 1990s rarely was there any mention of black English's deep imprint on American English. Yet linguists and other language experts know that America's language wouldn't be what it is—and certainly wouldn't pop as much—without black English.

"In the past, White society has resisted the idea," wrote Robert McCrum, William Cran, and Robert MacNeil in *The Story of English*, "but there is now no escaping the fact that [Blacks' influence] has been one of the most profound contributions to the English language."

"First, one cannot help but be struck by the powerful influence of African-American vernacular on the slang of all 20th-century American youth," Tom Dalzell wrote in *Flappers 2*

Rappers. "There were other influences, to be sure, on the slang of America's young, but none as powerful as that of the streets of Harlem and Chicago."

The linguist Connie Eble, author of *Slang and Sociability* and a college and youth slang expert at the University of North Carolina, Chapel Hill, calls the black influence on the American language "overwhelming."

White people (and not just the young) draw from a black lexicon every day, sometimes unaware of the words' origins, sometimes using them because of their origins. Here are just some of the words and phrases—born in different decades and now residing at various levels of popdom—that African Americans either coined or popularized, and, in either case, that they created the catchiest meaning of: *all that, back in the day, bling bling, blues, bogus, boogie, bootie, bro, chick, chill, come again, cook, cool, dawg, dig, dis, do your own thing, don't go there, freak, funky, get-go, get it on, get over, gig, give it up, groovy, heavy, hip, homeboy, hot, in your face, kick back, lame, living large, man, my bad, Micky D's, old school, nitty gritty, player, riff, righteous, rip off, rock 'n' roll, soul, tell it like it is, 24/7, uptight, wannabe, whack, Whassup?/sup?, Whassup with that?, when the shit hits the fan, you know what I'm saying?*

You know what I'm saying. Most of us talk, and all of us hear in the media some of that talk every day. Some phrases are said with an implicit nod to their source (*street cred, chill, You the man,* as well as a fist pound or high five), while others have been so widely adopted that they're beginning to feel sourceless (*24/7, lame, in your face*). *It's a black thang* has become everybody's thing, from *It's a dick thing* to (most offensively, considering who pushed it) "Virginia Slims: It's a Woman Thing."

But black vernacular didn't just add more lively, "colorful" words to the pop vocabulary. Much as marketing has influenced pop language, so black English has changed the American language in more fundamental ways. And that's what we're talking here—not about black talk per se, but about what happens when black talk meets, and transforms, the wider, whiter pop.

First and foremost, this language of outsiders has given us *cool:* the word itself—the preeminent pop word of all time—and quite a sizable chunk of the cool stance that underlies pop culture itself. Pop culture's desire for cool is second only to its desire for money—the two, in fact, are inextricably linked. (Cool may be first and foremost, but more on why it rules later.)

A second way African-American vernacular has affected the broader pop is that black talk has operated as a template for what it means to talk pop in the first place. As an often playful, ironic alternative to the official tongue, black slang has prefigured pop language in much the same way that black music has prefigured, and has often become, pop music. While there are important differences, some of the dynamics underlying black talk and pop talk are similar: Like black English, pop language sparks with wordplays and code games; it assumes that certain, often previously unacknowledged experiences deserve their own verbal expression; and it broadcasts the sense that only those who share the experiences can really get the words. For instance, black talk's running commentary on social exclusion is a model for pop talk's running commentary on media experiences.

Why do I say that pop is modeled on black and not the other way around? It's not just because black talk did these things earlier and still does them more intensely than pop, but as the original flipside to the voice of the Man, as the official unofficial speech of America, black talk is the object of pop talk's crush on everything "alternative" and "outsider."

There's an attitude in pop language that it is somehow undermining the stale old ways and sending a wake-up call to anyone who just doesn't get it. You can feel the attitude in everything from advertising's furious but phony rebelliousness to the faintly up-yours, tough-talking phrases like *Get a life* and *Don't even* think *about it*. It's not that these particular phrases are black or black-inspired, or that white people aren't perfectly capable of rebelliousness, anger at authority, and clever put-downs on their own. But the black experience, publicized more widely than ever now through hip-hop and its celebrities, has encouraged everyone else to more vigorously adopt the style of fighting the power—at least with the occasional catchphrase.

It may seem twisted, given American history, that general

pop language draws from the experience of black exclusion at all. But white attempts to *yo* here and *dis* there are an important piece of identity-and-image building for individuals and corporations alike. Today, the language of an excluded people is repeated by the nonexcluded in order to make themselves sound more included. As the mainstream plays the titillating notes of marginalization, we are collectively creating that ideal mass personality mentioned earlier: We can be part black (the part presumed to be cool and soulful, real and down, jazzy or hip-hop, choose your sound) and be part white (the privileged part, the part that has the luxury to easily reference other parts).

Related to all this imitation and referencing is the most noticeable way that pop talk is affected by black talk: Black talk has openly joined the sales force. At white society's major intersection with black language—that is, in entertainment—white society has gone from mocking black talk, as in minstrel shows, to marketing it, as in hip-hop. In the more than a hundred years between these two forms of entertainment, black language has by and large entered white usage as if it were a sourceless slang or perhaps the latest lingo of some particularly hep white cats, like the fast-talking disc jockeys of the 1950s and 1960s who purveyed black jive to white teenagers. Black language may have been the single most important factor in shaping generations of American slang, primarily through blues, jazz, and rock 'n' roll. But only relatively recently has black talk been used openly, knowingly, and not mockingly to sell products.

This would have been unthinkable once. Even fifteen or twenty years ago, car makers were loath to show black people in commercials for fear that their product would be tainted as inferior or, worse, as "a black car." Although many car companies are still skittish, by 2001 Buick was actually ending its commercials with the rap-popularized phrase "It's all good." (And by 2004, a BMW ad was featuring an interracial couple.) The phrase went from M. C. Hammer's 1994 song "It's All Good" to replacing "I love this game" as the official slogan of the National Basketball Association in 2001. Both Buick and the NBA have since dropped *It's all good,* but with their help the phrase massified, at least for a while. "It's huge" among white "sorority sisters and stoners alike," a twenty-seven-year-old white friend in Chicago told me in 2003.

So it's not all bad, this commercialization of black talk, especially if it can get the auto industry to move from shunning to quoting African Americans. But it comes laden with price tags. To read them, look at MTV, which has to be *the* major force in the sea change from whites-only to black's-da-bomb.

It may be difficult to believe now, but for years MTV wouldn't touch black music videos. The channel relented only under pressure, with videos by Prince and Michael Jackson. Black just wouldn't appeal to its white suburban teen audience, MTV explained. In 1989 with the appearance of the successful *Yo! MTV Raps,* that rationale was turned inside out, and—ka-ching!— black videos began to appear regularly. Since so much of MTV is advertising posing as entertainment (the videos are record company promotions, the parties and other bashes that appear are often visibly sponsored events), MTV has contributed significantly to two marketing trends: To the young, advertising has become an acceptable—nay, desirable—part of the cool life they aspire to; and a black, hip-hop-ish vernacular has become a crucial cog in the youth market machinery.

The outsider style is not solely black or hip-hop, but, at least in the marketing mind, a black package can be the most efficient buy to achieve that style. For corporate purposes, hip-hop in particular is a lucrative formula. Not only does the hip-hop black man represent the ultimate outsider who simultaneously stands at the nexus of cool, but much of hip-hop, created by the kind of people gated communities were meant to exclude, sings the praises of acquiring capitalism's toys. These paradoxes of racism are commercial-ready.

As the critic Greg Tate wrote on the thirtieth anniversary of hip-hop, "globally speaking, hiphop is money at this point, a valued form of currency where brothers are offered stock options in exchange for letting some corporate entity stand next to their fire. . . . Oh, the selling power of the Black vernacular."

When Sprite realized that teenagers no longer believed its TV commercials telling them that "Image Is Nothing" and that they shouldn't trust commercials or celebrity endorsements (said only half tongue-in-cheek by celebrities like NBA star Grant Hill), the soft drink's marketing department decided to up the ante. So, when you need outsider verisimilitude, who ya gonna call? Why, black rappers, of course, preferably on the hardcore side. Get *them* to testify to the soft drink's beyond-the-bounds, can't-be-bought spirit at Sprite.com launch parties (to be run later on MTV). Or get real kids, looking and sounding ghetto, to rap their own lyrics in TV spots about, say, "a situation that is not too sweet, which is an attribute of Sprite," as a Sprite publicist said. How else to get kids, usually white kids, to understand that you understand that they're sick of commercials telling them what's cool?

And so, while Sprite had long used rappers in its overall "Obey Your Thirst" campaign, now it pumped up the volume. Only by obeying the first commandment that image is everything can you become, as Sprite did by the late nineties, the fastest-growing soft-drink brand in the world. "Sprite has really become an icon," Pina Sciarra, then director of youth brands for Sprite, said on the 2001 PBS documentary *Merchants of Cool*. "It's not just associated with hip-hop, it's really a part of it, as much as baggy jeans and sneakers." Sprite, by the way, is owned by the Coca-Cola Company, the same company that agreed (around the time of the Sprite.com launch in late 2000) to pay $192.5 million to settle a racial discrimination suit by black employees, who accused the company of paying blacks less than whites for the same jobs and of discriminating in promotions and evaluations. (The company denied the allegations, but the settlement was one of the largest of its kind at the time.)

When whites talk black—or, just as commonly, when major corporations do it for them—it makes you wanna shout, *Whassup with that?!*

TERMS AND PROPS

Before I address wannabe black talk and other points where black language crosses over into pop, a few words about what "black language" and "black words" are.

I've been using the terms "black English," "black slang," "black talk," and "African-American vernacular" rather interchangeably, which, in plain English, seems OK. Yet, at the same time, each term is a bit off the mark.

No one phrase is the perfect vehicle to explain how a people speak, because "a people" don't all speak (or do anything) one way. That's one of the problems with the terms "black English" and "black dialect." "Black English" was more or less booted out of formal linguistic circles, because, as linguist Peter Trudgill wrote in the 1995 revised edition of his book *Sociolinguistics,* "it suggested that all Blacks speak this one variety of English—which is not the case." The newer scholarly term, African American Vernacular English (AAVE), has pros and cons: It "distinguishes those Blacks who do not speak standard American English from those who do," wrote Trudgill, "although it still suggests that only one nonstandard variety, homogeneous through the whole of the USA, is involved, which is hardly likely." The word *Ebonics* was created in 1973 by African-American scholars to "define black language from a black perspective," writes Geneva Smitherman, director of the African American Language and Literacy Program at Michigan State University. But the 1997 Ebonics controversy loaded the word with so much baggage (which we'll rummage through later) that, outside of some hip-hop use, it has become nearly immobile.

"Black slang" can't describe black language, because clearly most black language is composed of standard English. However, when referring to actual slang that blacks created *(my bad, dis),* "black slang" is the right term. Personally, I like "black talk" (which is also the title of one of Smitherman's books). Although, like any phrase starting with the adjective "black," it might suggest that all black people talk this way all the time, "black talk" (like "pop talk") is colloquial and flexible, encompassing vocabulary and then some.

In mixing up these terms, I take my cue in part from the Stanford University linguistics professor John Russell Rickford. Rickford's not hung up over what black language is called, though he favors "spoken soul," the title of his book (subtitled *The Story of Black English* and written with his son, Russell John

Rickford) and a term coined by Claude Brown, the author of *Manchild in the Promised Land.*

In *Spoken Soul,* the Rickfords spell out the dimensions of the language:

> In homes, schools, and churches, on streets, stages, and the airwaves, you can hear soul spoken every day. Most African Americans—including millions who . . . are fluent speakers of Standard English—still invoke Spoken Soul as we have for hundreds of years, to laugh or cry, to preach and praise, to shuck and jive, to sing, to rap, to shout, to style, to express our individual personas and our ethnic identities . . . to create authentic characters and voices in novels, poems, and plays. . . . The fact is that most African Americans *do* talk differently from whites and Americans of other ethnic groups, or at least most of us can when we want to.

If that approximates a definition of black language, what are "black words"? Word origins in general are difficult to trace, but the origins of black words are particularly so. In the dictionary-style *Black Talk: Words and Phrases from the Hood to the Amen Corner,* Smitherman writes that she did not include etymologies because "these are risky propositions at best when dealing with an oral language such as African American Language." Hampton University professor Margaret Lee, who published "Out of the Hood and into the News: Borrowed Black Verbal Expressions in a Mainstream Newspaper" in the linguistic journal *American Speech* and verified the black origins of each phrase with at least two sources, adds, "The approach Smitherman takes and I take is that these expressions and words were created by African Americans or were circulated in the black community before they went mainstream." In order to define black words that have gone pop, I would only add that a pop word is "black" simply if its most popular meaning or nuance was created by black people—for example, *bad* and *girlfriend* are pop when used with black nuance, but not pop when used conventionally.

Origins tend to get lost in the roaring mainstream. Some

words that seem white are black, and vice versa. For instance, until I looked into 24/7, I would have guessed its roots were cyber or maybe something out of the convenience-store industry. But 24/7 arose from a hip-hop fondness for number phrases. Rapdict.org lists some sixty number phrases, many of which are too obscure or gangsta to cross over; *411* is one of the few others that has gone pop. (A recent Mercedes-Benz magazine ad advised, "Get the 411.")

Bogus, which sounds so surfer, dude, dates back at least as far as 1798, when a glossary defined it as a "spurious coin," write David Barnhart and Allan Metcalf in *America in So Many Words.* "Its origins are obscure, but one guess that is as good as any is that it is from *boko,* meaning 'deceit' or 'fake' in the Hausa language of west central Africa. The word then would have been brought over by Africans sold into slavery here." In addition, some nuances that no one doubts are African American may run deeper in black history than most people, black or white, imagine. When *bad* is used to mean good, the meaning (though obviously not the word itself) is derived, Smitherman writes, from a phrase in the Mandinka language in West Africa, "*a ka nyi ko-jugu,* which means, literally, 'it is good badly,' that is, it is very good, or it is so good that it's bad!"

Meanwhile, some words that most people would identify as black, and that black people did indeed popularize, originated among others. Southern phrases in particular jumped races, "from black to white in the case of *bubba* and *big daddy,* from white to black in the case of *grits* and *chitlins,*" write the Rickfords. *Cat,* meaning a hip guy, is a dated piece of slang (though often on the verge of a comeback) that most people attribute to black jazz musicians; Ken Burns's television series *Jazz* states that Louis Armstrong was the first person to have said it. But, as Tom Dalzell writes, in "the late 19th century and early 20th century, *cat* in the slang and jargon of hobos meant an itinerant worker . . . possibly because the migratory worker slunk about like a 'homeless cat.' " However, it did take Armstrong, and then other jazz musicians in the 1920s, to introduce the word into broader usage. That old rap word *fly* (stylish, good-looking, smooth) was flying long before rap. "The most well-established slang meaning of *fly* was in the argot of thieves, where *fly* meant sly, cunning, wide-awake, knowing, or smart," writes Dalzell, who notes those uses of *fly* as early as 1724 and in *Bleak House* by Dickens in 1853. But again, *fly* didn't really buzz until black musicians picked up on it, beginning around 1900, well before *Superfly* in the 1970s and rap in the 1980s.

WANNABE NATION

Whether black-born or black-raised, black words are the ones that many white people are wearing like backwards baseball caps. That brings us to a particularly telling term that went from black to pop. *Wannabe* originally referred to people who wanted to be something they weren't; it was often said of a black person who wanted to be white. In Spike Lee's 1988 film *School Daze,* the conflict was between the dark-skinned, activist "Jigaboos" and the light-skinned sorority sister "Wannabes." Beginning around the time of that movie, *wannabe* was used by just about everybody to mean anybody who wanted to be somebody he or she wasn't—there have been surfer wannabes, Madonna wannabes, and dot.com start-up wannabes. But *wannabe* is not just a blast from decades past. More recently, "podcaster wannabes" have developed, and in just one week on TV and radio in late 2004, I heard of "artist wannabes," "geek wannabes," and "wannabe homeland security chief" Bernard Kerik.

Racially speaking, *wannabe* has reversed field. Since at least the early nineties, with hip-hop an entrenched, virtually mainstream hit, *wannabe* has been far more likely to refer to whites, especially teenagers, who want to be black or do the style. Sometimes called *wiggers* or *wiggas (white* plus *nigger/nigga),* black wannabes try to dance the dance and talk the talk. Even whites who would hate to be black will maintain the right to add the occasional black flourish. Some whites flash a black word or gesture like an honorary badge of cool, to show they're down with black people on certain occasions, usually involving sports or entertainment. Or maybe they do it because some of their best friends and some of the best commercials are flashing it, too. Or maybe they just need to know that black people like them. Take "Johnny and Sally," the fictitious white couple on the very funny Web site BlackPeopleLoveUs.com, which is full of "testimonials" to their racial bigheartedness. As one unnamed black man attested, "Johnny always alters his given name and refers to himself in the third person—for example, 'J-Dog don't play that' or 'J-Dog wants to know wusssaappp.' It comforts me to know that my parlance has such broad appeal."

African Americans aren't the only people whose parlance has broad appeal. Non-Latino blacks dabble in Spanish, Catholics in Yiddish, adults in teenage talk. Cultural skin is always permeable, absorbing any word that has reached a critical mass of usefulness or fun. The human species can't help but borrow—after all, that's how languages develop.

But whether we call it wannabe talk or the less derogatory crossover talk, something about white society's sampling of black speech is more loaded than the usual borrowing. Black vernacular's contributions to English are larger in number and run deeper linguistically and psychologically than do any other ethnic group's. And black English, born in slavery, resounds with our society's senses of guilt, fear, identity, and style.

Black-to-white crossover talk, which also began during slavery, is hardly new. But, like most pop talk today, it radiates a new gloss, a veneer in which you can catch the reflection of its increased market value. Black talk comes from something real— "serious as a heart attack," Smitherman says—but, whoop, there it is, sparking out of TV commercials, out of white politicians, out of anyone who has something to promote, spin, or get over.

"Chill, Orrin," the Democratic senator Patrick Leahy told the Republican senator Orrin Hatch when things got a little testy during a Judiciary Committee hearing in 1998. Behind the *chill* was something more than "relax." One white guy was momentarily able to harness and aim some soulful black power at the other white guy. Saying the black word says, I stake myself closer to black people and their righteous anger than you do. You're more afraid of them and their language than I am—so I win this moment.

"Go on, give it up!" the signs throughout Virgin Records

implored. *Give it up*'s "it" referred only obliquely to applause. (Used to introduce about every other musical act these days, the black phrase has long been a verbal welcome mat. "Everybody give it up for my very good friend Marion Barry," someone said on the old comedy series *In Living Color* in 1990.) "It" referred even more obliquely to sex. *(Give it up* originally meant "to agree to engage in copulation," according to the *Random House Historical Dictionary of American Slang [RHHDAS].)* No, this "it" meant your money—for "The Sacrifice Sale. Hundreds of titles: 3 for $26."

As recently as 2005, McDonald's, like many a corporation trying to sound more "urban," was getting it all wrong. "DOUBLE CHEESEBURGER? I'D HIT IT," read a McDonald's banner ad on ESPN.com. As mocking bloggers pointed out, the hip-hop slang actually meant, "I'd have sex with that cheeseburger."

It's not as if there hasn't been enough time to hit it right. Again, black style's market value jumped around the time *Yo! MTV Raps* debuted in 1989. In a TV spot that same year, the pasty white Pillsbury Doughboy performed a mean rap number. By 1994, Dan Rather (a magnet for every catchy, and uncatchy, turn of phrase that comes along) reported that political candidates were "dissing" each other. In 1999, a hip black guy insisted, for Wendy's, "This sandwich is da bomb."

Three years later, *CNN Headline News* asked the writers responsible for the crawl and other graphics that crowd its screen to inject some hip-hop. "In an effort to be sure we are as cutting-edge as possible with our on-screen persona, please refer to this slang dictionary when looking for just the right phrase," read a *Headline News* memo, according to the New York *Daily News.* "Please use this guide to help all you homeys and honeys add a new flava to your tickers and dekos." Among the phrases mentioned were *fly, ill,* and *jimmy hat,* for a condom. (A *Headline News* spokeswoman at the time said a mid-level producer sent the memo without top executives knowing about it.)

"You Go, Girl!" ran a 2004 headline in *Today's Christian Woman* for a story about finding supportive friends.

"She said she'd have more gay people in the White House. I'm like, 'You go, Teresa,' " a gay doctor said of Teresa Heinz

Kerry at an Ohio campaign rally. "Women to Heinz Kerry: You Go, Girl," an Associated Press headline read. For a brief moment there, Teresa was the nation's "You go, girl" girl.

You go, girl! is democratic and process-oriented—every girl is presumed to have the strength that can propel her forward. But what's a guy to do? When a man needs an equally exciting, gender-saluting pop phrase that expresses personal recognition, he's almost sure to receive the hierarchical, goal-oriented *You da* (or *the*) *man!* Both black and white men scramble to the top of the heap with this winner-take-all phrase. But in the media and off, it's increasingly white men who adorn one another with this verbal king's crown.

In the 1998 animated movie *Antz,* the ant voiced-over by Sylvester Stallone says to the Woody Allen ant, who has just saved his species' civilization, "You da ant!" And they exchange high-fives.

"You're the man!" Karl ("Bush's Brain") Rove "bellowed back into his cell phone" to Lloyd Smith, who managed Jim Talent's Missouri Senate campaign in the 2002 midterm elections, *Time* magazine reported. Smith had just told Rove that it looked as if Talent was going to beat Democratic senator Jean Carnahan, thereby guaranteeing the Senate to Republicans.

You da man! is now so common that when the sports columnist Frank Deford compiled his 2004 Thanksgiving Day list of things "I wish we still had," he included "golf tournaments that were played without idiots screaming 'you da man.' "

But white men still scream *You da man!* because the words (especially *da,* though it's not required) still suggest a wistful tableau of black folks testifying for white folks. Beyond giving a white man props for smiting a foe, *You da man* gives him authenticity clearance, momentary proof that, at the least, he's not the Man, an oppressive white authority figure.

It's better yet if a white guy can get a real black guy to testify for him (just like in all the movies that star a somehow emotionally stunted white hero who's made to see one light or another by a more soulful black sidekick). An ad campaign a while back made this embarrassingly evident. "The Colonel?" asked what intentionally sounded like a black male voice. "He da man!" The man, of course, was Colonel Sanders of KFC. He's dead, but in the late nineties the Colonel was not only revived as a cartoon character for TV spots, but he also became black (minus a pigment change). "Go, Colonel! Go, Colonel!" the voiceover jived. "The Colonel still has a pink face and white suit," Mark Schone noted on the radio show *This American Life,* "but these days the erstwhile Southern gentleman twirls his cane to . . . old school seventies funk. . . . In an ad campaign that began on his 108th birthday, the Colonel has cabbage patched, tap danced, rapped, and played basketball. . . . What's it mean when a redneck who dressed like a slaveowner comes back from the dead and gets funky?"

And what's it mean when right-wingers take a catchy phrase that points out racism to express their own sense of victimization? "But to you," "Aaron" wrote to "fazz" on rightwingnews. com in 2003, "facts don't matter because Abrams committed the greatest crime of all, he was guilty of BWC (Breathing While Conservative)." (That's Elliott Abrams, who was indicted for giving false testimony to Congress during the Iran-Contra affair, pardoned by Bush I, and recently made Bush II's top White House adviser on global democracy.) "Liberals and their Libertine fellow-travelers accuse Callahan of the one inexcusable crime in America: BWR ('Breathing While Republican')," "Illbay" posted on Freerepublic.com in 2002 about a pork barrel project involving Congressman Sonny Callahan of Alabama.

Breathing while Republican (or *conservative*) is based on the phrase *breathing while black,* the more prominent *voting while black* (which resurfaced during the 2000 and 2004 elections regarding attempts to suppress black votes), and the original *X while black* pop construction, *driving while black* (police using racial profiling to pull black people over on the road or to arrest them chiefly because of their race).

SPELLING B

Driving while black, itself twisted from *driving while intoxicated,* is simple, classic wordplay. And DWI to DWB to BWR is classic letterplay and codeplay. Coiled in most pop phrases—and especially in anything compressed further into initials (or numbers, like *24/7* and *411*)—is a Jack-in-the-box meaning that's just waiting to spring out. That is, the energy putting the pop in pop language comes from the power of codes. All language is codes, codes 'R' us and all that, but coded language is an African-American art form. The often double meaning of black phrases, the way some words may mean their opposite *(bad, dope, stoopid/ stupid)* developed among slaves who needed to talk to each other in front of the massa without him knowing Jack.

To carry the weight of a twisted meaning not on a word but on a single letter is to pack the code tighter. Altering a letter in an otherwise ordinary word can alter the world outlook. When *boys* went to *boyz,* so went Boyz II Men. The title of the 1991 movie *Boyz N the Hood* declared it was no suburban frolic. Young black musicians and hip-hop-influenced culture in general wear wayward words like visual rap. Hip-hop and R&B singers and groups have long been seizing the Z (Jay-Z, Outlawz, Limp Bizkit), crossing an X (Xscape, Xzibit), or otherwise kurupting the language (Kurupt, OutKast, Fabolous, Ludacris, Shyne, Mystikal).

Hip-hop didn't invent deliberate misspellings as a mild social subversion (remember the left's *Amerika,* the hippies' *freek?*) or as an attention-getting device (way before hip-hop, marketers were messing with the ABCs, from *Beanz Meanz Heinz* and Kool cigarettes to Kwik Save Foodstores and EZLern driving school). Wacky spelling may in fact serve the status quo quite well. In the late 1800s, a loose group of humorists called the Phunny Phellows "fed their Victorian audiences a bland diet of simple gags, sprinkled liberally with malapropisms, terrible puns, comic misspellings, blatant racism, stock characters, and shopworn topical jokes," wrote Kevin Mac Donnell in *Firsts* magazine.

But deliberate misspellings have long been used to declare some form of independence, however deep or shallow it might run. In the 1920s, young people "spelled 'rats' as 'rhatz!' and shortened 'that's too bad' to 'stoo bad,' " Dalzell writes, adding that even the famous *phat,* which seems the epitome of hip-hop spelling, has a surprisingly long history. *Fat* meant "rich" back in the seventeenth century, and examples of *fat* meaning "good," "cool," or "living well" have occurred ever since. As for the "ph," in a list of "Negro argot," *Time* magazine listed *phat* "as one of several 'adjectives of approval' " in 1963. But *phat* predated that. Dalzell found that around the turn of the last century "typesetters referred to type that was easily set as being *phat*. . . . Indeed, in 1885, the Post Express Printing Company in Rochester, New York, published the 'Phat Boy's Birds-Eye Map of the Saint Lawrence River' with a drawing of a corpulent boy."

Despite their varied history, creative misspellings today are mostly associated with hip-hop culture. So much so that in his 2000 movie *Bamboozled*, Spike Lee hilariously spoofed the trend. "I respectfully submit," one rapper tells his gangsta crew, "that we from now on, henceforth and whatnot spell black B-L-A-K, not B-L-A-C-K."

Hip-hop misspellings don't just reject select bits of standard white written style; they also reflect a history, beginning in the 1800s, in which standard writers ridiculed Negro speech with exaggerated misspelling. I'm not referring to the sympathetic, if imperfect, attempts at dialect writing in literature, as in *Uncle Tom's Cabin* and *Huckleberry Finn*, but rather to another, contemporary "trend in comic writing where southern speakers, especially blacks, were portrayed as uneducated or as figures of fun," as David Crystal writes in *The Cambridge Encyclopedia of the English Language*. "Dialect vocabulary and grammar (*hain't, saw* for *seen*, etc.) were used as well as misspelling, though it was the spelling which created the impact." Some of the impact of hip-hop's mangled orthography reflects that dis: Do the disapproved thing first; do it aggressively and obviously intentionally, b4 itz dunn 2 U.

And it's that unorthodox, defiant style that larger, nonblack marketing forces are now sucking image off of. If a company abuses the alphabet today, it's usually doing so to look hip-hop fresh, sometimes to look, dare we say . . . outlaw. Customized spellings that developed in part to subvert the Man's words are now copied by the Man's corporations almost as fast as they'll funnel benjamins to Congress to make them mo' money. (Hey, just like real gangstas!)

What's Black, Then White, and Said All Over?

In 1999, when Rupert Murdoch's Fox Family Channel launched two new cable channels, it fought the power by naming them the Boyz Channel and the Girlz Channel. (Both were soon zapped.) When it was still running, *Lizzie McGuire* was the most successful show on the Disney Channel lineup called "Zoog Weekendz." The STARZ!, BLACK STARZ!, STARZ! Kids, STARZ! Family digital movie channels add all caps and exclamation marks to convey their over-the-top Zness. Z bumped the old-skool *S* in DreamWorks' *Antz* (the name of Woody's "You da man!" ant, by the way, was "Z"). One of my favorite stupid attempts of someone to get down is the name of a spammer (apparently now deceased), "BestLoanz.com."

A quick trick to convince children that they're cool and that you, if you're a seller of stuff, are rad, is to call them "kidz" and otherwise buzz their brains with Zs; hence, the glitzoid Trollz dolls and cartoons (based on the 1960s cute-ugly Trolls); Bratz dolls (a massive seller); Nitro Battlerz (cars racing in battle domes and such); Kellogg's Gripz crackers and cookies; Hershey's Koolerz chewing gum, SnackBarz, and Twizzlers Sourz. On the health food side of the aisle, Hain's line of children's products is called Kidz, while EnviroKidz says it makes "The World's First 100% Certified Organic Cereals for Kidz."

Z—the purple of the alphabet, the last in line shall be first, the snap at the tip of the whip (Zorro's?)—is the letter that marketing relies on most to represent childlike fun, diversity, and all things hip-hop.

Z is unconventional, jazzy, but not really dangerous. Like Snoop Dogg's izzle, fo'shizzle ("for sure") pig-Latin-like lingo, Zs can be damn cuddly. (Snoop Dogg has dropped his "shizzolating." "I overdosed on it," he told *MTV News* in 2004. "I'm seeing it everywhere, you know what I'm saying?") For danger, citizens, you gotta get *X*.

X is pornography, the drug ecstasy, a former spouse, the signature of illiteracy, X out, cross out, the cross, an equation's unknown solution, off the charts, extra, extreme, and (in the exception exposing the rule) kisses. Generation X is the somehow canceled-out generation. *The X-Files* were stories of the paranormal too threatening for normals. *X Creatures* was a Discovery

Channel show about Loch Ness monsters, giant squids, and other excessive animals. The *X-Men*—whether the original sixties comic book or its later incarnations as animated TV shows and live-action movies—is a parable about "the Other," ethnic hatred, and race relations. (The X-men have a mutant gene that gives them great powers, but human society reviles them because they're different.)

But now outsiders are in (Outsider Art, by non-art-world, non-art-schooled, often black, and occasionally psychotic artists, draws big bucks). Exy is sexy—it's hardcore, outlaw, a black man, Malcolm X, Brand X. And today brands, rather than running from *X*ness, practically cut it into their foreheads with razors, probably Schick Xtreme III blades. *X* is death, like the Slug-X Trap for gardening. In a world of *Survivor, The Sopranos,* and Swift Boat Veterans for Truth, X or be Xed. When NBC and the World Wrestling Federation (now World Wrestling Entertainment) needed a name for their newborn, self-designated "outlaw" (and quickly Xed-out) football league, the choice was obvious: the XFL (and X marked the spot for its teams the Maniax and Xtremes). When Right Guard decided it needed another market for another deodorant, it created Right Guard Xtreme Sport. When Kraft's Jell-O sales declined, the company put the gelatin in push-up packages, named it X-TREME Jell-O Sticks, and took aim at kids: "They're extreme—yeah!" exclaimed the commercial. And when that foxy Fox needed a name for another cable channel, it chose FX. Yes, the name plays nicely on Fox, and if you happen to know that FX is Hollywood for special effects, you might get a goose bump. But more important, *F* looks cooler slapped up against a bad-ass *X*, the naive, open-mouthed *O* squeezed out all together. "Perpleed?" an ad for FX on a commuter train read. "What would life be like without the X?"

Well, it might not be quite so easy to sell in. In video games, X marks the spot for Microsoft's Xbox. On TV, the letter has done duty for *The X Show* (about relationships, guy talk, and big breasts), *Maximum EXposure* (about extreme activities—man eats live snakes, ex-wife attacks new wife), and, on the relatively staid History Channel, *Extreme History with Roger Daltrey*. "Beyond AM.

Beyond FM. XM" went a slogan for XM Satellite Radio. *XXL* is the name of the hip-hop magazine as well as the extra extra large size. *X* is a ride on the wild side that yet another XXL SUV swears it will deliver: A huge sign over Times Square read, "AS NOT SEEN IN THE HAMPTONS—NISSAN XTERRA."

For pure purchased *X,* look at the Jaguar X-Type, Infiniti's QX or FX45, or any vehicular X. *X* crosses the chrome on cars, says the automotive writer Phil Patton, because of "its connotations of 'experimental' and 'luxury.' " Or, in the case of XTerra, "Gen X and cross-country," he says. "The S in SE or SX is supposed to suggest 'sport,' but the SX also suggests sex."

OK, so *X* brands products. Earth to me: That's what popular symbols *do.* I guess I shouldn't be surprised to see *X* infiltrate newslike missives from media conglomerates, but when I saw the following, I almost had to slip on some Nike Shox to absorb the blow: A CNBC headline for a segment about international reaction to the U.S. invasion of Iraq was succinct, if not right out of the funnies: "World Reax."

So common is *X,* especially when referring to anything "extreme," that *X* has gone from out there to dead center—or, to restate that in pop, *X* is the new *edge.* Back in 2001, when ESPN's X Games (*X* stands for "extreme sports") were beginning to go global, even ESPN execs paid to propagate *X* were dissing the full *extreme.* " 'Extreme' is the old term," Ron Semiao, then in charge of ESPN's Global X division, told *Advertising Age* at the time. "These types of action sports have gone from being an activity of fringe groups to an ingrained part of a generation that influences its fashion, music, entertainment." He helped push for the rather uncatchy term "action sports." (Are there any other kind?) When Heinz's Bagel Bites, which was originally marketed to mothers, revamped to target *X*-attracted "tweens" (kids between childhood and teenhood), a Heinz executive said, "Action sports is a sport that embodies the lifestyle and personality of the Bagel Bites consumer." If true, this proves, finally: Edge is dead, long live the hole in the center.

Obviously, not everything *X* or *Z* is black or black-influenced. Extreme sports, in fact, are pretty darn white. Pornography appears in all colors. *Z* and *X* are mysterious and primal human qualities. But black, according to still-thriving stereotypes, is so often mysterious and primal, so often *Z* and *X*, that the corporate addition of those letters is black pepper for the white sauce.

Encouraged by the hip *X* and *Z* hopping around, other letter replacements have gained favor among wannabe companies— that is, they wanna *B*. I'm convinced the whole *B to B* nomenclature (meaning "business to business," the tag of telephone directories and other enterprises in which businesses deal directly with one another rather than with consumers) is a hit because it resonates with the black *B*s: *B-boy, B-ball,* and *B* as a form of address, as in "Yo, B, whassup?" (This last *B* was probably reduced from *blood,* "a positive term, noting the genetic kinship and shared bloodlines of African people," Smitherman writes.) Sure, it makes sense in this abbreviation-loving era that *business to business* would be punched down to *B2B*, as in B2BMarketingTrends.com ("to help marketing professionals stay abreast of B2B marketing trends," according to a press release). But *B2B* has become too popular for brevity to be the only explanation. *B2B* has spawned *B2C, B2B2C, B2G, B2E,* and *P2P*—"business to consumer," "business to business to consumer," "business to government," "business to employee," and "peer to peer" (as in electronic file sharing), respectively. All this B-bop can make any business sound less like it consists of a bunch of suits who bore one another at meetings and more like a crew of B-boys doing some def transactions.

B as short for *be* (along with *U* for *you* and *4* for *for*) has been around for ages (even pre-Prince). But this shading of *B* has been bumped up lately because of its increased use in text messaging as well as in hip-hop. "Now we can b alone," a man writes to a woman on a pager in a noisy concert crowd for a Verizon Wireless spot. A Burger King TV commercial had it both ways, with nods to hip-hop and electronics: "B Real. B Good," voiceovers sang as the lyrics were spelled out on-screen to make sure we C the Bs. "2 Go. BK4U." Bouncy and at the beginning of the alphabet, *B* is on the mild side of businesses that want their bit of blood.

When corporations misspell, they're trying to spell it out: We refuse to put letters together the way the authorities tell us to!

What's Black, Then White, and Said All Over?

Wannabe or crossover talk didn't begin with hip-hop, nor is lingo-lending from one group to another confined to blacks and whites in America. Whites talking some black is part of an apparently universal phenomenon that sociolinguists call covert prestige. This means that speakers of a "standard" language (whatever the language) "have favorable attitudes toward lower-class, nonstandard speech forms," explains the linguist Margaret Lee. "However, these attitudes are not always overtly expressed, and they may be subconscious, because they stray from mainstream—or overt—values about the perceived superior status of the standard forms." This occurs, she adds, "for the most part throughout the world—when new forms enter the mainstream, in fact, they usually come from nonstandard speech."

Males are more prone than females to imbibing some of that covert prestige. Perhaps that's because, as some studies indicate, males associate standard speech with femininity. "Females tend to use more 'correct' speech forms," Lee says. On the basis of a study in Norwich, England, Peter Trudgill wrote in *Sociolinguistics,* "A large number of male speakers, it seems, are more concerned with acquiring *covert prestige* than with obtaining social status (as this is more usually defined)." This may be, he wrote, "because working-class speech is associated with the 'toughness' traditionally supposed to be characteristic of working-class life— and 'toughness' is quite widely considered to be a desirable masculine characteristic."

Covert or otherwise, black-to-white (and white-to-black) crossover talk in America began during slavery, especially when slave children and white children played together. Most of that language was never recorded, of course, and we have to wait for the development of various media to see how black speech influenced the broader English. "Slavery made its own traditions of speech and vocabulary," McCrum and his coauthors write in *The Story of English.* The entry of black English—an amalgam of Africanisms, the trade English used on slave ships, and plantation English—"into the mainstream of American life began with the Brer Rabbit stories. Later it was to sustain its place there through minstrel shows, vaudeville, music hall, radio and finally the movies."

By the 1840s, minstrel shows had brought black language to large audiences and in the most overtly covert way possible. White men in blackface sang and told jokes using some variety of black language, often insulting imitations of it, to entertain whites. They were horror shows, "but minstrel shows were also the beginning of influence of African-American style on all America," writes Allan Metcalf in *How We Talk: American Regional English Today.*

Black musical forms—spirituals, ragtime, the blues—went on to spread black language to the larger public, but by far the most influential music, until hip-hop, was jazz. Jazz fed generations of slang. Jive, the jokey, mint-cool language that arrived with the swing jazz of the thirties and forties, was slang that went on to become the pop of its time, even spawning a number of dictionaries. Cab Calloway's *Hepster's Dictionary: Language of Jive* (first edition published in 1938) listed jive words like *beat* (exhausted), *chick* (girl), *hip, hype, groovy, in the groove, jam* (improvised swing music), *joint is jumping, mellow, pad, riff, sharp, solid, square, too much,* and *yeah, man.* In *The Original Handbook of Harlem Jive* (1944), Dan Burley wrote: "in the sense that [jive] came into use among Negroes in Chicago about the year 1921, it meant to taunt, scoff, to sneer—an expression of sarcastic comment," and he relates it to the "linguistic procedure which came to be known as 'putting you in the dozens.' "

The whites ("flappers" if they were women) who jammed the Harlem clubs in the 1920s, the jitterbug craze of the 1930s, and influential disc jockeys in the 1940s all contributed to making jive the lingo for black and white youth in the know. Listen, for instance, to this forties DJ: "Hiya cat, wipe ya feet on the mat, let's slap on the fat and dish out some scat. You're a prisoner of wov. W-O-V, 1280 on the dial, New York, and you're picking up the hard spiel and good deal of Fred Robbins, dispensing seven score and ten ticks of ecstatic static and spectacular vernacular from 6:30 to 9."

"A new language has been born," Lou Shelly wrote in 1945

in another jive dictionary, *Hepcats Jive Talk Dictionary,* "and with its usual lustiness youth has made jive talk heard from one end of the land to the other." This meant, as always, that corporate interests were moving in—a process then more likely to signal a phenomenon's demise than it does today. "The end of the jive generation," writes Dalzell, "could be measured by the fact that in 1946 Hallmark cards issued a set of 'Solid Sender' cards, 'groovy as the movie MAKE MINE MUSIC,' based on the 'Disney hepcat scene.' "

Though jive began to dive, it kept resurfacing in the slang of later groups. In describing the beat speech of the late-forties hipster, Jack Kerouac called it "a new language, actually spade (Negro) jargon, but you soon learned it." By the 1950s, Kerouac noticed that "even college kids went around hep and cool and using terms I'd heard on Times Square in the early Forties."

Jive, writes Dalzell, "would lay an important foundation for the slang of the hipster/beat movement of the late 1950s, the hippie movement of the 1960s and early 1970s, and to some extent the hip-hop/rap phenomenon of the 1980s and 1990s." "*Cap, fly chick, groovy, homey, hung up, icy, mellow, righteous, sharp, solid,* and *square* all endured quite nicely, playing major roles in the slang of the 1960s and the 1990s."

If the 1960s were the turning point in creating pop language of a different order, that was to a great degree because, simultaneously, black language was undergoing a renaissance and was developing an increased ability to cross over. This black force met up with the big two powers, mass media and marketing, and all three have played with and against one another ever since.

Smitherman describes this blossoming of black language:

. . . perhaps the richest period of linguistic innovation was the last half of the twentieth century, particularly the 1960s and beyond. The emergence of the Black Free- dom Struggle marked a fundamental shift in linguistic consciousness as Black intellectuals, scholar-activists, and writer-artists deliberately and consciously engaged in an unprecedented search for a language to express Black identity and the Black condition. This era was in fact the first period in the history of U.S. slave descendants when there was a critical mass of highly educated Blacks.

White people couldn't help but hear the newly invigorated black talk, she continues. "The 1960s was a defining moment in this cultural diffusion process with Motown, on the one hand, crossing racial boundaries with its music, and the Civil Rights Movement, on the other, crossing racial boundaries with its language and rhetoric of protest and moral confrontation, all broadcast live on the eleven o'clock news."

By the 1970s, black was beautiful enough to be in demand in the more liberal circles. As Gerald Boyd, the former managing editor of *The New York Times* and a black man, said in a round-table discussion about race, "When I started out in the early seventies, it was very popular to be black. Every white had to have one."

MEDIA BOND

Now, more than a generation later, does every white—or at least every white kid—have to be one?

In the late eighties, the hip-hop movement began to bring black style—music, dance, fashion, language—back harder than anything since the introduction of jive. However, as Dalzell writes, "Unlike the hippie movement where anyone could don a tie-dye shirt and become a weekend hippie, the hip-hop culture did not provide a lifestyle that most American young people could completely embrace. Simply put, white teenagers could not, as much as they might wish to, become black. They could and did, however, listen to the music, dress the dress . . . mirror the hair cuts, adopt the rap vocabulary suitable for their daily lives, mimic the cadence of street speech, and admire from a safe distance the lives of prominent black rappers and athletes."

What made both the mimicking and the distance possible were massive media and marketing, both of which have mushroomed since forties jive. Hip-hop is, for now, the leading culture (followed by various skateboard, drug, and online cultures) that white kids can draw upon to fight the power, be that their parents, their schools, the system, injustice, or the general what-everness of life. Which is why commercial powers want so badly to be associated, however tenuously, with hip-hop. (The truism about "brand loyalty" is, Hook 'em while they're young and you got 'em for life.) For the most part, that rented association is working. If hip-hop weren't commercialized and hadn't hit the pop stage (*stage* in both senses), most of these white kids wouldn't hear or see it enough to wanna be black in the first place.

How easily a word can hop from hep or hippie or hip-hop to shopping pop. In the year 2000, few pop words could compete with *Whassup?!* Perhaps that's because *Whassup?!* (the official Budweiser spelling) was the one phenomenon that most success-fully put black style through the marketing processor and coated every particle of implied transgression with a safety seal.

It was advertising, of course, that catapulted the sound into our faces. A Chicago copywriter caught a short movie by film-maker Charles Stone III in which Stone and some friends, cool black guys all, lay out deep, highly exaggerated *Whassup?!*s for every possible greeting. The ad guy, finding himself mouthing it too, figured, This is exploitable! and signed Stone to transfer his magic word to a client, Budweiser.

Said with tongue hanging out of mouth, the commercial *Whassup?!* was guttural and gross and funny. (Budweiser's spell-ing was wrong, Stone insisted; since the proper pronunciation is P-less, it should be spelled *Whaazzzaahhh?!* "If you make the P sound, your tongue can't be out," he told me.) After a climactic series of the guys growling *Whaazzzaahhh?!* to one another over phones and intercoms while watching a game on TV, the origi-nal spot ended with a sudden calm-down: "What's up, B?" Stone asked one friend over the cordless. "Watching the game. Hav-ing a Bud." "True. True," Stone replied. With the spots starring Stone's real-life pals, what emerged through this literally *lingua franca* was a lot of easygoing male bonding among some brotha buds.

(A note on origins: *What's up?* was not originally black. It goes back at least to 1838, Jonathan Lighter, editor of the

RHHDAS, wrote in a post to the American Dialect Society online discussion group. Nearly a hundred years later, the phrase went mass-pop when Bugs Bunny first uttered a crisp "Eh, what's up, Doc?" in *A Wild Hare* in 1940. But somewhere along the way, African Americans began to unroll *What's up?* into a more all-purpose greeting. By the seventies and eighties, Dalzell writes, long-haired white dudes were saying the blackened *whassup, s'up,* and *z'up.* Stone said he and his pals had been doing the mega *Whaazzzaahhh?!* for sixteen years before selling their shtick to Budweiser. But he feels strongly that it's more of a black thing than Bud's or his own. "Someone suggested to me that I should trademark it," he said. "If it ever came to that, I would hope that someone in the African American community would sue me.")

Whaazzzaahhh?! was just what the nation apparently needed on the eve of a new millennium. The sound instantly became an NBA refrain, a greeting on radio sports shows, the theme of an *SNL* skit (with Brokaw, Koppel, and Shaw *Whaazzzaahhh?!* ing each other), part of another easy question on *Who Wants to Be a Millionaire?,* and the basis of numerous Web site parodies.

Largely because of *Whaazzzaahhh?!,* sales for all Anheuser-Busch beers rose by 2.4 million barrels in 2000. Just as important, *Whaazzzaahhh?!* generated at least $20 million worth of free publicity, according to Bud's ad agency, DDB Worldwide in Chicago. (DDB calls this desirable state "talk value"—it means saturation buzz, a phrase that people use almost involuntarily. But since DDB wanted to reap benefits in case *talk value* acquired talk value, it did what Stone said he wouldn't with *Whaazzzaahhh?!*— it trademarked the term.)

Whaazzzaahhh?! clearly filled a catchphrase/catchgesture void. The Arsenio whoop and the high-five, pop as they still are, had already faded into background pop. The chest bump and the victory dance required actually getting physical. Men, especially sedentary sports-fan men, were ripe for a word that could reinvigorate their manliness, update them multiculturally, and refresh their irony.

And the very sound of the earthy, vomity *Whaazzzaahhh?!* was a perfect counterpoint to the entire high-pitched, beeping wired world. *Whaazzzaahhh?!* was disgusting, low-down, and as analogue as it gets—something to make primal *Fight Club* men out of digital midgets (the 1999 Edward Norton/Brad Pitt movie about wimpy white guys fleeing office cubicles and regaining testosterone by slapping each other around in abandoned buildings came out shortly before Bud's campaign), something to add thick yang to the whiny yin of cell phones and chirping virtuosity and everything eeeeeeeeeeeeEEEEEEEE. *Whaazzzaahhh?!* was grit thrown onto the computer screen, onto the very TV screen the ads ran on. That is—as racial myths still go—*Whaazzzaahhh?!* could make cool black men out of repressed white males.

But it took another spot of the many in Budweiser's campaign to make that perfectly clear. A bunch of preppie white guys—a sweater is draped over one's shoulders as he watches the "market recap" instead of "the game"—duplicate the plot of the original spot but instead of gutting out *Whaazzzaahhh?!*, they eke out a clunky *What are you doooo-ing?!* By the end, their war cry is very loud but very uncool, and the camera pulls back to show two of Stone's black pals watching these graceless wannabes on TV and looking at each other in disbelief. The spot, which debuted on the 2001 Super Bowl, was really funny. But think about what Budweiser was doooo-ing. It was telling its predominantly white customers that they could better identify with these loose, creative black men than they could with those ghosts-of-men honkies. Pouring on the covert prestige, it flattered white guys by telling them they shared the cool attitude of the black men— though, whew, they didn't have to *live* as black men. Drink Bud and get in touch with your inner black guy.

But not necessarily with an outer one. Because *Whaazzz-aahhh?!* was yet another way for white men, and women, to bond with black people without having to actually know any. Knowing *media* black people—actors, athletes, any celebrity will do—is so much easier. If white people can bond with media black people through a phrase or a gesture, we can all "celebrate" an idyllic racial harmony while ignoring real racial politics—assaults on voting rights, racial profiling, income disparities, leaving no African-American child behind.

But, hey, this ad's for Bud. Budweiser needed a hit of *Whaazzzaahhh?!* as much as many white people did. Never a big seller to blacks and without an indie bone in its image, the world's largest-selling beer, made by the world's largest brewer, could now say: These hops hip hop. Even though it's not true, true.

THE PAYING DUES BLUES

After just a year or so, *Whaazzzaahhh?!* became mere hall-of-fame pop—no longer "top of mind," as ad people say, but hauled out now and then to fill certain mental slots (like another Budweiser hall-of-famer, "I love you, man"). But within the *Whaazzzaahhh?!* campaign, particularly the preppie spot, lie the seeds of what's wrong with media-enabled crossover talk.

Yes, merging languages is great, and we're better off when "standard" English gets goosed firmly and frequently. Anyway, it simply wouldn't be possible for white people not to use black talk—it's part and parcel of American talk. But whether our national experiments in covert prestige are enriching or exploitative depends on the attitude that insiders bring to out-siders' speech. When white people are too tickled with their ability to reference black talk, when they treat it like exotica, when it's too trendy, too knee-jerk, too associated with the sell-ing of something (including oneself) and dissociated from the politics and history that forged it, then you have to ask, What are the hidden costs, and who reaps the profits?

In his show *You Are All Diseased,* George Carlin started in on theme restaurants like the House of Blues: "Burn down the House of Blues!" he said—it has too many white people playing the blues. "White people ought to understand they *give* peo-ple the blues. . . . A couple of terms used by lame white people: 'happens to be black,' 'openly gay.' When did 'urban' become synonymous with the word black? I don't think white women should be calling each other girlfriend. . . . 'You go, girl' should probably go along with 'You the man.' "

White people crowing "You the man" does not necessarily flatter black people. "Most black people are not delighted to have aspects of the language borrowed," the linguist John Rick-ford says. "They think of it as appropriated."

This isn't to say that all imitation of black or hip-hop talk is simply appropriation. Spreading words can spread the word—knowledge, empathy, and certainly the broader hip-hop culture. "It's something to see videos connect white kids in Utah to black kids in South Chicago to Croats and Brazilians," the hip-hop pioneer and former Public Enemy frontman Chuck D. wrote in *Time* magazine's cover story on hip-hop's twentieth anniversary. "This is the sound and style of our young world, the vernacular used in today's speak from scholastics to sports. . . . It's difficult to stop a cultural revolution that bridges people together." Those words began to sound prescient when, five years later, a rousing rap song, "Razom Nas Bahato" ("Together We Are Many"), became the theme music of Ukraine's pro-Yushchenko "Orange revolution."

Hip-hop truly is the young world's vernacular. But borrowing black language alone doesn't bridge people together. The bridges are often not so much between people as they are between people and the media. The college slang expert Connie Eble puts into perspective, for instance, the white use of the black term of address *girl*. "Well, *girl* is just used and that's all there is to it," she says. "It's one black phrase that has been taken over by white females, middle-aged secretaries around campus," as well as students. Eble once believed that the white use of *girl* and other black slang was a sign of hope. "At first I thought, Maybe race relations are improving after all. But I have absolutely no evidence that there is more mixing among the races than there ever has been. After researching it, I found that hardly any black slang entered the white vocabulary because a white student has encountered a black student. They've learned it from MTV, the movies, and rap songs."

What's wrong with whites gaining covert prestige through black talk isn't that it fails to bring the races together (that's too much to ask from any one trend or proclivity). What's wrong is that it usually allows whites to feel good about themselves without having to do anything particularly worthwhile. Such easily picked-up prestige encourages the belief that high-fiving or giving it up are the extent of political commitment that an enlightened person needs nowadays. Whites get to blacken up their act "at bargain-basement prices," as Smitherman writes. "They don't have to PAY NO DUES, but reap the psychological, social, and economic benefits of a language and culture born out of enslavement, neo-enslavement, Jim Crow, U.S. apartheid, and twentieth-century hard times."

DEARTH OF THE COOL

The matter of whites reaping benefits from black history brings us to the black-nurtured word and concept that has risen to a status above all others: cool, or rather a dues-free knockoff of it.

Cool is the tent pole of pop culture. Without it, desire flops around; money doesn't know where to put itself. Uttered by folks from two (I've heard it) to seventy, cool is both one of the most expressive concepts of our time and one of the emptiest.

Cool is not just a black thing, by any means. Garbo, Brando, and Eastwood, to name a few obvious cool white symbols, have projected it. Other languages have long had their equivalents—the French royalty displayed *sang-froid*, for instance, on the way to the guillotine. And *cool*, meaning warmer than cold, has been around since the Norman invasion. *Cold, cool, chill, glacier, gelato,* and *Jell-O* all go back to the Latin root *gelare*, meaning to freeze, congeal; by extension, to make rigid, unmoving, with the implication of restraint and control.

Exactly when *cool* jelled into the word we know today is difficult to say. But *cool* as an elixir of composure, detachment, and style is generally thought to have come of age during the era of Count Basie and Duke Ellington. In 1947, Charlie Parker came out with a track called "Cool Blues"; in 1950, Miles Davis, perhaps *the* icon of cool, brought out the album *Birth of the Cool.*

But the cool—the stance, the feeling, the vibe—that early jazz musicians exemplified goes back much further. "Cool is all about trying to make a dollar out of 15 cents. It's about living on the cusp, on the periphery, diving for scraps. Essential to cool is being outside looking in," Donnell Alexander writes in the essay "Are Black People Cooler Than White People?" "So in the days when [slaves] were still literally on the plantation they devised a coping strategy called cool, an elusive mellowing strategy designed to master time and space. Cool, the basic reason blacks remain in the American cultural mix, is an industry of style that everyone in the world can use. It's finding the essential soul while being essentially lost."

To pull off such a strategy, you'd have to at times appear unmoving; you'd have to chill. "A wooden-faced model is aristocratic in its roots," says the classicist Margaret Visser, author of *The Way We Are* and *The Geometry of Love*. "Kings and queens perfected an impassive public face as the look of power. If you have no expression on your face, other people interpret *you*—you are all things to all people." While the keeping of a cool public face by nonroyals is a relatively "modern phenomenon," Visser says, it was "adopted by black culture, people who were the opposite of aristocrats, though they knew how to use that to make themselves powerful."

Sometimes that impassive look can be gotten cheaply, by wearing sunglasses. Or by using other symbols—catchphrases, designer labels, a little something to entice other people to interpret you. The more that millions of people have chased the elusive cool, the more the word's meaning has been diluted. Perhaps the seeds of change were there in the sixties, when cool began to shift from a thing to admire to a thing to idolize. But somewhere along the way, *cool* ceased to be primarily a word denoting composure or detachment and became more an all-purpose murmur of approval (where it's sometimes written and pronounced *kewl*—a blend of *cool* and *cute?*). "That's cool," one might say when a cabby suggests taking Thirteenth Street across town instead of Fourteenth. "Cool," I say instead of listening when my son tells me an amazing fact about his Yu-Gi-Oh! cards.

Perhaps, too, *cool's* cool dissipated as people used it, as they will any fashion, not to cope with life as an outsider, but to enforce a popular-kids-in-class caste system. I used to say *neat*—until 1991, when I saw Madonna's tour movie, *Truth or Dare*. In it, Kevin Costner visited Madonna backstage and told her that her show was "neat." She acidly repeated the word, withering him on the spot for being an outdated creep and a disingenuous suck-up. This was not Madonna at her coolest. Cool, as Alexander further defines it, is "about completing the task of living with enough spontaneity to splurge some of it on bystanders." Ten years after *Truth or Dare,* the caste system *cool* got a comeuppance, of sorts, in another movie, *Save the Last Dance.* In this interracial teenage romance, the white heroine compliments a black friend on her clothes: "Cool outfit." "Slammin'," the friend corrects her, "*slammin'* outfit." I'm not sure, but I doubt that *slammin'* still rules. Such words of praise come and go, but in the grand mall of franchised pop, *cool* has outlasted them all.

As *cool* rose in popularity, it needed a chump. "*Square,* a vital word of the 1950s counterculture," Dalzell writes, "became by the dialectic process of slang a vital word of the 1960s predominant youth culture; it is richly paradoxical that kids whom Beats would have found quite square used the word to vilify those who were out of touch with the latest mainstream fashions, styles, and trends."

Today *cool* has everything to do with mainstream fashions, styles, and trends and very little to do with originality or art, much less with "trying to make a dollar out of 15 cents." And yet repeating the word's sound—its coo, its ooh, its refreshing pool—still gives the faint impression that the speaker is grooving to something the majority just doesn't get, that maybe he's even slyly artistic or, to veer toward another black-cultivated word of complexity, hip. John Leland, author of *Hip: The History,* says hip "refers to an awareness or enlightenment. It's the intelligence behind the mask [of cool's composure]." To that I would just add that cool and hip, as words and as forces, intertwine, overlap, and at times are indistinguishable, but that on the whole cool is central to pop culture, while hip influences it more from the sidelines.

Cool's opposite number among the pop superlatives is not *hip,* but *hot. Hot* and *cool* both convey the utmost in mass desirability, but *hot* doesn't know from detachment; it's all sex, passion, and hubba hubba. Magazine cover lines have hissed *hot* so

often that a women's magazine editor once told me his publication had nixed *hot* as being tepid. "Hot is unusable," he said
flatly. The moratorium must have lasted all of three months,
because the heavy-breathing *hot* is baaack. "What's Hot?" asks a
2005 print ad for (the co-owned) *In Touch* and *Life & Style* magazines. Citing each mag's sales stats, the ad answers: "That's hot!"
The lucre-and-loin-driven *hot* is simpleminded, and has none of
the paradoxes of *cool* (much less of the way more subtle *hip*).

No rich concept is without paradoxes, real and apparent.
Cool is rife with them. Paradox number one is that beneath the
frozen face of real cool, you're actually going with the flow
(no paradox at all for Buddhist cool). Paradox number two,
touched on earlier, is that borrowing from the excluded can
make you feel more included. This is less a paradox than a prag-
matic tactic for a market that needs outsiders (and even more
so, paradox itself) to sex up its merchandise. Even a few years
ago, who'd have imagined that GM and Ford would "trick out"
their autos with loads of bling to look like the car makeovers on
the MTV show *Pimp My Ride*? ("If you had big chrome rims a few
years ago, people thought you were a drug dealer or a pimp,"
Myles Kovacs, the publisher of the hip-hop car magazine *Dub*,
told *Newsweek*. "Now you could be a CEO.") Exuding excluded
cool can protect a seller from appearing, God help them, boring.
So market researchers, like those featured in Malcolm Gladwell's
now classic piece "The Coolhunt," stalk the ghetto for music,
garb, and slang to process into product.

If white people have made a fetish out of black cool, that too
goes back further than the jazz era, as Greg Tate reminds us.
In the introduction to the anthology *Everything But the Burden*,
he writes: "Capitalism's original commodity fetish was the Africans auctioned here as slaves, whose reduction from subjects to
abstracted objects has made them seem larger than life and less
than human at the same time." That paradox reverberates today
"in a market-driven world where we continue to find ourselves
being sold as hunted outsiders and privileged insiders in the
same breath."

Anyone who tries to resist the fruit of the coolhunts is bound to fail frequently. There's almost no way not to respond positively, at least momentarily, to marketed cool, whether in the form of a hip-hop Sprite spot or Nike's latest spectacle. We are really responding to presentations of grace—paid, staged, and third-hand though they may be. But in buying the product, we're not honoring cool, we're merely possessing its congealed representation—while the real thing evaporates from our credit-card-bearing hands.

"Most think cool is something you can put on and take off at will (like a strap-on goatee)," writes Alexander (ESPN once hired him to help hip-hopify its language). "They think it's some shit you go shopping for. And that taints cool, giving the mutant thing it becomes a deservedly bad name." Found in "advertising agencies, record company artist-development departments, and over-art-directed bars," this "ersatz cool," he adds, "fights real cool at every turn."

WHEN BLACK TALK GOES TO SCHOOL

White society's fetishization of black cool and black talk might go down easier if that society did not react so virulently when black vernacular left the neighborhood of entertainment and moved to more serious areas, like education. I'm talking, of course, about Ebonics.

In December 1996, the Oakland, California, school board approved a resolution to change how it taught African-American students who, the board said, spoke not a dialect of English but a separate, African-based language, Ebonics. On the face of it, which was as far as most of the press went, the resolution sounded like identity politics gone mad: calling a bunch of slang a separate language and proposing to teach it. Indeed, at first many blacks, most notably Jesse Jackson, in addition to most of the media and the larger public, trashed the plan.

Ebonics suddenly became the target of a rash of nasty cartoons, Internet jokes, and fuming commentary. Since the controversy arrived during the holiday season, several "Ebonics translations" of "The Night Before Christmas" began to circulate on the Net, like this one:

> I looked out thru de bars;
> What covered my doe;
> 'spectin' de sheriff;
> Wif a warrent fo sho.

> And what did I see;
> I said, "Lawd, look at dat!"
> Ther' wuz a huge watermellon;
> Pulled by giant warf rats!!

The "Ebonics Lectric Library of Classical Literature" Web site (no longer active) introduced itself thus: "Since the recent decision to make Ebonics (Ebony-Phonics) a second language in our schools it has become obvious that e-bliterations of the classics will be required. We will cover here the greater works of world Literature (Litershure) in the hopes of bridging the gap between English and the new Slanguage."

With the general consensus that Ebonics was broken English and teaching it meant the triumph of black special interests, the mockery and stereotypes were suddenly viewed as a healthy dose of politically incorrect humor. "The nationwide roar of laughter over Ebonics is a very good sign," John Leo wrote in *U.S. News Online*.

But most of the outrage against Ebonics was based on the erroneous notion that the Oakland schools had proposed to teach Ebonics and to ignore standard English. Although the resolution was ambiguously and poorly written—a clearer, amended version appeared a few weeks later, partly at the urging of Jackson, who subsequently supported the plan—the idea was never simply to teach Ebonics. Rather it was to compare and contrast the "home language" (Ebonics) of academically failing students with "school English"—that is, to draw on their vernacular to help them master standard English. If teachers ignored the children's home language—or, worse, ridiculed it—the thinking went, the students were less likely to be open to learning the English skills they so desperately needed. The strategy was endorsed by the Linguist Society of America as "linguistically and pedagogically sound."

"The Ebonics controversy confirmed that linguists—whether or not they describe themselves as 'Afrocentric'—are generally united in their respect for the legitimacy and complexity of the language spoken by many African American children," write the Rickfords, who are generally supporters of Ebonics in the classroom. "This perspective clashed with the more widely held public opinion that Ebonics was simply slang and gutter talk, or the product of laziness and carelessness."

Like all languages and dialects, black English follows consistent rules and a system of grammar, most linguists agree. Even vocal opponents of using Ebonics to teach English, like the linguist John McWhorter, say that black English is not simply "bad," "broken," or "inferior" English. Standard English, or the standard version of any language, is but one of many dialects itself. "One of those dialects is chosen as the standard one not because it is somehow 'better' or 'more correct' in the eyes of God, but because it happens to be the one spoken where the center of power coalesces," McWhorter writes in his book *Losing the Race: Self-Sabotage in Black America.* "We have no trouble understanding that a tiger is not a 'degraded version' of a leopard but simply another variation on 'cat'; we do not see house cats' lack of a mane as meaning that they are 'broken' versions of lions. In the same way, Black English is not 'bad standard English' but just another kind of English."

The reason for discussing the Ebonics battle here (in a book that's not about specific dialects themselves) is to look at how conflicts over language and race surface in pop language and the politics that pop can't help but speak of. For whatever you think of Ebonics as an educational tool—and you can find arguments and studies that support or derail it—you have to ask, Why the heat? Why the ridicule at the very mention of Ebonics?

Some of the contempt stemmed from ignorance (augmented by the vast majority of the news media, which seemed to willfully ignore the facts, a story the Rickfords detail in *Spoken*

Soul). But some of the vehemence was due to a frustrated racism, to prejudices whose outlets of expression had been closing off for years. Condemning Ebonics was a safe way to finally voice anger at and fear of black people and their increasingly confident presence in American culture. Over the last couple of decades, most white people, unless they were outright white supremacists, had been feeling that if they were uncomfortable with black individuals or music or style, they could voice their criticism only gingerly or had to cloak it in disagreements about policies and programs, like affirmative action, welfare, or classroom Ebonics. While I really do believe that you don't have to be racist to oppose any of these programs, if you *are* racist, occasionally have such inclinations, or are just afraid of black people, then mockery of Ebonics can supply convenient cover. (The Ebonics controversy also came, McWhorter reminds us, a few months after the O. J. Simpson verdict in his criminal trial, when white anger at black support for Simpson was at a peak.)

For black opponents of Ebonics, the situation was more complex. For many African Americans the squabble over Ebonics replayed a long-held ambivalence toward their language. The other side of black pride is black shame, something that being treated as subhuman for centuries can engender. "The variously named vernacular of African Americans does have a remarkable capacity to elicit denial and shame from blacks (not to mention others)," write the Rickfords. Arguments among blacks about "talking proper" rise up regularly, they add. "During the Harlem Renaissance of the 1920s," for instance, "debate raged among the black intelligentsia, with Langston Hughes endorsing and exemplifying the use of vernacular, and Alain Locke and others suggesting that African Americans ought to put the quaintness of the idiom behind them and offer the world a more 'refined' view of their culture. These enduring attitudes reflect the attraction-repulsion dynamic, the oscillation between black and white (or mainstream) poles that W.E.B. Du Bois defined a century ago as 'double-consciousness.' "

(If one response to speaking a laughed-at language is to make it bolder and tougher, as hip-hop does, an opposite response might be to brood silently. After the Supreme Court decision against letting Florida recount votes in the 2000 election, during which the Garbo-like Clarence Thomas asked nary a question, the Court's sole black justice discussed his previously unexplained shyness on the bench with a group of high school students. He said his reticence came from fear of being made fun of for speaking his native Gullah, the creole of the coastal Carolinas, in his otherwise all-white seminary class.)

The attraction-repulsion among blacks toward black English has its parallels among the public at large. "Americans of all types tend to bad-talk soul talk, even though it is the guts of the black music they so relish," write the Rickfords. "Appreciating sung soul is one thing, but appreciating soul as it is spoken is something else entirely. . . . In fact, middle America has quite often jeered those who speak 'jive' in the same breath and with the same enthusiasm that it has grooved to black sounds a la Bessie Smith and Mahalia Jackson and Ray Charles and Lauryn Hill."

There is, however, one other form of black speech as widely grooved to as black song lyrics: individual words and phrases that have evolved from black-only slang into everyone-owns-a-piece-of-it pop. Even middle America holds on to these words as if they were talismans of the soul of a people.

None of this is to say that Ebonics itself is pop. The black talk that turns into pop, whether through the avenues of jive, civil rights, or hip-hop, did indeed begin as Ebonics (or whatever you want to call it), but the pop process has stripped that talk of its other dimensions. "The part of black language that is used by the general public is vocabulary," John Rickford says. "But the core elements of Ebonics or black language, which are the distinct grammar, phonology, and pronunciation patterns—that's not being borrowed to any significant extent, because you have to be living it." Since white people gravitate primarily to the vocabulary—with very occasional pronunciation exceptions as in *You da man* and *gangsta*—Rickford doesn't believe that popularization will be the death knell for black talk: "I don't think it has a powerful effect, at least not on black language itself. Anyway, people are always creating new terms—there's a premium on that in black English."

New terms, dwelling on the periphery, tend to have authenticity cred, and some of them, too, will eventually undergo the media glamour treatment that makes them pop. It might be a drag in real life, but marginalization can be marketable—if it's packaged right. Or, as the writer Khephra Burns put it in 1997, speaking of the students who were supposed to be at the center of the Ebonics brawl: "It can't help our children to be told at every utterance that their mode of expression—which is intimately linked to their identity—is wrong, wrong, wrong, when others who plagiarize them are getting paid."

Don't Even *Think* About Telling Me "I Don't *Think* So": The Media, Meanness, and Me

T erry Gross, the host of NPR's *Fresh Air,* was interviewing a French journalist about how she covered the war in Chechnya. Her tale was fascinating, I wanted to hear more, but I was rushing to leave the house. The journalist said the Russians' excuse that they were fighting guerrillas was an utter lie. "The reality is, it's a full-scale war. The citizens are suffering." On "suffering," I turned off the radio and, in my head, I said to her, "That's too bad. But nothin' we can do about it now, so let's just get over it."

Those idiotic words were a product of my busyness, not of my sympathies (which were This *is* too bad and it's disgusting to suggest that anyone should "just get over" Chechnya). My glib, fake toughness was also the product of a larger cultural habit— an urge conditioned by years of sitcom put-downs, advertising zingers, rabid political campaigns, and mob moments throughout the media. When people are talking about something you'd rather not think about, as often as not, you cut them off with a verbal stun gun: a pop phrase, usually on the peevish side. The small cruelty gives you a cleaner break. Your distance from the speaker is confirmed, and any guilt, ambivalence, or annoyance they might have stirred in you is dispelled. The percussion of the phrase's pop! signals the end of the minor disturbance, helps you to . . . just get over it.

What part of that last paragraph don't you understand? Do I have to spell it out for you? Repeat after me: This chapter is about pop weapon words, about what happens when high dudgeon meets entertainment and when one's own meanness—*meanness* in the senses of both malice and commonness—meets the media's. This chapter is about how the media course through our speech and thought, and how the glamour and irony that often come with media comebacks and make us sound so smart can actually make us dumb.

All pop expressions, by definition, give off some media glow, but not all throw off stinging sparks. The feisty words and phrases here—often the poppest of the pop—are like tiny fists, pop in the sense of "I'll pop you one!" Serving our defensive and offensive language needs, they're snappy *and* snappish, PR-ish *and* POed. They're our licensed buzzphrases that, loaded with killer inflections *(Yeah, right; Oh, puh-leeze; End of story)*, chop down any and all assaults on the sensitive modern ego.

Every day, Americans are belting out more of these in-your-face catchphrases to semantically sic it to someone or something. Conversations, e-mail, lovers' quarrels, PTA meetings, can barely be conducted without our resorting to one of these media-darling ripostes. A whole nation barking Hollywood retorts—creepy, but so useful. In the daily battlefield of misunderstandings and bickering disagreements, locutions like *In your dreams, Whatever,* and *Duh* are our Nerf-like weaponry. When you're blind with anger or exasperation, you just grab the nearest item from the arsenal. When a friend of mine was leaving her building and failed to hold the door for another resident trying to enter, she got a disdainful "Hel-*lo*?!" When the radio plays something I don't like, I smite its audacity with two words— "Ex*cuse* me?"—and a push of a button. My power is restored.

Phrases like these aren't just clichés. They're more like a bad case of televisionary Tourette's—involuntary, canned punch lines that bring the rhythms of sitcom patter into everyday experience. As media scatter the patter, they become part of our shared response to the little frustrations of modern life. More and more, that response tends to be a dismissive pique, as these buzzbarbs verbally roll up the window on any nuisance that might come tapping at the tinted glass.

ARMED AT THE TEETH

Teed off that some people thought her babysitter was more involved in her child's life than she was, the actress Melanie Griffith complained to *InStyle* magazine about a visit to her daughter's piano instructor. "The teacher started making arrangements with the nanny. And I said, 'Hello! Excuse me, I'm the mother here.' "

"What part of 'Stop that right now' don't you understand?" a grandmother says to a toddler at Rite-Aid.

"What part of 'It's *your* phone that rang' don't you understand?" a man, through gritted teeth, says to a woman at a supermarket.

"What part of 'Stay the hell out of my life' don't you understand?" a woman asked her father on the (short-lived) Fox show *North Shore.*

"Dad, when I grow up I want to be a pilot just like you," a young boy tells his father as the TV commercial's sentimental music swells. "You have to work hard, son," his father, in pilot's uniform, tells him. "I know, Dad. Not everyone gets to fly for JetBlue." "Son," Dad says with sorrow, "I don't fly for JetBlue." With his hand the kid makes an "L" on his forehead, cries out, "Loser!" and stalks off. In response, Dad makes a "W" (thumbs together, index fingers out) and silently mouths, "What*ev*er."

"Oh, my God, Puffy is *sooo* two years ago," one of "New York's best-known fashion editors" said of the Puff Daddy (P. Diddy) line of clothing.

"I'm tired of Aspen," Donald Trump said. "Aspen's over."

When former secretary of state Colin Powell appeared before

a congressional hearing on the war in Iraq, Representative Sherrod Brown of Ohio compared Powell's war record favorably to that of "a president who may have been AWOL." "Mr. Brown," Powell retorted angrily, "let's not go there. Let's not go there in this hearing."

"Isn't she a little young? Sex with a minor. Don't go there," read a billboard in Virginia. It was part of the state's 2004 public service ad campaign to remind men that sex with a minor is against the law.

"I thought you were sexy—you suck," a female contestant told Simon Cowell, the sharp-tongued judge on *American Idol*, after he told her: "Great voice, personality 4½."

In a Visa ad running during the 2002 Winter Olympics, a U.S. Olympic bobsled team brings its sled to a sudden halt because a cute little bunny is crossing the path. A voiceover reminds us this is the *women's* bobsled team. But one of the gals quickly disabuses us of the notion that women are too kind to compete: "This happens in competition," she says, "he's toast!"

Not one but two grown women have told me that they actually want some guy they don't like to ask, When can we see each other? just so they could say, at least once in their lives, How's never?

At a diner, a pretty young woman says to a pretty young man, "It's just the same old thing. I need adventure, excitement. I'm suffocating." "OK, you can drive," he says, handing her the car keys. She's finally in the driver's seat of the Hyundai Santa Fe—a pleasure so great, she won't give up an iota of control. So, as the guy reaches to change the music, she strikes: "Don't even *think* about it."

The mother of a six-year-old boy said that when she asked his school to apologize for punishing her son for kissing a girl schoolmate, "The principal laughed and said, 'I don't *think* so.'"

Does it ever get just too snotty? A 1998 radio ad for Canon Canada drew dozens of complaints for the sort of words we hear every day. The spot began with a woman asking, "So, what do you think of my presentation?" *The Wall Street Journal* reported the rest:

A girl who sounds about 12 years old answers, "Really, Mom? It's Stone Age." She proceeds to tell her mother she needs a Canon printer and reels off the technical specifications like a seasoned pro.

Mom, a little deflated, replies that all printers are probably much the same. The daughter's response: "Hel-*lo*?!"

After hearing about a few more of the printer's features, Mom asks, "How'd you get so smart?" Daughter replies, "I'm a graduate of grade seven. Duh!"

(After a barrage of phone calls from angry parents, the ad agency rewrote the spot, cutting *Hel-lo?!* and replacing *Duh* with a feel-good line that could have worked as the ending of any Hallmark spot. The substitute phrase came from the same system of prefab responses but out of the opposite tap. Now when the mother asks the girl how she got so smart, the girl says, "Guess I inherited it.")

It's as if all these people, from across North America, are speaking the same dialect. And they are: Together these phrases form the dialect of the demagoguery of everyday life. Drawing on the thumbs-up or thumbs-down power of the imaginary crowd, pop weapon words are a quick and easy show of force. At least for the moment we wield them, we can feel as if we're dealing with conflict and taking control. Not being in control—that's our real worst nightmare.

COOL FIRE

The *appearance* of control, after all, is fundamental to the appearance of cool. We need words and phrases that not only seem to control a situation but that also make us seem as if we're not trying to. If handled with skill, such words can allow a speaker to sound cool while feeling hot. One's anger or impatience is tempered by the words' entertainment value; the words' indirect route to their target buys them time to release some heat.

Without a modicum of song and dance, the weaponry would

be the harsher, usually unpop, sound of *fuck you, asshole,* and the like. (Not that *fuck you* and *asshole* aren't sometimes most effective pop, but more on that soon.) It's the difference, for instance, between a direct "I'm going to kill you!" and an indirect "Make my day"; between "Stop it right there!" and "Don't even *think* about it!"; between "You worthless piece of shit!" and "Get a life!" The threatened one has to work a tiny extra beat to figure out what the speaker is somewhat elliptically referring to; he might also be momentarily stunned by the crack of the silent applause. The speaker, meanwhile, can float for that beat, and, if he's got rhythm, then sting like a bee.

What with all these weapons, threats, and stings, I don't mean to imply that these are literally dangerous words; they're not equal to the sticks and stones that break our bones. Occasionally they'll lead to sticks and stones, but for the most part, we're just talking about the age-old ability that humor has to chill violence. As sublimated punches, pop punch lines are mall-fightin' words, ruff tuff stuff that would much rather disarm an opponent than take up arms against him.

With their emphasis on cool and entertainment, weapon words may evoke the black tradition of playing the dozens, the verbal game of exaggerated, funny insults (like "Yo momma is so dumb she thought a quarterback was a refund," as Geneva Smitherman writes). But despite their apparent similarity to the dozens, and to less formal, more hip-hop variations like snappin, most of today's weapon words are not particularly black.

Yes, black slang is the largest influence on American pop language (nice, mean, or neutral), but if any one source gives weapon words their particular lilt, it's white kids of a generation ago. "The slang of the 1970s and 1980s was, until the emphatic influence of rap and hip-hop in the late 1980s, for the most part free of the influence of black street vernacular," Dalzell writes. "Instead, youth slang of the 1970s and 1980s relied in large part on the clever, sardonic use of standard English." Today, it's still this twisting of meanings and pinching of inflections of plain words *(Hel-*lo?!*, I don't* think *so)* that propel their ammo and ups them to weapons-grade pop.

That's not to say that a sardonic accent is just a white thing.

As with pop language in general, regardless of who coined the weapon phrases, everyone says them. The habit simply doesn't recognize racial, class, age, "lifestyle," or ideological boundaries. The 2001 movie *Baby Boy*, for instance, written and directed by John Singleton, a black man, has plenty of black phrases that have gone on to various degrees of pop *(It's all good, bling bling)*. But the movie is just as full of the zingers that populate most Hollywood fare and most of our lives *(He*l*lo?, "He*l*lo, is anyone home?, Yeah, right, I don't* think *so, Whatever)*. A line in an LL Cool J song: "What's ya worst nightmare, Black?" A white militia code name in the nineties for a possible counterattack on the feds: "Project Worst Nightmare."

You don't even have to be particularly belligerent to speak this armored brogue. As long as you occasionally bask in the reflected light of the TV, movie, or computer screen (or surround yourself with people who do), you're there, girl!

PERSON NOUVELLE

It's as if there's a new personality that many of us wear like a clean white T-shirt and pair of khakis. This savvy, fresh personality might, depending on the individual, sound a bit hip-hop or a tad surfer, now and then dip into Valley Girl or, wittingly or not, vamp into drag queen. It's less important which identity is sampled than that the sample produce a winning comeback in a timely manner. You don't have to be the sharpest tool in the shed—as long as you're trained to say things like that. Even if you are not particularly clever, it's important to make clear that you can summon the big laugh track in the sky, especially when defending an ego under duress.

People, meet the Person Nouvelle, a pop-culture ethnic of indeterminate heritage; a pastiche of lightly donned identities and a vast knowingness (if often shallow knowledge); a population that includes more of us than we like to admit (myself and loved ones included). This newish kind of person is someone who can swing a media reference, who can kick in with irony and has come to expect it, who can be both tough competitor and

Don't Even Think About Telling Me "I Don't Think So"

vulnerable victim; it's someone who might even have the commercial cojones to know how to market him- or herself, at least over e-mail, pager, or phone. You need not possess all of the above abilities to be a Nouvelle. Only one trait is really required: that, on a fairly regular basis, you vibrate with autonomic media responses.

Take, for example, the cast on the second season of *The Apprentice*. During just the few minutes while I was flipping in and out of an episode, they said: "I'm going to push you outside your comfort zone . . . outside the box" (Maria, a marketing executive, to others on her team). "Money shot right there" (one guy, of a woman being photographed for a jeans catalogue). "No-brainer" (Caroline to Trump about his decision to fire not the customary one person but two). "Andy stepped up to the plate" (Trump, in reply, on why Andy wasn't among the banished).

Persons Nouvelles are a much more diverse group than the small minority who audition for or star in their own reality shows. Cutting a swath through all socioeconomic categories (though not including all members of each category), the Person Nouvelle transcends them all. The PN is defined less by what brands he buys or what values he holds (i.e., none of this red state/blue state dualistic drivel) than by how much influence media and marketing have in his life. It doesn't matter which piece of media or marketing you prefer—Fox News Channel or NPR, Wal-mart or Nordstrom, TV evangelists or TV bad boys. It's not which, but how much. How much do you cough back up the stuff you've been imbibing? How much do you understand life and politics through the language, imagery, and constructs of the media you dwell in? You might be a Nouvelle if . . . you answer, Uh, don't go there.

Marketing and media are the amniotic fluid of the Person Nouvelle, providing his knowledge base and cushioning his interpretation of the world. And marketing and media inevitably promote nouvelle traits, because (1) many Persons Nouvelles work in those two professions (and even if they don't, they live in what Earl Shorris has called, in the title of his book, *A Nation of Salesmen*), and (2) the paradoxes inherent in the nouvelle personality create "needs" that only a sale seems to fulfill.

In his ideal incarnation, the Person Nouvelle is different yet popular, indie yet corporate, daring yet nonthreatening, rock solid yet light. He needs to telegraph one paradox or another in a way that calls attention to his uniqueness while allowing him to consume something used by millions of fellow Nouvelles. Like a really cool sneaker ad, the PN wears some kind of alternative stripe—an attitude, a tattoo, a choice of words—that makes him even more acceptable to the mainstream.

The minty hint of paradox is perhaps best illustrated by the Celebrity Nouvelle. That celeb might be Cameron Diaz or Rosie O'Donnell one year, Vin Diesel or Carson Daly the next—that is, a famous person who, by displaying something a little off-center (Cameron, flaky but strong; Rosie, pissed off but accessible; Vin, tough but sweet; Carson, distant but reliably there), can come off as that most commercial-friendly of entities, the hip mainstream. Mass media love certain kinds of paradox because they, the media, can claim to resolve the apparent contradictions. Dramatic conflict is built in; the media supply the happy ending: how the kid who's different becomes popular and dresses better *(About a Boy)*, how the nonconformist recluse joins the world *(Shrek)*, how any character moves from outside to inside, from resistance to "buying" in.

And because so many Celebs Nouvelles gladly pitch products, their alt has a limit: How different or threatening or anticapitalist can any of them be, we figure, if they're just out to make a buck?

The commercially compatible Person Nouvelle has evolved because we live in an increasingly commercial, transactional culture. As more things in life besides actual products become commodified—political access, college papers, pollution rights, identities (as in "identity theft"), scandals (Tonya Harding and Paula Jones end up in a boxing match for Fox TV; in prison, Martha Stewart plans her reality show), even simplicity (services, products, and magazines that are supposed to help you escape the overcommodified world)—the number of transactions between humans, and between their technological surrogates, rises sharply. More transactions means more need to establish a position from which to better deal. A person juggling dozens of transactions a day (getting a parking space, health insurance, a kid into preschool; cutting through traffic or automated telephone prompts; choosing DSL or cable, low fat or low carb; deciding to sell or buy, to stand or remain seated for the pregnant lady) needs a new kind of language. Ideally, this language should provide more effective methods to persuade and cajole, and to gloss over what we don't want known. It should be a language with a built-in shield and a quiver of arrows slung, as casually as possible, over the shoulder.

Casual, or at least the appearance of it, is important. It can defuse the tension of all those transactions, make you sound less like Gray Davis and more like Ah-nold (if I weren't right now aspiring to "caj," as some say, I'd write his full name). And pop casual, like all pop, is bipartisan. While liberal Hollywood Nouvelles might still "do lunch," neocon Beltway Nouvelles want to "do" Syria or Iran, as a follow-up transaction to doing Iraq—even though, when the Iraqi war began to falter, Defense Secretary Donald Rumsfeld insisted, "I don't do quagmires." Most pols, since they're Nouvelles to varying degrees, do the *do*. George W. Bush said, "I don't do nuance," while John Kerry said of the dirty campaign that would later hit him, "Listen, man, I fought in Vietnam and I know how to do mud. I'm ready for them." Though, of course, he wasn't.

You have to skip back a presidential election to see a more truly caj, better-equipped Nouvelle at work. John Ellis—writer, blogger, and business consultant, and a first cousin of George W. and Jeb Bush—was in charge of Fox News Channel's election-decision team in 1999. Fox, of course, was the first to declare that Bush had won Florida, an announcement the other networks scurried to repeat. That premature decision was retracted within hours because the race was too close to call, but it created a set of assumptions impossible to retract: that Bush was the winner, that Al Gore had a loser's "L" burnished on his forehead, and that any subsequent numbers or facts to the contrary were aberrations. That is, Ellis, instrumental in setting Bush's dubious victory in motion, is one transactional dude.

And he talks like one. Two days after Election Day, the then-forty-seven-year-old Ellis spoke with the *New Yorker* writer Jane

Mayer while padding around his house, she writes, "in gym socks, khakis, and a baggy navy sweatshirt," and he produced speech as casually pop as his clothing. Ellis said that early in the campaign he believed Bush was so incompetent that Gore could've stopped him cold with just the right zinger, which Ellis supplied after the fact. "I kept wondering," he told Mayer, "why, during the debates, Gore didn't just turn to Bush and ask, 'What, exactly, is it about peace and prosperity that you don't like?' " Referring to the possibility that the Democrats would demand an actual re-vote in West Palm Beach, he said, "I just can't imagine that they want to go there." (They didn't.) During the nail-biting election night, he said he spoke constantly with George and Jeb in Austin from Fox headquarters in New York: "They were, like, 'How we doin'?' " And when he first projected Florida for his cousin, "Their mood was up, big-time." "It was just the three of us guys handing the phone back and forth—me with the numbers, one of them a governor, the other the President-elect. Now *that* was cool."

Ellis's pop talk wasn't limited to weaponized remarks (like *What part of X don't you like?*, *[Don't] go there*, and arguably, *big-time*), but then, nouvelle speech isn't. We speak the whole pop enchilada, affecting a tightening of the screws here, an adolescent nonchalance ("Now *that* was cool") there. Weapon words figure in as only a part—albeit the sharpest part, the tip of the arrow—of the Person Nouvelle's talking repertoire.

THE VERBAL SUV

If the weaponized pop of the Person Nouvelle were a car, what kind would it be? Something very *That's* his *problem* and yet also *Hey, dude*, something intimidating yet popular. Why, this language would be an SUV! (The more benign pop talk might be a cartoony bright New Beetle or an ironically retro PT Cruiser.)

Both weapon words and SUVs turn on a showy overkill: the slammin' comeback when you don't get your way, the truck-sized vehicle to pick up the mocha latte. The meaner pop and the bigger SUVs create many of the same effects: They can make drivers feel insulated from life's potholes, and they block the vision of those traversing streets or sentences by less bulked-up means. And both weapon words and SUVs rule despite weaknesses stemming from their position high off the ground: The SUV is prone to rollovers because of its high center of gravity; weaponized pop, composed of canned, media-distributed punch lines, is not very "grounded" in one's own thought and is likely to leave its operators running on intellectual empty.

OK, I might be hitting the gas on this metaphor a little hard. But there's no doubt that the words and the vehicles arise from the same desire to arm oneself, a desire that marketers and the media frequently mine for financial gain.

SUVs were not just born beefy. Automobile market researchers "had been greatly influenced by Dr. Clotaire Rapaille, a French-born medical anthropologist who has worked as a consultant to DaimlerChrysler, Ford and General Motors," *The New York Times* wrote. "He said sport utilities are designed to be masculine and assertive, often with hoods that resemble those on 18-wheel trucks, vertical slats across the grilles to give the appearance of a jungle cat's teeth and flared wheel wells and fenders that suggest the bulging muscles in a clenched jaw.

"Sport utilities are designed to appeal to Americans' deepest fears of violence and crime, Dr. Rapaille said." They are " 'weapons' and 'armored cars for the battlefield,' he said. An ad for one SUV, the Lincoln Navigator, promoted it as an 'Urban Assault Luxury Vehicle.' " As we navigate our overbooked, competitive lives, the concept of an Urban Assault Luxury Verbalization describes many a *You're so over!* or *Don't even* think *about it!* (The comedian Bill Maher has more concisely equated car and attitude by calling SUVs "fuck-you-mobiles.")

But why the need for such overwrought cars or comebacks? Usually originating from real people and not corporate anthropologists, weapon words aren't as consciously designed as weaponized vehicles are. But both car and word are shaped by the same societal habits. As the linguist Deborah Tannen writes in her book *The Argument Culture,* there is "a pervasive warlike atmosphere that makes us approach public dialogue, and just about anything we need to accomplish, as if it were a fight. It is a tendency in Western culture in general, and in the United States in particular, that has a long history and a deep, thick, and far-ranging root system. It has served us well in many ways but in recent years has become so exaggerated that it is getting in the way of solving our problems." The argument culture "rests on the assumption that opposition is the best way to get anything done."

The media are a major culprit in the maintenance of "programmed contentiousness," Tannen writes, because they frame every issue into two opposing sides, even though the geometry of most issues might be better described as "a crystal of many sides." But the media, whether telling fictional or real-life stories, are dependent on two sides, because dualisms fit dramatic and ancient conventions (protagonist/antagonist, good/evil). When George W. Bush called Osama bin Laden "the evil one" and Iraq, Iran, and North Korea the "axis of evil," Bush (or, rather, his writers) was taking a language tip from our most pop president, former star of TV and film, Ronald Reagan, who of course dubbed the Soviet Union "the evil empire." We prefer our evil with banality banished: us-good/them-bad plays better as sport and gets higher ratings.

In the more personal realm of the Person Nouvelle, growing up in an entertainment-based, two-sided world makes it more likely that you'll see yourself as suffering some brute's insensitivity. You're the good guy, the put-upon one, the heroic victim. Or perhaps you see yourself as the plucky protagonist in a sitcom who's not going to take it anymore! Either way, shortly before the conflict is resolved, you finally get up the gumption to tell the brute *off*, and the words to zap him with come to you as if from heaven (but more likely they're from Disney), as they seem to in, say, *Toy Story*'s big revenge moment. Woody, the heroic toy cowboy, has mobilized all the toys that Sid, the vicious kid, has maimed. For the first time in his little plastic life, Woody must break the toys' sacred rule to never speak in front of a human, and he tells Sid in a slow, threatening growl that scares the bejesus out of him: "Plaaay nice!"

One of the best-known sources of our dualistic, programmed contentiousness is America's adversarial system of justice. It has become adversarialism on steroids for the same socio-psycho reasons underlying the clenched jaws in vehicle design, politics, business, sports, and personal fights. "Many attorneys feel they have to engage in scorched earth tactics because the other side does it," Tannen writes, "just as journalists feel they have to cover a sensational story because the competition is doing it. This is what Gregory Bateson called 'symmetrical schismogenesis'— each person does more and more of the same thing in reaction to the other."

Just as America's no-holds-barred adversarial system of justice has pumped up the larger argument culture, so our no-holds-barred system of entertainment has made our justice system more adversarial. Real judges, lawyers, and clients have begun to imitate the media's version of courtroom dramas, says Richard Sherwin, the author of *When Law Goes Pop: The Vanishing Line Between Law and Popular Culture.* "I have nothing against entertainment and I love popular culture," he told *Stay Free!* magazine, "but I worry when the law becomes synonymous with entertainment so that if you don't entertain, you're not convincing."

He says judges have told him "that when *L.A. Law* was at its peak, they not only expected lawyers to dress that way, but they expected two-and-a-half-minute summations. You know, 'Let's make this peppy.' But what happens when you put stuff on the screen? You abide by the esthetics of the screen, you have to make things work using visual production values, and that changes everything. It changes politics, it changes journalism, it changes law."

And, of course, it changes language. But that pop equation— if you don't entertain, you're not convincing (which might be stated, Entertain or lose)—was in the making long before we had TV, movies, the Internet, or any mass media at all. Before all that, we had the media of movement itself. The sweep of American history tilted toward the establishment of a single national popular language, in part to protect its mobile and often foreign-born speakers from the suspicion of being different.

"Instead of becoming more divergent, people over the bulk of the American mainland continued to evince a more or less uniform speech," Bill Bryson writes in his book *The Mother Tongue*.

> Why should that be?
> . . . First, the continuous movement of people back and forth across the continent militated against the formation of permanent regionalisms. . . . Second, the intermingling of people from diverse grounds worked in favor of homogeneity. Third, and above all, social pressures and the desire for a common national identity encouraged people to settle on a single way of speaking.
> People who didn't blend in risked being made to feel like outsiders. They were given names that denigrated their backgrounds.

He goes on to list *wop, kraut, yid, dago, kike, mick,* and *paddy.*

CROWDS AND LOSERS

Today that person who is not going to be treated like an outsider but an insider needs a language that allows him to blend in, as Bryson says, and one that also helps him differentiate himself from the "real" outsiders, a language barbed enough to fence off those who still can't get with the program, whatever that might be at the moment. The need for a vernacular that's camouflaging as well as teeth-baring becomes stronger, I'd hypothesize, with sheer population growth.

As each of us is surrounded by more and more people whom we know less and less well, as we realize there's no escaping the numbers of lives and our lives as numbers, as our busy world putt-putts out more atomizing experiences (from spending our days in cubicles to hearing the cash register, instead of the person behind it, thank us), we risk feeling like little nobodies, distant from the center of power, or any center at all. But by emulating that distance with ironic detachment and pugnacious punch lines, we try to immunize ourselves from it, to prove that we are not a bunch of sheep. *I'm outta here! Gimme a break! I'm going for it!* The sensation of control and independence that's there for the speaking makes it harder to see that most of these bellicose bleats are prepackaged, too.

The apparent contradiction of trying to counter atomization by using its instruments is a consequence of the ancient, never-ending tug-of-war between the individual and the crowd. This war is closely related to the anticorporate corporate advertising mentioned earlier, those campaigns that swear you can express your unique personality by buying the same individualistic product as millions of others do. With the right come-on, Coke or Nike can release the James Dean or the Eminem in each of us; with the right phrases and intonation *(No way, José, Bring it on, You gotta walk the walk),* we can express a freewheeling, cowboyish bucking of the system.

Taking on qualities of the crowd even while insisting on one's individuality has rarely been more pithily expressed than in the United States Army's slogan "An Army of One." Sure, it sounds oxymoronic, but only if you forget Rambo. The previous, more New Age slogan, "Be all you can be," created by the NW Ayer ad agency in 1981, emphasized too much individual, not enough team player, and no swashbuckling at all. But "An Army of One" (from a new agency, Leo Burnett) inflates a regular guy into a superhero of enormous proportions. Today's soldier may have been sent to war without enough fellow troops or armor to cover his ass, but, according to commercial fantasy, he's the brave loner who's never really alone. Encompassing multitudes, he's the true American crowdboy.

And so mass media resolve another paradox. But in reality, individuals and crowds rarely blend so harmoniously. The crowd will always gang up on selected individuals (or races, ethnicities, or nationalities; in 2003, guided expertly by the Bush administration, it ganged up on the French). That's how the crowd, and the crowd in each individual, can feel its own status. There's a weapon word for those individuals cast out of the crowd, or never let in, a word that avoids any group slurs and that the media promote even while they exalt people who are "different":

loser. Wearing the wrong clothes or making the wrong business decision is more shameful than adultery once was, for a scarlet "L" is showing up on foreheads across the nation.

On the animated sitcom *The Family Guy,* the teenage daughter hates a dress her mother picked for her. "Why don't I just wear an 'L' on my forehead?" the girl tells Mom. "Loser! Loser! Loser!" a bunch of sea animals taunt SpongeBob SquarePants. (My young son immediately does the same to me.) Calling someone a loser can get ornate. A friend tells me that his teenage daughter and her friends in Berkeley make a "W" with their thumbs and index fingers, bring their index fingers together to form an "A," move index fingers back apart and turn hands upside down for an "M," then with one hand shape an "L." You don't get it? What a major loser.

In the print ad for the 2000 movie *Loser,* the star, Jason Biggs, made an "L" over his own brow. Biggs played a nice small-town boy nervous about moving to New York City after winning a college scholarship there. "You've seen that *Seinfeld* show, right?" he asks his dad. "It's just like that. They all got that sarcastic humor." Of course, when a movie calls its title character a loser, that's our cue that the word's being used unfairly and that we should be on his side. And we are. So much so that when he survives humiliations by dorm bullies (who lob him an "L"), holds on to his morals, *and* gets the girl, I felt relief and I actually said to myself, He's a winner!—which I was supposed to say.

You might expect these playground taunts from kids or in entertainment targeting them. But then you see a grown woman with a big black "L" on her forehead appearing in a print ad for Genesys, a company involved in "interaction management solutions." "She's delighted to be offering both phone and online customer service," the ad reads—then it whispers: "(Doesn't she realize she's actually driving her customers nuts [?])." The helpful woman is really a pathetic loser, the ad explains, because "if your voice and online customer service systems are unable to share information, it's like the left hand not knowing what the right hand is doing. Which is enough to drive your customers away."

Loser's unfair, it's mean—but, fortunately, advertising reminds us that we have other weapons with which to retaliate. When the airline pilot whose son L'd him because he didn't fly for Jet-Blue shot back with a "W" for "What*ev*er," he was not being immature—he was just caught up in the symmetrical schismo-genesic arms race. (Of course, advertising is always telling us that the best defense against loserdom is prevention—just consume the right product in the first place, sucka!)

Meanwhile, in non-TV life, a friend tells me that her thirty-six-year-old brother made an "L" on his forehead when referring to somebody; another time, he made the related "C" (short for "Like I really care," which is close to *Too much information,* or *TMI*—said when someone goes on too long about their prob-lems or other intimacies).

So which came first, the real-life word *loser* or the media word *loser*? Almost certainly the first, but like I really care. The more pertinent question is, Why does the loser cross the road and start using words like *loser* himself? To get to the safer side. The person who fears attack by the crowd or being lost in it, or fears that he gives off TMI like so much B.O., may become fluent in the language of the crowd in order to blend into it. Then again, many uncrowdlike people with no particular fear of crowds also draw from the common arsenal. The stinging come-backs are always close at hand and not likely to be misinter-preted. What gives a weapon word like *loser* its power is the knowledge that it can and will be used by millions. The "L," the "W," the "C," the *Hel*-lo?!, the *Duh*—each allows any person to be an army of one.

MEDIABORGS

The crowd I've been referring to includes people we actually know, of course, but it also includes millions of imagined people we know only through the media. The media represent, or, rather, *are* that crowd in our lives. And the melding of that crowd and the individual is positively cyborgian.

When I'm really plugged in—when I effortlessly utter a phrase that I sense will persuade another person, or when I have an experience that "seems like a movie"—I often get the feeling that I'm *literally* plugged in, that an invisible tube connects my brain to a hovering source of mass media that's feeding me words, images, ideas, frames of reference, and all my knee-jerk reactions. It's as if this source's silicon were coating my synapses and I become, in an ongoing morphing process, part myself, part media. (I realized only after writing those sentences that the hovering and morphing, the images of invisible tubes and silicon synapses are themselves fed by media sources, like *Star Trek* and *The Matrix*—which just proves what a mediaborg I am.)

But the mind-meld between an individual and the media is not a matter of neo-humanoids just blurting out whatever Microsoft or Clear Channel orders us to through implanted electrodes, at least not yet. The words and ideas do not flow only one way. The media's in me, but "me" is also in the media. We and the media are (though I hate the word, because it seems itself borg-generated) interactive. If mankind is an extension of the media, the media still are and always will be, as McLuhan said, extensions of man.

That's to say, clever constructions don't simply trickle down from movies, ads, and talk shows. Almost invariably, pop language bubbles up from "the people" and is relayed back to them by the media. These trade routes become continuous feedback loops of lingo. Even the phrase *Show me the money,* so identified with the 1996 movie *Jerry Maguire,* came from outside the media. The movie's writer and director, Cameron Crowe, said he heard the then–Phoenix Cardinal Tim McDonald say it in 1993 to an agent before he was traded to the San Francisco 49ers.

It does, however, take the media to make these phrases the lingua franca. The origins of a particular buzzphrase may be boardroom or locker room, but once the media pollinate it, it can become part of our collective reaction to the annoyances and difficulties of everyday life. "Show me the baby," I heard a woman say of her unsuccessful fertility treatment. (*Show me the X* is perfect for expressing transactional frustrations of all sorts. In 2002, well after *Jerry Maguire* came out, a friend of mine complained, "I work my ass off at this job. I'll do what you say, just show me the money." That same year, I saw "Show me the data!"

on a T-shirt for a children's autism foundation, and heard a blonde coo, "Show me the color" in a TV spot for L'Oréal soft permanent color gel.)

We the people and they the media coproduce the vernacular. People create the slang and the new inflections; then the media, controlling the means of mass distribution, turn some of those tropes into pop. (Once in a while it works the other way— the media coin a phrase and the people spread it, *Where's the beef?* from a Wendy's commercial being the most famous example. Some say that Jim Carrey invented, not just popularized, the loser "L" in his 1994 hit *Ace Ventura: Pet Detective.* Knowing a catchword's marketing potential, Carrey has tried to come up with a trademark gesture or phrase for most of his movies. Before it even opened in 2003, *Bruce Almighty* got some giggly publicity for a certain way he pronounced *Gooood!* The movie did well, but *Gooood!,* difficult to imitate, was a major loser.)

The media may rarely coin a phrase, but they are more than mere delivery boys. They perform an alchemy of their own on a word. Regardless of whether pop words are inspired by "the street" or a copywriter's deadline, it's the sense of golden media coursing through them that gives them a glamour, altering how we hear them, say them, and experience ourselves saying them.

Media glamour has long been known for its ability to make a personal activity—be it scrubbing your tub, rafting the rapids, or making love—feel like a secondhand event, something to be experienced in "quotation marks": While you do something, you (and perhaps imagined others) are watching yourself do it, just like you watch people do similar things on TV and in movies. Media glamour works pretty much the same way on language.

It used to be that the occasional French word picked up by English-speaking tourists lent the tourists a panache that they could carry back home like a souvenir; dropping a French phrase gave them a sense that they were part of a more dazzling *monde.* Today that momentary transcendence comes from repeating not French but a snappy phrase that's been on TV or in a movie. (This phenomenon is a little like those tacky print ads that read, "AS SEEN ON TV!"—when the only thing seen on TV was that same company's television ads.) Uttering certain TV- or movie-kissed catchphrases pumps us larger, brighter, hotter. The words connect us to the power source, and they allow us to join the ongoing national audition to be as clever as our friends on *Friends*.

Anyway, that's the hope. But whatever these phrases gain in glamour, they tend to lose in wit. It may be regular people who create verbal weaponry like *loser* or *whatever*. But by the time the phrases become TV celebrities, and regulars start saying them on a regular basis, the words' native charm is hard to detect. It has been replaced by the familiar and ultimately dumber sound of the dissy, pissy sitcom comeback.

SITCOMS AND THE DUMBED-DOWN PUT-DOWN

Television has catapulted catchphrases to stardom before: *Get Smart* spread *Would you believe . . . ?* and *Sorry about that* into near universal use in the late sixties. *Here come da judge* and *Verrry interesting*, from *Laugh-In*, and *Be careful out there*, from *Hill Street Blues*, had their runs. Sergeant Friday's *Just the facts* is still with us (most prominently in headlines that have anything to do with fax machines).

Nor are the combat-ready catchphrases of this chapter anything new to TV. From Ralph Cramden's *To the moon, Alice!* and a different *Alice*'s *Kiss my grits!* to Archie Bunker's *meathead* and *dingbat*, the colorfully hostile utterance has long been a television staple.

But today's TV catchphrases, whether innocuous or killer, are different from those of the past in a couple of ways. Over the last twenty or so years, TV catchphrases have become less particular to any one show or character and more transferable to all shows and characters, and to real life itself—a glibness for all seasons. Secondly, compared with earlier barbed witticisms, the current crop smarts without having quite the smarts. Both these changes—more one-size-fits-all, less wit—are caused in huge part by the insertion of marketing into every media moment.

Why pick on sitcoms when so many other televised forms—

talk shows, dramas, commercials, and, the supposed sitcom slayer, reality shows—also traffic in dumbed-down put-downs? Because sitcoms are the heaviest users and distributors. Minute for minute, commercials outpop sitcoms by far, but sitcoms have more minutes to fill. Reality shows and talk shows, which depend on real people to say real things under pressure, do indeed produce both positive pop (*Go girl!* and *Go for it!*, for instance, are big on *Fear Factor*. "You're the man!" one contestant told another, as the latter rather cheerfully emerged from a tubful of scorpions) and weapon pop (dismissing a rival's chances of winning Joe Millionaire's heart, Heidi sneered at the woman, saying, "He's mine. [bleep] Get over it." On PBS's *Frontier House*, a teenager in one family said that the spoiled father of a competing family should "get a life"; at another point that paterfamilias told someone else to do the same). But the pressures in sitcoms are scripted, and the scriptwriters themselves are under pressure to produce as many comedic clashes between battling egos as possible. So they reach for the bottled yuk more often. With decades of the habit under their belts, sitcoms have established the role and rhythm of our put-downs, in reality shows as well as in reality.

There used to be at least two other scripted forms of entertainment that relied on weaponized pop as much as sitcoms: variety shows and stand-up comedy. "That sort of confrontational banter works well in the short skit of variety shows and in stand-up comedy, especially when dealing with hecklers," says Gerard Jones, author of *Honey, I'm Home! Sitcoms: Selling the American Dream.* "But the variety show disappeared and the spirit of stand-up took over a lot of sitcoms, like *Roseanne, Home Improvement,* and *Seinfeld*." That leaves the sitcom standing up for the put-down.

For a brief history of the role of the sitcom put-down, I spoke at length with Jones, who says that the sitcom catchphrase began, like so much else on TV, with radio.

"With early radio comedy, you have for the first time an instantly transmitted mass language and people taking a great enjoyment in participating in that language," Jones says. "If somebody was laughing inappropriately, the perfect retort was

'T'aint funny, McGee.' That's from *The Johnson Wax Program with Fibber McGee and Molly,* one of the most popular sitcoms in the thirties and forties. George Burns's line to Gracie Allen, 'Say good night, Gracie,' became a way of shutting someone up who was silly. I've known people of my dad's generation who still say that occasionally.

"But between those radio show catchphrases—and there were a lot of them—and the early seventies, there was a long period when TV sitcoms were trying to become more naturalistic and less vaudeville-driven. The running gag and the signature catchphrase, which radio had gotten from vaudeville, were deemphasized."

Catchphrases had "pretty much disappeared from the TV sitcom, with a few exceptions, like *The Honeymooners,*" he says. "But they weren't on *I Love Lucy,* they weren't on *That Girl,* or even *The Beverly Hillbillies.* Who can remember a line from *Bewitched?*" What about *The Brady Bunch?* I ask. Don't people who watched it as teenagers still quote from it a decade or two later? "*Brady Bunch* fanatics might quote lines from the show," he says, "but there was nothing that jumped over the fence to become a real catchphrase."

All in the Family, debuting in 1971, changed all that, Jones says, with "a return of a vaudevillian, stagey feel and the big gag line, especially from Archie—'Stifle yourself, Edith,' or calling someone 'Meathead.' Largely because of Norman Lear, you find the return of the gag line: *Dy-no-mite* from *Good Times* or *This is the big one!* from *Sanford and Son.*" (Sanford was referring to the heart attack he feigned whenever his son annoyed him.)

But our relationship to catchphrases was a bit different back then. Those lines didn't become part of people's *reflexive* language. "Everyone knew where the catchphrase came from, and if you said it, you were consciously putting on that character's traits," says Jones. "What seems to have happened lately, either in the creation or distribution of phrases, is that they've become detached from a particular character. We know 'as if' got a boost from *Clueless* [the 1995 movie], and now you can feel cute and youthful by saying it, but you don't necessarily think of those characters. When Seinfeld got a hold of *yadda yadda yadda,* it had already been out there and you can say it without being a *Seinfeld* character. But if you said *'Stifle yourself,'* you *were* Archie Bunker."

Norman Lear–like insult humor—the running gag that lets off steam about generational, racial, sexual, or political friction—caught on in large part because it arrived during the early seventies, when national anxiety over Vietnam, civil rights, women's roles, and Watergate was boiling. "It was a bitchy time," Jones says, "and people found it very liberating to express this outrage," even if it came out like irritability as much as anything else. By the mid-seventies, Lear's peeved and aggrieved gag approach became codified and cutified by producers like James Komack *(Chico and the Man, Welcome Back, Kotter).* "Komack tried to create catchphrases that teenagers would say to each other, like *Chico and the Man*'s 'Get out of here and take your flies with you.' But none really stuck." (One from that era that did stick for a while, he says, came from Garry Marshall's *Happy Days,* as eight-year-olds across America imitated Fonzie's "Aaaaay," said with backward-jabbing thumb.) This more mechanized put-down humor, with the occasional hit phrase, says Jones, "was such an easy way to attract attention and get a teenage audience that by the eighties there hadn't been a lot of work on smarter, subtler sitcoms."

Mechanized but glamorized comebacks merged well with, and were undoubtedly egged on by, the look-out-for-number-one-and-screw-everyone-else ethos of the "greed decade." If put-downs helped sell sitcoms, why not base entire shows on them (along with their close personal companion, sexual innuendo)? For sheer abrasiveness, the sitcoms of that era outdid any since, says Jones. "I think eighties sitcoms were nastier, especially work ensemble shows like *Talk Radio,* where the whole function of the characters is to put somebody down. In *Who's the Boss?,* Judith Light played a woman whose mother did nothing but make acid remarks about her and horny remarks about Tony Danza."

Overuse eventually softened the disparaging word, and shows began to mix a slightly more anodyne put-down throughout the whole comedic formula. In nineties sitcoms, especially those about attractive single professionals, snippy comebacks were belted out so often that they became the yuppie yodel. One episode of *Cybill* (Cybill Shepherd's show on CBS), for instance, called out *Hel-lo?!*, *Oh, puh-leeze*, *Get a life*, *Yadda yadda* (well before *Seinfeld*'s *yadda* episode), and *Haven't we had enough fun yet?*

Impatient, irritable catchphrases are also echoed in the titles of sitcoms and, to a lesser extent, movies. Such sitcoms, at some point on the air or in the planning stage, include *As If, Get a Life, Get Real, Get Smart, Gimme a Break!, Just Shoot Me!, Oh Grow Up,* and *You Don't Know Jack.* Among the catchphrase movie titles are *Get Over It, Showtime, Whatever,* and *What Planet Are You From?*

When the goal is to get a laugh every time the characters look at each other, demand will outrun supply, and the lesser sitcoms, especially, will grab phrasal filler off the shelf, preferably from the cooler section. "It's the difference between creation and cool-hunting," says Jones, "a shift from a writer making up a line to a writer legitimizing something that people are already saying—which I think results in stupider lines. There's some wit to the older ones. 'To the moon!' isn't great, but the real humor of that line was in Alice's reaction. We could identify with her not responding to him, looking dour and unfazed by Ralph's threat. Whereas 'I don't *think* so' is more an effort to seem cool."

Packaged gibes not only write the dialogue for you, they potentially make money. If the target audience is already speaking the same lines at home, the hope is they'll be flattered— their words AS HEARD ON TV!—and thereby the show's ratings and ad revenue will rise. As revenue goes up, something comes down—not inevitably, but often. To understand how the all-purpose put-down can dumb down, and what marketing has to do with it, look at *Friends.*

One of the highest rated shows during its ten-year run, *Friends* is *the* model sitcom for and about the young demographic that advertisers crave. That's why, as of the show's penultimate, 2002–2003 season, each of its six stars was making $1 million an episode, record-breaking sums for an "ensemble sitcom" (as distinguished from single-star shows; Kelsey Grammer of *Frasier,* for example, reportedly earned $1.6 million an episode during the same period). More important, by the time *Friends* went off the air, it had the most expensive thirty-second ad spots of any prime-time show.

Persons Nouvelles par excellence, the *Friends* characters spritz put-downs on one another like Evian facial spray; the insults don't bruise so much as they make the air seem to glisten. Rachel reminds Monica that a valentine a boy left in Monica's locker way back in high school was really meant for Rachel. Monica looks dubious, so Rachel says: "Hel-*lo*?! Like he was really going to send you one!" Joey, the not-too-bright soap opera actor, has almost finished an interview with *Soap Opera Digest* when the reporter asks him what his favorite soap is other than his own. "I don't watch soap operas," he blurts out. "Excuse me—I have a life!" *I don't* think *so* has appeared on *Friends* almost as much as its famous guest stars, and often by way of the insecure Ross. He asks one of the girls whether she really believes she can defend herself after one karate class, then answers rhetorically, "I don't *think* so." When his all-thumbs buddies offer to babysit his infant son, Ross replies, "I don't *think* so." On the show's 2003 season finale, the friends shot at one another three *I don't* think *so*'s, three *ye-ah*'s, and one *loser.*

I admit, I've laughed a few times, literally a few, at *Friends,* usually at one of Phoebe's absurdities. The show's as easy to munch on as Frosted Flakes. But mostly I stare and wonder at the high-paid vapidity, and Jones reminds me why. "*Friends* is an awkward compromise between the vaudeville approach of making people laugh with gags and valorizing the audience by showing them an idealized version of themselves," he says. Looking smart (i.e., cool) is part of that ideal, but being smart is not. Joey is a sweet stud, but with a few bulbs missing; babelicious Rachel is no brain surgeon, either. Monica and Chandler, married to each other, are comedically and intellectually the Blandlers. Phoebe's wacky associations do show a creative flair. But only Ross, not a brain surgeon but a "paleontologist," evinces some thoughtfulness, or at least a healthy frustration with his friends' denseness. (After all, he doesn't *think* so, therefore he thinks.)

But then, dumb lines can add up to smart marketing. While there have been notable exceptions—popular shows with intelligent humor, like *Seinfeld, Bernie Mac, The Simpsons, Everybody Loves Raymond*—the logic of the dumbed-down put-down in sitcoms (and sitcomish movies and life) works something like this:

"If you're trying to make characters seem hip and idealized, you can't make them more witty than the audience itself," says Jones. "If they're too witty you lose that 'relatability,' as TV people say, and so the characters becomes less witty, less intelligent, less superior to other people. So rather than build your dialogue around the cleverest things you can think of, which is how comedy writers used to work, you build it around what you've heard in the dorm, in the mall, or on other TV shows.

"You end up trying to milk a devastating put-down out of something that is quite trite or witless. So the stupid line is supposed to have more power than it does."

Then, in order for us to suspend disbelief and trust that the put-down is as funny as the laugh track, the timing, and the reaction shot of a character's arched brow tell us it is, we have to put a few IQ points on hold. All those familiar comedic lights and bells send a signal that *other* people (the crowd) think the put-down is funny—so maybe there's something wrong with you if you can't get with the program. You might not like the program, it might be canceled tomorrow, but for the time being (to borrow from a fratboy-mean knee-slapper), it's on TV and you're not.

SLAMMIN' CLAMS

So dependent on pop language are sitcom writers that they even have a word for overused jokey shticks: clams. Clams are slightly different from clichéd put-downs, but the overlap is significant.

"Some of the biggest clams you saw over the last few years," says Jack Burditt, who has worked as a writer on *Frasier, Just Shoot Me!,* and *Watching Ellie,* "are 'a few good men,' 'I see dead people,' and 'Dead man walking' " (from the films *A Few Good Men, The Sixth Sense,* and *Dead Man Walking,* respectively). "Usually clams come from movies, but not always," he says. " 'I'm putting you on decaf.' That became a big one. One character says that to another when someone's acting wild." Some clams hail from other TV shows, like these large flashes in the pan: "You are the weakest link, good-bye" (from *The Weakest Link*) and "Is that your final answer?" *(Who Wants to Be a Millionaire).* Other clams derive from history's verbal highlights: "Houston, we've got a problem," "Read my lips," "kinder, gentler," "what the definition of *is* is."

Clams lie in a phrase's structure as well as in the frequency of its repetition, says the television writer and producer Peter Tolan (who most recently coproduced *Rescue Me* with Denis Leary). "For instance," he says, "the naming of a past presidential admin-istration as a time gauge of how long it's been since something happened: 'He hasn't gotten laid since the Ford administration.' Anything 'from hell' is a clam: 'the fiancé from hell.' It's com-pletely overused."

Why "clams"? I wondered. Catchy (but) Lame Attention Maximizers? Short for "exclamation"? Because clams stink when exposed too long to the air? The genesis is indeed a bad clam, but not necessarily a smelly one, says Tolan, who co-coined the word with Michael Patrick King when they were working on *Murphy Brown.* "We were sitting around a table pitching ideas, and we'd groan whenever someone brought out a bad joke. If you think back some years ago, in a sitcom someone would say, 'Where's Steve today?' and someone else would answer: 'Oh, Steve won't be in. He had some bad clams.' I don't know why that was supposed to be funny—maybe that's why the word *clam* got enshrined."

" 'Did I say that out loud?' is an infamous one," he adds. "It wasn't a clam the first time—it was genius." No one's sure, but it was probably first said out loud on TV by Cliff, the mailman, on *Cheers.* "If you said something outrageous, you followed up with 'Did I say that out loud?' as a way of allowing yourself to say the unallowable," says Tolan. "But it was so good writers started repeating it." (Chandler on *Friends:* "Sometimes I wish I was a les-bian. [beat] Did I just say that out loud?")

"The first time around, a clam is usually just a clever way of saying something, and so clever people, like sitcom writers, remember it," says Tolan. "They don't even know where it's from, they just start saying it."

Plugging a clam into a script is not an unconscious act, however; TV writers are nothing if not deliberate in choosing words. But ultimately writers use pop language for the same reasons we all do, only more so: deadline pressure to entertain and a desire to not have to think. "Sometimes when doing a TV show, there comes a point in the season when you're just tired, somebody will say 'Carter administration,' and in that moment you'll do it," Tolan says. "Even good people can stoop to clams."

Nevertheless, moratoriums are possible. "Each time you're on hiatus and you get back together in June, everyone talks about things to avoid," says Burditt. "I remember when I was on *Just Shoot Me!* a while ago. The first day we gathered, we said no Viagra jokes. We did not have a Viagra joke that year."

Clams are similar to, at times identical to, pop put-downs. Both forms exist to connect to an audience, but there are differences. "A clam has to be a joke or at least reaching for a joke," says Tolan. How about put-downs like *Don't even* think *about it, Duh, Ye-ah, Whatever*—are those clams? "Not necessarily. When you say *I don't* think *so* on a sitcom, more often than not, you're not going for a joke. *Duh* and those others are more attitude things. You can use them all the time."

Pop put-downs, because they're less formally jokey and more able to snap on to any line anywhere anytime, tend to last longer and appear more often both on and off TV than do clams. (How often have you said *Hel-lo?!* or *What part of X don't you understand?*, as opposed to *Did I say that out loud?* or *Houston, we've got a problem?*) Clams are pop, but not quite as pop as media-glazed weapon words, if only because clams aren't on the tip of the public's tongue.

Some phrases are too close to call. *Don't go there,* which Burditt says "is now considered a sitcom clam," and *the [blank] from hell,* which Tolan labels a clam, I consider prototypical weapon phrases. "*Too much information* is a clam," says Tolan. "Well, it has one little foot in each area."

As for my pet-peeve peevish put-down, *I don't* think *so,* it has so colonized the collective brain that it doesn't even occur to writers to flag it as a clam or a cliché of any sort. Burditt: "I've never heard anyone on a sitcom say, 'Don't use *I don't* think *so.*' "

LAUGHING ALL THE WAY TO THE LAUGH BANK

There used to be another word for words that guarantee a boffo response: *claptrap* ("any artifice or expedient for winning applause," as well as "pretentious and insincere or empty language," according to the dictionary). Beyond clams, weapon words, or words of any kind, sitcom language has laid an extensive trap for claps: cadence itself.

Even if the words are as plain as the prairie, sitcom dialogue is likely to bob along with a particular rhythm—the timing of the set-up, the beat before the rejoinder, the tension of laughter lying in wait.

"Sitcoms have their own language now," says Tolan. "It's like French. I've been in motel rooms where I can hear the TV through the wall, I can't make out one word, but I can tell it's a sitcom from the inflections. The words are unintelligible, but you know there's a laugh coming."

Over a lifetime of watching TV, we have all internalized the standards—what's "on" or "off" in an almost electrical sense, just how long a pause needs to be pregnant.

That's why *Friends,* which occasionally ran episodes with few or no stock pop phrases, could never shake its overall stock pop *phrasing.* Ross might have missed an opportunity or two to say *I don't* think *so,* but the cadence of the snippy retort is in the show's DNA (to use a popism). Chandler and Monica have just returned from their Hawaiian honeymoon and are about to enter their apartment. Still wearing his aloha outfit, Chandler tells Monica sincerely, "Before we go in, I just want you to know I love you. I had a great time on our honeymoon, and I can't wait to go in there and spend the rest of our life together." Monica: "You're really sticking with the shell necklace, huh?"

Those exact words will never turn up on another TV show, but the instant switch of sentiment, from sincerity to ridicule, is so ritualized that the audience is programmed to laugh (and to think Chandler is dorky). Same with the sheepish mea culpa. A slightly jealous Rachel asks Monica about a guy they both had crushes on in high school: "When were you going to tell me that you were going out with Chip Matthews?" Monica takes a beat and replies, "Now?"

The rhythmic and verbal tropes of sitcoms were determined in part by the belief that a live studio audience would stimulate the home audience to laugh. It's all about the money: More laughs can translate into higher ad rates. So just in case the studio audience was bored, sitcoms invented the laugh track.

A laugh track is any prerecorded laughter and can be put to different uses, says Tolan. "Some producers will just go into a laugh bank"—stored hilarity from an audience responding to a different show altogether. "If you never shoot with an audience, they will use a laugh track. If a show is shit and is shot in front of an audience but no one laughs, they will use a laugh track."

However, not all sitcom laughter is completely fake. "Most is actually recorded from mikes hanging over the same live audience watching a show," says Tolan. "But you never know if those laughs fell exactly where they did on the night of the filming. During the editing process, lifts are made in the piece that disturb the natural flow of the laughter, and so sometimes laughs have to be replaced or moved from one joke to another. In other words, the whole bloody enterprise is corrupt."

But lately the peppy sitcom cadence has been calming down, because some shows have dumped the laugh track, the audience, and the shticks that play up to it. These shows (among them *Curb Your Enthusiasm, Malcolm in the Middle, Bernie Mac,* and two that Tolan worked on, *The Larry Sanders Show* and *The Job*) use a single camera, which means they're shot more like a movie. With every shot, the angle and lighting are laboriously changed, making it difficult to shoot in front of an audience. (Most sitcoms are shot with four cameras, allowing the show to go on at a pace that will accommodate a studio audience.) But if you eliminate the live audience, you're free to write and perform without pausing for audible appreciation. Laugh-track-free comedy might seem like jumping without a net, but it has been on TV forever: Cartoons rarely use laugh tracks (the painful *Scooby Doo* excepted).

The absence of a laugh track can make a show come across as "quality," but it doesn't guarantee good writing (see the 2002 sitcom *Leap of Faith*). Nor does the presence of a track necessarily hinder good writing *(Seinfeld, Everybody Loves Raymond).*

Whether a sitcom uses a laugh bank is less important than it once was, because after watching television for more than half a century, we now carry laugh ATMs in our heads. They tell us when and how much laughter we can withdraw and into which feuding characters to deposit our exasperation or goodwill.

The same system also provides 24/7 real-life access. There's a light, rubberband-like tension in the way we talk: A situation or a rhythm summons the internal laugh bank and then we follow its prompts—with a joke, a put-down, a phrase.

MASTER OF ITS OWN GUFFAW

Sitcom language doesn't have to be so programmed. The gleaming exception to the rule is *Seinfeld.* In fact, language was one of the show's recurring subjects. *(Seinfeld* was never for a moment "a show about nothing," the blurb that George and Jerry used to pitch their fictional sitcom. But "a show about nothing" became the entertainment press's shorthand for the real show and then a catchphrase in its own right, as knee-jerk a refrain in stories about *Seinfeld* as *yadda yadda yadda.)*

Not only was *Seinfeld*'s repartee much better than most sitcoms', but the characters were always commenting on the oddities of words, particularly those that filled their own niche's nouvelle vocabulary. (Jerry to a girl: "I'm lactose intolerant. I have *no* patience for lactose.") There were entire episodes about a phrase (most famously *yadda*), and in the process of naming a previously unnamed behavior, attitude, or quirk, *Seinfeld* coined phrases: *close talkers, shrinkage, master of my domain, soup Nazi, Not that there's anything wrong with that.*

These neologisms of "Seinlanguage" (as Jerry Seinfeld's best-selling book was called) were actually spoken less frequently than the common pop put-downs, which *Seinfeld* engaged in along with mediocre sitcoms—a *Hel-*lo?*!* here, an *I don't* think *so* there (as Jerry told an unctuous magician who wanted to borrow him for a trick). Or Elaine's friendly but aggressive *Get out!* yelled while shoving one of the guys whenever he told her something unbelievably good or bad. (A somewhat more recent incarnation of *Get out!* is the equally amazed *Shut up!* Two characters said it in the movie *Loser,* as Julia Louis-Dreyfus, who played Elaine, later did in her post-*Seinfeld* sitcom, *Watching Ellie.*)

Seinfeld dips into the big pop put-down pool because its characters occupy the same savvy transactional universe as do *Friends'*. But the two shows, now masters of the rerun, write in opposite directions. In *Friends* the writing always veers toward the test-marketed center, where the audience is prone to identify with the characters and to laugh away their shared, whimsically portrayed obsessions. In *Seinfeld* the writing is out there, as out there as Kramer (*Friends'* Phoebe is a poor woman's Kramer), revealing in Machiavellian detail the petty transactions that plague or make the characters' days. You've hoarded your favorite brand of contraceptive sponges because they're going off the market; your supply is limited, but you meet a guy you want to have sex with—what tests can you run to see if he's "spongeworthy"? If you're at a party and a barely touched éclair is sitting in the trash can and no one can see you, should you go for it? It's not just that *Seinfeld* predicaments are more honestly selfish and its humor smarter than other sitcoms'. But the same pop phrases that in lesser comedies are pleas to "relate" are used in *Seinfeld* to expose the nuances of our spurn-worthy narcissism. The *Friends* crew, always fondling the lacy edges of sentimentality, grow as characters; *Seinfeld's* never do.

(I'm going to say something possibly stupid, possibly stunning. Have you noticed that over the last ten or fifteen years, the titles of the very best TV shows that are also huge hits are all based on lead characters whose surnames start with *S*? The big hitters: *Seinfeld, The Simpsons, The Sopranos, The Daily Show with Jon Stewart, SpongeBob SquarePants.* Not blockbuster but of high quality: *The Larry Sanders Show, Mr. Show.* Or forget surnames and think of quality hits that start with *S* [and end in *X*]: *Sex and the City, Six Feet Under.* And forget quality and think of the shows that are among the most successful in their genre: *Survivor;* the Super Bowl. *S* is one of the most frequently used consonants in the alphabet, but still . . .)

Don't Even Think About Telling Me "I Don't Think So"

If indeed most TV clams come from movies, as the sitcom writer Jack Burditt says, that may prove a point made by the linguist Geoffrey Nunberg. TV catchphrases aren't as recyclable as those from movies, he said in a *Fresh Air* commentary on NPR, because when TV shows end their prime-time run, the lines begin to sound decrepit, while movie phrases are "always detaching themselves and entering the language under their own steam." He cites the Bette Davis line "What a dump!" from the 1949 film *Beyond the Forest;* "It seemed like a good idea at the time" from *The Last Flight* (1931); and "We don't need no stinkin' badges," which, as he says, is actually a slight misquote from *The Treasure of the Sierra Madre* (1948)—all phrases we still use, though we have little if any sense of their source. Then, he adds, there are "the famous lines which people can still identify but which they use without really quoting the movie they came from—'I could have been a contender'; 'Make him an offer he can't refuse'; 'What we have here is a failure to communicate'; 'Go ahead, make my day.' " Of course, some TV catchphrases do stick, he says, like *Seinfeld*'s "Not that there's anything wrong with that."

I would add only that the relatively fewer TV phrases that have entered the language under their own steam tend to scream, *The Simpsons!*): *Whoo-hoo!* (to express joy or a victory), *What the hootman?!* (to express incredulousness, and one of my favorites), and of course, *D'oh!* (I'm an idiot! How did I make that mistake?). When *D'oh!* (or *Doh*) entered the updated online edition of the *Oxford English Dictionary* in 2001, the press excitedly sent the news around the world, as if the entry had given all of TV a degree from Oxford U.

One-of-a-kind phrases from movies may be more likely than television's to endure. But when you get away from those unique lines and look at the more generic comebacks that TV has merely spread, rather than coined, TV's influence is everywhere, including the movies.

The proliferation of TV pop weaponry is quite evident if you compare two animated Disney movies made nearly fifty years apart: *Peter Pan,* released in 1953, and its 2002 sequel, *Return to Never Land.* In the first, far superior movie, the closest examples of prefab pop phrases I could find were Captain Hook saying to Mr. Smee, "You blithering idiot!" and later shrieking, "I'll get you for this, Pan, if it's the last thing I do!"—not terribly pop even for its time (written before, during, and after World War II).

In the sequel, Wendy's hard-headed young daughter, Jane, doesn't believe in Peter Pan and disses him all the way, setting in motion the crank-it-out crankiness that replaces actual comedy. Peter Pan's first words to Captain Hook, as the villain is about to throw Jane overboard to the octopus: "In your dreams, Hook!" When Peter pushes Jane to fly before she's ready, she fires back, "Don't even *think* about it!" Peter to a Lost Boy who can't stop blubbering: "Put a cork in it!" Jane to Peter, who falsely claimed he didn't want to make her angry: "Oh, grow up. . . ." A sniveling Hook to Jane: "My sources tell me you wish to return home." Jane: "You got *that* right." To win Jane's trust, Hook complains that Peter is an insensitive jerk. "Tell me about it," she replies. When Peter and Jane finally become friends, he jokes that he's braver than she, and she says, in the flat pitch that's become a trademark for cynical, "Right." Hook asks his intimidated crew, "Who's the bravest pirate, boys?" and they pump their fists and shout Arsenio-audience style, "Hook! Hook! Hook! Hook!"

My complaint isn't that although the movie takes place during World War II, the characters are hurling twenty-first-century comebacks. (One of my favorite such movie anachronisms is in *Titanic.* Circa 1912, Leonardo DiCaprio presses Kate Winslet to tell him whether she loves her fiancé, and she responds, "We are not having this conversation!") I do find the unpoetic license jarring. But my real beef is that moviemakers believe that if they don't supply soddenly familiar dialogue, the audience won't relate—a formula that makes the whole enterprise a more middling, insipid experience. It's also a sign that other little lies probably lurk in the script.

The franchisable put-down wasn't born yesterday. Movies were plugging in pop phrases even before they were plugging products, even before six-year-old Drew Barrymore said (with perfect cynical pitch), "Gimme a break" in 1982's *E.T.,* so famously strewn with free ads for Reese's Pieces. But the two kinds of plugs often appear in the same movies, because they're born from the same urge to sell.

Watching old movies convinces you that sitcomatosed movie language isn't inevitable. In her book *Fast-Talking Dames,* Maria DiBattista, a professor of film studies and English at Princeton, focuses on the dialogue in 1930s and 1940s movies, especially those starring smart, accomplished actresses, like Katharine Hepburn, Barbara Stanwyck, and Rosalind Russell, whose characters spoke an inventive, vivid language, often slang. Moviemakers were aware of audience demand, but they weren't limited by it, DiBattista writes, especially in the early years of the talkies: "The newborn talkies were hungry for words after the long fast imposed by the silents. Hollywood scrambled to find writers to satisfy moviegoers who sought to hear how modern men and women did or *should* sound. The fashioning of a language suited to American realities was not just the business of studios eager to create and keep mass audiences. It was a job that engaged highbrow culture as well." She notes some of the writers who wrote for Hollywood (albeit with varying degrees of satisfaction): Nathanael West, Dorothy Parker, Lillian Hellman, Dashiell Hammett, Raymond Chandler, P. G. Wodehouse, F. Scott Fitzgerald, William Faulkner.

Movie talk today suffers not so much from a dearth of good writers but from the assumption of producers and writers, bolstered by market research, that flattering and exciting audiences is more profitable than challenging them. What matters is that language creates an almost physical sensation, often the pleasant one of numbing out. "Wisecracks still ricochet off movie soundtracks," DiBattista writes, "but too often they are severed from their roots in actual harsh or bitter experience. They are zingers offered for the sake of the zing, not for the hard truths and obdurate realities that we otherwise could not bear to hear of outright. The smart talkers of today's movies, mimicking the monologism of stand-up comedians or the one-liners of sitcoms, rarely aspire above the level of the put-down."

The put-down not only puts down and suppresses an adversary, it puts aside anything we'd rather not think about. "We gravitate toward these kind of phrases," DiBattista adds, "because it's an easy way of dispatching any of the complications of our lives."

WORDS WITH WHICH TO WHACK

Sometimes you *want* characters to talk in the meanest, media-saturated lingo because that's how they routinely punch through the fog of their days. Mobsters, for instance, at least the movie and TV kind, spit out tough-man pop like nobody's business. And this makes sense, because gangsters were among the original slangsters, especially in the old days. "Invention of slang words by the literati of the dominant culture appears to be meager; most of them, it seems, are borrowed from underworld sources," H. L. Mencken wrote in the 1936 edition of *The American Language*.

Now, however, media gangsters talk like Persons Nouvelles talking like them. "Do the math," mob boss Robert De Niro tells his shrink, Billy Crystal, in *Analyze This*. Some guy wants to kill De Niro: "I don't *think* so," he says. Crystal suggests that in one of De Niro's dreams he was acting like Fredo the coward in *The Godfather*. De Niro: "I don't *think* so."

And the pissed-off pop that comes out of Tony Soprano's mouth—fuggedaboudit! But seriously, one of *The Sopranos'* great themes is that Tony and his crew are like us, trapped in the frustrating transactions, large and small, of a capitalist, materialist society. Minus the threat of violence, Tony's explosion at his wife because she doesn't remember his preference in orange juice options—"lots of pulp," "some pulp," or "no pulp"—could have been a *Seinfeld* routine. Meanwhile, the Sopranos' yuppie, non-Mafia neighbors are tickled pink to mouth mob words like *whack*.

And speaking of *Analyze This*, the *[Blank] this!* construction has been providing words with which to whack for a while now. *[Blank] this!* surfaced well before De Niro and Crystal's

1998 movie—Michael Moore published *Downsize This* in 1996, and he didn't invent the phrase—but the movie did inspire a bevy of similarly in-your-face dares.

Privatize This! In response to President Bush's efforts to "personalize" Social Security, *Privatize This!* quickly hit the blogs, appeared in headlines, and became the name of a Web site (privatizethis.com) paid for by the Democratic Congressional Campaign Committee.

Outsource This! is the title of a Jason Alexander Internet short film for the Communication Workers of America, a logo on coffee mugs, and the occasional pop in headlines, like "Outsource This: The Dems Smell Blood" in *BusinessWeek.*

HIGHJACK THIS, FAGS. Navy crewmen "painted 'hijack this, fags' on missiles headed toward Afghanistan," and the Bush administration was forced to apologize, as David Talbot wrote in *Salon.* (The first word was actually misspelled "highjack," as a photo of the missile shows.)

Fear This! The bumper sticker and windshield decal is often applied to monster pickups, as if their size alone didn't instill the desired trembling. But it's not just the vehicle we should fear. After the invasion of Iraq, I spotted on the rear window of a small car a large "Fear This!" decal in a red, white, and blue stars-and-stripes motif.

Scan This! In the first month that police began scanning visitors to Tampa's entertainment district with facial-recognition software, one hundred faces per minute, protesters "wore masks, shot the international finger award and said, 'Scan this!' " complained the project's coordinator, Detective Bill Todd.

Recount this! quickly went up on T-shirts just days after the 2000 election.

Hey ARNOLD: GROPE THIS—You lose! A woman held up this handwritten sign at a Schwarzenegger rally on the eve of the California recall election. It refers, of course, to Schwarzenegger's alleged history of groping women.

[Blank] this! is an acceptable way to say Fuck you! But usually it's a *fuck you,* Tom Dalzell says, "to a particular constituency"—corporations that outsource, Bush, small cars, small countries,

Arnold. I asked linguists and lexicographers, but no one's quite sure of the phrase's derivation. But the much-longer-standing *Fuck this!*—the one that emphasizes *fuck* rather than *this*—is surely a contributor. Wherever it came from, *[Blank] this!* is one of those heavy-weapon phrases that, while most people get it and might even use it, is favored especially by people who are paid to write.

Screenwriters, speechwriters, copywriters, press release writers, journalists—professionals whose livelihood depends on using words to entertain and persuade—have brains that are stuffed with catchphrases, clams, clichés, puns, rhythms, and verbal crutches of every kind. Playing with the words can be imaginative, great fun, and, of course, art; too often it's hackneyed and encourages the stupidity of our fellow man, and ourselves.

I can tell you why I, as a journalist, have used pop clichés. Sure, I've done it to save time and out of desperation when I couldn't think of anything more original to say—that is, out of laziness. And sometimes I've told readers, in essence, to "talk to the cliché," because cliché talk is such a tenacious, heavily rewarded habit (besides money, rewards include getting through a sentence with rhythm intact) that I'm not always aware I'm doing it. But I've also used clichés more consciously and for less excusable reasons, such as swerving to avoid reader skepticism. If, when writing (or, heck, when talking), I suspect I have inconsistencies or loose ends in thoughts, I might plop in a cliché to create an emotional distraction, so the reader (or listener) won't notice that I've missed a beat of fact or logic. I can cover up, or so I've been betting, with a *stronger* beat. (For instance, on occasion I have placed the slightly dramatic *In the end* at the end of a story to imply that fact and logic have delivered me to a point, a closure, when in truth, I just didn't know how else to end. I have not stooped, however, to the sunset-evoking *at the end of the day,* the chorus of bloviating TV talk-show pundits, though I admit it serves the same purpose.) Such sentence savers are the verbal equivalent of waving a shiny object to get a child's attention, something writers do with grown-up audiences all the time.

Shiny writerly objects can be pop even though, as with *[Blank] this!,* it's primarily wordsmiths who use them. Such pop-but-not-populist words include *dish* (when referring to gossip), *gravitas,* and *wordsmith.* However, some words that are by, for, and about the media, like *soundbite* and *spin,* have swelled way past their professional confines.

When talking about the tics and tricks of writers, pundits, and other media heads, I'm talking about the talk of the "chattering classes," that small, self-enclosed group given—more than other people are—to throwing out clever soundbites, especially biting ones. These may be the only people, in fact, who use the term *chattering classes,* which is meant to lightly disparage those who produce nothing more useful than verbiage. While *chattering classes* seems to me to be a form of self-criticism, or more likely, colleague criticism, to many chatterers it's self-flattery. After all, in our classless society, we're a class—and that's classy. (Not to mention that *chattering classes* is slightly kinder than some of the other names we're called, like *elites* and *effetes.*)

Chatterers chatting about chatterers—claustrophobic, but from whom else can you get good dish on the folks who produce the movies, TV shows, Web sites, and ads that inundate you? And once in a while, the media's parodies of their own dependency on catchphrases can make for some funny writing.

In a Snickers Crunch commercial from 2001, a street vendor sells little windup dolls who repeat clichés. Customers request a particular cliché-spouting doll and stomp on it. Somebody smashes a doll who keeps blabbing, "Talk to the hand"; someone else, "Whassup?!" (Some clichés concern relationships: "I love you, but I'm not in love with you.") "Need to crunch something?" the voiceover explains. ". . . Crunch this." Since the campaign slogan "Hungry? Crunch this" is itself a pop-angry phrase, this spot was a rare instance of deploying peevish pop against other pop that people are peeved at.

Nothing in the media, however, lampoons the media's pop put-downs better than *The Simpsons*. Here, for instance, are Homer and Marge, as usual, watching TV.

HOMER: So, Marge, ready for another episode of *Don't Go There?*

MARGE: I'm tired of that show. But I've been hearing good things about *Talk to the Hand.* [reading from her TV guide] Tom Shales says, "The writing snaps, crackles, and pops."

HOMER: OK. Whatever takes my mind off my life.

In another episode, Apu, the convenience store owner, is trying to increase his sperm count by cooling his testicles:

HOMER: Hey, Apu, sitting in the ice-cream cooler, eh?

APU: . . . chilling my loins. I'm increasing my chance for impregnating my wife.

HOMER: Too much information. Thanks for the mental picture. Why don't you tell us what you *really* think?

APU: Will you stop spouting those hackneyed quips?!

HOMER: [a few moments later] Hel-*lo?*! . . . Thanks for sharing! More than I wanted to know!

These hackneyed quips also tell us what *The Simpsons'* writers *really* think about their own influence in passing pop phrases on to the masses, like the aforementioned *D'oh!*, as well as phrases that Bart popularized (though didn't coin) in the show's early days: *Been there, done that; Outta my way, man; Don't have a cow, man; Cowabunga!; Ay, caramba!* (the last three are so Bart-specific that you rarely hear them anymore).

At play with the power of its word, *The Simpsons* has become, to the surprise of the chattering classes, a religious touchstone, used in church sermons and college courses on religion and philosophy, where readings have included *The Simpsons and Philosophy: The D'oh! of Homer,* edited by William Irwin, and *The Gospel According to The Simpsons: The Spiritual Life of the World's Most Animated Family* by Mark I. Pinsky. Dropping *Simpsons,* Harry Potter, or even *Seinfeld* references into a spiel can wake up the flock or classroom, of any persuasion. *The Simpsons* and Harry Potter, especially, have proven as useful for evangelicals railing against the characters' supposedly anti-Christian ways as for progressive clergy hailing the characters' relative enlightenment. This flock-rousing feat is testimony in part to the power of mixing celebrity with even a drop of the spiritual, something we've been aware of at least since John Lennon declared that the Beatles were more popular than Jesus. Celebrity—be it human, animal, or phrasal—supplies our talking and thinking points and does so in a slogany way that increases the chance we might actually retain them.

But even more important than celebrity in contributing to *The Simpsons'* religious vibes are its commentaries on pop culture. *The Simpsons* does one of the jobs that religion (as often represented by the show's joyless Reverend Lovejoy) falters at: It pulls back the veils to reveal the truths about the most transcendent forces in our lives—family, community, and God, sure, but mostly television, the only force that encompasses them all. As Homer once drooled when he and his coveted box made up after a fight, "TV—mother, father, secret lover!"

The Simpsons' catchphrases are funny for the same reason that its jokes about God, family, and community are funny: They mock the way our pieties are often rhetorical covers for their opposite. When Homer says to Apu, "Thanks for sharing," he means it sarcastically, of course, as most of us now do; the phrase is meant to shut off any communication from Apu that might verge on the personal. Homer's cascade of pop put-downs is light antisocial behavior posing as light social communication, just as Mr. Burns's recycling plant is a thin veil for a toxic waste dump and Mayor Quimby's political bromides camouflage his personal graft. Homer's monumental self-centeredness is reflected in the thought-foreclosing aspect of pop language: Say what you have to in order to get what you want, consume it, and go numb. "Look, just give me some ice cream," Homer tells Apu, who hands him a container he has been sitting on. Homer: "Um, how about one not touching your ass?"

XPLOSIVE POP

Animated art like *The Simpsons* is about as pop as it gets. Unencumbered by deadening detail, all big colors full of air, cartoons, like pop phrases, float the promise that you can pop through their blown-up version of life to some bit of truth.

All this popping, wham-bam punch lines, and popgun weaponry—it's time to look at the word *pop* itself, an onomatopoeic masterpiece with both cartoony fun and primal aggression built into it.

While the adjectival *pop* in *pop culture* comes from, as the people know, the word *popular* (and that from the Latin *popularis*, meaning "of the people"), *pop* as a noun and a verb comes from the Germanic-based Middle English (*poppe*, "a blow," and *poppen*, "to strike"), and there its origins are considered imitative, or onomatopoeic. The verb's many other dictionary definitions include "to make a short, quick, explosive sound: *The cork popped*"; "to put or thrust quickly"; "to shoot; fire at." Pop the Latin and Middle English meanings into the oven and you might come out with "a popular explosion" or, to name a few of the word's pop cultural manifestations:

The pro wrestlers' pop. This is the moment when performers jolt the crowd. Or as one wrestler explained on the PBS show *Merchants of Cool,* "Pop means when that crowd pops, when they react—pow!" A colleague elaborated: "It's like a shot reaction, you know, they don't really expect it, so you may get that surprise out of them. Just like when you catch somebody coming around the corner and you jump out and whoa!"

The marketeers' P-O-P. It stands for *point of purchase*—the place where you buy something, or a sales promotion at that place, like the coupons that flag you down from supermarket shelves or the bulky cardboard displays that you bump into and perhaps topple. POPeteers insist that such store paraphernalia are no small matter, as in these (weaponized) headlines from a catalogue for a P-O-P trade show: "Without P-O-P your brand is toast" and "News flash: 70% of all purchase decisions are made in-store." In a retail landscape that's "been completely overhauled," the copy reads, and "with the overall consolidation of retail, the most effective way to woo the American buyer is at the point-of-purchase. So brands today need to be powerful, stealthy, and absolutely ruthless in-store. . . . You've got to dig in and play mean."

Pop-up ads. Taking P-O-P to more obnoxious extremes, these are the windows that suddenly appear while you're online, flashing, covering up the site, and otherwise intruding. The ads may have spawned as many lawsuits to stop them and software to kill them (with pop-fun names like popupcop.com and popupbegone.com) as they have drawn customers.

Pop-up graphics. The small printed messages appearing on the show *Blind Date* or the late *Pop-Up Video* from VH1 are meant to reveal the real deal on paramours or performers. Just bursting to divulge the onscreen characters' grimy little secrets, the popped-up word is presumably more trustworthy than the manipulative live-action visuals surrounding it. These pop-ups may be little more than mean-spirited gossips, but when print busts through with such a *pow!*, it comes across more like a truthsayer of pop culture.

POP (Protect Our Privacy). In 2002, this grassroots group in North Dakota fought against the selling of financial and health data. Fortunately, with the help of such a pop acronym, protecting privacy can take on populist overtones. Unfortunately, the ravaging of privacy comes out of a stronger impulse, indulged in by both individuals and corporations: to just pop a name into a computer and—presto!—out comes the data needed to spy on or sell to anyone in the world.

Linguistically, *pop* is one trifecta of a fun-loving, fist-wielding word. When short for *popular, pop* is a "clipped" word, and as such it is energy compressed, ever ready to bolt out of the gate. *Pop* is also a palindrome, a word spelled the same way forward and backward, like *mom, wow,* or *Bob* (which I'll later argue is the poppest name of all). And most pertinently, *pop* is an onomatopoeic word made of plosives. *Pop* sounds like what it means because of its plosive *P*'s. Plosives are consonants whose sound is formed when part of the vocal tract completely closes, stopping the air flow, and "the soft palate is raised. Air pressure thus builds up behind the closure, which is then released explosively," as David Crystal, a leading language authority, writes in *The Cambridge Encyclopedia of Language*. The plosives, also called stops, are *B, D, G, K, P,* and *T;* and the last three, as "voiceless plosives," create a more intense "noise burst," Crystal writes. All plosives are most forceful in a word's final position.

Pressure released in noise bursts—this pretty much describes how the pop put-down works. "I'm trying really hard and doing my best," says Speaker #1. "Oh, I don't *think* so," Speaker #2 says (in a put-down that pivots on an exaggerated, voiceless final plosive). The put-down stops the flow of conversation, thus building pressure in Speaker #1. But in Speaker #2 (and, if one is present, the audience) pressure is released through this noise burst (a burst that, whether funny or not, we *associate* with humor and that we respond to with sounds and facial expressions that others associate with our getting the humor). The pop put-down is a physiological act.

OK, *pop* is a plosive and as physical as all get-out—so? Well, consider that so are the expressions for other things primal—for instance, the basic "dirty" sex words: *fuck, cock, prick, dick, shmuck, tit, boob, cunt, bootie,* and *butt* (though, notably, not *ass* or *asshole*). *Sex* (pronounced *seKs*) itself peaks on a *K* plosive. (The plosive *K* also explains some of *X*'s e*K*streme popularity.)

Then there are the "disgusting" bodily function words: *shit, piss, fart, vomit, throw up, burp,* and the childlike *poop* and *yuck.*

The very sounds of the sex words and the bodily function words convey a breaking through, a penetrating, a popping, or, in the case of body parts—*prick, boob, butt*—a popping out. The onomatopoeic process is, after all, a primal process.

If the pressure ramps up enough to result in an actual physical act like hitting, then you practically trip over the plosives. Jumping down the thesaurus under the verb *hit* (and skipping the relatively few exceptions like *flail, hammer,* and *lather*), we hit *bat, batter, beat, belt, blast, blitz, box, buffet, bump, clap, clip, clobber, clout, club, crack, dab, ding, flax, flog, hook, jab, kick, knock, KO, lob, pelt, pop, pound, punch, rap, slap, smack, sock, swat, tap, thump, thwack, wallop,* and *whack.* My thesaurus was written before WWE's *SmackDown!* show blitzed us with *smackdown,* but it's one of the poppest—in this case, the most commercially hip—hit words of all (although as a noun), as in this *New York Post* headline about a real estate dispute: "Two luxe malls in Fla. smackdown."

Likewise, the best-known words for "hard" drugs have the plosives' harder sounds: *smack, junk, crack, crank, coke, poppers,* and *dope* itself, while the best-known words for "soft" drugs have plosives like *pot, weed, ectasy,* or *X,* as well as softer sounds like *marijuana, grass.* (I say "the best-known" words for drugs because, by definition, only those words can reach pop status; but the scores of lesser-known slang words for drugs draw from sounds across the board.)

And when the point is purchase, marketing whizzes must be aware of plosives' primal appeal. What else explains why so many sneaker names punch their presence into the world the way hardcore sex words do, with lots of guttural, aggressive *K* sounds? Nike, Reebok, BKs, Cons, Keds, ASICS, Etonic, Skechers, Ryka, Brooks, even the shoe named after an officially nonaggressive country, K-Swiss. (And look at how *sneakers* kicked the soft ass of *tennis shoes,* which many of us in the Midwest grew up calling them.)

K and fellow voiceless stops, *P* and *T,* get noticed, and when they're selling sneakers, their noise bursts help create a muscular, sexy image out of a nothingness (and a lot of global sweatshops). It's as if the plosives were built-in exclamation marks on the toes of the shoes, the better to kick butt with. That the most existential advertising tag line in history, Just Do It, stops on a voiceless plosive is pretty fuckin' *K* itself.

Plosive popularity is not just my auditory hallucination. Crystal finds plosive domination in another category of names: "Plosives are much more likely to be found in male endings *(Bob, David, Dick, Jock)*" than in female names, which, he writes, tend to end in gentler vowel sounds. He also notes that male names usually have fewer syllables than female names and are likelier to be monosyllabic—a brevity, I'd suggest, that accentuates a plosive's pop.

Poppycock! many linguists would cry. They pooh-pooh "sound symbolism"—the idea that certain sounds convey certain meanings. "It's fairly common for nonlinguists to think all words have some sort of intrinsic meaning based on their sound, so linguists are constantly fighting this lay notion" and often over-reacting to it, says Leanne Hinton, a University of California, Berkeley, linguistics professor who co-edited the book *Sound Symbolism*. But linguists' slap at in-your-face sounds doesn't mean that the *B, D, G, K, P,* and *T* punch isn't there. "As for sex words ending in *K*, I'm not sure I want to stick my neck out as to why," says Hinton. "But I can see that sound symbolism is playing a role with 'hit' words. In fact, it's a universal tendency, because it really is an imitation of the sound. . . . If you go to comic books in other languages and look at the sound-effect words for hitting, you'd find that they have a fair number of stops or plosives in them."

POOP HAPPENS

Dirty words, even when used to put somebody down, rarely amount to pop put-downs. Because dirty words are restricted on broadcast television and radio, they cannot easily attain pop status. It must be said, though, that as taboos have fallen away, some obscenities have entered the halls of mainstream pop, the very flash of their notoriety getting them past the bouncer.

But before looking at the profanity that does flirt with pop, we should note that dirty words are being pulled in two seemingly opposite directions more than usual these days. On one hand, bad words (along with glimpses of nipples and lower backsides) are being fined, banned, or threatened with as much, and they're so seriously clucked at in the public sphere that everyone but the Christian Coalition wants to scream them at the tops of their lungs. On the other hand, mainstream marketing is still fooling around with taboo language (albeit with more trepidation than just a few years ago) in order to capitalize on the words' nearly irresistible bad-boy daring.

Pretty much up until the halftime show at the 2004 Super Bowl, when Janet Jackson's breast was fleetingly exposed (the Federal Communications Commission flogged CBS parent Viacom with a $550,000 indecency fine), a few bad words were staggering toward popdom by appearing on prime-time network

TV. In the nineties, the formerly forbidden or avoided *crap, ass,* and *bitch* began doing occasional guest spots, most famously on *NYPD Blue.* On the relatively unrisqué *Everybody Loves Raymond,* the vulgar *crap* teamed up with the sacred *holy,* as *Holy crap!* became the signature phrase of Ray's father. In 1996, long before her troubles began, Martha Stewart did a promo for a David Letterman special, saying of him, "There goes one funny son of a bitch." Even scatological wordplay made it on to network TV with 7 Up's "Make 7 Up Yours" campaign, as the comedian Orlando Jones pointedly paused when saying, "Make 7 . . . Up Yours." "The problem with 7 Up was it just wasn't being consumed by the younger set," an executive on the campaign told me when it began in 1999. For this target group, *up yours* is "not scatological," he added. "It doesn't have shock value. Fourteen-year-olds think it's cool. We had a major increase in sales for the first time in years." (The campaign stopped running in 2004, but not because of a new, post–Super Bowl propriety, a spokesperson for 7 Up insisted: "The brand was repositioned based on consumer insight. It was not based on consumer complaints.")

You were even getting the occasional really dirty word on prime-time network TV. In 2001, after much deliberation, NBC allowed a character on *The West Wing* to call the president's father a "prick" ("I got a secret for you, Mr. President, your father was a prick who could never get over the fact that he wasn't as smart as his brothers"). In 2000, on CBS's *Chicago Hope,* Mark Harmon said *shit.* Two years later, on *NYPD Blue,* a character prefaced *shit* with *bull.* Worse than that was said, sort of, on *Action* in 1999. The short-lived Fox sitcom coyly advertised its daring with "the first all-out barrage of four-letter words ever unleashed on broadcast television—all of them bleeped out, but easy enough to lip read," *The New York Times* wrote.

Network shows had been getting sexually more daring, if only because they were competing with cable, where all kinds of poop hits the fans. In 2001, Comedy Central's *South Park* devoted an entire episode to the shunned *shit,* with characters saying it out loud 162 times. The idea was to ridicule the arbitrariness of taboos. And, of course, *shit* and its XXX partner, *fuck,* are regulars on other cable channels; on HBO, the two are veritable pop stars, especially when seasoned with comic attitude ("What the *fuuuck?*" "Shit happens"). But even when the words are spoken humorlessly, the sheer frequency of *fuck* and *shit* on cable has turned them into pop put-downs for the adult-language crowd. The characters in *Six Feet Under* have said *fuck* so often that it is, in effect, their *I don't* think *so.*

You can even make the case that because dirty words were the original antipop—*the* thing not commercially acceptable— they were primed to eventually rise to top pop. The taboo-to-pop trail has been trekked before. "*Fuck* probably reached its zenith during the Second World War," Bill Bryson writes. *Snafu,* soldier shorthand for "situation normal all fucked up," is still said today, and in the most proper of circumstances, to mean a messy mistake. But back then other acronyms disguising *fucked up* were also common, such as *fubar* ("fucked up beyond all recognition") and *fubb* ("fucked up beyond belief").

As various media have slowly, tentatively become more tolerant of *fuck,* the word has lost its sharpest sting. Until rather recently, I even believed that *fuck* coulda been a pop contender. Jesse Sheidlower, the author of *The F-Word* and editor-at-large of the *Oxford English Dictionary,* wouldn't go that far. But, as he told me (before George W. Bush was a presidential contender), "the word's impact has been diminishing for several decades, and it's very widespread. I don't know if I'd call it a pop word in the way you're talking about, but it's getting close." In 2005, he added that *fuck* "is still going in that direction," despite the current backlash against dirty words. "The fact that they're cracking down means that it's common enough that they feel the need to crack down."

It's also common enough to bunt into commercial use. In the early nineties, I was rather shocked to hear *fuck* spoken in an in-house marketing video for a major sneaker brand. Since 1997, *fuck* has been in print ads and on T-shirts, dyslexically, as FCUK, the acronym for French Connection UK. In 2005, FCUK magazine ads in England showed a young couple sitting on a bed in their underwear; attached to the pages were fold-out samples of the company's "fcuk her" and "fcuk him" perfumes with instructions to "open here to try fcuk her" and "open here to try fcuk him." As the novelty of the brand's name has worn off, the ads have amped the innuendo—so much so that the most embarrassing thing about the campaign is its own desperation. Revenues for FCUK had dived in late 2004 (the British company blamed its clothing, not a surge of morality). So when the UK's self-regulatory ad group slapped FCUK on the wrist for the perfume ad, the scolding provided much-needed confirmation that the clothing company was bad, really bad.

Dirty words are the bad boys of language, and as rebel, indie, and bad-boy style—just the style, mind you, not the real thing—serve as marketing assets, so do their verbal counterparts. If *fuck* actually goes corporate, we're fugged. How else will we express disdain, ridicule, and complete, utter frustration?

But in trying to banish dirty bad words, the extreme right may have inadvertently saved us from a weakened, commercially tamed *fuck* and put some fire back in its belly.

The conflagrations over sex and language are now culture-war lore. At first, when U2 singer Bono said, "This is really, really fucking brilliant" on winning a Golden Globe award, and NBC carried his exuberance live, the FCC let it pass: *fucking*, it decreed, was used as an adjective "to emphasize an exclamation." But then came the nipple that launched a thousand censorships (easily, if you count the media's innumerable self-censorships and calls by lawmakers to extend indecency rules to cable and satellite TV)—and the FCC overturned its decision, declaring the word indecent regardless of context.

After being hit with record FCC fines for indecency violations, the media conglomerate Clear Channel dropped Howard Stern's raunchy show, spurring Stern to leave broadcast altogether for Sirius Satellite Radio. On Veterans Day in 2001 and 2002, ABC ran the World War II movie *Saving Private Ryan* without incident and without cutting the frequent *fuck*s and *shit*s that accompany battle. However, for Veterans Day 2004—after the ostensible "moral values" election, but while the country really was at war and soldiers really were screaming expletives—the conservative American Family Association complained about *Ryan*'s language and violence, prompting sixty-six ABC affiliates to drop the movie for fear of FCC reprisals. (After Veterans Day came and went, the FCC dismissed indecency complaints against the 159 affiliates that did air the movie.)

In an age when media conglomerates have never been so huge or so few, the suppression of dirty words may be only the visible tip of more significant suppressions. As Frank Rich wrote about the *Private Ryan* case, "If these media outlets are afraid to show a graphic Hollywood treatment of a 60-year-old war starring the beloved Tom Hanks because the feds might fine them, toy with their licenses or deny them permission to expand their empires, might they defensively soften their news divisions' efforts to present the graphic truth of an ongoing war?"

Such decency now grips the land. But while the George W. Bush right wing may have FCCuked-up our ability to say bad words in certain venues, it can't completely reverse the forces of history. "Swearing," writes Geoffrey Nunberg, "has always flourished most luxuriantly in ages when it could count on a strain of middle-class delicacy to work against." This pattern is unlikely to change, because "the prudes and the profaners are locked into an eternal co-dependence."

So even as ABC apologized for actress Nicollette Sheridan's locker-room towel drop in a *Monday Night Football* promo, the ratings of her show, *Desperate Housewives,* continued to soar—in the supposedly blushing red states as well as in the sin-loving blues. Months after Bono exclaimed the F-word, grandma Barbara Bush, apparently a fan of the rock star, giddily snapped his picture during the Clinton library festivities. Although the FCUK brand may be in decline, American sales for PHUK sweatshirts (standing for Planet Hollywood United Kingdom) were "very strong," according to the clubby restaurant chain. And just weeks after the *Private Ryan* F-word flap, ads for *Meet the Fockers* sent a rollicking substitute F-word over the airwaves, and the comedy broke all Christmas Day box-office records.

You can always count on the return of the repressed, even from the would-be repressors' chosen leaders. Vice President Dick Cheney, a pro at pop put-downs (he singlehandedly revived the fading *big-time* and, as detailed earlier, his "Saddam is toast" remark helped convince the Saudis to give their blessings to our invasion of Iraq), is also a pro at easing himself out of a profanity snafu. Cheney had told Senator Patrick Leahy—on the Senate floor, no less—to "go fuck yourself" or "fuck off" (reports vary). But he didn't have to say "My bad" in order to avoid fines, public censure, or eternal damnation (real GOP men never apologize). All Cheney had to do was to lend the bad Bono word some new bona fides, which he did by attesting on Fox News to the word's therapeutic effects. "I expressed myself rather forcefully," he said, "felt better after I had done it."

Well, he put his finger on it. Profanity flaps will come and go, yet dirty words will never die: They make us feel better.

Fuck may or may not have a career in corporate relations, but one of its younger siblings already has an office suite. The only semi-banned *suck* has been following the yippie-to-yuppie path as if it were still networking with the late Jerry Rubin.

Suck can still evoke collective memories of its wilder past— *suck* means lots of things, including fellatio, and is integral to the homophobic *cocksucker.* But *suck*'s sexual meanings have dimmed as society's more nouvelle, argumentative concerns take over. *Suck* as a general put-down was well established before *Beavis and Butt-Head* came along, but MTV's animated miscreants gave it institutional status as *cool*'s opposite number. It's not that *suck* means "uncool," exactly, but it became the cool way (if for many, the only way) to say that something is bad, undesirable, or worthy of scorn, just as *cool* is the way to say that something is good, desirable, or worthy of praise.

As Internet *suck*-sayers—such as all the sucks.com domains (like AtkinsDietsucks.com or Oreillysucks.com) and the hundreds of "Things That Suck" lists ("Gifts That Suck" and "Movies That Suck with a Passion" on Amazon's Listmania)—jumped on the *suck* truck, *suck* began to lose its dirty-word quality and to sound, at its worst, like an all-purpose complaint for disgruntled consumers. At its best, it's a fight-the-power battle cry for people who aren't going to take it anymore, like "Walmartsucks.org."

Whoops. My premise that *suck* is a shell of its wild past self is wrong, because *[X] sucks!* didn't necessarily begin as a phrase with sexual connotations, contends the Duke University linguist Ron Butters. "I do not deny that, say, *suck donkey dicks* is a part of the pejorative history of *X sucks!*," he writes. "But I *do* object to the assertion that the fellatious origin is the *only* source of pejorative *sucks* in English: pejorative *sucks* has a rich heritage, of which fellatio is only a part." For instance, Butters says, there are *suck eggs, suck air, sucker,* and *sucker punch,* and he testified to as much in the 1991 court case of a junior high school student in Norfolk, Virginia, who was suspended for wearing a T-shirt that read, "Drugs Suck." In any case, for most young people today *suck* is supersized pop but not particularly sexual: A 1992 study by Teresa Labov showed that *[X] sucks!/ It sucks being [X]!,* primarily as a nonsexual pejorative, was the most highly recognized slang term in use among high school students at the time of her survey.

Nonsexual, perhaps, but vulgar enough to ban on a spot basis. Presumably, CBS censors didn't blink when, on the *CBS Evening News,* a friend of Nathan Ross Chapman, one of the first soldiers killed in Afghanistan, said of him, "No matter how bad it sucked, he made you laugh." On the other hand, the crass commercial world occasionally runs from its own progeny. In a Mike's Hard Lemonade TV commercial, monsters kidnap a guy's wife, and one of the guy's pals, product in hand, commiserates with him at a bar, saying, "Well, that sucks!" The *sucks* and the shock-jock-like joke that a wife is less important than a good drinking buddy were designed to prove that Mike's is not wuss juice but a most extreme beverage. However, in an age of mean (= malicious), mean (= common) media, *Well, that sucks!* isn't shocking. What is mildly surprising, though, is that in 2002, in order to air on ABC, Mike's had to change the punch line to "Well, that stinks!"

(Actually, what should be shocking, but isn't, is that this entire fruity, spiked beverage category—Mike's has a 5.2 percent alcohol content, about that of most beers—is a hit with underage drinkers because the sweetness disguises the taste of the hootch. The American Medical Association recently warned that these drinks were luring teenagers, especially girls. As liquor marketers usually recite in binds like this, they deny that they want to suck in the too-young—the ads, the language, the sugar are meant to attract only adults. But the word for the category, in and out of the industry, sure says "teen spirits": *alcopops.*)

Fuck, shit, and the like aside, most plosive put-downs are not forbidden; they're bidden, and they trot insouciantly across the media everywhere. They range from juvenile name-calling, like *stupid, jerk,* and *idiot,* to commands to stop, like *shut up, shove it,* and *stuff it,* all so common now they barely register. (Though a little tweaking from the Central Laugh Bank can pop them up again. "Donkey, two things, OK?" Shrek says to his annoying sidekick. "Shut. Up." Peals of laughter from three-year-olds.) And there are sarcastic comebacks. When she was first coming out, Rosie O'Donnell informed the audience at a comedy club that she was gay; a woman in the audience replied, "Big whoop." You want plosive put-downs like that on your side, because in a smackdown culture, they practically guarantee you, as Rosie, George Tenet, and most of us have said in other contexts, a slam dunk.

WHEN NICE WORDS GO MEAN

Put-downs don't have to end in plosives (duh); they don't have to contain plosives at all (only a loser would claim they do). The urge to verbally swat life's misdemeanors out of the way is now so strong that even nice words, with no trick letters, are doing it.

Isn't this special? Some of the polite little expressions that not so long ago stood for niceness itself—*excuse me, hello, please, thank you,* and *good*—have, by a gerrymandering of their inflections, turned into their evil, easily offended twins. Of course, the world brims with insults more fearsome than *Hel-*lo*?!* But their unexpected inversion from banal nicety to brass knuckle gives these words a passive-aggressive sting.

Excuse me? Steve Martin's *Ex*cuuuuse *me!,* which at least made fun of itself, has been pretty much bumped by the serious, huffy *Ex*cuse *me?,* much too impatient to pronounce all those *U*'s. The accent is still on the second syllable, but it's not as exaggerated as Martin's. This *Ex*cuse *me?* might be accompanied by a raised eyebrow or two, indicating that the speaker is astounded at some fool's transgression. The inquisitive ending is purely rhetorical, the purpose being to say, How dare you! (In the penultimate season of *Friends,* Phoebe and Mike break up, and each begs a friend to keep them apart. But when the two kiss, Mike's guardian tells Phoebe's guardian, Monica, "You're not doing your job!" Indignant because she had tried so hard, Monica glares at Mike and spits out, "Ex*cuse* me?")

It's difficult to say why a shift in accent and punctuation changes a pleasantry into a dagger. Perhaps a heavier *cuse* causes *ex*cuse to sound more like *ac*cuse, as in "I accuse *you* of not excusing yourself to *me.*"

Polite *Excuse me*'s still abound, of course. But the outraged *Ex*cuse *me?* has given birth to an *Excuse me* halfway between polite and offended, the one that says, "You're *weird.*" In that nouvelle milestone *You've Got Mail,* Meg Ryan rhapsodizes about how her online love interest (Tom Hanks) wrote her about "bouquets of sharpened pencils." On hearing this, Meg's baffled assistant replies, "Ex*cuse* me?"

Hel-*lo*?! As Meg and Tom banter on by e-mail, she asks him the-media-is-the-personal questions, such as "What is it with men and *The Godfather?* Hel-*lo?*"

When not said as an opening greeting, *Hel*-lo?! is a way of saying, Wake up! Get real! Get lost! and, ultimately, Good-bye! Conscious of its own pop, *Hel*-lo?! (again, emphasis on second syllable) is headline-ready: "Subways and Manners? Hell-o-o!"— headline of a *New York Times* column. "Hel-lo: School Shootings Are SO Two Years Ago"—headline for a piece in the online *People Who Matter* ("America's Collegiate News Source").

NBC's Web site used to list the following as a "Finchism"— that is, something catchy said by David Spade's character on *Just Shoot Me!:* "Hel-lo! Hel-lo! Would you stop saying that?! It wasn't clever ten years ago! What makes you think you have a fresh spin on it?"

Regardless of spelling or punctuation, *Hel*-lo?! is very much about fresh spins and the shame of old ones. Indeed, this *Hel*-lo?! is the diva descendant of the less heavily accented, Greatest Generation *Hello?,* which isn't really about spin or being culturally offended at all. Both demand that some idiot wake up. But the older *Hello?* (still very much with us) is peeved to distraction because someone is not paying attention. "Hey, buddy—hello?!"

my father barks at drivers he deems too fast, too slow, too reck-
less, too cautious. Sometimes he switches to "Hello? Chaim
Yankel?!" (two male names used, Leo Rosten wrote, in a "somewhat condescending way of addressing a Jew whose name you do
not know"). The diva *Hel-lo?!* is also peeved at attention not
being paid, but what really yanks its vowels is those who REFUSE
TO GET WITH THE PROGRAM! Next to the Greatest Gen
Hello?, today's *Hel-lo?!* is voguing down the runway, swaying those
O's into Outraged and Offended.

Puh-leeze! Pulleeze! Please! Any of these may still serve two
masters. *Puh-leeze* (to settle on one spelling) still functions as
a polite if extreme plea (a variation of Zsa Zsa's "Puh-leeze,
dah-ling").

Puh-leeze, however, is more likely to do indignant, à la "You
must be joking," "Yeah, right," or "Gimme a break." "Rock Hudson as iconic hero? Puh-leeze"—a line in a *New York* magazine
review of *Far from Heaven*. "You reviewed over 150 albums for
your record guide and the best cover story you could come up
with was Sum 41? Puh-leeze"—letter to the editor of *Now Toronto*.

A cool, goateed Apolo Anton Ohno, a gold medalist in the
2002 Winter Olympics, is doing some serious skating in a TV
spot as his voiceover speaks: "Am I a speed skater? Yes. Did I
skate when they said I couldn't skate? Yes. Did I skate my way to a
World Cup victory? Yes. Could I have even skated this far if I ever
did drugs? Please." His *please* is not elongated, but as the somber
last word of the ad, it's all the more drop-dead. Which is the sen-
sory effect desired by the Partnership for a Drug-Free America,
creators of this ad (as well as "This is your brain on drugs. Any
questions?").

Thank you! is not nearly as prickly as *Puh-leeze!* or *Hel-lo?!*
(nor as easy to search for online). Said with an audible breath of
relief, heavy on the first word, *Thank* you! is actually a gush
of appreciation to the person or entity who—finally!—corrected
or slapped down an offending person or thing. When Representative John Conyers of Michigan called the pursuit of Clinton's
impeachment "psychopathic," I immediately said, "*Thank* you!"

A variation of this avenging *Thank* you! exudes a sense of
entitlement. The gals on *The View* were talking about a cop who

was dumped from the force because he was "too smart." "I want a cop with triple-digit IQ," said the comedian Joy Behar, a *View* co-host. "I don't want some moron defending my life, *thank* you!"

Dry goods. It's not just that *bad* means good in a hip-hop sense, but *You're good* means "You're good at being bad" in a post-mod sense. You tell someone "You're good" not when he's been virtuous, but when he's been so sly, sneaky, or manipulative that you can't help but salute in admiration. "You're good," the guy tells the girl after she tricks him into getting out of the Ford Focus so she can drive it. In *The Sweetest Thing*, the Cameron Diaz character fantasizes that the lead man tries to woo her first by promising her cunnilingus every hour on the hour ("Yeah, right," she imagines herself responding dubiously), then by removing all the calories from her ice cream. "Oh, you're good," she'd tell him, right before letting herself fall in love.

You're good (He's good or *That's good)* might also say, "I appreciate your clever trick, but I won't be taken in by it." In *XXX*, the Vin Diesel character tells the bad girl (before she becomes good as well as his love interest), "Oh, you're good, but not that good."

" 'That's good,' Mr. Clinton drawled in appreciation at the question of 'What, if anything, [*sic*] you'd like to say to Monica Lewinsky' now that her life has been 'changed forever?' " It was the sort of press conference query that, had the sex scandal not existed, "might have occasioned one of Mr. Clinton's classic 'I-feel-her-pain' responses of empathy," Francis X. Clines wrote in *The New York Times*. " 'That's good,' the President slowly repeated instead, rolling the 'ooo' as if savoring a sip of inviting, but lethal, moonshine. 'But at the minute I'm going to stick with my position: I'm not commenting.' "

Those *ooo*'s allow anyone to savor the illusion that he's a cool detective, always one step ahead of a worthy adversary. Humphrey Bogart made it so. As Sam Spade in *The Maltese Falcon* (1941), Bogart tells the duplicitous Brigid (Mary Astor) how much he admires her prowess at lying. "You're good," he says, amused. "You're *very* good." A little earlier, when she begs for his help, he says, "You won't need much of anybody's help. You're good. It's chiefly your eyes, I think, and that throb you get in your voice when you say things like 'Be generous, Mr. Spade.' "

Such pedigreed cool makes saying *You're good* feel so good that why save it just to compliment the naughty? It's also the chip of praise we dispense for any transaction surprisingly well executed. When my neighbor's husband remembered to bring my son's lunchbox home in the carpool in addition to their own child's, my neighbor told him, "You're good." The phrase makes completing a chore sound like a foxy move in a master plan, and makes those of us clued in to it savvy players indeed.

Even when this *good* refers to a straight-out skill, the word retains a flat, astringent pronunciation that drains it of sentimentality. Nouvelle marketing in particular likes to set us up with this underwhelming *good*. It helps prevent consumers from feeling suckered—even while prying open our jaws in awe. The sound comes across even in writing. An ESPN promo showed Tiger Woods, as the words on screen read: "This Just In . . . He's Good." (That two-part phrase also pops up in other sports.)

In 2003, AT&T created the slogan "Talk Is Good" for an ad campaign. It's not that anyone thought talk was bad or that talk needed repositioning. But the schmaltzy old reach-out-and-touch-someone AT&T, a financially wounded, blubbery giant, needed liposuction. Lean with understatement, "Talk Is Good" tries to get away with suggesting that running up higher phone bills is not so bad.

This dry *good*—which has more to do with skill and added value than with virtue or "moral values"—is about as good as *good* gets in a complex world where, especially for the moral relativists among us, it's hard to know what's good anymore. Laughing a bit, a man in his late thirties says hesitantly, "This is a good thing," as he's told by an appraiser on *Antiques Roadshow* that the used Steuben glass candlesticks he paid $20 for sell for $1,800 to $2,200 retail.

This *good* can also serve as a kind of Post-it to remind us of the important things we may have forgotten in the daily rush of our acquisitive transactions, or our politically acquiescent ones: "*The New Republic.* Unconventional is good." The magazine's tagline began running during the 2004 election year.

Reminder *good*s got a huge boost from Martha Stewart. "It's a good thing," she would remind us about whipping up our own wine or trellis organizers. "Good Things" was the name of a Stewart sweepstakes, the title of a section in her magazine, *Martha Stewart Living,* and part of the title in a few of her books.

But even before Stewart made it her signature line, *It's a good thing* had a tinge of irony: Hey, if a thing's so good, why do we have to neurasthenically remind ourselves of the fact? A jokey element in the phrase *good thing* goes back at least to 1930, when *Punch* published a satirical history of England, *1066 and All That,* according to which, "103 Good Things" dot the isle's past, starting with the "Roman Conquest" itself and "the memorable Roman law, 'HE WHO BATHS FIRST BATHS FAST,' which was a Good Thing, and still is." That's more Monty Python than Martha, but some of the shtick stuck. When Martha's insider trading scandal broke, nearly every TV news headline predictably used *It's a good thing* against her to imply (without having to prove it, of course) that she had done a bad thing. *It's a good thing* has emitted more irony and lost that much niceness ever since.

It's as if we're afraid to accept something as an outright good, either because we can't believe our luck or because we're surrounded by so many claims of goodness. So we say and receive *good* at an angle, deflecting its fullness and reflecting our conviction that everyone—Martha, you, me—is playing an angle.

GO HOMELAND! GO HOMELAND!

Then there are the weapon words that aren't put-downs so much as crank-ups—actual fightin' words that rev the emotions for aggression aimed at live enemies rather than squeaky egos. The last large round of such real weapon words that have become pop—*evildoer, axis of evil, regime change, weaponized, Shock and awe, Why do they hate us?*—was forged from the violence of September 11, 2001, Afghanistan, anthrax, and the invasion of Iraq.

These words were supposed to defy mockery and, initially spoken in solemn tones, most did enjoy a brief honeymoon.

Until, that is, irony was injected by jaded media types like myself, always in need of trendy phrases like *Shlock and awe,* and by teenagers, also always in need of trendy talk and who, in the months following 9/11, according to *The Washington Post,* "might have called a messy bedroom 'ground zero,' a mean teacher 'such a terrorist.' A student is disciplined? 'It was total jihad.' Petty concerns? 'That's so Sept. 10.' And out-of-style clothes? 'Is that a burqa?' "

At least the first two hundred times around, subverting an anointed phrase can help metabolize one's fear or undermine authority. The Bush administration's *regime change,* for instance, was asking for it. "Regime change begins at home. Vote!" was the anti-Bush response during the 2002 midterm elections. Soon after it left the gate, Bush's boorish *axis of evil* ran into ridicule ("Axle of Evil" was the clever title of an article about SUVs). *Axis of evil* was eventually exiled from straight use when one of its three targets, the North Korean leader, Kim Jong-Il, had the audacity to take it seriously and went into nuclear brinksmanship. *Evildoer* has also been slapped silly, although that hasn't eliminated the brave new habit, among politicians and the public, of calling others evil. "One of Bush's worst faults in rhetoric (to dip into that cornucopia) was to use the word [evil] as if it were a button he could push to increase his power," wrote Norman Mailer.

But two warward words have endured few or no irony attacks.

Even while jokes about "homeland insecurity" became de rigueur, *homeland* by itself pretty much does what it was recruited to do: create a hush. *Homeland* beckons as it threatens. You're either in the homeland or in one of the homeland's detention centers. This is made possible by the word's complex personality.

At its worst, *homeland* sounds totalitarian. The Soviet Union used to (and Russia still does) refer to itself as the homeland (as well as the Mother- and/or Fatherland). When South Africa's apartheid government wanted black tribal groups out of the way, it drew some lines in the bush, moved people in, and told them those territories were now their homeland. The German word *Heimat,* which means homeland, was a favorite of Nazi propagandists and still crops up among neo-Nazis. But at its best, *homeland* sounds like a new line of Campbell's soups.

Maybe Bush's advisers decided to go with the foreign-sounding term for the new homeland security agency (and later the Cabinet-level department) because, while they might have been indifferent to the word's totalitarian tilt, they were all ears to the media success of *homeland*'s Midwest cousin, *heartland*.

Heartland appeared in so many headlines and TV news banners during coverage of the 1995 Oklahoma City bombing—like Fox TV's "Terror in the Heartland"—that the Heartland virtually became America's new name. (Indeed, the Fox News Channel liked it so much that it later debuted a political talk show called *Heartland with John Kasich*, hosted by the former Ohio congressman.) That heart began beating loudly back in the Reagan years, at first implicitly in his "Morning in America" reelection ad and all the gauzy beer commercials escorting it; later it was spoken outright in Chevrolet's "Heartbeat of America" campaign, where *heartbeat* was an oblique dig at the "heartless" Japanese automakers. Advertising's arteries never stop working. In that infamously lazy August before the September 11 attacks, President Bush, who douses his rhetoric with as much *heart* as *evil*, actually gave his month-long vacation a slogan: "The home to the heartland tour." (He has also claimed to "know Secretary Rumsfeld's heart" and to "see [the Russian president Vladimir Putin's] heart.")

Then, just weeks later, heart/home/land found a higher calling. *Homeland* caught on overnight, at least among reporters and commentators, who began saying it on cue when referring not just to the newly proposed agency but to our country, as if *homeland* were common parlance. "We haven't had another major attack on the homeland in the U.S. since September 11," Monica Crowley of the Fox News Channel said (redundantly) in defending Bush's security measures.

However, *homeland* is not tripping off the tongues of those who aren't Beltway blatherers—it's too Teutonic, said even Peggy Noonan, George Bush I's "kinder, gentler" speechwriter. So what did she propose? "My own imperfect nominee," she wrote, "is Heartland Security, which unfortunately sounds like an Omaha-based insurance company, though maybe that's not all bad."

Aside from the complication that Heartland Security might leave the two (suspiciously un-American) coasts vulnerable to attack, I'd argue that Noonan is half wrong. *Homeland* is reassuringly Omaha-like *and* frighteningly Teutonic. In naming patriotic power entities, the point is to beckon and threaten, to shake carrot and stick. Like *heartland, homeland* evokes images of folks huddling in front of a hearth in a prairie house built of big, solid, indestructible stone. Like *Heimat* (and especially *die verlorene Heimat,* "the lost homeland" of nostalgic German lore), *homeland* suggests that it will one day bring back the life we lost on September 11, even if it has to trample our civil liberties to do it. The world might hate us far more than we imagine and for reasons we still can't fathom, but now we have a word to protect us (even if the budget and policies of the Department of Homeland Security don't).

WAR WORDS YIN AND YANG

If *homeland* sets a "We're good people" tone for our defense policy, *Let's roll* does likewise for our offense. *Let's roll* in the "original sense of get rolling had to do with the wheels of conveyances, horseless and otherwise, and dates back to the 16th century," William Safire has written. "Let's roll!" I'd say to my son when we finally pulled out of the driveway. But I don't say it anymore, because it evokes the memory of Todd Beamer.

"Are you guys ready? Let's roll," an operator heard Beamer say to other passengers aboard hijacked United Flight 93 right before they rushed the terrorists. The passengers' heroism caused the plane to crash into a Pennsylvania field instead of, presumably, the White House or the Capitol. It's chilling to know anyone's next-to-last words, and the chill has not yet worn off. That's why, for the most part, *Let's roll* is still too sacred to be treated ironically.

But not too sacrosanct to be politicized and merchandized.

The phrase's utility was obvious to George W. Bush's speech-writer when, in Atlanta on November 8, 2001, Bush cited Beamer's "last known words" and made them the last words of his speech: "We will no doubt face new challenges, but we have our marching orders. My fellow Americans, let's roll." This is powerful language. Soon afterward, a caller on the liberalish *Leonard Lopate Show* on WNYC public radio in New York said, "When Bush said 'Let's roll' I was ready to sign up for the military for about five seconds. And that's a lot for me."

In his State of the Union address two months later, Bush tried to squeeze more juice out of the words, as a call to banish immoral, undoubtedly left-leaning hedonism: "For too long our culture has said, 'If it feels good, do it.' Now America is embracing a new ethic and a new creed: 'Let's roll.' "

Other politicians have tried to capitalize on *Let's roll*. After the 2002 midterm elections put Trent Lott back in the saddle as Senate majority leader, Lott said, "We're ready to get to work. As I've said to others, 'Let's roll.' " (Of course, shouting out words that have the percussion to rally the troops, regardless of what they actually mean, is what later got Lott fired as Senate leader.)

Let's roll is the only slogan I know of as powerful as Nike's "Just Do It." Both take a group of plain words said by almost everyone to urge us to be decisive in life's most existential moments.

Like rolling into a dealership. For weeks after 9/11, GM ran ads for cars (including the SUVs that make us so dependent on Arab oil) with the slogan "Keep America Rolling." In the year or so following 9/11, everyone from mouse-pad sellers to fireworks makers was filing applications to use *Let's roll* in their names. Lisa Beamer, Todd Beamer's widow and the author of the book *Let's Roll*, formed the nonprofit Todd M. Beamer Foundation, in part to protect the phrase from exploitation. (But she did allow its use as the slogan of Wal-Mart's employee motivation program and, more controversially, by Florida State University's 2002 football team.)

As if it were a gift from an epic movie, *Let's roll* helped prepare us emotionally for invading Iraq, linking Beamer's heroism to the Bush military and, in a more subterranean way, 9/11 to Saddam Hussein. Of course, during the war in Iraq and in the buildup to it, *Let's roll* was not a star, not like, say, *Shock and awe*. But having already seeped into everyday pop, *Let's roll* was repeated that much more easily by the man on the street and the pundit on the beat.

" 'Let's roll!' went up the cry in Molly's bar, New York, as President George W. Bush concluded his declaration of war, on screen," reported *The Observer* of London.

"Let's roll, already!" Bill Steigerwald began a column in the *Pittsburgh Tribune-Review.* "Who cares what those Euro-weenies in Paris think?"

At pro-war rallies, signs went up that read, "God bless our troops" and "Let's roll."

Shortly after Bush gave Saddam forty-eight hours to get out of town, major religious right player Gary Bauer wrote, "Overnight polls show a spike up in the support for the President's Iraq policy, with over 70% of the public saying, 'Let's Roll!' "

"Way to go! Lock and load, kick butt, take the body count, and let's roll!" a woman whose former husband served in the first Gulf War said as she watched the bombing in Iraq on TV.

The blogger on 18r.blogspot.com also enlisted *Let's roll* into a march of words: "Let's roll, let's burn down the torture chambers, and motherfuckers, bring it on."

Despite the company it keeps, *Let's roll* is not one of those brutish tanks of a phrase. The weapons maker Northrop Grumman might have even preferred *Let's roll*, had the Beamer foundation allowed it, over the words it parachuted into a TV commercial during the tense months leading up to the invasion of Iraq. After touting its computer systems for "information warfare," comparing them to "a cool game," the Grumman spot ended, astonishingly, with a pro-wrestler-like cry of "Bring it on."

Bring it/them/'em on is such a reliable weapons system that months later when President Bush said "Bring 'em on"—referring to the insurgents attacking American troops in Iraq—he was initially admired for his toughness almost as much as he was chastised for inviting assaults, which did indeed escalate. (After his reelection, Bush said he regretted the words.) *Bring it on* dates back further than the 2000 movie *Bring It On,* but that film about black and white rival cheerleading squads raised the phrase's media quotient high. It's probably just coincidence, but only days before Bush told the bad guys to bring 'em on, *Charlie's Angels: Full Throttle* opened—that's the film in which angel Cameron Diaz told evil ex-angel Demi Moore, "Bring it on, bitch!" This taunt travels fast: Just days *after* Bush's *Bring 'em on,* the press secretary for Governor Gray Davis of California explained his boss's feelings about a recall election: "His attitude is, bring them on."

Actually, in February 2003—before Bush's taunt to insurgents and, indeed, before the war began—presidential candidate John Edwards defended his career as a trial lawyer by saying, "And so, Mr. President, if you want to talk about the insiders you fought for versus the kids and families that I fought for, here's my message to you, Mr. President: Bring it on."

John Kerry didn't bring *Bring it on* aboard until everyone else above had, in November 2003. While campaigning in Iowa during the primaries, Kerry would say, "If George Bush wants to fight this election on the issue of national security, I've got three words for him that he does understand: Bring it on." Thrilled to see him almost as fired up as his then rival Howard Dean, the crowds would chant, "Bring it on! Bring it on!" The call-and-shout continued sporadically until Election Day.

The story of how Kerry found his own personal *Bring it on* is telling about the caution of the candidate and his top adviser, Bob Shrum. In its behind-the-scenes postelection issue, *Newsweek* tied Kerry's first *Bring it on* to "a marked improvement in the candidate."

> Kerry's speechwriter, Andrei Cherny, had been trying to think of a way to convey that Kerry was ready to go toe to toe with President Bush on national security, the Democrats' weakest front. The expression "Bring it on" popped into his head. He wrote the line into a Kerry speech to be delivered to the Democratic National Committee in October, but Shrum crossed it out. "Bush-type bravado," he sneered—too undignified for Kerry.

But with the press reporting his campaign in melt-
down, Kerry needed to do something to change his
soporific style, and at the Jefferson-Jackson Day dinner
in Des Moines on Nov. 15 [2003], he used Cherny's
"Bring it on" line. The crowd loved it. (Kerry later apologized to Cherny for not using the line earlier. "I was
wrong," he said. But a few weeks later Cherny was purged
by Shrum as a [former campaign manager Jim] Jordan
holdover whose punchy style did not suit the candidate.)

Though the tragically out-of-touch Shrum never should have
barred *Bring it on* (or other aggressive moves, like immediately
counterattacking the Swift Boat Veterans for Truth ads; Shrum
advised, Wait), his observation was half correct: *Bring it on* was
not a natural for Kerry. Kerry was always more of a *Let's roll* kind
of guy. It was too late, of course, to use that Afghanistan-era war
cry. But the two weapon phrases exemplify a difference between
the two candidates (Bush, the *Bring 'em on* blusterer; Kerry, the
reluctant but determined *Let's roll*er) and between the two wars
(the unnecessary and unjustified destruction of Iraq; the necessary and justified invasion of al-Qaeda's haunts).

Let's roll is yin to the *Bring it on, lock and load* crowd's yang.
It's a simpatico call to action, a sensitive but nonweenie way to
be aggressive. *Let's roll* rooollls like the river, establishing you as
a compassionate combatant, as a goin'-with-the-flow guy who's
gotta do what a guy's gotta do, be it in war, politics, or sales. *Bring
it on,* its chest thrust out so far it risks toppling over, is, for the
moment, the battle shriek of the Argument Culture.

WAR AND IRONY

At the same time, the relative lack of irony in *Let's roll* and *homeland* makes clear how rare in pop culture the *un*ironic weapon
word is.

Irony, as a concept and as a word, has taken on a generational role nearly as important as cool. You might even say that
irony is the poor dude's cool. If you can't be cool or plausibly

imitate it, you can usually pull off ironic (just say, "Yeah, right") and get a temporary cool pass.

Even before September 11—the date on which irony was so wrongly believed to have died—we were obsessed with what our irony was doing to us. Was it saving us from suffocation by sentimentality, or was it poisoning our souls with its acid drippings?

Derived from the Greek *eiron* (defined by various dictionaries as "dissembler," "one who hides his or her true knowledge or capabilities," or "ignorance purposely affected"), irony has, of course, always been with us.

And there has always been irony both high (the sharp rhetorical tool that can enlighten people or expose hypocrisies) and low (the frivolous stuff of easy detachment or sheer play). The more prolific low is where irony is most likely to express itself through a ready-made phrase. *Not!,* to take one of the piddliest examples, may have peaked with the 1992 movie *Wayne's World,* but you'll still hear it now and then. (More recently, a drier, statement-contradicting *not* has arisen: "I'm going to put this parenthetical in the notes at the end of the book. Or not." *Or not,* spoken without excitement but perhaps with a smile, is said to show that you may change your mind; the bang shot *Not!* is said to show that you're pulling legs.) *Not!* may seem very nineties ironic, but it was also very 1890s ironic. It has been found in print as early as 1893, when "An Historical Parallel—Not" appeared in the *Princeton Tiger.* Other early quick-switch wits listed by *The Random House Historical Dictionary of American Slang* include "That confounded rarebit I ate . . . is making me sleep lovely. NOT!!!" from 1908 and "He's a fine neighbor—not," from 1910.

But just a few years later, in response to the horrors of World War I, irony found more important work; in fact, irony shaped our modern sensibility itself, the critic Paul Fussell argued in *The Great War and Modern Memory.* "Every war is ironic because every war is worse than expected. Every war constitutes an irony of situation because its means are so melodramatically disproportionate to its presumed ends. In the Great War eight million people were destroyed because two persons, the Archduke Francis Ferdinand and his Consort, had been shot. . . .

"But the Great War was more ironic than any before or since," Fussell wrote (in 1975), because "it was a hideous embarrassment" to "the Idea of Progress" and a reversal of it. Fussell quoted Philip Gibbs writing in 1920 that people "had been taught to believe that the whole object of life was to reach out to beauty and love, and that mankind, in its progress to perfection, had killed the beast instinct, cruelty, blood-lust, the primitive. . . . The war-time humor of the soul roared with mirth at the sight of all that dignity and elegance despoiled."

From such "a collision between innocence and awareness" modern irony was born, Fussell wrote. "Irony is the attendant of hope, and the fuel of hope is innocence. One reason the Great War was more ironic than any other is that its beginning was more innocent." (An "index of the prevailing innocence," he said, was "a curious prophylaxis of language. One could use with security words which a few years later, after the war, would constitute obvious *double entendres*. One could say *intercourse,* or *erection,* or *ejaculation* without any risk of evoking a smile or a leer.")

"I am saying," Fussell concluded, "that there seems to be one dominating form of modern understanding; that it is essentially ironic; and that it originates largely in the application of mind and memory to the events of the Great War."

Today we're not so innocent. Our Idea of Progress has shriveled to an almost solely technological one. Our hopes have been blown into dotcom, Wall Street, and Enron-like "bubbles"—invariably financial in nature and inevitably burst. Reaching out to beauty and love, mankind striving toward perfection—huh?

With innocence gone missing and awareness focused like a laser beam on what's on TV, the two stand little risk of colliding. So our ironies become smaller, lower, and, as they do, we giggle with our guard up instead of roar with mirth.

When a sharp irony does manage to cut into a deeper vein, the bleeding is quickly staunched by political or corporate PR and an obedient press. The distracted public barely feels its sting. At a question-and-answer session for troops on their way to Iraq that was closed to the press, a soldier asked Donald Rumsfeld a question about armor. When the defense secretary told the soldiers, who were being wounded and killed for lack of armor. that "you go to war with the army you have, not the army you might want or wish to have," it seemed for a moment as if the public would be thunderstruck by the irony: Rumsfeld himself had pared down that army for his and Bush's and Cheney's war of choice. But no. Instead, most media redirected suspicion to a reporter who had helped the soldier phrase his question.

We've had plenty of wars since Fussell wrote that all wars are ironic. But each war, and each major crisis, since Vietnam has become more of a media event than the one preceding it, the gruesome details sucked into the media machine, which then spits out spinning television graphics, melodramatic music, blabbing pundits, polls that make us puny, and an ever brighter, more blinding screen between us and the thing itself. We still need irony to help us feel the horrors of war, but before irony can cut to that it has to cut through the screen, and it is barely scratching.

As the media absorb more irony about themselves, our own little knives get dull. Anyway, we figure, the self-mocking media help us digest the mass, crass nature of the things we buy and buy into—so why not sit back, quip back, and enjoy the show?

It's not that we have no skepticism about commercial news or entertainment. Constant hype has conditioned us to wedge some space between media representations and what we suspect is actually true—without (and here's the beauty part) our ever having to think about what *is* true. "First we tell you what happens and then we make a joke about it," said a writer for the Web site Television Without Pity, which runs sarcastic summaries of your favorite or most hated shows. "That's, I think, a very Gen X attitude toward the media—we're watching it, but not enjoying it the way you meant us to." That's payback!

Irony means never having to say you believe. You can establish that cool by, say, distancing yourself from your own actions or by claiming falsely to be lying. To lie about lying equals honesty, right?—but without any embarrassing earnestness. When caught in a mistake, an exaggeration, or an out-of-character act, we say, "I must have been smoking crack," "Did I just say that?" or, shruggingly, "I lied."

But too-easy cynicism and too-easy belief are two sides of the same wooden nickel. The American people and media are just as quick to doubt sincerity as they are to believe in angels, miracles, stock markets that never fall, wars without repercussions, and life without pain. We use one excess to shield us from the other. Many of us adults are like the little girl at the beginning of this book who trusted her Fortune Teller when it predicted I'd become a movie star, and who, at the same time, was certain that once I reached superfame I'd never deign to give her my autograph (in her words, "I don't *think* so"). All the magical thinking for and all the magical cursing against can exhaust our powers of nuanced thought, driving us further into commercial entertainment's pleasant and/or depressive numbness—and making us even less responsive to life's sharp ironies.

And it's no irony that one of the easiest ways we have of describing the frivolous low kind of irony is a superfamous person himself. David Letterman's name first came to be shorthand for the ironic smirk, then a shining example of New York courage when, on his first show after September 11, he spoke with moving sincerity and even cried on camera.

But just as irony began long before Letterman, so the backlash against it started before 9/11.

IRONY IS TOAST

In 1988, Mark Crispin Miller succinctly described the shallow pose of detachment as "the hipness unto death." "The old children of the Sixties half-recognize an emanation of their own self-irony—the corrosive cynicism of those who have had to trash the ideals of youth so as to keep on shopping."

Irony and ridicule are "enfeebling," "agents of a great despair and stasis in U.S. culture," David Foster Wallace wrote in 1993. Irony "tyrannizes us," it's "the new junta."

The movie *What Planet Are You From?* exemplified "an era enervated by the ironic ideal. (Wouldn't it be ironic if irony destroyed our ability to make one another laugh?)," Richard Schickel wrote in *Time* in 2000.

At a management retreat in the mid-nineties, *Newsweek* editors found themselves debating their own use of irony. "One of the things we talked about was whether the whole culture and tone of the magazine was too smart-ass—is this something the readers are going to get sick of?" a former *Newsweek* editor recalls. "We were talking about whether we—and the media in general—had the courage to be earnest. Snarkiness is something to hide behind."

One result of *Newsweek*'s self-analysis was a cover story on the "Queen of Nice," Rosie O'Donnell, and a purported trend. "Her new show is a hit—and she never bashes anyone. But she's not alone," the cover read. "From Hollywood Moguls to rap music, nasty is out. Nice is in." (The national niceness soured, even before Rosie's jabs at other celebrities and her fights with the publishers of her eponymous magazine earned her a new sobriquet, which she wore proudly. "The bitch," she said, "ain't so nice anymore.")

"The 'Queen of Nice' piece was as much about *Newsweek* and journalism in general as any real trend," the former *Newsweek* editor says. "Our discussion didn't translate into a lot of real changes in thinking about stories or editing them. Some thought smart-ass could be intellectually lazy, but we also knew that it was a good way to make things readable and funny."

No wonder so many journalists for whom irony is Match Light for their prose attacked Jedediah Purdy, author of the 1999 book *For Common Things: Irony, Trust, and Commitment in America Today*. "The ironic individual practices a style of speech and behavior that avoids all appearance of naïveté," Purdy wrote. "By the inflection of his voice, the expression of his face, and the motion of his body, he signals that he is aware of all the ways he may be thought silly or jejune, and that he might even think so himself. His wariness becomes a mistrust of language itself. He disowns his own words."

Others before him had said as much, but Purdy did so without an ironic safety net. He was bravely unfunny about a supposedly funny thing and was therefore left open to exactly the kind of damning charges that David Foster Wallace had described years earlier. "Anyone with the heretical gall to ask an ironist what he actually stands for ends up looking like an hysteric or a prig," Wallace wrote. He'll be called "dead on the page. Too sincere. Clearly repressed. Backward, quaint, naive, anachronistic." (And, in fact, as *The Christian Science Monitor* pointed out, "Purdy-pounding has become something of a favorite pastime among critics . . . he's been compared to Dickens's Uriah Heep and called 'insufferably smug.' The *New York Observer* dismissed his book as 'garbage,' and warned, 'get ready for a gassy, sanctimonious, post-ironic age.' "

Not brave enough to handle such name-calling, I always write with a net. Sometimes nets turn into trampolines, making language fly, and that is one of life's great pleasures. But too often my bounce is just an inch high, relying on phrases that nod to a pop phenom we're all supposedly familiar with. Take, for instance, the opening lines of two paragraphs in the last section: "Today we're not so innocent" (I know a Britney Spears song!) and "Irony means never having to say you believe" (I can reference *Love Story*, though I never saw it!). The references aren't particularly fun (not to mention, they're ancient), and for me, tapping them was less pleasurable than utilitarian: Whew, transitions from previous paragraphs made. (I'm goood.)

Whether out of art, habit, or fear of being thought uncool, most of the media in the nineties resisted the call to give up callow irony. Any irony backlash was pushed down by an anti-irony backlash. And so the media's occasional nausea over its own irony continued to build—until 9/11, when it was hurled out.

Nearly the day after, the hand-wringing began. Were we permanently more serious, never to say anything as irreverent as *Hel-lo?!* again, unless it was directed in no uncertain terms at Osama bin Laden? Roger Rosenblatt believed so, writing, "One good thing could come from this horror: it could spell the end of the age of irony."

Most infamously, because he was a chief purveyor of irony, *Vanity Fair*'s editor, Graydon Carter, announced the "end of the age of irony. . . . Things that were considered fringe and frivolous are going to disappear." (Later, embarrassed, he joked that he was talking about "the end of ironing.")

What's fascinating is that so many jumped so quickly on the death-of-irony bandwagon, that in the midst of terror and real deaths anyone stopped to consider irony and its fate at all. Irony runs that deep, and that shallow. Irony may be the dominant form of modern understanding, as Fussell said. But here we were treating it like Winona Ryder, like a scandal-ridden celebrity whom everyone loves to pull down.

Irony might have been buried alive, only to rise stiffly from the crypt, but for a few days it was easy to believe that it really had died. Terror scares the mind games out of you. When addicts hit bottom, the first thing they do is swear they'll never drink or gamble or binge again. And so for a short time, our understanding split into the ultimate What's Hot/What's Not list: life-and-death vs. lifestyle, feeling Letterman vs. glib Letterman, jihad vs. jerking off, primal vs. postmod. Irony came to stand for a willful emptiness that put us in grave danger.

WAR BETWEEN THE IRONIES

But that's because we were focused on the prevailing low irony, not the rarer high irony. The first we swish around like mouthwash to cover up what we fear are unfashionable feelings; the second is the more biting kind that chomps into (the often fashionable) lies, hypocrisies, and denials.

In the days after the World Trade Center fell, not everyone in the media forgot about the more honorable irony. In *Salon,* David Beers called for us to drop the "low-grade irony" of flip disengagement and to take up a "skeptical Ironic Engagement." "We need a profoundly ironic outlook to avoid being swept up in the new jingoism, to see that the best intentions might lead us further astray, to protect ourselves from the manipulative propaganda that envelops us in wartime."

And, as Beers pointed out, while some who "peddle[d] a cheapened grade of irony over the past couple of decades" were now stoning it in the public square, guess who was riding to irony's defense? "In peaceful and prosperous times," Jedediah Purdy said in an interview less than two weeks after September 11, irony is a way of "keeping the passions in hibernation when there is not much for them to live on, but another kind of irony can also work to keep dangerous excesses of passion and self-righteousness and extreme conviction at bay."

But after September 11 and the war in Afghanistan, self-righteousness and extreme conviction worked to keep high-grade irony at bay. If World War I forged hard, painful ironies, 9/11 sent them into hiding, as the low-grade took their place. Surveying the year and a half in culture after September 11, Michiko Kakutani wrote in *The New York Times,* "Greeting-card sentimentality and snarky, knee-jerk irony proliferated with abandon this year. . . . In the past, hard times and historical uncertainties have often galvanized the artistic imagination . . . but thus far, the cultural fallout from Sept. 11 has ranged from the negligible to the tacky."

Culture, politics, and journalism cowered before the intimidating, Ashcroftian "patriotism": Advertising pressure forced Bill Maher's *Politically Incorrect* off ABC; newspapers fired writers and cartoonists for criticizing Bush; a mall had shoppers arrested for wearing antiwar T-shirts; right-wing campaigns tried to crush Bush critics like the Dixie Chicks and France; *Saturday Night Live* played it even more safe. Irony that was truly politically engaged only occasionally braved nonprint media appearances—on Maher's subsequent show on HBO, in Michael Moore's movies, on *The Daily Show with Jon Stewart.* (My favorite, Air America Radio, and especially the Al Franken and Marc Maron shows, arrived later, in the spring of 2004.) September 11 and the wars that followed became, in effect, an excuse for *more* escapism into searing conflicts not our own, like those in the ever increasing number of reality shows and celebrity scandals.

The aggressive pop language that turns on snarky irony hasn't really changed since 9/11, either. Oh, maybe for a while the lightheartedness was more forced. But overall, weapon words were no more traded in for nicer, more sincere language than SUVs were for safer, more fuel-efficient cars. The JetBlue ad in which a boy called his father a "loser," the Olympics Visa ad that would've made "toast" out of a little bunny, the majority of pertinent put-downs in this chapter—all appeared after September 11.

Along with the attitude, *snarky* the word has been riding

high, especially with the rise of blogs, as RJ Smith pointed out in *Los Angeles* magazine. Blogs can operate "like the cool clique in high school. . . . Everybody starts talking about what the cool kids are saying. Since about every blog I've looked at recently has used snarky—means witty, cheeky, though more often is used to mean snotty—the word has taken on a new life."

Still, some in the mainstream media have been more cautious about how glib to get. *Time* magazine used to run the "Winners & Losers" column, pop-talking snapshots of the week's well-knowns ("winner" Julia Roberts: "You're soooo Erin Brockovich. Wins scrappy legal battle to get her dotcom domain name"; "loser" Marisleysis Gonzalez: "Loses latest and [almost] last appeal to keep Elian. Get a life, girl; your 15 minutes are up"). *Time* pulled the plug on the column after 9/11. "After September 11, the Notebook section [the opening few pages of short items] took on a much more serious tone, and we ended a lot of the more tongue-in-cheek stuff," said the section's editor, Richard Zoglin.

By early 2003, the magazine felt it was safe to run another zippy sum-up. "Anxiety Meter" measured how worrisome the week's events were in a color-coded, Homeland Security–like ranking of "severe," "high," "elevated," "guarded," and "low." But after the government announced a real Orange Alert (the one that came tied in a bow of much-ridiculed duct tape), the meter quietly disappeared.

On the other hand, *Newsweek* never stopped running its even more dismissive "Conventional Wisdom" column. Giving up or down arrows to its victims, CW punctures with as much pitbull pop as ever. A down arrow to Eminem: "White rapper dominates MTV awards but loses cool at ribbing by comic puppet dog. Grow up." Another to Howard Dean: "The Perfect Train Wreck: Betrays his core by firing Trippi and hiring lobbyist as campaign manager. Blog that." Another column ended different items with "Get used to it," "Stick a fork in him," and "Slick."

When, in 2005, the Bush White House tried to stick a fork in *Newsweek*—really, into the independence of the press—by blaming the death of seventeen people on *Newsweek*'s story about Koran abuse at Guantánamo, the CW gave *Newsweek* a down arrow: "Qur'an-in-toilet story gets magazine all wet. At least according to one anonymous source."

To many readers, including me, CW is the best thing in the magazine, because it heckles the hackneyed thinking of the media's conventional wisdom. But the attitude elsewhere in the magazine, and in media the world over, usually just mirrors the CW without offering any wisdom about how conventional it is. The resulting tone, despite *Newsweek*'s declaration that "nasty is out," can be middle-school snotty. In an item on possible carcinogens in potato chips, *Newsweek* wrote that the World Health Organization "suggested a balanced diet that includes fruits and vegetables. Duh." When laddy mag *Stuff* included the actress Lindsay Lohan among its "It Girls" of 2005, the gossipy blog whatevs.org sounded like one of the snobs in Lohan's movie *Mean Girls:* "HELLO, 2004 was her year."

We're unlikely to ever give up our sneering put-downs, because, as *Newsweek,* whatevs.org, most media, and I have done, we confuse smart-ass with smart.

Which leads to the highest irony about low irony: It sounds intelligent, but it can make us dumb.

I DON'T STINK SO

A snappy put-down sounds as if you've done some quick thinking. After all, it takes a brain operating at a higher order to select the right response from among the preapproved cool options.

Not! One night in an online fan forum of Fox TV's *24,* fans were foaming that the soap operaish subplot about Jack Bauer's daughter, Kim, took up too much precious time. I rabidly agreed, though I didn't necessarily want her murdered or tortured as some others did. Then came the comments of Killer462, who was less pro-Kim than he was anti-anti-Kim, as he tried to verbally kill those who hated her. "HEY ITS A TV SHOW," he wrote, "DONT SHOW SIMPOTHY FOR HER SHES A TV CHAREC-TOR. THEY R REFERING TO HER CHARECTOR AND FACE IT SHE IS A COMPLETE IDIOOT AND SO ARE SO GET OVER IT AND GET A LIFE."

I don't quote him verbatim to prove he's stupid. I do it to show how the pop *get* phrases at the end can idiootically snuff debate and how irresistible such phrases are when we have to punch our way out of a corner.

Whether peevish put-downs are la-la ironic or take-no-prisoners angry, the effect is similar: They whisk you out of a discussion through a trapdoor and pretty much foreclose further thought and subtleties.

Most, but not all, weapon words fall into one of two categories (which bear no relationship to the two kinds of irony, except that bipedal mankind likes to peddle notions in pairs): the dismissives and the obvious slayers.

Yeah, right, for instance, handily dismisses the quality or feasibility of an idea or thing. *Ye-ah,* on the other hand, attends to the idea or thing's glaring obviousness. By questioning the mental creds of anyone who'd make such a gaffe, obvious slayers can be harsher than dismissives. While Killer462's *Get over it* is a dismissive ("That idea sucks"), his more personal *Get a life* is an obvious slayer ("You mean you're still obsessed with *that?* Move on, loser"). Either way, he at whom the words are directed should ideally feel enough shame that he slams the door on his own thought.

Yeah, yeah, I've been dissing *I don't* think *so* all along. So it behooves me to examine what it is about the phrase and its dismissive cohorts that makes me say, "Man, that is so annoying."

I need look only at my own head. Recently I got so excited looking at old houses with a house-hunting friend that I thought I should chuck writing and become a real estate agent. Then, realizing how antithetical that would be to the rest of me, I said to myself, "Don't go there," followed immediately by "Don't even *think* about it." The only thing stopping me from tripping right into "Oh, I don't *think* so," "Get over it," "Get real," "Yeah, right," "No way!" "Hel-*lo*?!" "In my dreams," "Puh-leeze!" and/or "What am I *think*ing?" was the realization that I had no nonpop way of expressing how implausible such a career switch would be. "Nah, not a good idea" or "Unrealistic" had no oomph, and only oomph could block this train of thought.

Don't Even Think About Telling Me "I Don't Think So"

I don't think *so* and its fellow discontents are the new *no*. It's not enough to say "I disagree" or "Please don't do that"—the proposed notion, whatever it is, must suffer. Pop dismissives have virtually blasted a new neural pathway that we must take whenever we want to respond in the negative.

An upside-down clown (head near his knees, butt up where his head should be) walks into a bar, orders a Bud Light, and, much to the disgust of other patrons, drinks it through his (clothed) butthole. The clown then asks for a hot dog. The bartender instead delivers the punch line: "*I don't* think *so.*"

Donald Rumsfeld, asked by *NewsHour*'s Jim Lehrer whether we need more troops in Iraq (this was in September 2003), says: "Do you want to do what the Soviets did in Afghanistan and flood it, flood the zone as they say in football, flood it with 300,000 people and lose—and become an occupier, be oppressive, be everywhere, be in everyone's business? I don't *think* so." Later Lehrer asks about stories "that you've grown testy and defensive about criticism." Rumsfeld gives his version of events and asks back, "Is that testy, Jim? I don't *think* so."

"Don't even *think* of parking here" is the injunction on some New York City street signs. The warning has spread to other towns and to church sermons. "That's what God the King says to Evil: 'Don't even think of parking here!' " said the pastor at North & Southampton Reformed Church in Pennsylvania, while the preacher at the Gospel Light Baptist Church in Albany, Georgia, told his congregants, "Don't even think of parking at the place of immorality."

A magazine ad for Mohegan Sun, a Connecticut casino, showed a picture of people gambling like crazy. The headline reads, "We also have a coffee bar. (Yeah right. Like you'll need more stimulation.)"

Walking in Manhattan a few years ago, I saw a homeless man sitting on the sidewalk of West Forty-second Street, watching a high-heeled prostitute strut by. She glared at him and said, "I don't fucking *think* so."

Of course, dismissives don't always try to ridicule or vigorously prohibit. Much depends on context, voice, and facial expression. There are degrees of dismissiveness, particularly of *I don't* think *so,* which has been around long enough to have gone through several cycles.

Originally, *I don't* think *so* wasn't even a phrase. Attitudinally neutral and with no inflection, it was a mundane comment on a par with *yes, no,* and *maybe*—what we can call IDTS I.

Maybe one day a long time ago someone blurted out an absurdity—"It will snow in July" or "The U.S. will start a war with a country that didn't attack it"—and someone teased the absurdist with a singsongy "Oh, I don't *think* so." We don't know how or when this sarcastic offspring, IDTS II, was born. Because inflection is all in II, linguists and lexicographers are hard pressed to find early written citations of it. We do know, however, that Macaulay Culkin gave *I don't* think *so* a big push by uttering it twice in the top box-office hit of 1990, *Home Alone.* (Maybe that's why IDTS II became a minor celeb in *Home Improvement,* which debuted the following year. As Tim Allen's sidekick, Al, actor Richard Karn was originally slated only for the pilot of that highly popular sitcom. But when "Al's trademark line, 'I don't think so, Tim,' landed the biggest laugh of the pilot, Karn's fate with 'Home Improvement' was sealed," according to Karn's Touchstone Pictures bio.)

Nor do we know exactly how emphasizing the word *think* creates dismissiveness. Perhaps *think* suggests that he who speaks the phrase has been logical about the issue at hand and has deduced that it sucks. In any case, the effect is like striking a bell: The gong of its Wronnng! warns all comers that whoever says "I don't *think* so" first is nobody's fool.

IDTS II has become so common that it is, as linguists say, getting bleached, and that has produced a third-generation *I don't* think *so.* In IDTS III, *think* is barely if at all emphasized. III sounds like I but feels more like II, a tired II. It's listlessly ironic, sometimes mumbled. IDTS III seems to be forced to perform, to play out a contentiousness, when all it really wants to do is to say nicely, "I disagree."

Don't Even Think *About Telling Me "I Don't* Think *So"*

Both dismissives and obvious slayers want to show that you can't pull the wool over the speaker's eyes, but the latter also try to pull the rug out from under the target's feet.

Duh is the leader of this pack and is older than it may seem. *Duh* originally referred to the sound a dunce might utter. "It began as an outward expression of a slow-witted cartoon character's mental processes, as in a 1943 *Merrie Melodies* movie: 'Duh . . . Well, he can't outsmart me, 'cause I'm a moron,'" Barnhart and Metcalf write in *America in So Many Words*. This is the *duh* in *Floriduh*.

Later, *Duh* came to be not just a sound a moron might utter, but an exclamation of annoyance at a comment so obvious that only a moron would make it. The problem with being obvious, however, isn't stupidity per se. It's that making an obvious remark is the act of an unclued-in weakling, someone still excited over last year's fashions. The strong will pick up the scent and come in for the kill.

Media and marketing love to *Duh* it up, because doing so pits them as sexy, populist action figures against the wussy bureaucrats who overexplain what everyone already knows in deadening studies and reports.

A female voiceover speaks the following words as they appear on-screen: "Did you know studies have been conducted spending millions of dollars over years and years to find out what most guys think about 24 hours a day?" Then over the logo for Playboy TV: "Duh."

In recent print ads for Microsoft Office, human office workers walk around with dinosaur heads—the point being that they're technologically ancient. "Should we upgrade?" one dinoperson asks an apparently hipper dinoperson, who replies, in one ad, "Duh" (and in another, "That's a no-brainer").

Duh's less publicized peers include the preteenish *news flash* ("News flash," a doctor tells two tipsy residents on the NBC comedy *Scrubs*. "You can't drink and go to work. You're not airline pilots") and *You think?* (Donkey notices how Shrek puts a "wall" between himself and others, and tells him: "I think this whole wall thing is a way to keep somebody out." Shrek: "No, do you think?").

Likewise, when *yeah* divides into two syllables it becomes a *duh* (or a *du-uh*). "Would you say they're ideologically driven?" Jon Stewart asked his guest, Al Gore, about the Bush administration, in 2002. Gore leaned in, smiled, and said in his best Valley Girl imitation, "Ye-ah." Laughs from the audience (perhaps some relieved laughs that he didn't answer the question sincerely). Gore has said *ye-ah* before, to sound loose and not as self-conscious as he is, and to appeal to a younger crowd. Then, of course, the question deserved such an answer, and many of us would have given it one. Gore's problem using pop putdowns, to this day, is that he sounds like he doesn't believe in them beyond their service to him as a performer. He isn't, to his credit, a true pack attack animal.

George W. Bush is. Not only is he at home with adolescent barbs, but he won't or can't diplomatically dandy them up, a lack of finesse that has won him points as a "straight shooter." I agree with those who say his language, especially his mispronunciations, is not a political weakness but a bonding agent to populist regular guys (even as he sics 'em with elitist corporate policies). Bush's verbal weaponry often amounts to what *The New Yorker*'s editor, David Remnick, has called his "rhetoric of irritation," like saying of Saddam Hussein, "I am sick and tired of games and deception." Dick Cheney has praised Bush the "cowboy" who "cuts to the chase." Referring to various evildoers, Bush has said: "Smoke 'em out of their holes," "Hunt 'em down," and "Wanted: dead or alive."

But Bush, who has also been known to say *fabulous* a lot, is actually more the suburban cowboy. As former Bush speechwriter David Frum (who wrote the first two words of the "axis of evil") said of his ex-boss, "He can be very sarcastic. . . . [A]t one point I sent him a note that had the phrase 'I've seen with my own eyes' in it, and he circled 'with my own eyes' and wrote beside it in big letters, 'Duh.' " (Which makes Bush both a better editor and a nastier taskmaster than his image would suggest.)

WORDS DON'T KILL DISCUSSIONS, PEOPLE DO

But perhaps I'm not being open to phrases that blunt discussion. I mean, these phrases can be extremely useful, providing comic relief and relief from propaganda.

A good defense of *Duh, Yeah, right,* and gang comes from Kirk Johnson, who wrote that his twin eleven-year-old boys taught him that "television commercials can be rendered harmless and inert by simply saying, 'yeah, right,' upon their conclusion. Local television news reports are helped out with a sprinkling of well placed *Duh*s, at moments of stunning obviousness. And almost any politician's speech cries out for heaping helpings of both at various moments."

Though it takes more than a few sarcastic grunts to render ads or politicians harmless (it takes something like political involvement), I agree that weapon words, quickie mantras, and "talkback" are a healthy *immediate* response to commercial and political lies. When I get spam that reads, "savan, You have been approved. Cash Grant Amount: $10,000–$5,000,000," I mutter, "Yeah, right," and I feel empowered, not part of the herd but a black sheep who is exposing vile, naked greed.

But . . . baaa, baaa. My *Yeah, right* will inevitably be folded right back into one marketing come-on or another that grumbles "Yeah, right"—to get me to identify. These phrases roll past our defenses like Trojan horses. As cathartic as it may feel to blurt "Duh," doing so can confer a false sense of immunity, leaving us more susceptible over the long run to better-disguised vile, naked greed.

One of the best arguments for pop language in general comes from the Harvard psychologist Steven Pinker. "When the more passé terms [of slang] get cast off and handed down to the mainstream, they often fill expressive gaps in the language beautifully," he wrote in his book *The Language Instinct.* "I don't know how I ever did without *to flame* (protest self-righteously), *to dis* (express disrespect for), and *to blow off* (dismiss an obligation)."

Filling expressive gaps is indeed a great virtue of pop language. But, I asked Pinker by e-mail, when it comes to put-downs in particular, what is the effect of having so many slam-dunk phrases continually popping off in our face? As those words shove their way to the front of our vocabulary, do they prevent more nuanced or smarter conversations from getting through? "If someone cuts off intelligent discussion with one of these put-downs," Pinker responded, "I wouldn't blame the put-down; I'd blame the person. (The problem may be not the language per se, but the general coarsening and increased aggression of inter-personal interaction, at least as portrayed on TV.)"

He's right: Verbal popguns don't kill intelligent discussion; people do. But with huffy sound bites at their hip, people kill it more efficiently. And when they're socially rewarded for doing so, people are more likely to repeat the enjoyable sensation, be the target quite deserving or not.

And isn't there a feedback loop at work here? With so many automatic weapon words in circulation, we are incrementally creating a person more in the words' image. You don't have to be an Old Europe structuralist to get the idea (usually associated with Heidegger or Lacan) that "we don't speak a language, a language speaks us." Or that, at least, it speaks us as much as we speak it. "Our language puts blinders on us," says the linguist Robin Lakoff, author of *The Language War*. "The way we construct language influences the way we see reality, and reality influences language."

MEAN, MEAN MODULAR MACHINE

The language influencing our reality and the reality influencing our language are both increasingly mean. I've referred a couple of times to the two senses of the adjective *mean*. Usually it's used to mean malicious, cruel, intended to hurt. But there's the less often used sense of *mean* as middling, common—a definition that *Webster's Third New International Dictionary* traces back to the first: "destitute of distinction or eminence: COMMON, LOW, HUMBLE; destitute of power or acumen: ORDINARY, INFERIOR (a man of mean intelligence), SHABBY . . . LOW-MINDED, IGNOBLE, BASE, STINGY, CLOSE-FISTED, characterized by petty selfishness or malice: contemptibly disobliging or unkind."

So middling *mean* and malicious *mean* are related and, often enough, join forces at destitute-of-acumen *mean*, or stupid. Every time we try to sound common—in order to gain acceptance, say, or to avoid discussing a difficult issue—we are ignobly volunteering to be men and women of mean intelligence. Cruelty to others need not be involved; the unkindest cut may be to ourselves.

The temptations to sound a little stupid are powerful. A first-year high school teacher I know had a crush on the principal, a married man, who was unaware of her feelings. She knew that soon he was going to ask to observe her class. The very idea of him watching her threw her into a tizzy. "So in my head I prepared what I'd say if he insisted on it," she told me. "I'd say something like, 'I'm not comfortable in front of you.' If he asked why, I'd say, 'Don't go there'—as the only thing I could do to make this look like it wasn't a personal experience I was having, to make it stereotyped, to make it common, like an emotion that 'everyone has.' " (By the time he asked, her crush had vanished, and she just said, OK.)

Pop weaponry is not only destitute of distinction—it's less distinguishing. Painting with a broad brush has its plusses, pro-*duh*ster Johnson says: "Duh and yeah right are matchless tools of savvy, winking sarcasm and skepticism: caustic without being confrontational, incisive without being quite specific."

But being caustic and incisive without confronting or offering specifics, going for brand-name insults because that's all the vending machines carry, is not particularly smart. It's a modular meanness. "We're so reducing language to a gesture, and we only know what the crudest sense of that gesture is—'Oh, they're putting me down,' 'Oh, they like me,' " says Maria DiBattista. "Comedy and wit can be cruel, but this is cruelty without any accompanying perception about what it is that's so wrong."

For even if these weapon words were the nastiest bomb mots on earth, who'd want a civilization without frequent hits of wicked wit? The real reason modular meanness grates isn't the cruelty—it's the modularness. Multiple-choice zingers are thought replacements; they'll do the thinking for us. Entertaining but mechanistic, wise-ass but anti-intellectual, they stun the synapses and bully their way to a spurious consensus.

WHAT AM I *THINKING*?

I'm not so idealistic as to believe that thought replacements are suppressing original, brilliant, creative thoughts. After all, as the eighteenth-century English artist Sir Joshua Reynolds is quoted as saying, "There is no expedient to which a man will not resort to avoid the real labour of thinking."

Nevertheless, the market and our self-image put a premium on words and attitudes that *pass* for thinking. The easiest way to pass is simply to refer often to thinking, brains, and the like.

In fact, the words *think* and *brain* are beneficiaries of a curious phenomenon: Some words appear more as the reality they stand for appears less. For instance, *community* is all over the place as actual communities are disappearing. It's as if reciting the word often enough makes the labor of creating the reality unnecessary. Likewise with *think* and *brain*.

"Think PlayStation!" Vin Diesel's character shouts in an action scene in *XXX*.

"Think different" is the famous Apple slogan implying that the computer can make you as singular and nonconforming as Einstein, Gandhi, and other superstars of civilization (whose independent thought surely would have led them to flame Apple for using their photos as posthumous endorsements).

"Rethink TV" is DirecTV's new slogan.

"Rethink 50+" is a slogan for AARP publications.

"Rethink those dinner plans," a Boston Market TV spot advises.

"I would gladly pay the $23 million Liza is suing Viacom for (if I had it), just to make *sure* her 'reality show' never reaches the airwaves. . . . What were they thinking!?" asked a letter to the editor of *Entertainment Weekly*.

R. Foster Winans, the former *Wall Street Journal* columnist convicted in the eighties for passing insider tips to traders, said of Jayson Blair, the *New York Times* reporter who lied in published stories: "If I could talk with him, I would have to ask: 'What the fuck were you thinking? You know you're going to get caught!' "

"Real easy," Lynne Rossetto Kasper said of a recipe on her public radio show, *The Splendid Table*. "This is not brain surgery."

I'm not knocking Kasper, I like her, but I *knew* she was going to follow "real easy" with "brain surgery." I didn't know, however, that the convicted identity thief who spoke to CBS News was going to say of his trade, "It's very easy. It's something you don't have to be a rocket scientist to do."

"Oh Jesus, I can't wrap my brain around that thought yet," said Halle Berry on the possibility of winning an Oscar for best actress in 2002 (which she did).

No-brainer is such a no-brainer for advertising that between just late 2002 and mid-2003 the word lit up ads for Mitsubishi, Mercury, and VW; Road Runner High Speed Online, Optimum Online, and Charter Pipeline High Speed Internet; an AT&T calling plan, the Nextel National Connect Plan, and Telecom USA, one of those 10-10 deals. "A no-brainer," the actor John Stamos said in the last. "What's a no-brainer? Everyone knows what a no-brainer is. You don't have to think about it." Is this marketing nirvana, or what? What once was called "impulse buying"—not asking whether you need a product, not comparing products, just going for it—now sounds like a smart move.

For a while in the nineties, young Hollywooders with perfect vision were wearing eyeglasses with plain, noncorrective lenses, in order to seem serious and not just like hollow heads. These phrases are like that eyegear, tokens of thinking.

Think about it. For all the references to thinking—*I don't think so, no-brainer, clueless*—for all the surgeons and rocket scientists you don't have to be, for all the things you can't wrap your brain around, even if you are a brainiac, for all the other things you're told to not even think about, isn't the real message of these phrases simply "Don't even think"?

After all, only an inflection, a pause, and a question mark separate "I don't *think* so" from "I don't think—so?"

CHAPTER 5

The Great American *Yesss!*

For those who manage to vanquish an adversary or have a win of any sort there is a totally positive victory cry and (in contrast to the bounty of negative weapon words) really only one totally positive victory cry. You know it, you say it, America roars it.

"Yesss!" said a friend of mine when she won a bid on a house "by just that much."

"Yesss!" hissed Michael Douglas—one arm pumping the word, the other draped around wife Catherine Zeta Jones—when Barbara Walters asked what he did on learning that Catherine was pregnant.

"Yesss!" yelled a contestant on a promo for *Millionaire* (in its glory days *Who Wants to Be a Millionaire*).

"Yesss!" I whisper as I get a kink out of my back.

"Yesss! Yesss!" whoops Jack, the flamboyant foil on *Will & Grace*. The question was Whom does cute guy Barry want to date—Jack or Will? Confidently expecting Barry to choose him, Jack shouts, jumps up, and performs a full-body *Yesss!*—even as

Barry replies, "Will." "What?" Jack says, doing the sitcom double-take.

Few days have been more yesssful, however, than February 10, 1997. That's when Denise Brown said on *Nightline* that the guilty verdict in the civil case against O. J. Simpson, her former brother-in-law, "really made me kind of yes." She made a tiny fist that barely moved. That same day, after Lemrick Nelson was found guilty for causing the death of Yankel Rosenbaum during the 1991 riots in Crown Heights, Brooklyn, Yankel's brother Norman told Fox News, "I could imagine my brother going, 'Yesss! Yesss!' "

These were both quiet *Yesss!*-es, spoken with a bitter jubilance. But whether roared or whispered, accompanied by an arm motion or just straight from the mouth, in response to a murder conviction or a good parking space, *Yesss!* seems to be the absolutely best way to express—and to experience—victory.

Winning doesn't feel as complete, as real, as registered if not punctuated by a *Yesss!* In a world obsessed with winning and losing, saying *Yesss!* is to have an avenging *Amen!* on our side. When even a minor obstacle caves in to our will, we suddenly click from victim to victor, an ejaculatory sound enhancing the thrill, our arms pumping like knockout punches not actually thrown for an audience not actually there.

Other sound-gesture combos—like the Arsenio Hall arm-cranking *Woof-woof-woof* or the adolescent finger-in-throat-with-gag-noise to indicate vomitous—come and go, but a big triumphant *Yesss!* is the one we can't say no to.

THE PEAKS OF *YESSS!*

Though most of the public is *Yesss!*-ing as much as ever, there was a time when the action-affirmative was even bigger in the media than it is now. Throughout the 1990s, *Yesss!* was the emotional climax of scores of TV shows, commercials, movie trailers, and, most feebly, movies themselves.

In just one night of watching TV in the mid-nineties, I caught *Yesss!*—sometimes solo, but usually paired with an arm—

emitted by a winning contestant on MTV's dating-game show *Singled Out,* by a character on *My So-Called Life,* and in ads for Miller Lite's Super Bowl inflatable chair, the instant scratch game Three Point Play, Neutrogena's Clear Pore Treatment, and the National Hockey League.

Expressing desire and gratification at once, *Yesss!* erupts from the core of the commercial infrastructure, and so it is a no-brainer for actual commercials. (In fact, *Yesss!* and *no-brainer* cover the same territory, with one difference: As a spurious form of logic, *It's a no-brainer* tries to fake out the brain. *Yesss!,* however, ignores the head altogether and aims straight for the gut: I Want! I Have! I Yesss!) The commercial leverage of *Yesss!* is innate—the word simply can't be said without an exclamation point, and associating a brand with such excitement is advertising's point. In fact, so many TV spots peaked on *Yesss!* during my long *Yesss!* ad-watch between 1996 and 2002 that the following list only skims the surface:

Yesss! was shouted and/or hissed by: a little girl when her mom agrees that, thanks to her conference-call-ready cell phone from AT&T, they *can* go to the beach after all; a boy when his parents decide to buy a BMW from BMW of Manhattan; a kid playing with Matchbox cars; a mother who finally gets her off-spring off to school with the help of Glad Bags; John Lithgow in a promo for *Third Rock from the Sun;* Moesha in a promo for *Moesha;* a sleepy man and dog who won't wake up until the man's wife offers them Edy's ice cream; a man as he grabs an O'Doul's beer from the fridge; a kid in a Honey Bunches of Oats ad; someone in a Doritos spot; Michael Jordan, for his cologne, as he putts a golf ball into a plastic cup in his living room; a golfer on a green, for a Charles Schwab retirement fund, as he drops a ball into the hole; Santa, for Celebrex, as he sinks a putt at a home he's delivering presents to. (Since the painkiller was later linked to heart problems, rotund Santas probably should have been staying clear of the drug.)

CLOSURE AT THE MOVIES

Movie characters don't *have* to be Celebrexing a putt in order to shout *Yesss!* (someone in the Kevin Costner golf movie *Tin Cup* *Yesss!*-ed for a much lesser victory). As a hole-in-one emotion, a *Yesss!* or two has become as much a Hollywood convention as a sidekick or a romantic interest. *Home Alone,* the 1990 popularizer of *I don't* think *so,* is even better known for making *Yesss!* a star. In three separate clusters, Macaulay Culkin yelled, arm-pumped, and/or jumped *Yesss!* to celebrate his outwitting of the burglars.

Yesss! went on to provide a measure of closure in *Disclosure* (1994) as Michael Douglas, long before his *Yesss!* to Barbara Walters, whooped it when his character finally triumphed over sexually harrassing villain exec Demi Moore. Two years later, a rather muted *Yesss!* sounded in *Independence Day* (a stripper got a stalled truck to start).

Despite its age, *Yesss!* is still finding work in the industry. In *Legally Blonde 2: Red, White & Blonde* (2003), Elle phones her fiancé during the Harvard law class he teaches to tell him she rented Fenway Park for their wedding. His students cheer when he announces, "I'm getting married under the green monster! Yesss!" (There was actually more pop language—*No biggie, It was genius, I don't* think *so, Don't even* think *about it,* a few *Omigods,* and the admittedly funny "Is bill-writing super fun, or what?"—in the sequel than in the 2001 original. In *Legally Blonde,* Elle's "Me! Yesss!" on learning that she won a coveted law firm internship shared the stage only with "Am I on glue?," which Elle asked her ex-beau when he called her dumb.)

TRAILERS TRADEMARK TRIUMPH

Yesss!-ness is a quality basic not only to pop character and plot— a neon sign that conflict has been resolved—but to movie marketing itself. Combine the advertising *Yesss!* with the movie *Yesss!* and you've got the trailer *Yesss!* Given that hundreds of scenes can be edited into an ad for a movie, it is notable that great numbers of comedy and action flick trailers, especially, pop in scenes with a *Yesss!* To mention but a few trailers (whether for television, theatrical, or video/DVD release) that climaxed on *Yesss!: Aladdin, Rumble in the Bronx, The Burbs, The Next Karate Kid, Striptease,* and *The Nutty Professor,* as well as, from above, *Tin Cup* and *Legally Blonde* (that "Me! Yesss!"). More recently, Hilary Duff exhaled *Yesss!* in a trailer for *The Perfect Man.*

"This movie's a winner!" a trailer *Yesss!* is really saying, as it tries to drive the movie into blockbusterdom. The desperate search for blockbusters has been making Hollywood movies stupider for decades now, pretty much since the seventies "golden age" of movies ended and the era of corporate media mergers began. "As the huge debt created by mergers was added to the rising costs of making little but blockbusters, the risks of making a film forced the businessmen to be risk averse, to play to the least critical audience: teenage boys with disposable income," the veteran screenwriter/director Frank Pierson said in his University of Southern California film school commencement address in 2003.

It's not just the young natives who require easy-to-understand movies. Hollywood is trapped on the lowest-common-denominator runaway train because (what with escalating star salaries as well as merger and blockbuster costs to cover) it must sell more product overseas, where boldface English can cut across cultural barriers. Luckily for the media giants, *Yesss!* is the internationally recognized sound for "The hero wins! You can feel good!" Since the formula by and large works, the studios can scream back at critics, "Subtitle *this*!"

By the time a film reaches a commercial editor or producer who cuts and pastes it into an ad, the formulas have so thickened that they leave little or no creative latitude.

As an editor who worked on the *Tin Cup* trailer said, "We did it a hundred different ways before we got the finished cut approved. But somebody saying an exuberant *Yesss!* from the movie was always in the trailer at some point. It may have come following a kiss or somebody doing a put-down, but it kept popping up."

"*Yesss!* says it all with the arm motion and the one word," added Kevin Wagner, a former vice president of creative advertising at Miramax. "That's a producer's dream, to get something so clearly defined. It's an exclamation point at the end of a sentence. You have shot, shot, shot, then exclamation point. Or like Jim Carrey saying 'Smokin' ' in *The Mask.* We look for nuggets like that. We're like, 'Oh, thank you.' " Plus, *Yesss!* is great for rhythm, Wagner said: " 'And just when you thought all was lost— *Yesss!*' It fills a beat right between two lines."

In 1997, when Peter Adee was in charge of trailers at Buena Vista, he explained the *Yesss!* explosion by saying, "It's the quickest way to communicate the coolest thing that could happen." By 2003, Adee, now president of worldwide marketing for MGM and overseeing trailer production, told me that *Yesss!* is still cool. "Oh, God, yes," he said. "There are no rules in making trailers, but it's still valid to say that the exclamation *Yesss!* with the arm gesture is as excited and as positive a thing as you can do."

THE BARK OF THE UNDERDOG

Even so, I haven't observed *Yesss!* in quite as many trailers, commercials, or sitcoms as in the nineties.

But if *Yesss!* has peaked, it has slid down only a few yards. The middle-aged phrase hasn't lost its vital role, just its newcomer sheen. No younger, stronger victory cry has come along to take its place—and we need *something* to express consumer and/or competitive jubilance. When the salesman hands a customer the keys to a new Toyota Camry in a 2002 spot, what else could she do but repeatedly jump up and shout, "Yesss! Yesss! Yesss!"? That same year, when the duplicitous tabloid TV reporter played by Winona Ryder (that's revenge entertainment!) scores a coup over the hapless Adam Sandler in *Mr. Deeds,* she double-arms a silent *Yesss!* behind his back. In either case, other victory cries, like the old-fashioned *Yay!, Hurray!,* the ironic *Whoo-hoo!,* or the rather laid-back *All riiight!,* just don't convey the spiritual glory of getting your way.

Movies are so dependent on the drama of *Yesss!* that they'll gladly risk anachronism. In the 2003 film *Seabiscuit,* Tobey

Maguire, alone in his hospital bed in the 1930s, hears on the radio that the jockey riding Seabiscuit for him has won a race. Three times he shouts "Yesss!," hitting the last one the hardest (and hitting the bed rather than arm-pumping). In Hollywood, of course, anachronism is no risk at all, because (1) audiences don't care about such things, and (2) on this particular anachronism rides something that audiences do care about: assurance that they're the good guys and always were, despite any news to the contrary.

Seabiscuitmania, which first struck during the Depression and again in the new millennium with Laura Hillenbrand's best-selling book and the hit movie, is the "story of American pluck in the face of overwhelming odds," as the writer Traci Hukill has put it. The story's real-life "cast of underdogs . . . had a go at the sport of kings and beat the bluebloods at their own game." But, she continues, "This is not 1937 and America is not a nation of underdogs. We are Rome after the fall of the Republic, at the peak of our powers. . . . By all indications we have become that overbearing entity it was once our calling to unseat. Yet the myth demands that we be cast as the hardscrabble underdog, individually and collectively."

It is *Yesss!*'s job to express and promote that myth. And the myth is not about to dump its best spokesman ever.

This isn't to say that the plucky-underdog myth is a complete fabrication, a media trick designed to fool the masses. The story is founded on a historical reality and spirit: American can-doism, optimism, and a never-ending faith in opportunity. The nation couldn't have been built without large dollops of such *Yesss!*-ness. But somewhere along the line, *Yesss!*-ness became reduced to a badge of our Americanism, proof of our very humanity. (That applies even if you're an android. In *Star Trek: Generations,* Data gets an "emotion chip" so he can understand humor. When the *Enterprise* destroys the evil Klingon ship, the movie cuts to Data, who shouts "Yesss!"—which proves both that the chip works and that he's, almost, one of us.)

Precisely because the myth flows from something real, it's that much easier to exploit. In ways both genuine and hyped, unconscious and deliberate, certain powerful forces—namely, gambling, sports, and (to a different extent) sex—revolve around the Great American *Yesss!,* and thus ensure its longevity.

ALL BETS ARE ON FOR *YESSS!*

As a significant beneficiary of optimism and opportunity, gambling is now considered less a sin than a stress-reducer (as the would-be virtue czar William Bennett initially maintained after he was outed as a habitual gambler) and, morality aside, a necessity. From state lotteries that are supposed to fund public education (but don't always) to President Bush's efforts to replace Social Security with private investments to the new majority of adult Americans who play the stock market either directly or through pension funds, gambling in one form or the other is increasingly seen as the only way of getting ahead in a world stacked against you. We're all playing the slot machines of life.

On the slim chance that we do beat the house, our pressurized hopes gush like an oil well. It's a sensation screaming for a sound. The sound doesn't *have* to be *Yesss!,* but should equal its force. "Let's see some red, honey!" the dice-rolling *Sex and the City* alumnus John Corbett shouted in a promo for *Lucky,* his short-lived show about Vegas on FX. Yanking his arm down and across, Corbett ended the spot with a *Yesss!*-like "Yeah!"

Lucky portrayed gamblers as addicts, but, overall, gambling has been getting virtuefied. Not just because it's so pervasive that we try to find ways to accept it, but also because it has been renamed—now it's the less rattling, even hip *gaming.* The American Gaming Association showed it's got game by going on the linguistic offensive: "While some people assume the word gaming was created as a way to 're-invent' the casino industry, history tells a different story. The word 'gaming'—defined as the action or habit of playing at games of chance for stakes—actually dates back to 1510, predating use of the word 'gambling' by 265 years."

Perhaps, but press-release-writing.com tells how, history be damned, it's the connotations, stupid. For "a client who ran an Online Gaming Company . . . [w]e couldn't extol the benefits the reader would derive because there is no guarantee in gambling. What we could do was go along with the 'gamesmanship' of the experience. . . . Our [press release] heading was 'All Bets are On for Aladden [*sic*] Casino Online Gaming with State-of-the-Art Software.' We tied in the words 'bets' with 'Casino' and 'Gaming' to create a mood. 'All Bets are On' creates a positive feeling. . . . We used the word 'Gaming' rather than 'Gambling' because it has a more positive connotation. 'Gaming' sounds like fun, a game, a pastime while 'gambling' denotes risk, a negative tone."

WHEN MARV MET MOLLY

Positive feelings, fun, games, pastimes . . . ah, sports—a field even richer in *Yesss!* gushers than gambling is. As more of us live life as a series of events that can be won or lost, performing a *Yesss!,* even when alone, can feel like getting media coverage of your own private touchdown.

In sports lie the origins of *Yesss!* as we know it. It was, of course, the sportscaster Marv Albert who popularized the excitable, drawn-out *Yesss!,* though, as he explained to *Sports Illustrated,* he did not invent it. "There was an official in the NBA in the '50s named Sid Borgia. He was a very animated official who would go through gyrations when someone scored a basket. He would say, 'Yes!' and if a guy was fouled, 'And it counts!' I remember early in my career during a Knicks playoff game Dick Barnett [a Knicks player] hit what was called a fallback baby jumper that banked in at the buzzer at the end of a quarter and I just happened to say, 'Yes!' People started to repeat it back to me and I started to incorporate it. It just seemed natural."

A year or so after much of the media had blared Albert's 1997 sex scandal in humiliating detail, a TV spot let loose a fusillade of *Yesss!*es to announce his return to MSG. (The media—they're at your throat or at your feet; you're their celebrity in exile or their comeback kid.) What more natural word than *Yesss!* with which to signal the resolution of the whole crapoid drama. (Albert has since left MSG, for unrelated reasons.)

The Great American Yesss!

While no other sportscaster has made *Yesss!* his own shtick, the word has remained as much a part of sports culture as multi-million-dollar corporate sponsorships. Announcers, players, and fans still shout it; ads for teams still try to score with it. (In a 2003 Kansas City Chiefs football spot, men run wild through a super-market, convulsively yelling, "Yesss! Yesss! Yeah, baby!" on hear-ing that the Chiefs have won.) Meanwhile, an entire sports network baptized itself with the word: the YES network (Yankees Entertainment and Sports network).

A sense of the crowd seeps into all pop language, but it soaks those words and phrases that have anything to do with sports.

There are (at least) two reactions to living in a sports-entertainment dominion: Join it and be one with the crowd, or—fearing that every stadium roar will devolve into a stampede—run from it as fast as your nerdy feet allow. Yet in *Yesss!* these opposing urges coexist: *Yesss!* aligns you with the massest of the mass—you're a regular guy, unimpeachably American—and, at the same time, *Yesss!* conveys that you're an indomitable individual prevailing over the idiots, the established order, the gathering mob. The beauty of *Yesss!* is that it allows all us underdogs and outsiders to overcome the odds—without seeming the least bit odd.

Yesss! is not the sports world's only MVP. From Mel Allen's "That ball is going, going, gone" to Spanish soccer's *Goooooollll!*, ritualistic phrases are like prayers. In an article about how "sportscasters evolved from experts to baby sitters for a nation of lonely guys," the writer and sports fan Peter de Jonge says the TV shows (like ESPN's *SportsCenter*) and the phrases (like "Good to see you. Got to GO!" for a home run, or "for a point guard leading the break a reference to LL Cool J: 'Push-ing it and pushing it and pushing it good' ") serve a higher pur-pose. "With the floor of the world falling out from under us," he writes, "it's comforting to turn on a show that uses the one lan-guage in which we're fluent, that never makes us feel ignorant, apathetic and disconnected."

Nor is *Yesss!* the only sports phrase that has saturated the wider society. *Slam dunk,* believed to have been coined by the late Los Angeles Lakers announcer Chick Hearn, *a Hail Mary pass,* and *behind the eight ball,* for instance, have all gone way past their sport.

But *Yesss!* is one of the few pop words from sports—or any realm—to day in, day out appear with a physical gesture. (Several gestures, really. The arm pump, a sort of arm-sized V-for-victory sign, leads Team *Yesss!*, but the clench-fisted players also include the straight-armed overhead jab and the lifted bent arm that rotates or beats.)

Other victory gestures abound, from the two-fingered *V* sign and the bouncy chest-thump to the rich array of end-zone dances. None of them, however, has a steady word buddy.

The following is ridiculously speculative, but perhaps the word *Yesss!* and the arm gesture evolved together because the underlying emotion is so primal that it needs a bodily motion to complete it. Really primal. For before there was can-do-ism, gambling, or even sports, there was sex. And who knows, maybe even *Yesss!*-ful sex, victorious in scaling the peak, all physical and spiritual, all Molly Bloom yes yes yes YES!

It is true that the sports *Yesss!* and the climactic sex *Yesss!* are vocalized differently—the former tends toward forceful hisses, the latter toward breathy moans. And unlike the sports or lifestyle-victory *Yesss!*, the sex *Yesss!* does not appear with an illustrative gesture. (But then, one's limbs are already pretty well occupied.)

Unfortunately, even this transcendent sexual *Yesss!* has been stolen from literature and the most intimate of experiences, and turned into another seen-by-billions marketing gimmick. One of the first spots in Clairol Herbal Essences' "totally organic experience" campaign began with a woman washing her hair in an airplane lavatory. Though it's unclear how she got such luxurious lather from the sink's trickle of water, cleaning her scalp feels so darn good that, acting out the throes of orgasm, she screams "Yesss, Yesss, YESSS!" Clairol girls have gone on to find their C-spot in showers at the gym and in courtrooms (three guys help a female lawyer wash her hair to satisfy her "urge"). In a Spanish-language ad, a woman shampoos under a jungle waterfall, her ecstasy baffling the onlooking monkeys. Although the male voiceover is in Español, the woman does not scream *"Siii, Siii, SIII!"* but "Yesss, Yesss, YESSS!"

Absurd? Of course. And yet evidence for shampoo-stimulated female orgasm exists. Linda Kaplan Thaler, head of the Kaplan Thaler Group and creator of the campaign, said her ad agency convened a focus group of women to find out how they felt about washing their hair. Not much came up. Finally some women indicated that it felt "good." Add to that the inspiration of Meg Ryan's famously fake orgasm in *When Harry Met Sally,* and a new, mainstream (Clairol is owned by straitlaced Procter & Gamble), product-enabled orgasm was born.

IN ARM'S WAY

But perhaps that campaign is no more absurd than my campaign to prove a primal relationship between *Yesss!* and the arm that escorts it. Maybe I'm wrong and this coupling isn't based on sex at all, but on sports, specifically (as some men I know figure) on referee hand signals.

Sounds plausible. But my referee hand signal adviser, the sportswriter Jeff Z. Klein, author of *Messier,* says, "I know all the hand signals for all the sports, and there's no connection. There's just not that kind of gesture. And referee hand signals by definition don't denote celebration."

So forget referees, but look at the players, Klein suggests. "I saw the gesture in hockey in the late seventies, early eighties. Someone scored a goal, and he'd pump his arm while gliding along on one skate—and the opposite knee would come up as well, thrusting upward."

Whether or not the multilimb pump originated with hockey (and Klein says he doesn't know), there's still the question of why, out of the myriad of victory gestures, this particular one attached to *Yesss!*

No one can really know this sort of thing. But follow, for a minute, the aggressive and sexual behavior of the good old naked ape. Desmond Morris, who wrote *The Naked Ape* and other

books tracing twentieth-century human behaviors to their primate roots, has described what may in fact be a grandfather of
the *Yesss!* arm pump. He has written that the "forearm jerk"—
bent arm, fist clenched, jerks upward or outward as palm or fist
of opposite hand slaps crook of bent arm's elbow—is used extensively in Europe, especially the south, to say "Up yours!" or "Fuck
you!" "The forearm with its clenched fist represents a super-
normal phallus and its jerking movement imitates the thrusting
of the penis," Morris and his co-authors stated in *Gestures: Their
Origins and Distribution*. As "a phallic threat," the forearm jerk "is
remarkably similar to certain displays of monkeys and apes . . . a
symbolic way of saying 'I am dominant over you.' "

Symbols are nothing if not evolving. "The very size of [the]
penis-substitute leaves no doubt about the omnipotence of its
owner," they continued. "This may explain why this gesture has
become so popular in recent years and why it seems to have
eclipsed—in certain regions, at least—the much more ancient
obscene insult, the middle-finger jerk" (which "was so popular
among the Romans that they even gave a special name to the
middle digit, calling it the impudent finger: *digitus impudicus*").

In Britain, though, the forearm jerk is more likely to signify
male sexual arousal and is usually performed out of a woman's
sight as a vulgar comment to other males, meaning "a bit of all
right" or "I'd like to do her," according to *Gestures*. "It is a sexual
gesture about a sexual feeling, whereas the phallic threat is
a sexual gesture about a hostile feeling." Meanwhile, a "third
major meaning for the forearm jerk," mostly in Scandinavia,
Germany, Austria, and Tunisia, is a Popeye-like "I'm strong, look
at my muscles."

When Morris and his colleagues wrote *Gestures*, published in
1979, they noted an up-and-coming gesture.

> At sporting events recently, a subtle blend has developed
> between the phallic erection of the forearm and the sim-
> ple, muscle display. A triumphant winner, in his moment
> of elation, can often be seen to bring his bent forearm
> up into the stiffly bent, muscle-bulging posture, and to
> do so in such a way that there is something inescapably

"erectile" about the action. . . . This puts it into a special category of its own. It is not directed at the opponents, or defeated rivals . . . nor is it a comment on sexual arousal. It is done for the benefit of the winner's teammates or his fans, and is in effect a comment on, or a celebration of, his sudden moment of dominance.

What they describe is functionally identical to the V-shaped arm pump, though with the arm somewhat higher. In the 1995 *Bodytalk: The Meaning of Human Gestures,* Morris added a bevy of victory arm actions, including the "fist beat": "The clenched fist is raised high in the air and then delivers a powerful beat, forward and downward. . . . It is derived from the primeval overarm blow that is common to all mankind." But the classic arm-yanking-toward-the-torso *Yesss!* was still not cited.

I'll give the gesture's genesis a stab: Elbow pulled down and back, fist tightened, biceps enlarged—the arm pump (as distinguished from the overarm blow) looks pretty much like how an arm prepares to punch. Let's say a primate has just beaten his rival. Now that he doesn't have to actually execute a punch, he might briefly keep his bent arm close to his body, perhaps repeating the prepunch motion, "pumping" his arm in order to draw out the satisfaction and savor his win. (Mimicking the excited heart's faster beat, the arm pump also suggests that the victory wasn't cold and ruthless but heartfelt and personal, as a plucky underdog's win should be.)

If this repetitive motion were then to meet a word—especially one with an elongating hiss—the primate could further enhance his sensation of triumph. The word would serve as the gesture's bullhorn, the gesture as the word's steroid.

As for when *Yesss!* and the arm pump hooked up, we can only guess that it was sometime between the 1950s, when Sid Borgia was shouting the *Yesss!* that Albert said he later took up, and the late 1970s, when Klein first saw the arm and leg pump in North American hockey and Morris first saw the closely related celebratory forearm in British sports. By the late 1970s, the word and gesture had probably noticed each other in the mass media.

But just as the middle finger in some parts of the world is too puny an insult, so the *Yesss!* arm-and-word partnership is not always emphatic enough for a livin' large win. Sometimes the double arm pump is called for, or, better, the hockey player's full-body *Yesss!* We are nouvelle naked apes now, and some of our hardest-won victories concern not one's rivals or turf, but one's time. That is, many of our victories are transactional (getting the info, the Web site, the break we need) and therefore ripe for advertising. But another *Yesss!*-cum-arm in an ad can get lost in the crowd. The following print ad wasn't going to make that mistake.

A bespectacled, business-suited woman is pumping one fist-clenched arm hard; the other is grasping a report. One leg is also in pump position—the knee is bent and raised, its high-heeled foot hooking behind the supporting leg's knee. Her head is doing the "I'm goood" downward nod: eyes squeezed shut, chin jutting out, lips pulled back in the teeth-baring smile that the aggressive *S*'s of *Yesss!* demand.

What in the name of the American dream caused *this* response? "Can you imagine spending more time doing business—by spending less time copying?" asks the headline for the digital copier company.

"YES, IKON!"

CHAPTER 6

Populist Pop and the Regular Guy

ey, guys: I owe you. Big-time. So I'm gonna stop talkin' the talk and start talkin' 'bout the talk that walks the walk.

That's right—this chapter is about language that seems immune to the media's glossy corruption, about words and phrases that come straight from the hearts and guts of regular guys. These words are a little bit country, a little bit rock 'n' roll, a little bit NASCAR, a little bit Ace Hardware. Giving off an easygoing toughness, they're the salt-of-the-earth working stiffs of pop language. They ring true. But even this creative vernacular eventually goes pop and, in a heartbeat, what was poetry becomes PR.

Listen up: Regular-guy talk has been turned up a notch, gotten glittery, become guyismo. Most of us, even the elite snobs, want to be down-to-earth, unpretentious good guys—and we want to signal that we are. The advertising of our authenticity is a paradox perhaps best expressed by the logoed, regular-guy baseball cap—still, after all these decades, worn by black and white, good ol' boy and metrosexual, construction worker and lobbyist, celebrity and nobody.

From our pickup trucks to our Pabst Blue Ribbon, from our "gear" to our cargo pants, from the California recall election to the Seattle café-sitters' vote against an espresso tax (to fund daycare and preschool programs), we're all halfway populist regular guys now. We all deserve a break, a tax break, a brewsky, a few words of baseball-cap yap to make us feel like the real deal. On that, there's no daylight between bubbas and Hollywood agents.

Since most of us, including the bubbas, are to varying degrees now nouvelle (that is, crackling with autonomic media responses), the presumed antidote to too much nouvelle—tough but heartfelt regular-guy talk, imagery, and merchandise—is in high demand. So even if populist pop sometimes sounds Southern, no way is it going south. Because the marketplace, especially the political one, has not yet squeezed all the regularness out of the regular guy.

THE REMARKABLE, MARKETABLE UNMARKED GUY

Why are regular guys, be they Joe Average or Joe Schmo (each has won his own eponymous reality TV show), so desirable? Because guys—the actual males and the word *guy* itself—are "unmarked."

I don't want to get too egghead on you, but . . . every language has linguistic forms that indicate the standard, the normal state, the basic theme on which other forms are but variations. For example, as the linguist Robin Lakoff points out, singular nouns are unmarked, while plurals are marked with an *s*. Present-tense verbs are unmarked, while generally the past tense is marked with *-ed* and the future tense with *will*. This seems like such common sense, Lakoff says, that we don't think about it, much less question it. Marking gets more controversial, however, when we get to gender or race. *Actor* is unmarked; *actress* is marked. *Whites* are unmarked; *nonwhites* are marked (and marked with a negative).

To be unmarked may not sound like much, but it signifies

power, the power of the presumed normal. Meanwhile, the marked are presumed to be exceptions, secondary, maybe even weird.

Commercially and politically, guys (white guys, that is) are the great unmarked, or, to use the parlance of credit card come-ons, preapproved. They are considered the norm, a powerhouse of neutrality, from which women, children, and even "men" are variations. Guys are different from the serious, rather grandiose men, as Dave Barry explains in *Dave Barry's Complete Guide to Guys*. Superman is a man, he says; Bart Simpson, a guy. Dober-man pinschers are men; Labrador retrievers, guys. Geraldo is a man; Katie Couric, a guy. Unlike men, who may have vision things and ideologies, guys are easily trusted (and their populist potential is courted and copied) because they're passionate only about their immediate wants and needs, like sports, beer, and pizza. And as long as we're talking straight-up stereotypes, guys are likable, kinda comical, and, underneath it all, decent.

The word *guy*, however, began life as a creep. The first defini-tion of *guy* in the *Random House Historical Dictionary of American Slang* is "a grotesque-looking, ill-dressed, or ridiculous person . . . a fool." This guy is based on Guy Fawkes, leader of England's Gunpowder Plot (1605), who has been annually hanged or burned in badly attired effigy on Guy Fawkes Day, or Bonfire Night, ever since. The fool *guy* evolved into "a comical or joking fellow," and later mellowed further into just another word for "a man or boy; fellow," eventually becoming so bleached that the outcast became incast. "He is a social leper. . . . He isn't a 'regu-lar guy,' " the *RHHDAS* quotes a 1924 citation. As the un-leper, *guy* was mass pop well before TV took over. "It is one of the few words—*okay* is the only other polite one—that *all* Americans feel belong to them," the *RHHDAS* quotes a writer from 1954.

But a funny thing's happened between *guy* and *guys*. While for the most part the singular *guy* continues to stand for male unmarkedness, the plural *guys*—as in *Hey, guys* or *you guys*—has generously opened its gates to the marked masses: women, ethnics, immigrants; hell, even the occasional criminal—and, within limits, accepts them all as OK. *Guys* in this broadest sense confers a safe, ageless shmoo-like quality on adults as well as children, judges and jurors as well as family and friends. "Can you guys call me Monica?" Monica Lewinsky asked those assembled before her grand jury.

Why does *guy* get so loosey-goosey after just one little *s*? Most societies need a way to informally address groups of people that signals friendliness and nonbelligerence, and we do have *y'all* and *folks*. But Boomers and younger generations wanted a plural of their own—*y'all* is geographically limited; *folks* can be overly folksy. *You guys*, though, has the region-free, media-borne quality we prefer. As jjoan ttaber wrote in *The Vocabula Review*, "you guys, a childish form of address popularized by children's television during the 1950s, was carried into adulthood by hordes of baby boomers who didn't know how to give up the habit." The habit grew up along with the larger tendency toward inclusiveness. Young people who address older people as *you guys* "might even be prompted by the best of intentions—namely, to make their interlocutors feel younger and, therefore, more acceptable," ttaber writes. "In turn, older people who aren't necessarily trying to imitate young people, but who wish to be liked by them, accommodate their young interlocutors by speaking as they speak."

SEX AND THE SINGULAR *GUY*

The magnanimity of *guys*, however, falls off as its *s* does. While the singular *guy* occasionally designates a female as regular (and that's not new: "She is a 'real guy.' You'd like her immensely," Eugene O'Neill wrote in 1927), the singular word is overwhelmingly a guy thing. Within this males-mostly club, *guy* is still quite generous. Slapping a fellow's back with a *guy* is one of the most reassuring things you can say about him. For instance, *a black man* and *a black male* are the very definition of marked (this person is not just a man but a race, and because both phrases are associated in police reports and the news with "criminal," this person is not just a man but a suspect). But *a black man* sheds some marks when he is renamed *a black guy* or *this black guy*. Used by whites as well as by some blacks, *this black guy* can be a friendly or neutral way to refer to a black man whose name you don't know (though it's all too easy to use it to *pass* for friendly or neutral when the speaker is anything but).

You really do want a *guy* watching your back. Such instantly all right and often self-named guys include: *Family Guy* (the animated sitcom), The Art Guys, The Sports Guy, The Tech Guy, The Book Guy, The Comic Book Guy, The Merch Guy, and hundreds more. And despite the malevolent title character in Jim Carrey's *The Cable Guy*, we invariably call a real cable serviceman "the cable guy" in a more or less genial way. Larry the Cable Guy is the bawdy but endearing redneck comedian on *Blue Collar TV*. To be called "a [blank] guy" can plunk a male from any occupation or background right into the heart of affable knucklehead America. (On the other hand, *guy*'s potential for nauseating cuteness became apparent when the kidnappers [and subsequent murderers] of the *Wall Street Journal* reporter Daniel Pearl communicated with news organizations through the e-mail address kidnapperguy@hotmail.com.)

It is *guy*'s assumed moral OKness that got William Safire going on how *bad guy* "lost a little badness. Perhaps," he wrote, "that is because the word *guy*, which used to connote a macho male (from the name of the 17th-century British terrorist Guy Fawkes), is becoming sexless."

Dude, don't blame the dames. It's true that *bad guy* can seem a bit good. But dollars to donuts, *bad guy* lost its badness because of the regularizing effect of *guy* (not to mention that we don't always know who the bad guys are anymore), not because of *guy*'s occasional inclusion of fems.

Anyway, neither *guy* nor actual guys are giving away the farm. Even while *Hey, guys* and *you guys* open up some borders, the singular *guy* is tightening security on other fronts, hoping to gross out the invaders of inclusiveness by leaving up toilet seats, spilling stale beer, and just living large in fartmeister city.

Keeping women out, resisting feminization and the "eternal feminine," is job one for *guy*. It's related to job two: The word guarantees that its bearer has reached an acceptable threshold of masculine regularness—that is, he's probably not gay.

Men's magazines that dare not be mistaken for gay adore

guys. For years, *GQ* had a posse of guy departments: "Guy Tech," "Guy Style," "Guy Food," "The Single Guy," and "The Married Guy." On its Web site, *GQ* pitched itself with the help of the straight man's close companion, "guy stuff": "GQ. It's about fashion. It's about style. It's about journalism. It's about guy stuff." With time (and a new editor), *GQ* lost most *guy*s. But the word performed an invaluable service, especially when paired with the word *style,* as it is for "The Style Guy," *GQ*'s last *guy* standing. *Guy* is so frankly code for *heterosexual* that the author of a book on men's style told me he made sure to include *guy* in the title to signal that the book isn't what you might think.

The first to expose the code to the open air was the flamboyantly straight *Maxim.* "The time has come for all guys to come out of the locker room," the "laddy" mag from England declared in a manifesto called "Guy Pride" for its inaugural U.S. issue. "Don't be ashamed of that fetid jockstrap and those toxic sweat socks. Leave that toilet seat up proudly! The time has come not only to live openly guy, but to embrace the whole guy lifestyle." The manifesto concluded, "Guys: we're here, we leer, we drink beer."

Cargo, the all-products, no-articles men's shopping magazine (based on its Condé Nast sister success story, *Lucky*), goes for a different kind of guy, the famous "metrosexual"—a hetero male who dresses well and might even wear cosmetics. But to get this guy to flip through a magazine that promotes pubic hair waxing, Botox, and compulsive shopping, he must be assured it won't make him look gay. "That's a real anxiety guys have," *Cargo*'s editor, Ariel Foxman, said on the magazine's 2004 launch. Hence *Cargo*'s working-man title and items like "Honey, does this embroidered shirt make me look gay?" (One shirt was deemed "way gay," another "no-way gay.") Semicloseted about its fear that it will be mistaken for gay, *Cargo* still mustn't alienate its potentially large gay market, and so it dabs on a little self-mockery like a male mascara.

The success of *Queer Eye for the Straight Guy* made it OK for straight men to use products once thought to be gay, *if* they did it in a sufficiently dopey way. In fact, *Queer Eye*'s limited friendship between gays and guys reinforces rather than weakens the demarcation between them. Though the title flirts with the image of gay men sexually checking out straight men (which is indeed the theme of some gay porn with *guys* in the title), the show's recurring moral is that the Fab Five won't do a thing without the straight guy's permission—other than fuss over his irrepressible schlubbiness.

THE PRESTIGIOUS SLOB

And irrepressible it is. You might say that as society has become more casual, it's finally catching up to the original ill-dressed guy. Hanged in effigy? Ha! He became an icon of hanging out, bringing us casual Fridays, pants that hang off hip-hop butts, and the right of middle-aged people to wear pajamas on airplanes. To dress "guy" shows, at the least, that you're not an uptight "suit."

And if you *are* slick, elite even, you'd better cover your ass— literally, as in a print ad for the Territory Ahead clothing catalogue. An otherwise neatly tucked-in shirt with one side yanked out is shown under the headline "PART SNOB, Part Slob." The company sells "a somewhat upscale fashionable line of products for men who are not comfortable with the notion of fashion," explains Trevor Pitchford, who writes the catalogue copy. "We do clothing in better fabrications that address the snob, but a lot of it is that elastic waistband stuff, so it fits roomy," for the slob. He says the company's "Guy Stuff" line of washed-down luggage— "Guy Stuff Gear Bag," "Guy Stuff Gym Bag," and so on—"sells like crazy, and that name figures into it."

The populist vibe of guys and the importance of being unfancy, if not also part slob, are central to the career of the NFL commentator John Madden. An "empire unto himself," with "the most popular sports video game ever" as well as endorsement deals with Ace Hardware and Outback Steakhouse, Madden "is a genius masquerading as a meathead," writes Peter de Jonge. Madden is a fine football analyst, but "his far more crucial TV talent is as a populist. . . . Somehow in the course of a football game, Madden lets you know it's O.K. to be fat, even borderline obese, no big deal to be ugly, bearable to be lonely."

"For Madden the word 'guy' is the cornerstone of his world-view and saturated with affection and respect. . . . [H]is ex-players are 'my guys' and when I ask him if he sees himself as a journalist, he succinctly disabuses me. 'No,' he says. 'I'm just a football guy.' "

Madden *is* a real guy, really believing that games aren't won and lost by "former high-school homecoming kings," as de Jonge writes, "but by the grunt labor of the less conspicuously talented everymen in the middle."

Grunt labor is also the source of the toughness of regular-guy talk. That is, a lot of *guy*'s ismo goes back to the concept of covert prestige.

Mentioned earlier in the context of how white people use black speech to sound cool, covert prestige also applies to how middle and upper classes use worker speech to sound tough. "Working-class speech," the linguist Peter Trudgill wrote, ". . . seems to have connotations of or association with masculinity." The equation, he found, is working-class = tough = masculine. And the Norwich, England, men in Trudgill's study were "at a subconscious level" so "favourably disposed to nonstandard, low-status speech forms . . . that they claim to use these forms or hear themselves as using them *even when they do not do so.*" (Italics Trudgill's.)

But when Randall Terry, the extremist antiabortion pro-tester, attacked Governor Jeb Bush of Florida for not defying the courts to keep the brain-dead Terri Schiavo alive, he definitely did use a regular-guy locution and made explicit its connotations of masculinity. "If Governor Bush wants to be the man that his brother is," Terry said, "he needs to step up to the plate like President Bush did when the United Nations told him not to go into Iraq."

I MEAN, HEY

Today "low-status speech forms" are used not just covertly (below awareness), but overtly (with awareness, à la Terry) and, as they spread across the media, hyperovertly (with irony).

I mean, hey. The most common guy word after *guy* is an

equally short half-grunt of a word: *hey*. An editor of mine once called *hey* the white *yo*, and I think that's right. (*Yo* is not strictly black, I know. Its origins have been variously ascribed to African languages, Spanish, or Italian, and to Philadelphia, Sylvester Stallone's hometown in *Rocky*, which made *yo* so popular. But in the eighties and nineties, *yo* became more associated with hip-hop, from which it has been gaining prestige ever since.)

As a multipurpose interjection, *hey* has been used for hundreds of years "to call attention or to incite, to express interrogation, surprise, or exultation." Considered low-class, even crude by some ("Hay is for horses," children have long been reprimanded), *hey* has had toughness to spare. By the 1970s *hey* had updated its skills and become used "affectedly for emphasis," especially after a *but*, according to the *RHHDAS* (citing "But, hey, that's the kind of guy I am" from 1974, as its earliest *But, hey*).

Hey is now the mot juste when aiming for easy edge, which makes it a stock media character. *Hey* might play it mock rude, sort of thirties tough-guy gangster movie, or *hey* might go for roll-with-the-punches relaxed: "Hey, You Never Know" (New York Lotto's best-known slogan). It's intrusive because the speaker is so cutely crude: "Hey, the dog's red, not the beer" (Red Dog beer). For many people, especially younger generations, *hey* has replaced *hi*. Compared to *hey*, *hi* sounds as if it wants commitment.

But *hey*'s most important duty is to help anyone be a momentary populist. This hardy little trowel of a word breaks up sentences to level the conversational playing field: Wedge in a *hey* and hedge against sounding elite. Hughes Norton, Tiger Woods's former agent, explained why his client at the time would not postpone his vacation by one day in order to honor Jackie Robinson at Shea Stadium at President Clinton's request, saying, "We talked about the pros and cons, hey, this will be perceived as snubbing the President, when the President calls most people drop everything, blah, blah, blah. But this is really a tribute to Tiger Woods's single-mindedness and individuality that he was able to say, 'Hey, this is something that's been scheduled for a long time.' "

It's not surprising that one company selling those trendy

variants of the baseball cap, the mesh trucker hat, gave them the brand name HEY!hats. (Trucker hats haven't quite held on to their hey. First they were blue collar; then around the time Justin Timberlake was photographed wearing one, they acquired a blue-collar chic, which caused the one-step-ahead chic to shun them.)

REAL GUYS LIKE TO SAY "ROADKILL"

Hey's gone Hollywood, but the prestige of other rugged-guy talk is still more co- than overt, as we subconsciously borrow the muscle of real tough guys' speech to make us sound more convincing, including to ourselves.

"Companies have no choice," said an expert who was talking about paying big bucks to ward off the expected (but fizzled) Y2K disaster. "It's either ante up or you're going to become roadkill."

Roadkill rose along with *information superhighway* in the 1990s, when Microsoft and others kept warning that the former would be splattered across the latter if we didn't get hip to this innovation or that. But, funny—*roadkill* still walks the earth, while *info highway* isn't heard of much. Maybe that's because *roadkill* has a real as well as a metaphorical meaning. The shock jock Todd Clem, aka Bubba the Love Sponge, for instance, beat animal cruelty charges for castrating and killing a boar for a promotional "roadkill barbecue." (That's not why Bubba later became roadkill himself; in the post–Janet Jackson frenzy of propriety, Clear Channel fired him for raunchy, "inappropriate" language.) Full of actual blood and guts, *roadkill* says all you need to know about the tough guy in each of us: You drive, you kill, you drive on. That's the way of the road.

Roadkill is also an automatic hee-haw about the dumbness of animals who even *think* about crossing the road. Meanwhile, the word gives humans a refreshing whiff of the woods. People love to say *roadkill*, makes 'em feel like hunters. Laugh at me, but I even feel a little tough every time I look at the folder I labeled "Roadkill."

At this more macho end of the guy-talk spectrum, there's an affinity for phrases that seem to face reality with a swagger:

Going south. For anything (prices, health, popularity) that decreases, as in "The economy is going south." While *going north* hasn't gone far, *going south* has gone north because it evokes a guy in a pickup really going South, where real men dwell and where folks know how to talk real. "Put some South in your mouth" usually refers to food, but it might as well be about talkin' regular guy.

Pile on. An unfair thing to do, as in "Piling On Rush," the title of Larry the Cable Guy's defense of Rush Limbaugh. The negative command, *Don't pile on,* is related to the less vivid but quite guy *Get off my case* and *Don't give me a hard time.*

Big time. As a noun, *big time* is small pop: "[Julia] Roberts Comes Back to the Big Time with 'Smile' " (Fox News.com headline). As an adjective, it's bigger: "To those who know, [Pete] Rose remains a big-time loser" (*International Herald Tribune* headline). As an adverb, biggest: "But the Drudge smear, so far, has pretty much bombed big-time" *(New York Press).* Of course, the adjectival and adverbial forms got a major boost when then presidential candidate George W. Bush called the *New York Times* reporter Adam Clymer a "major league asshole" and Dick Cheney responded, "Yeah, big-time." By intentionally repeating *big-time* in public, Cheney later turned the embarrassment into an applause line.

Zip and **nada.** Though *big time*'s opposite in size, these words are tough little numbers, telling us, "Hold on! Sit down! This is how excruciatingly nonexistent or unlikely something is." Often used in threesomes with *zilch, nothing, zero,* and/or *squat,* they crush expectations into dust. "Zip. Zilch. Zero. That's carbs we're talking. Because Sugar Free JELL-O Gelatin has none" (2004 TV commercial). "Zip. Nada. Nothing. That's how much down payment you may need to buy that dream house" (on-hold phone recording for Countrywide Mortgages). A Google search shows *zip* slightly outnumbering *nada* as the leader of the trios of nothingness. But the Spanish-coolio *nada* is definitely the star, inspiring other foreign words—*nyet, niente*—to occasionally enter this country's language.

I owe you/You owe me; payback/payback time; no daylight between A and B; ass on the line. Each in its own way draws a line in the sand to emphasize the finality of some flat-out reality.

In a heartbeat. A *heartbeat* shows the tenderness behind the toughness and a desire or conviction so strong that only a fraction of a second is required to act.

Walk the walk. The top tough talker, this phrase promises to separate the honest real guys from the loquacious deceivers. Asked why conservatives should vote for him rather than other GOP candidates in a 2000 New Hampshire primary debate, George W. Bush said, " 'Cause unlike other people on this stage who talk the talk, I have walked the walk." Later, as president, Bush was criticized for funding African AIDS programs with significantly less money than he had earlier promised. "I think it's truly unfortunate," Congresswoman Nita Lowey (D-NY) said, "that the President talked the talk but wasn't willing to walk the walk." Of course, absolutely anyone or any company can hawk with this talk. "Janus walks the walk," Janus investors said in a 2004 TV spot.

As the dishonor of just talking the talk indicates, much of the toughness in guy talk derives from its brevity. In classic less-is-more fashion, dropping words from a phrase or syllables from a word increases its brawn: *Ohio plates* instead of *Ohio license plates; a drive-by* instead of *a drive-by shooting; We card* instead of *We check your I.D. card* ("We Card" is the slogan of Philip Morris's campaign to advertise how tough it is on underage cigarette purchasers); *chopper* instead of *helicopter* ("victim caught in the chopper" and "chopper crash" are among the chopped words on local news); even *pop the trunk* instead of *pop open the trunk.* It's as if all of us, advertisers and newscasters, were seen-it-all cops on the beat.

Of course, the jargon that most occupations develop to save time also bonds its members by creating an insiderness—if you talk that dropped-syllable talk, you're a regular guy within the group. (When I say "graf" instead of "paragraph" or "parens" instead of "parentheses," I feel like I'm part of a hard-hitting bunch of *Front Page* reporters.)

Droppin' letters, words, and sylls also exemplifies what Maria

DiBattista calls macho minimalism. "There's an endemic paranoia in American pop culture about words, particularly words that seem polysyllabic, erudite, or somehow not of common parlance," she says. " 'Macho minimalism' describes the way this paranoia plays itself out—we associate the quiet, silent, even tongue-tied type with honesty, and someone who knows how to use words with someone who wants to con us. That's one reason the Western is so notoriously a nonverbal form, full of yups and nopes."

So if real guys don't waste words, they sure as hell don't quibble about pissant shit. Maybe that's why *No problem* is Guy International for a response to a request, for "You're welcome" or for just getting it done ("No root. No weed. No problem"— Roundup herbicide slogan). Immigrant cab drivers and cashiers, eager not to get kicked out of the country, learn this early on. It's always nice to hear *No problem;* it means no confrontation, no argument. Though once in a while when I hear it, I hear the omission of a threat, a suggestion that if things had gone a little differently it just might've been a problem.

An interesting thing about *No problem:* When Españolified to *No problemo* or clipped to *No prob,* it goes from guy to guyismo—as has the Regular Joe himself, at least as he's portrayed in the media.

THE YO OF JOE

To market the unmarked guy, it helps to give him a name, namely *Joe.*

Joe has long been the tag for the ordinary workingman— Average Joe, G.I. Joe, Joe Six-pack, Joe Blow. The appellation of averageness used to be *John* ("I never was however much of John Bull. I was John Yankee and such I shall live and die"—John Adams, 1778), and of course we still have *John Doe,* a prostitute's *john,* and *john* as a toilet (a function *joe* once fulfilled, too). But for unknown reasons, *Joe*'s presumed clean-slate plainness overtook *John*'s, leaving *Joe* to personify the most typical version of whatever identity or quality followed: Joe Citizen, Joe Lunchpail,

Joe College, Joe Broke, Joe Schmo, or Joe Public (the guy that George Bush said wouldn't understand the CIA's case for WMD). As a first name, *Joe* isn't as common as it once was, but that faint outdatedness only makes it riper for postmodern picking. Even Joe Lieberman tried to ride the trend, telling crowds that his presidential campaign in 2004 had "Joe-mentum" (though it went Joe-where).

You could say the *Joe* revival began with Joe Camel, the retro coolster dromedary who sold so many Camel cigarettes. The testicular-looking cartoon character was so popular with children, in fact, that by 1997 the FTC had to kill him. Starting in 2003, however, not one, not two, but three unreality TV shows were named in his honor: NBC's *Average Joe* (fat and/or unhandsome guys vie to win the heart of a "beauty," not just against one another but against a surprise contingent of "hunks," one of whom an Average Joe actually refers to as "Joe Smooth"); Spike TV's *The Joe Schmo Show* (a vote-'em-out-of-the-house series in which everyone but "Joe" is an actor in on the joke); and the show that launched Joe TV, Fox's *Joe Millionaire* (a Joe Six-pack fakes being filthy rich to get gold diggers to cat-fight over him).

The joke of *Joe* and the prestige of the slob were mixed together and flavored with an homage to other rockin'-guy marketing in a 2004 spot for Ragu Rich & Meaty sauce. Joe Frazier, Joe Piscopo, and Joe Theismann hang out in bathrobes and jerseys in a wreck of a living room, bouncing out a sound poem in the rhythm of Budweiser's *Whassup?!* ads: "Hey, Joe." "Yeah, Joe?" "Have you seen Joe?" "No." "Cup of Joe?" "Thanks, bro." "Joe?" "Hello!" "Joe!" "Joe!" "Joe!" "Yo!" "Yo!" "Yo!" The doorbell rings and a now-slick Joe Millionaire (real name: Evan Marriott) points to himself and says, "Joe!" Frazier replies, "I don't *think* so," and slams the door. See, dapper Evan is not a *sloppy* Joe— which is, the voiceover says, "just one of the many recipes you can make with Ragu Rich & Meaty." (Ragu walks the walk to show that there's no daylight between it and regular guys: The year before, it had John Madden promoting "All-Madden Ragu Tailgate Recipes.")

LOVE THAT BOBSTER

If the name for the working-class regular guy is Joe, the name for the middle-class, not so sloppy regular guy is Bob. *Bob* covers nice, pleasant, nerdy, OK, appropriate, good neighbor, boring, middle of the road. Bob is that famous nondescript guy; he earns his unmarkedness just by being bland. In this, Bob evokes his ancestor, the 1950s Organization Man.

But (to use advertising's pop term for social change) this is not your father's Bob. The Organization Man wore a pencil behind his ear; today's Bob wears a sprig of irony, placed there by a pretty publicist he met at the one media party he ever attended. Willingly or not, this nice square has come to be an Everyguy marketing device. As such, Bob's original contributions to regular guy talk amount to zip; rather he *is* a word, a campy commercial and artistic symbol for "the rest of us."

Bob and the rest of us, however, are frustrated. We believe we're more than average. We're more like Bob Parr, the insurance company paper-pusher who's forced to pretend to be on par—until he busts out and turns into his amazing former superhero self, Mr. Incredible. The animated hit movie *The Incredibles* argues that society's insistence that "everyone is special" is a crock, because, as Bob's son Dash says, "When everyone is special, no one is." And yet Bob Parr, the name and the notion, is not so special, either: He got where he did only by standing on the shoulders of dozens of media Bobs before him.

Bob Parr's forebears weren't superheroes, but most rose above averageness one way or another, often with the aid of a retail product. Bob made his big commercial debut in an early 1990s spot for Nissan Sentra: A guy drives through traffic like a king, with signs reading "Bob's Expressway," "Yield to Bob," and "No Parking Except for Bob." In 1997, a commercial for Pentax cameras centered on Bob Dole and other Bobs at a "Bobfest." Microsoft once named some software Bob. "Bob, pig farmer" turned up in a Super Bowl ad for Breathe Right nose strips. Despite the snoring, girls want him: "I found my Bob through *The New York Times*," read a 2001 ad for the paper's personals. An infant named Baby Bob was created in the late nineties to promote the now-defunct Web site Freeinternet.com, and he was reborn in 2005 as the "spokesbaby" for the fast-food franchise chain Quiznos.

Bob has also made a name for himself in entertainment and the arts. There is Bob performance art (by the nerd-hipster comic duo known as Premium Bob), Bob theater *(See Bob Run),* and Bob TV. Between ad campaigns, in 2002, Baby Bob briefly had his own, eponymous sitcom on CBS; *God, the Devil and Bob,* a 2000 NBC animated series, was pushed off the air by religious groups and low ratings; the short-lived 1998 ABC series *Maximum Bob* was based on the Elmore Leonard novel of that name; and the animated kids' show *Bob the Builder* on PBS joined us from England. And those Bobs descended from such attitudinal ancestors as the a cappella group the Bobs, Letterman's dog Bob, and the Church of the SubGenius icon, J. R. "Bob" Dobbs.

Bob is clearly not as populist as *Joe* (unless you squeeze 'em together as *Joe Bob*), but *Bob* is more pop, arguably the most pop name ever. Like much pop entertainment, *Bob* is about low-expectation, nonthreatening satisfactions. Compared with the working-class Joe, or every Tom, Dick, and Harry, who have a somewhat carnal presence (they have heavier *hey*), Bob is safe, more sexually and politically neutered. His are the politics of no politics, which can work for the right: *Bob Roberts* is the Tim Robbins movie about a folksinging, greed-is-good "populist" running for the Senate. Even better, BOB doubles as a childlike play word: five friendly circles, bobbing but made topple-proof by their boring symmetry, spelled backward or forward—it's all the same!

As we can be if we buy these branded names. I mean no offense to the real Bobs out there, but how do you like your soul's slipcover being used like this?

On the other hand, if you *want* to enter the poposphere (and your name's not Bob), stir in *-ster.* Ever since *Saturday Night Live* gave the suffix a showbiz push, *-ster* has been turning people and things into more approachable, Boblike entities, about as threatening as hamsters: "Third Reich Flickster Resurfaces" (a CNN headline on the hundredth birthday of Leni Riefenstahl). *-Ster* allows anyone to "reinvent" himself with a third-person bobblehead identity. "The Colbster is still alive. I love you" (Colby to his mother on *Survivor II,* when the cast was allowed to e-mail folks back home).

Joe and *Bob* are retro fantasies designed to get us to tune in, maybe buy in. But *dude* comes from real guys saying *dude,* and only later did marketing slither in and spread the word. In this, *dude* is more like *guy.* The two, in fact, are near synonyms, separated chiefly by a scrim of irony.

Probably derived from *duds* for clothes, *dude* early on meant an "over-refined or effete man or boy who is pretentiously concerned with his clothes, grooming, manners, etc.: dandy," as the *RHHDAS* says. Out West, a dude was a city slicker, a guest at a "dude ranch." " 'Don't send me any more [drawings of] women or any more dudes,' grumbled the young Frederic Remington at school in 1877, preparing for his career as a Western artist. 'Send me Indians, cowboys, villains or toughs,' " Barnhart and Metcalf write in *America in So Many Words.*

But *dude* eventually hopped on *guy's* path, coming to also mean simply a male, a fellow. The slang waxed and waned until black dudes in the sixties revived it (to mean *man* or *cat*), and from there *dude* served surfers, from whom the word acquired a goofy if not also stoned glitz.

So *guy* and *dude* both began as marked men, though from different sides of the fashion aisle: *guy,* the poorly dressed fool; *dude,* a fool for dressing too well. (Today dudes are likely to be portrayed as the bigger slobs, as is "The Dude," played by Jeff Bridges, in *The Big Lebowski.*)

Being the fool, though, helped *guy* and *dude* survive. The fool's self-deprecating humor evokes a likable chap, good company—at bottom, an unmarked male. *Dude* in Michael Moore's best-selling book *Dude, Where's My Country?* immediately signals a laid-back attitude that precludes the liberal "shrillness" the right so loves to attack. And like *guy, dude* has spawned a flurry of suddenly more comical occupations and preoccupations (the Public Defender Dude, the Deranged Video Dude, A Jewish Dude with Conservative Attitude—online guys all), and has amassed so much likability that it can loan itself out, no prob: *Hey, dudes* and *dude* alone often apply to women. Drew Barrymore's co-star in *Fever Pitch,* Jimmy Fallon, said of Drew and her beau, the drummer Fabrizio Moretti, "Neither has any pretension about them. They're two cool dudes who totally enjoy each other."

Dude's and *guy*'s target markets overlap, but differ at the edges in age and attitude. *Guy* is hardworking, mainstream pop; *dude* is flashy, media-darling pop, more a youth specialty (tickling mainstream media to no end), like the once cultish "Dude, You're Gettin' a Dell" ad slogan or the Ashton Kutcher movie *Dude, Where's My Car?*

Dude 'tude allows *dude* to work gigs that *guy* doesn't. Like *Oh, man!* or *Oh, boy!, Duuuude!* is an exclamation based on a word for a male. This comes, as Ron Rosenbaum points out in an essay on *dude,* from "Whoa, dude!"—"where the awestruck 'whoa' is encompassed within the elongated 'Duuuude!' "

As for irony, the stereotypical guy is without it, while the stereotypical dude *is* it. To address someone as *dude,* Rosenbaum writes, is "a sign of ironic respect for that person's ironic sensibility."

"WHAAAAT?" HE SAID

The jackass (aka a lout, a boor, or a jerk, and proud of it) is generally less likable than the guy or the dude. But presented as a regular guy gone X-treme, especially in the gross-out department, he's eminently marketable. Celebrated jackasses include Howard Stern, John Belushi, the late-night talk-show host Jimmy Kimmel and his former *Man Show* co-host Adam Carolla, most pro wrestlers, and, of course, the guys in the MTV *Jackass* series and 2002 movie, both of which jacked up the word *jackass.* Two of those guys went on to star in *Wildboyz,* an MTV nature show in which wild animals clawed them, pissed on them, and bit their butts.

But that's not where the toughness of the jackass lies. Rather he has developed a tough inner hide. By his unspoken threat that he could do or say something outrageous at any moment, the jackass blunts the bites of criticism, leaving him relatively unscathed, and unmarked.

He is not, however, without redeeming social value. At his best, as in Stern's more illuminating moments, the jackass can humorously reveal what he'd insist is the truth—that we're all greedy, selfish pigs, energized only by blind comfort and instant gratification.

The jackass message can really rock with Joe Six-packs, teased by an abundance of commercial delights. "If you don't have a lot of money, you're not a player," Susan Faludi, the author of *Stiffed: The Betrayal of the American Man,* has said. "That's what the culture has taught young men. It's hard to feel like a grownup man. Maybe there is comfort in believing that it's O.K. to be a boorish kid with a baseball cap turned backwards forever."

All of us, women and men, jerks and gentlepersons, can on occasion find comfort in that. And so any of us might indulge in the language of the jackass. Next to the tough guy, the jackass is a nonstop chatterbox. But I can think of only two verbal hallmarks of the jackass, both arising from when he tries to weasel out of responsibility.

When reminded of something he'd rather not deal with, the pop jackass will probably say, "Whaaaat?" If you don't feel the emotion behind it, this word can be difficult to pronounce. Beyond drawing out the *a*'s, the speaker should hit a note of impatience at the mere suggestion that he did anything wrong. *Whaaaat?* says that the guy feels vaguely guilty but the irresistible charm of his semi-admission will clear him handily.

Whaaaat?'s are probably as old as guilt, but they began to really wad up TV and movies circa 2000. In the 2001 movie *Shrek,* the animated ogre represents most regular-guy stereotypes: tough, slob, jackass (wipes his butt with the pages of a fairytale book), and, underneath it all, lovable. All of which is contained in his perfectly pitched *Whaaaat?* The word so suggests the type that a trailer for *Shrek 2,* the top-grossing movie of

2004, turned on the wolf from "Little Red Riding Hood" saying, "Whaaaat?" as the camera spots him disguised as Granny. (I quote Shrek and crew a lot because, although he's a cartoon and the movies are shrines to programmatic cool, I'm attracted to the guy.)

When a jackass does get caught, he's equipped with a phrase that's the pop language equivalent of an insanity plea: he "behaved badly." *Men Behaving Badly* was a late-nineties NBC sitcom (based on a British sitcom and novel by the same name). The American version was quickly canceled, but *men behaving badly* lives on as a headline ("men" sometimes replaced by "women," "animals," or "Microsoft") and as an organizing concept for naughty but forgivable activity. When some sixteen women accused him of groping them, Arnold Schwarzenegger, then running for governor of California, said, "Yes, I have behaved badly sometimes." With so many of us associating *behaving badly* with light comedy—and with Arnold's older pop phrases being recycled for the campaign ("Hasta la vista, Gray Davis!")—his behavior sounded less ominous than simply finely tuned to the larger, brighter pop life.

THE POLITICS OF PIZZA

Because guys are so unmarked, marketers and politicians want them—their money, their votes, and rub-off from their preapproved personalities. The problem for pols, however, is that guys don't necessarily vote one way (a white male drift toward the GOP not quite withstanding) or vote at all. Anyway, this guy is likable *because* he's apolitical. You could even say he's politically apolitical, by which I mean he has an active antipathy to abstract thinking. His prevailing ideology is Don't have one.

Call it the swing vote, the undecided vote, the soccer mom, security mom, or NASCAR dad vote. I prefer to call it the pizza vote, which represents a broader demographic classification, one that includes the regular guy in each of us. Ordering, eating, and enjoying pizza—even just saying the word—is our slice of populist life.

The politics of pizza suggest no particular policies whatsoever. But to establish oneself as a pizza kind of guy is nevertheless the gut goal of politics—national, local, or office.

In the nineties, after fractious negotiations over a new union contract were finally resolved at *The Village Voice,* a management guy was eager to dispel any lingering ill will from the staff. So did he give a speech or engage in tête-à-têtes? Come on—he ordered pizza for everyone! And that pretty much quelled the militant crowd. Pizza-resolved conflict is common, I know. But that a few pies mollified even us supposedly crazy lefty *Voice* types indicates that pizza transcends all political categories, yet serves each of them.

When we decide to take action, we order pizza—in our sedentary consumer lives, ordering pizza *is* walking the walk.

When we want to feel like a mensch, we mention pizza. *Pizza,* like *hey* and *guys,* is a great leveler.

When we want to ward off suspicion or seem like we're busting through the BS, we broadcast our hearty appetite for this, the food of the guys.

A few years before he was executed for blowing up the Oklahoma City federal office building, prisoner Timothy McVeigh portrayed himself as a regular guy—"I'm just like anyone else," he told *Time* magazine. And his complaints about the FBI could be settled in regular-guy fashion. "If I could meet with FBI Director Louis Freeh," McVeigh said, "I would tell him we better order out pizza because it's going to be a lengthy meeting."

Bill Gates began publishing a journal in *Slate,* the Web magazine he then owned, when Microsoft came under investigation. In the "faux populism" of his "insistently just-folks diary," as Frank Rich put it, the richest man in America wrote "of eating hamburgers and pizza, of spurning stretch limos for cabs, of struggling to get into a tux."

The more you desire pizza, no matter its condition, the more guy and less elite you are. That explains *Cold Pizza,* a weekday-morning sports-talk-and-ribbing-around show that debuted in 2003 on ESPN2, which was desperate to shore up its ratings.

Also launched that year was Cartoon Network's *Teen Titans,* a DC Comics show about teenage superheroes. Their motto:

"Truth, Justice, and Pizza." It equates (quite accurately) something we love to consume with "the American way" that it replaces.

WHO'S ON TOP(PINGS)?

Pizza may be our most easygoing food, but the punishment for not eating it or its culinary buddies—or not eating them the right way—is severe. On the primary campaign trail in Philadelphia, John Kerry was caught asking for Swiss cheese on a Philadelphia cheesesteak. This was no small sin to Rush Limbaugh, who excoriated "the French-looking John Kerry" and "reputed Vietnam veteran" for not going with the standard Cheez Whiz.

"You might ask, 'Rush, what's the big deal?' " Limbaugh's Web site read. "The big deal is these are the guys who tell you that they are at one with you, that they understand the plight of the middle class, feel your pain, etc. In truth, they're far removed from you—and they don't want to be anywhere near common folk. They think they're better than all the people in 'flyover country.' You can tell that this cheesesteak looks very foreign to Kerry." (Kerry later struck back by saying, "There are two ways for you to have lower prescription drug costs. One is you could hire Rush Limbaugh's housekeeper, or you could elect me president of the United States.")

It doesn't matter that Limbaugh, a multimillionaire, once boasted that his favorite Bordeaux is Château Haut-Brion '61, at about $2,000 a bottle, even as he slammed Kerry for the uncommon-folk infraction of getting $75 haircuts. With such day-in, day-out demagoguery, Limbaugh has done more than any one person to establish Republicans (the party of Big Business) as populist and unmarked, and to establish Democrats (once the party of the working guy) as elitists and marked—as deviations from the standard and the good, as . . . deviants.

But, the hope goes, liberals can erase their marks with a slice. Bill Clinton, who never would have made Kerry's faux pas, knew that certain foods *are* pop language, a true lingua franca that can help us digest the world, including economic policy. At a White House correspondents' dinner during the 1996 presidential campaign, Clinton asked, "Suppose . . . you go home tonight and you decide to order pizza. Who do you trust to select the toppings? Bob Dole or Bill Clinton?" (*Time* magazine followed up, and it was Clinton 54 percent, Dole 26.)

TALKIN' NORMAL

By and large, though, liberals "have a namby-pamby way of saying things," as Moore wrote in *Dude, Where's My Country?* "It's like we invented our own language—and it annoys the hell out of anyone we're trying to get to listen to us. Knock off the PC mumbo jumbo, quit trying to be so sensitive and just say what is on your mind. Less wimp and more OOMPH!"

Of course, let-it-rip populism was once the province of progressives and liberals. The populist urge, often based on resentment of those in power, has historically been harnessed by the right, left, and center. In 2004, Democrats, largely inspired by Howard Dean, tried to reclaim it, to little avail. Without going into the actual, twisted politics of contemporary populism (which often fills the pockets of the powerful in the guise of empowering the little guy, as Thomas Frank explains so well in *What's the Matter with Kansas?*), it is fair to say that in recent decades populist *language* has been more a dog of the right. This is for two reasons.

First, by emphasizing action, populist pop language appeals to right-wing sentiments. "Talk is cheap, actions speak louder than words, poetry is for old maid schoolmarms, and real men (action heroes, strong, silent hunks like Clint Eastwood and Sylvester Stallone) . . . 'never settle with words what can be accomplished with a flamethrower,' " John Haiman writes in his book *Talk Is Cheap*. That conservatives have been associated with vivid "action talk" (the millions of exceptions notwithstanding) and liberals with plodding "reason talk" (eloquent exceptions like Al Sharpton notwithstanding) has often been attributed to the two sides' fundamentally different thought processes. People who lean right (George W. Bush) tend to see things in terms of black and white, right and wrong, good and evil, while people who lean left (John Kerry) see grays, nuances, complexities—all diluters of oomph. Now, this absolutism-versus-relativism duality itself might be a black-and-white dichotomy, and I'm ambivalent about possibly seeming to endorse it, but it works for me, more or less.

Second, the right gets more mileage from populist pop language because the language is popular. This isn't a mere tautology. When something is popular, the implication is that power and authority are on its side—as you had better be, too, unless you want to be ignored or trampled. Right-wing populism, as Frank writes, "is today triumphant across the scene; politicians speak its language, as do newspaper columnists, television pundits and a cast of thousands of corporate spokesmen, Wall Street brokerages, advertising pitchmen, business journalists and even the Hollywood stars that the right loves to hate." This language would not have beaten competitors in the marketplace of ideas (as the free-market right likes to say) if it didn't have the sense of a threatening crowd behind it. Populist pop language is not all stick, however. The carrot offered its users is acceptance into the fold, where it is comfortable, familiar, and, above all, safe. That is, populist pop offers the reassurances of traditional Republican conservatism.

Populist talk needn't involve actual pop phrases, though they help. The key is the ability to use words forcefully, and to create, if necessary, a gaping hole between Us and Them, which neatly echoes black-or-white absolutes. A phrase like "I don't know about you, but here we do things like . . ." isn't mass media pop, but it can stop you cold. Or take the mixed plain and pop words of a Mississippi man who was asked by a National Public Radio reporter why he supported the former lobbyist and Republican National Committee chairman Haley Barbour for governor (Barbour won): "If you lived here you wouldn't ask that question. . . . Haley is a homeboy," this presumably white man said. (*Homeboy* originated as black English, according to the *RHHDAS*. It went on to be used by black and white Southerners, and later rose to pop status via hip-hop.) "How do you expect us to feel about him?"

Whew. Whatever the reason liberals don't talk that way, they intermittently try to. A year before the last presidential election, *The New York Times* reported that House Democratic leaders "have spent the past several months conducting focus groups and polls in an effort to develop a national message—a turn of phrase that will appeal to the swing voters who are crucial to the party's prospects in 2004."

Until that pizza-perfect phrase is found, if you can't always talk regular, at least say *regular* a lot, as John Edwards did during the Democratic primaries, referring often to "regular people" and pointing out his history as one. (A possible real populist, Edwards also went for the harder stuff. "We ought to cut these lobbyists off at the knees," he said regularly in his primary stump speeches.) *Regular* is a smarter choice than *average* or *ordinary*, which no one wants to be anymore, and certainly wiser than the still vaguely pinko *working people*.

And *normal*? The right lays claim to that golden egg. Most famously, in a piece defending Clarence Thomas's supporters and attacking Anita Hill's, the former Reagan and Bush I speech-writer Peggy Noonan established not only who is normal but also that normal people use action, not words. There is, she wrote, "a total perceptual split between the chattering classes . . . and normal humans . . . , between clever people who talk loudly in restaurants and those who seat them." For example, J. C. Alvarez, the regular-guy gal who testified for Thomas, was part of the "real, as opposed to the abstract, America." If Alvarez was ever sexually harassed by her boss, Noonan decided, Alvarez "would kick him in the gajoobies and haul him straight to court."

Yeah, right, like that's going to happen. When was the last time a sexually harassed woman got movielike justice by going for the "gajoobies"? (And, hey—what kind of word is *that*? I don't know about you, but around here we just don't talk that way.)

CHAPTER 7

The Community of Commitment-Centered Words

J ust when it looks like we've talked ourselves into a solipsistic stupor of wicked-cool comebacks and beer-gut guy talk, a bunch of civic-hero words comes riding to the rescue. These words seem to put the focus back on the commonweal, engaging us as involved citizens in big, earnest, inspirational tones: *Community! Empowerment! Giving back!*

This is regular-guy talk in reverse: abstract, larger than oneself, and seemingly politically and socially committed. As a banner strung across a street in downtrodden Orange, New Jersey, read: ORANGE NIGHT OUT AGAINST CRIME: LET'S TAKE A PROACTIVE APPROACH FOR COMMUNITY WELLNESS. You might not want to have a beer with words like these, but they conduct a larger pop chorus than you might imagine.

I hope it's appropriate to be transparent here: I had some issues naming this group of words. Should I call them goo-goo (good government) pop, because they strive to summon our higher, public-minded selves? Or maybe halo pop, because they lend an aura of virtue to whatever they touch? Both are accurate, but neither is truly inclusive. My philosophy is to choose a name that is accountable, that I'm comfortable with, and that, above all, reflects what we're talking about when we talk about the conversation we're having with ourselves.

A DIVERSE COMMUNITY OF WORDS

I hear you: This language is usually called politically correct. Depending on subject matter and degree of tin ear, it might also be called doublespeak, crunchy granola talk, or bureaucratese; euphemistic or deadening. Sometimes it's still called psycho-babble, and its psychotherapeutic origins are evident in *dysfunction, closure, appropriate behavior, sharing, having issues, in denial, feeling your pain*.

But for the most part, the language in this chapter is not strictly psychobabble. It's broader than that; drawing from an array of social sciences (and the studies and committees shaping them), it's more a sociobabble. With roots also in the business world (we *negotiate* deals and reality; we follow *agendas* for meetings and schemes), literary criticism *(subtext, the narrative)*, and, of course, government and politics *(transparency, accountability, no child left behind)*, this is a diverse community of words, mixing jargon and tone from various fields into a smooth parlance to contain the mess of social problems.

And to imply solutions: Many of these words have become chants of magical thinking. They might not bring us any closer to solutions, but that's not the point. We speak them in order to *feel* like we're improving things. Remove the word *psychological*, and R. D. Rosen's description of psychobabble, from his 1977 book of that name, applies to most sociobabble: "It's an idiom that reduces psychological insight to a collection of standardized observations, that provides a frozen lexicon to deal with an infinite variety of problems."

Nor is this language strictly PC as we usually think of the term. Right-wingers jerk their knees to it almost as much as the supposedly Birkenstock left does, and often more effectively. "One of these days there's got to be closure," Caton Dawson, the chairman of South Carolina's Republican Party, said of Trent Lott's many apologies for praising Senator Strom Thurmond. "It's a big national conversation," the conservative commentator Maggie Gallagher said of gay marriage. "Thank you for sharing that with us," George W. Bush, visiting a faith-based homeless shelter, said to an addict who described how he'd found recovery through Jesus.

As with many suffix-friendly phrases, *faith-based*, the label for Bush's preferred approach to help the needy, is quietly PC-driven. Like the name of the popular Web site "raptureready. com," *faith-based* is an expedient odd-coupling of the godly and the bureaucratic—the first element being solidly fundamentalist; the second, a secular-humanist favoid. But perhaps nothing better demonstrates how the political right retools crunchy PC pop for its own purposes than this pair of *community-* and *based*-based phrases: *reality-based community* and *faith-based community*. The latter has been around for quite a while, but *reality-based*, with or without *community*, is a bold newcomer that the faith-based community has apparently created to act as the Cain to their Abel. Now an ironic T-shirt slogan, *reality-based community* first emerged in 2004, when the journalist Ron Suskind was interviewing a senior adviser to President Bush. The adviser clearly didn't care for Suskind or his ilk. As Suskind wrote in *The New York Times Magazine*:

> The aide said that guys like me were "in what we call the reality-based community," which he defined as people who "believe that solutions emerge from your judicious study of discernible reality." I nodded and murmured something about enlightenment principles and empiricism. He cut me off. "That's not the way the world really works anymore," he continued. "We're an empire now, and when we act, we create our own reality. And while you're studying that reality—judiciously, as you will— we'll act again, creating other new realities, which you can study too, and that's how things will sort out. We're history's actors . . . and you, all of you, will be left to just study what we do."

Yet, curiously, for all their differences, the two bases speak the same PC tongue. Like all pop language, PC pop is used by people of any persuasion as long as it helps them persuade. When the Democratic New Jersey governor Jim McGreevey came out as gay, he polished the edge off the word by announcing he was "a gay American," a focus-grouped phrase that shifts the emphasis from sexuality to civil rights. Civil rights–centered expressions are also popular with conservatives. The phrase *hate speech,* for instance, made a comeback starting around 2003, not because of a resurgence of antiblack or antigay slurs, but because liberals began to talk bad about Bush. As the linguist Geoffrey Nunberg explained, "Conservatives use 'hate speech' in the way they use words like 'diversity' and 'bias,' in the hope that the moral valence that the terms acquired in the context of civil rights will persist when the words are applied to partisan divisions, even if their meanings are altered in the process."

Left or right, as history's actors or its students, we use this language ʰbecause it works—and so we don't have to. Frank Luntz, the GOP tactician and pollster who used to run voter focus groups on MSNBC (often using technology, he said, "to measure on a second by second basis exactly what words, exactly what phrases [from politicians' speech] the American people like and dislike"), made this clear in a memo, titled "The Language of the 21st Century," that he sent to Republican members of Congress in 1997. On closing the gender gap, for instance, he wrote: "I do not subscribe to the notion that we must change our substance or create a separate women's agenda. Listening to women and adapting a new language and a more friendly style will itself be rewarded if executed effectively and with discipline."

Obviously, neither seventies social workers, nor eighties MBAs, nor twenty-first-century political operatives invented this new language and more friendly style. The word *multicultural,* for instance, has been around at least since 1941, primarily "as an antidote" to nationalism, write Barnhart and Metcalf. For centuries, the military has been firing off euphemisms (and "the nine years of Vietnam refined that practice to an art," as Ken Ringle wrote in *The Washington Post.* "Such terms as 'plausible deniability,' 'collateral damage' and 'friendly fire' entered civilian discourse half a world away from the war"). In a pinch any of us will cover up raw truths with verbal pasties. In apologizing for yanking off Janet Jackson's Super Bowl bustier, Justin Timberlake famously coined the term "wardrobe malfunction."

TAKING PUBLIC WORDS PRIVATE

Regardless of which bureaucracy, ideology, or publicity crisis the babble bubbles up from, the words are out there because someone believes they sell. And when they sell, it's not because the words are sexy. Quite the opposite: These monkish words forswear any desire or selfish motive whatsoever. They seem to stand above the fray of the personal—an effect they achieve by the mechanism of making the public private. Many of these words and phrases once had a social, public meaning, but they're increasingly used to suggest a collective emotion from which an individual, an interest group, or a company can benefit. Using them implies your goals are actually those of a principled, rather altruistic multitude, which you just happen to represent.

One of the best examples of such artificially sweet speech is provided by an artificial sweetener. In 1996, the PR executive Pat Farrell told a Public Relations Society of America conference about how, as a former brand manager for Monsanto's NutraSweet, he altered the brand's image with a few language nips and tucks. "After many years of defending the ingredients using hard scientific facts," the company grew "frustrated by its inability to change the conversation," he said (and I quote from the journal *PR Watch*, which reported on Farrell's speech):

> The company had for years described Nutrasweet as "an artificial sweetener." But artificial, said Farrell, "conjures up cancer, headaches, rat studies, laboratories, dueling scientists, allergies, epilepsy, you name it, none of which are very appetizing."
>
> . . . Armed with this knowledge, Nutrasweet cre-

ated "sweetspeak." Said Farrell, "Words such as 'substitute,' 'artificial,' 'chemical,' 'laboratory,' 'scientist' were removed forever from our lexicon and replaced with words such as 'discovered,' 'choice,' 'variety,' 'unique,' 'different,' 'new taste.' "

Using sweetspeak, Farrell gave an example of how Nutrasweet now responds to the question: How do you know aspartame is safe?

The answer: "Aspartame was *discovered* nearly 30 years ago. Since that time, hundreds of *people in our company* and *elsewhere around the world—people with families like yours and mine*—have *devoted themselves* to making sure *consumers can be confident* of their *choice* when they *choose* the *taste* of Nutrasweet. *People* have looked at *our ingredient* in every which way possible and *we encourage* that because we want *consumers* to be *comfortable* when they *choose* Nutrasweet. That has been our *commitment* for *nearly three decades,* and it will *always* be our *commitment.* You can *feel confident choosing* products that contain *our ingredient,* but if you don't, you have other *choices.*" [Italics are mine.]

My commitment is to state that at times we all choose sweetspeak as our communication choice. But this language isn't always so insidious. At its best, sweetspeak, halo pop, goo-goo pop, PC pop, or sociobabble—*you* choose!—provides expression for the previously unnamed or inadequately named. *Inclusive, hands-on, diversity*—like all pop, they're terrifically handy. *Your inner child,* for all the goofs on it, is irreplaceable. And aren't we better off with *in denial* than with nothing?

At its worse, sweetspeak's excruciatingly thoughtful tone camouflages the seller's intention to get you to stop thinking, to stop truly choosing and just buy the damn thing. In particular, the phrase *freedom of choice,* deregulated from the halls of democracy to the strip shopping centers, now applies chiefly to your freedom to choose Diet Coke or Diet Pepsi (both chockful of aspartame) or the kind of bread you want for a submarine sandwich (recent Blimpie ads bop to the Devo song "Freedom of

Choice," which was once a sardonic rip at just this sort of corporate takeover of civic language).

Often, sweetspeak has a medicinal aftertaste. When I first had a child, I joined a playgroup that was part of the cleverly named organization F.E.M.A.L.E., or Formerly Employed Mothers at Loose Ends. But the national leadership decided the name was "negative," so they came up with Formerly Employed Mothers at the Leading Edge. By 2000, the acronym F.E.M.A.L.E. itself was deemed too militant-sounding (were they thinking of SCUM [Society for Cutting Up Men] in whose name the crazy feminist and sole SCUM member Valerie Solanas shot and wounded Andy Warhol in 1968?). After heated debate, F.E.M.A.L.E. was anointed Mothers & More: The Network for Sequencing Mothers. I kept saying "sequestered mothers." But no: *sequencing* means that once you worked; when you had a kid, you worked less or not at all; and later you might work again. *Sequencing* also allows the careful to avoid saying the sometimes politically touchy "stay-at-home mom."

AN ALPHABETICAL SEQUENCING

In and of themselves, these might be fine words, nice words; but as they've become overused, they've become too nice. They're not simply euphemisms, neutralizing the negative. These words go further: They glorify the banal. A quality of mass illusion permeates them. The rule of thumb is that the rarer a social virtue—community, empowerment, diversity—the more we invoke its name, as if that could summon it into being. Whatever the reality, reciting these words makes us feel a whole lot better about ourselves.

Below are other words and phrases that lend a halo effect to anything they touch.

Acceptable and **appropriate**. *Acceptable* and *appropriate* (sometimes appearing in tandem) are psychobabble that's been to business school, and are used as often to refer to behavior in a loved one as to the terms of a leveraged buyout. The ways to express approval (or disapproval) are gradually narrowing down to these two barbed-wire Miss Manners dolls. "That's not accept-able!" parents shout at their two-year-olds, for whom the words would seem to be an especially lame form of censure. I swore I wouldn't resort to *not acceptable* because it's really just PC for *bad, Don't,* or *Stop.* But I have. Because *acceptable* and its permutations pervade the air, they work. Of course, *acceptable* often makes per-fect sense. If the Israelis and Palestinians reject each other's pro-posals, one would say the proposals are not acceptable to the other party. But *acceptable* and *unacceptable* cover all sorts of situa-tions in which acceptance isn't the salient point. The Metro-politan Museum of Art in New York City had to temporarily close its Egyptian tombs to visitors because the large crowds "put the humidity at unacceptable limits." *Unacceptable,* for all its dip-lomatic restraint, now sounds its own note of opprobrium—something is so beyond the pale that the very idea is offensive to our inner authoritarian. Maybe the humidity was just too high.

Ditto for *appropriate,* but more so. "Always Appropriate" is a company offering "Image and Etiquette consulting for the real world." There is the Consortium for Appropriate Dispute Resolution in Special Education, the National Center for Appro-priate Technology, and on from there to organizations or com-panies for Appropriate Development, Appropriate Transport, Appropriate Rural Roads, and Appropriate Solutions. Some are attempts to expand on the concepts behind *sustainable* and *renewable,* but even in these positive senses you can almost hear *appropriate* gnashing its teeth as it scolds, "There are rules, and rulers with which to measure your adherence to them. Now get in line."

Agenda. I don't quite understand why *agenda* has overtaken near synonyms like *plan, list,* and *program.* Perhaps it is because *agenda* has in it a bit of *agitate* (they share the same Latin root, *agere,* for "to drive, do") and therefore seems a more "proactive" way to get down to business. For whatever reason, *agenda* is the favored corporate and political sweetspeak of the moment. The former commerce secretary Don Evans assured the National Association of Manufacturers, "Your agenda is our agenda." John Edwards told the 2004 Democratic convention, "We can strengthen and lift up your families. Your agenda is our agenda."

But like Edwards's "two Americas," there are two *agenda*s. One lends a halo; the other, a pitchfork. Depending on whose agenda it purportedly is, an agenda can be a good thing or can suggest insidious plots, as it does when right-wingers casually mention "the homosexual agenda." Context is all, even within the same few sentences. "God has graciously granted America—though she doesn't deserve it—a reprieve from the agenda of paganism," Bob Jones III, president of the fundamentalist Bob Jones University, wrote to George W. Bush after his reelection. "Put your agenda on the front burner and let it boil. You owe the liberals nothing. They despise you because they despise your Christ."

Celebrate. We used to celebrate holidays and special occasions. Now, undoubtedly encouraged by Kool & the Gang's 1979 party-hearty standard, "Celebration," we celebrate anything we feel kindly toward or that needs promotion: "Celebrate the Child," "Celebrate Recovery," "Celebrate Canada," "Celebrate Self" (campaigns, companies, and/or Web sites all). The sell in *celebrate* is usually in the forefront: "Evolving artist or fashion plate? We celebrate both" (an ad for *People* magazine under a photo of the newly slicked-up singer Jewel). "Celebrating Your Choices" (the 2004 motto for the Whole Foods Special Diets Series). Or maybe your choice is to "Celebrate Capitalism (tm)" in the Disney town of Celebration, Florida. The goody-goody *celebrate* is related to the Hallmarkean habit of nominees at awards ceremonies and performers everywhere to applaud themselves, which is part, I think, of the self-esteem movement—if you don't sell, uh, celebrate yourself, who will?

Center. I first noticed the power of halo words at a convenience store in the early seventies. Displayed behind the checkout counter was a small cardboard poster stapled with packages of condoms and labeled "Family Planning Center." *Center* is such old and fundamental sociobabble that it would seem to have no pop left. But I maintain that *center* still exerts a force by fulfilling the human needs to find balance and to feel that we're at the center of what's happening, if not also of the universe.

Community center arose in 1915; later came *shopping centers, information centers,* and the most all-encompassing, *lifestyle centers* (aka retirement homes). All sound good and civic for bringing people together. But it was the destruction of town and city centers by suburban sprawl and "big box" stores that created more need to slap a *center* on the replacement architecture. "When Wal-Mart determines that one of its traditional discount stores is unsuitable for an upgrade," writes Bloomberg News columnist Ann Woolner, "the company simply abandons it to build a larger Supercenter nearby."

Center has always had a New Age element about it; in yoga and other body movement classes, instructors advise, "Find your center and move from there." From there it's not a big leap to finding a spiritual center. As *center* got a second wind as *-centered*, it became a bit easier to find God through *God-centered education*, *God-centered marriage*, and *God-centered parenting*. Yet for all the ways that *center* fulfills us, *fulfillment centers* are not places of worship but places from which companies stock and ship orders.

Comfortable. We expect to be comfortable—to live in a comfortable home, to make a comfortable income, to "contribute at whatever level is comfortable for you," as the WNYC public radio fund drive asks. It's so important we stay in our *comfort zone* that, rather than state that we don't like something, or in fact loathe it, we say, "I don't feel comfortable with that." No one will be offended, goes the theory, if you're just obeying little distress signals from your tummy.

Among those who left the CIA during the upheaval spurred by its new chief, Porter Goss, were two undercover officials who directed "spying operations in some of the most important regions of the world and were among a group known as the barons in the highest level of clandestine service," *The New York Times* reported. "A former intelligence official described the two as 'very senior guys' who were stepping down because they did not feel comfortable with new management." It would be bizarre, indeed frightening, if these top-notch, presumably tough spooks quit because they weren't "comfortable." But that is how we, be we spies or writers characterizing them, process an entire range of disagreeable emotions.

It's up for grabs which shaped this euphemism more: the

psychotherapeutic tip to "talk from your feelings" or our consumer sense of entitlement that we should always be without want. Either way, the word's popularity helps others earn comfortable incomes. As the Web site adbanter.com said, "If consumers feel comfortable purchasing online, they will keep coming back online, creating more opportunity for marketers."

Community. Hands down, the leader of the public words gone private is *community*, which can now be defined as two or more individuals who so consecrate themselves. The word *community* has risen roughly in inverse proportion to how far actual communities have fallen; there's so much desire out there for something that modernity hasn't bulldozed that we're only too eager to take this verbal hologram for the real thing.

And so whoever the rounded, glowing word lands upon seems a bit valiant; whatever the endeavor, it is ennobled. Sightings over the years include "the polling community," "the criminal community," "the venture capital community," "the swinger community," "the listening community" (for those who eavesdrop on cell phone conversations), the aforementioned "faith-based" and "reality-based" communities, and, of course, from the nonplace where this kind of thinking is the default drive, "the online community" and "the blogging community." *Community* is a Web site word for "discussion group." But that's nothing. Advertising itself equals community: "It's not an ad, it's a COMMUNITY," declares an online ad for *LA Weekly*'s personals ads.

Globalization, suburbanization, and the Internet have all popularized the idea of nonphysical communities, pushing cup-of-sugar-borrowing, townhall-decision-making neighborhoods to the margins of the definition. But there is a more emotional shift in the meaning of the word as well, away from one describing an indiscriminate mix of people living near each other, for whom proximity fosters mutual concerns and responsibilities, to something more about personal choice and self-realization. "The communities that have some importance to me," an interior designer told *Metropolis* magazine in 1996, "are communities of intellect or spirit. They are the design community, the artistic community, the psychologically aware community, the health-

conscious community, the nonviolent community, the ecologi-
cally sound community."

Soft-leftish identity politics like that have contributed to *community*'s spread, and the word, with its emphasis on collective
over individual values, is indeed the liberal's crowning glory. But
the right also goes for the gold: "You can support The Heritage
Foundation's efforts to strengthen and expand the conservative
community in America. Click here to help." And despite its *common* cousins, *commune* and *communism, community* is unfettered
capitalism's favorite humanizing device. Citizens may have been
transformed into consumers in large part by "the advertising
community" and "the marketing community," but at least they
live in a cozy, caring world with "the banking community," "the
investment community," and "the lobbyist community." ("The
talk of the town in the lobbyist community," Robert Novak once
said on CNN, "is a report that Congressman Billy Tauzin [may
succeed] Jack Valenti as the motion picture industry's chief lobbyist in Washington." Actually, Tauzin went on to a much greater
conflict of interest. The former chair of the House committee
that regulates the pharmaceutical industry, and one of Bush's
main men in pushing through the overhaul of Medicare to
Big Pharma's specifications, Tauzin became the president and
CEO of the pharmaceutical community's top lobbying group.
Novak, of course, went on to out an undercover member of the
intelligence community, while Novak's fellows in the journalism
community took the legal heat for him.)

Throw away any modifiers and *the community* becomes a pro-
toplasmic living entity that we have only to tap for moral guid-
ance. In a *Seinfeld* episode, Elaine worries what people will think
if they discover she dumped a man after he had a stroke: "I'll be
ostracized by the community!" Jerry: "Community? There's a
community? All this time, I've been living in a community. I had
no idea."

The "commercial real estate community" is especially prone
to call upon this higher-power sense of *community*. "Lifestyle
villages," for instance, are retail-cum-residential developments,
usually upscale apartments and condos built atop upscale stores;
the idea is to bring an instant urbanity to the burbs. "Com-

mercial developers," William L. Hamilton wrote in *The New York Times*, "like to call these shopping villages 'communities,' " although the lifestyle village he featured, Santana Row in San Jose, "will not have public parks, day care or senior-citizen centers, schools or community boards. . . . Santana Row will have no church, but there will be an imported 18th-century French chapel, selling flowers."

Yet real communities do exist. After 9/11, and especially in the New York area, the word transcended its publicity, and communities, even "the community," became palpable. And well before 9/11, physically dispersed groups have honorably been called communities—the black community, the Asian-American community, the Jewish community—because history, not just professional or financial interests, gave them more in common than not.

But even when the nomenclature seems worth striving for, don't we often overstate the case? Why not use other words that, depending on context, can actually be more descriptive: *neighborhood, group, movement, association, profession, network, industry, circle, field, constituency, public, enthusiasts*? In fact, why not go for broke and name the entity—investors, artists, lobbyists—without any appendage?

Robert Putnam, whose book *Bowling Alone* examined the decline of civic participation in America, once told me, "The word [community] has become so vague and banal and meaningless, I try to use another term—social capital, which means social networks of connectedness, of reciprocity and trust . . . but as a people, we don't seem to want to give up this word for something we long for—a sense of warm, cuddly connectedness to people with whom we share things in common."

Whether community is vanishing or merely evolving, fear of its loss is what keeps us hosannaing its name. The word's quasireligious overtones may reflect an authentic yearning, but too often we're reaching less for spiritual kin than for self-amplification: We want to see our individual selves turned into a multitude—a thousand others who shop on E-bay or blog all day. We're not alone; our values are validated.

Anyway, who wants to do anything if instead you can say it?

You don't have to attend PTA meetings, do volunteer work, or even vote, because you're already part of "the corporate community," "the gambling community," or "the Fox News community." You've done your duty by pronouncing the word.

Conversation. "One of the animating ideas behind *Fast Company* was a new conversation about business," said a "From the Founders" column in the business magazine *Fast Company.* "As the context of business changes, so must the conversation. . . . In that spirit, we've spent the past few months sponsoring, participating in, and capturing a variety of new conversations from coast to coast."

The centrist Democratic Leadership Council holds an annual "National Conversation" conference. The subtitle on early prototypes of Tina Brown's now defunct magazine, *Talk,* was "The American Conversation." The Gay and Lesbian Alliance Against Defamation (GLAAD) advises older gays and lesbians, "Play into this huge national conversation we're having about civil marriage, same-sex parenting and equality—this conversation isn't going to go away for a long time."

And neither is *conversation,* the reigning halo pop for *talk, debate, discussion, discourse,* or *dialogue* (except when it's a foot-stamping "I'm not going to have that conversation!" as the spoiled Omarosa once said on *The Apprentice*). *Talk's* too informal, *dialogue* and the rest are too high-falutin' to carry the social and political freight. But *conversation* (*co*-based, like *community,* with a *com-* or *con-* prefix that means *with, jointly, together*) is soothingly mutual and pluralistic. And on occasion it still means an everyday conversation.

It's as though the new national *conversation* has been chatting with *what we talk about when we talk about [blank].* This rather contemplative conversation starter was popularized by the Raymond Carver short story that supplied the title of his 1981 collection *What We Talk About When We Talk About Love* (which Amazon.com called "the most well-known short story title of the latter part of the 20th century"). It implies that there's something we're *really* talking about when we ostensibly talk about X. Or it proposes to more precisely define something, as in this message in an online forum: "when YOU say update, what do you mean? what do we talk about when we talk about a Google update?" I've also seen (on Google) the following words at the end of WWTAWWTA: tenure, narrative, family, Barbie, knowledge, wine, money, mentoring, New Media Studies, weather, MIT.

Diversity. *Diversity* was much needed to freshen up and bring nuances to *integration*. But watch out who says it; like *African American, diversity* can provide convenient cover for opponents of the very things it stands for. As James Traub wrote in *The New York Times Magazine*, " 'Diversity' must be a very, very good thing; President Bush used the word, or a variant of it, 10 times in his speech last month announcing that the administration would seek to have the Supreme Court declare the undergraduate admissions policies [using affirmative action] at the University of Michigan unconstitutional." And a note of sarcasm can turn *diversity* into racist code. During the 2000 election, an independent group ran a pro-Republican TV spot in Kansas City, where a school desegregation battle was being fought. The ad featured a white woman talking about removing her son from a public school that had "a bit more diversity than he could handle."

Empowerment. While it may sound like a holdover from the sixties, *empowerment* never lost its groove. At an organized Manhattan sex party in 2003, one man complained about the women, "If you're going to keep making them more empowered, then I become a commodity." In the 1990s, Nike referred to its ads for women's sneakers as an "empowerment" campaign (Nike cooled the empowerment talk when it started to get slammed for depowering third-world women in sweatshops). While *empowerment* loves women and is a natural for politics (it too began on the left and migrated rightward, Nunberg says), the word also fancies spirituality and corporations. At a Burger King retreat, "Dana Frydman, vice president of product marketing for Burger King, was injured [walking over white-hot coals, an exercise 'intended to promote bonding'] but had no regrets about the event she helped organize. 'It made you feel a sense of empowerment and that you can accomplish anything.' " By emphasizing process (a good thing), *em* softens some of *power*'s bully quality, and can make anyone a David against a Goliath.

Giving back. *Charity* and *volunteering* are popular, but *giving back* is pop, because (1) the phrase resounds more with the modern truth that in a transactional society it's all a quid pro quo, and (2) the giver can take back some good PR. (Some companies even spend more money advertising their charitable donations than they actually donate.)

On *The Apprentice,* Donald Trump (a real estate developer who, as Frank Rich wrote, "cares little about who is displaced or whose view is blocked by his slabs of phallic architecture") stood in front of the Wollman ice-skating rink that he helped rebuild for New York City and told his aspiring execs, "It's all about giving back, giving back to the city, and now you have a chance to give back." That is, the contestants got a chance to organize a celebrity charity auction, in order to win more fame and a job with Trump at a $250,000 starting salary.

Today few of us can give to charity without the two-word mention of *why* we're doing so. But *giving back,* invariably *to the community,* is especially useful for companies that roll over communities. "Wal-Mart has been very fortunate in our profits and success, and it's time to give back," a Wal-Mart manager said regarding his store's donation of $500 worth of napkins, cups, and other goods to a Boca Raton, Florida, soup kitchen. Wal-Mart seems to believe that repeating "give back to the community" will lull those fearful that the store will give it *to* the community. In Ontario, Ohio, where Wal-Mart was seeking approval for a supercenter, a company community coordinator not only dangled the giving-back bait but essentially said that the larger the floor plan, the larger the largesse: "One of the biggest things is that every store in the company gets a specific budget to give back to the community, based on store size and sales." (*Give back,* by the way, should not be confused with *givebacks,* like those in health benefits that Southern California supermarket chains eventually got from striking grocery workers in 2004. The chains said they needed to cut costs—largely to compete with the forty new Wal-Marts planned in the region over the next five years.)

Good Corporate Citizen. When companies give back, it's because they want to be seen as *good corporate citizens.* "We recognize that we manufacture and market a product that is addictive and causes serious diseases. . . . But that doesn't mean that we can't be a good corporate citizen," says a Philip Morris Web site. Another company with a checkered past says on its site, "Exxon-Mobil strives to be a good corporate citizen and a good neighbor in the communities where we do business around the world." I find this fascinating: As citizens complete their transformation into *consumers,* the corporations they consume from are taking up the mantle of *citizen.*

I am, faces, and looks. This is what PC pop looks like: "Bill Jones is the face of the old Republican Party," said Toni Casey, one of Jones's opponents in the 2004 GOP primary race to unseat the California Democratic senator Barbara Boxer. "I am the face of the new Republican Party." (The new face lost to the old one, and both lost to Boxer.)

I am the face of, another left-born, right-borrowed construction, evolved out of a need to "put a human face on" the facts and statistics surrounding diseases and social problems; hence, *I am the face of breast cancer* (or AIDS or hunger). The idea is to offer so much specificity, through faces or other representations, that you have to empathize. A similarly worthy goal is behind the phrase *This is what [blank] looks like,* with words like *democracy, justice,* or *an imperialist, colonialist occupation* filling in the blank. (Sometimes the goal is just to make more money, like the line "This is what $1,594,649.21 looks like!" from guide2casino. com.) With *This is what [blank] looks like* we may have a coiner. Gloria Steinem wrote in *New York* magazine: "A reporter said to me, kindly, 'Oh, you don't look 40.' And I said, just off the top of my head, 'This is what 40 looks like—we've been lying for so long, who would know?' "

At times, representation itself disappears, and *I* becomes the thing it was once just the face of. "I Am Ann Taylor" is the line over photos of different supermodels (none named Ann Taylor, who is, by the way, fictitious) in a recent campaign for the clothier. Employees of the accounting firm Arthur Andersen held signs and wore T-shirts reading "I am Arthur Andersen" outside the federal courthouse where a judge ruled that a trial would begin on "a charge that the firm obstructed justice in the Enron investigation." ("I am Arthur Andersen. And you are Arthur Andersen. And everyone here is Arthur Andersen," David Turnley wrote in AlterNet. "And this great mass of throbbing human flesh on spaceship Mother Earth is Arthur Andersen. And, together, we will ride the balance sheets into the sun.")

Issues. When I hear *issues,* I reach for tissues. For in psychobabble, these are not issues in the news (where controversies are often dismissed as "nonissues" by those at the center of the storm), but emotional problems from one's childhood. In halo pop, *issue* has replaced *problem* because it removes *problem*'s negative vibe and because, by implication, the difficulty isn't quite anyone's fault but the issue's fault. *Issue* is on such autopilot that we use it as a synonym for any glitch, no matter how issueless. "A little louder!" someone in the audience shouted to the speaker (a psychologist) in a school auditorium. Realizing that the microphone was too low on its stand, he said, "I think the issue is . . ." Trailing off, he raised the mike.

Lifestyle. Lifestyle, as a word and concept, is the crux of nouvelle identity. We are the people, after all, who needed a stylish new word (and *lifestyle* has *style*) to make our transformation from citizens into consumers sound more enlightened and less narrow than we may suspect it is.

Lifestyle wears a halo because it's the result of *choice, your* choice, like something you pick up at Bed, Bath & Beyond. If you can choose styles of espresso makers or garlic presses, you can choose a style of life.

You can also choose what you want *lifestyle* to mean. The Lifestyle Store is "the most complete gold prospecting and outdoor equipment supplier on the Internet." The Life Style Movement is for "all people of goodwill who aspire to live in a way that reflects the ideals of justice for our Earth." The LifeStyle Channel is for people into food, wine, gardening, leisure, or pets. "Lifestyle villages" are high-end retail/residential real estate developments (see *Community*), while "lifestyle centers" are retirement homes. Just trying to cut carbs can qualify as a lifestyle: Carb Slim Bites, says the package, are "Candy Bites For The Low-Carb Lifestyle!" Not so fast, says the LifeStyle Company, a weight loss and fitness Web site: "While most companies give little more than lip service to the term 'lifestyle' we have defined lifestyle and we are The LifeStyle Company."

It may wear a halo, but *lifestyle*'s no angel. *The lifestyle* is also code for being heavily into a particular sex scene. One woman who goes to those empowering sex parties mentioned above "counts herself a full-fledged member of what insiders refer to simply as 'the lifestyle.' " "Generally speaking," says FetishAnalyst.com, "Lifestyle BDSM [bondage, domination, sadism, masochism] people are more healthy emotionally than non-Lifestyle people who are trying to achieve the same agenda." However, others resent applying *lifestyle* to their sexuality. "It really just bothers me if gays and lesbians put down our life by calling it a 'lifestyle,' " the blogger Redwaterlily sensibly notes. "A lifestyle you can change, but I can't change who I am. And I don't want to either." Hence, a bumper sticker from Lesbian Worlds: "Because it's a life, not a lifestyle."

Long before *the lifestyle,* the terms *the life* and *in the life* were used to refer to homosexuality, prostitution, drug addiction, and the criminal underworld. The more marketing-friendly *lifestyle* goes back to the use by the German sociologist Georg Simmel of *Lebensstiles* in his 1900 study of money, *Philosophie des Geldes.* *Lifestyle* was already big pop in the eighties, when Robin Leach's *Lifestyles of the Rich and Famous* both cemented the word's association with affluent consumption and helped it survive the ridicule phase that most long-lived pop inevitably encounters. (If *lifestyle* were a major joke, we never would have seen the late-nineties men's magazine called *Icon Thoughtstyle;* on the other hand, the publication died.)

What *lifestyle* may have lost over the years in rich and famous pop, it has gained in mainstream breadth ("Community von Body-Lifestyle!" reads an otherwise German-language Web site), to the extent that we can't think without it. On CNN's *TalkBack Live* a while back, a man said he disagreed with the anti-abortion argument because it would "force a lifestyle" on women. When used outside the context of consumption, *lifestyle* sounds odd, a smooth flat thing, with none of life's texture or dimensions. And, of course, it completely cuts death out of the picture.

But then *lifestyle*'s job, much like compulsive shopping's, is to build an attractive wall between you and death, to distract you with endless choices of accessories, appliances, and amenities. So even if you fit none of the lifestyles above, you can still enjoy a lifestyle—the Lifestyle Lifestyle: media, technology, and entertainment at your fingertips, rarely having to touch anything that hasn't been processed, promoted, and/or encased in hard plastic. Cell phone, TiVo, remote control; Google, iPod, rock 'n' roll!

Offended. Rather than say we're sorry for something we did, we often say we're sorry if what we did "offended" someone. Of "mistakes were made" caliber, *offended* is a tool to distance oneself from actually apologizing, as if the worst offense were to someone's sensibility. And even that was never "intended." "I am really sorry if I offended anyone," Janet Jackson said, succumbing to the ritual. "That was truly not my intention." "It was not our intention to offend anyone and we apologize if anyone was offended by the card," a spokesman for the credit card issuer MBNA said in 2004. (MBNA canceled a card using a World Trade Center image after 9/11 victims' families complained.) One might call such transgressions crass or exploitative, insensitive or innocent, as the case may be, but does it occur to anyone that the transgressors *intended* to offend? They intended to increase profits, publicity, or whatever; to offend people would usually get in the way of their goal. No, more than anything, these acceptable and appropriate a-pop-logies just sound legal-eagled.

Philosophy. It's not enough to have an idea, a set of rules, or even a gimmick—you gotta have a philosophy. "The Catalina [Yachts] philosophy means listening to our customers and doing our best every day." "Home Depot has a four-part merchandising philosophy." These days you actually can dab yourself with philosophy: "Philosophy" is a brand of upscale beauty products with clever, lowercased product names like "eye believe," "the present," and—a phrase that once dismissed the idea that beauty could be purchased—"hope in a jar."

Haloes float over not just specific words but, more subtly, certain parts of speech, especially the verb. With our walking-the-walk value system, physical action is pretty much considered prima facie good, and verbs are as physical as words get. In a zenny way, verbs are also metaphysical. As the architect and (real) philosopher Buckminster Fuller wrote in the poem "God is a verb": "God is a verb / the most active / connoting the vast harmonic / reordering of the universe / from unleashed chaos of energy."

Perhaps it's with such goodness in mind that sociobabble goes big for "verbing"—making a verb out of a noun, as in *to partner* or *to dialogue*. But whatever virtue the verb form may communicate, verbing itself has turned out to be a target of ridicule, and not just among professional word watchers. As an old Calvin and Hobbes cartoon said, "Verbing weirds language."

However, there's nothing weird or wrong about verbing at all. "In fact," Steven Pinker wrote in *The Language Instinct*, "easy conversion of nouns to verbs has been part of English grammar for centuries; it is one of the processes that make English English. I have estimated that about a fifth of all English verbs were originally nouns. Considering just the human body, you can *head a committee, scalp a missionary, eye a babe, nose around the office, mouth the lyrics . . . arm the militia, shoulder the burden, elbow your way in, hand him a toy*," and so on. And you may remember not so long ago when the now-common *to host* and *to contact* were frowned upon.

Pinker pointed me toward what really irks about verbing—not so much the words themselves, but the kind of people who, we believe, mouth them (other than ourselves, of course). After all, it's primarily the newer instances of verbing that grate, and perhaps that's because they're associated with the newer people (the Nouvelles), who tend to be "early adopters" of phrases like *liaisoning, Let's calendar that!*, or, as some news people say, *efforting*. ("We want to take you to the White House now," Anderson Cooper said on CNN, "where our correspondent Chris Burns is efforting reaction on this morning's Baghdad blast. Good morning, Chris.")

For instance, *parenting*, fairly or not, suggests to many a different kind of parent than the kind they grew up with, who was probably a noun-solid, holdable mother. The parenting woman, on the other hand, is stereotyped as too much verb, running around putting her career first or sandblasting through household management and only occasionally intersecting with her offspring to share some fun-inducing quality time. (Though she, like me, probably feels poked and buffeted by such an intensely prioritizing parenting lifestyle.)

Living in such a busy-biz world, we're likely to occasionally seek language that slows down and warms up our clinical speech—an efforting that can lead to more verbing. "Here's the invitation for the training session," said an e-mail from a vendor to one of the top accounting firms. "You certainly may wordsmith it as you see fit." Ah, ye olde *wordsmithing*, way more sweat-o'-the-brow than *writing* or *editing*. Wordsmithing is perhaps best anviled at the Hamlet on Olde Oyster Bay (an amenity-filled, gated " 'lifestyle' community" in Plainview, Long Island, that Elliot Monter, president of the Holiday Organization, its developer, admits is "10 miles from an actual bay." But that's a nonissue: With the addition of a five-acre body of water, says Monter, "it is themed architecturally to [the] turn-of-the-century North Shore Oyster Bay area").

When the virtuous verb meets leadenly literal goo-goo marketing, you should hop, skip, and leap away. The Centers for Disease Control has been running a series of public service ads showing kids bicycling, skateboarding, and tap-dancing as a voiceover offers advice like "Everyone has a verb. . . . No matter which verb you choose, do it your own way." The campaign slogan is "Verb. It's what you do." But what are these ads supposed to do? This five-year, taxpayer-funded, thus far $275-million campaign is how the CDC figured it could best fight childhood obesity. The campaign's AOL-sponsored Web site (verbnow.com) suggests, among other kid calorie-burners, that children watch the Verb TV ads that sent them to the site in the first place. But you can't expect a very verb-vigorous attempt to get children off their butts when one of McDonald's ad agencies, Publicis Groupe, handles the campaign, or when, as *Slate* said, "the campaign's corporate sponsors are a virtual Who's Who of the couch-potato industry—in addition to AOL, they include Disney, DC Comics, Primedia, and Viacom." So nix any jeremiads against staring at screens all day or eating from school vending machines filled with junk food (McDonald's and Disney partner with Coca-Cola). But celebrating verbs? That's the ticket!

INGING TITLES

A far more successful form of verb appeal is the *ing*ing of titles, especially of movie titles. It was no big deal when *Bringing Up Baby* did it in 1938 or even when *Pumping Iron* did it in 1977. But by the 1980s, *Eating Raoul* (1982) and *Educating Rita* (1983) were Establishing Formula.

Raoul and Rita were followed by *Romancing the Stone* (1984), *Desperately Seeking Susan* (1985), *Raising Arizona* (1987), and *Driving Miss Daisy* (1989, based on the 1987 play of the same name). Eventually all *ing* broke loose, and most kinds of entertainment were taking running leaps to their title characters, like *Chasing Amy* (movie), *Judging Amy* (TV show), and *Regarding Amy* (art show). There's something about Amy. But given the last decade or two of movie, TV show, TV movie, and play titles (and we're not even counting magazine articles or books, such as Ed and Lois Smart's 2003 *Bringing Elizabeth Home*, about their kidnapped daughter), Amy's not alone. To wit (and not in chronological order): *Drowning Mona, Serving Sara, Kissing Jessica Stein, Crossing Jordan, Watching Ellie, Chasing Papi, Owning Mahoney, Killing Zoe, Boxing Helena, Capturing the Friedmans, Surviving Grace.*

There are lots of exceptions, but while females are drowned, watched, crossed, judged, killed, and boxed, males do tend to get more supportive treatment: *Raising Arizona* (a boy's name), *Raising Victor Vargas, Raising Dad, Raising Cain, Finding Forrester, Finding Nemo, Regarding Henry, Being John Malkovich, Waking Ned Devine, Spinning Boris, Saving Silverman,* and *Saving Private Ryan,* with *Saving Grace* and *Saving Jessica Lynch* among the exceptions.

After all those, you might think producers would be too embarrassed to repeat the tic. But since just early 2004 came the CBS movie *Raising Waylon,* the TV Land series *Chasing Far-rah,* and the theatrical movies *Raising Helen, Being Julia, Chasing Liberty,* and *Imagining Argentina.* Never a community to be embarrassed anyway, Hollywood loves such titles because they're "high-concept"—like high-concept pitches *("Star Wars* meets *The Terminator"),* these titles distill and market the movie in a few provocative words.

So titling is pop, but is it halo pop? Yes, because it raises our expectations of the entertainment ever so slightly, nudging TV shows more toward movies, movies more toward serious "films." The aesthetics and aspirations we usually associate with indie movies *(Chasing Amy, Being John Malkovich)* drift over to the most mainstream product *(Saving Silverman, Crossing Jordan)* because they are cast from the same titular template.

More than most, this particular halo is formed out of grammar. In *Judging Amy,* for example, you have a missing subject and the missing helping verb *to be,* followed by *judging,* which here is both a progressive participle verb (its action is continuous) and a transitive verb (it is acting on an object, *Amy).* Were the title a sentence, it would read: *I Am* [He Is/They Are] Judging Amy. Omitting the subject adds an intrigue, suggesting perhaps a narrator, an unknown agent, or an unseen but overseeing presence (the judicial system? the community? God?). The absence is a breeze of McLuhanesque cool for your brain to heat up, maybe with a bit of poetry of your own.

And echoing philosophic works à la (sort of) Descartes's *Meditations Concerning First Philosophy* or William Gass's *On Being Blue,* the progressive-participled entertainment seems vaguely progressive—action-filled, to be sure, but also contemplative, observing the action from one level above: *Meditations Concerning Waylon; On Kissing Jessica Stein. Ing*ing makes a title seem vaster, ratchets it up a nuance or two toward grand, artful, good for you. And with that I am . . .

Closuring chapter.

CHAPTER 8

Digit Talk in the Unit States of America

A man looks out from a Rolaids commercial and says, "Today we're so busy even our stomachs multitask—as in heartburn, acid indigestion, and [embarrassed pause] gas." How do you spell relief? D-I-G-I-T-A-L P-O-P L-A-N-G-U-A-G-E.

Digital pop is not just a bunch of e-mail- and computer-related words like *multitask* (or *bandwidth* or *interactive*) that we use only because digital technology has beeped into every corner of our lives. Digit pop also includes nontech but core-value business buzz *(win-win, opt, think outside the box)* that we *use* digitally in order to experience the satisying click of a binary beat.

FAQ: Uh, OK. But how does digital pop language provide relief—and relief from what?

Long answer short: Digital pop can cool the burning heart, neutralize the acid indigestion of too much information (TMI), and release the gaseous fear that even proactive multitasking won't make life manageable.

Optional content: We all live in BusyWorld. BusyWorld is bombarded by TMI, which, to quote Rolaids, generates "gas that causes uncomfortable bloating and pressure." Every trend, hope, dread, every fragment of gossip, news, politics, advertising, whatever, whips through our mind/bodies as we rush through our day jammed with work, shopping, traffic, cell phones, bills, e-mail, scheduled fun—the rush of rushing, sickening and great. And through it all, keep your eyes on the prizes: profits, efficiency, speed. As Homer Simpson enthused about being able to type *y* on a keyboard instead of *yes,* "I just tripled my productivity!"

The binary, either/or nature of digital language provides relief by breaking down and calming down the rush, isolating its elements into seemingly prioritized, contained units—separate lexical cubicles that keep us safe from info overload. Ah. The bloating and pressure subside. A sense of control returns. Technology's utopian promise of a clean, well-lighted space—a space epitomized by the computer screen—finds verbal expression in digit pop.

Take-home message: All pop language is somewhat digital, in the sense that if you pop the right media-tested word into place, you maximize access to the desired response. But, IMHO, the pop content in this chapter links to digital deliverables with value-added solutions.

EITHER LOL OR LOLL

Even if you don't want to communicate that way, at times you do, because digital-free living is no longer an option. You don't need even a single silicon chip to live digitally. Vitamin pills, for instance, are digital nutrition, extracted from their analogue context—that is, food. Likewise, working out on StairMasters is digital exercise, isolated from games, sports, or moving much through space. "Teaching to the test"—that's digital, because students are less likely to learn about subjects than about how to take tests. Digital living emphasizes information distilled from context and ends detached from means.

Clocks are the best-known examples of the digital and analogue modes of representing information. With clocks that are analogue (from the Greek *analogos,* for "proportionate"), you tell time by observing the position of the "hands" relative to the dial, or "face"—context conveys meaning. On digital clocks, numbers or "digits" (from the Latin *digitus,* for "finger" or "toe") appear discretely, relative to nothing and (to quote the title of the George W. S. Trow book) within the context of no context. Joshua Meyrowitz defined the two modes in *No Sense of Place:* "Digital systems are based on discontinuities—either/or. A number is either a 3 or a 4, but not both. A word is either one word or another. Analogic messages, in contrast, are continuous; they are based on the principle of more or less."

Like the sides of other complementary opposites—yin and yang, right brain and left brain, female and male—analogue and digital both have advantages and disadvantages. Since I got a digital thermostat, I can actually control the heat. I much prefer pushing radio buttons and immediately getting my programmed stations to fiddling with dials and wasting precious seconds away from, say, Al Franken (although I do miss ever happening upon an unprogrammed surprise). And just in terms of sound, analogue communications can sometimes drone and moan, loll and lull.

But lolling and lulling are also a source of analogue's (by comparison) Southern charm. Analogue language communicates without a net (net), allowing serendipity as well as static to get through. But those rich, manifold rhythms are slowly vanishing, ordered out by a staccato, ticker-tape beat. Lan-guage-get-ting-chopped-up-en-cod-ed-&-de-con-tex-tu-al-ized. In a word, digital.

TECH TICKER TALK

A lot of digital pop comes directly from specialized computer and online jargon or from plain words that are used for techlike purposes. But such technically technical phrases don't reach digit-pop status unless they've spilled over to the general public for general talking purposes, as have these:

In the system. Customer service reps will often say, "You're in the system now." And that's supposed to be good. Because the system is a company's computer system, not the prison system, not the oppressive "system" of the sixties. No, today *in the system* means you're covered, you and your information won't be lost (though your identity is more likely to be stolen). You're electronically tucked in.

I don't have the bandwidth. "Shut up!" a friend says she wants to shout when she hears this. "Just say, 'I'm too tired,' 'I don't have the energy,' 'I don't have the time.' "

Content. I admit I'm frightened by how easily people took to *content.* Even writers didn't rage against the eunuchized synonym for their profession: *content provider.* Maybe they were thinking that if you were a content provider, at least you were a provider— you had a job, you could feed your family. Abide and provide. You were in the New Economy mix, up there with health-care providers—and doctors still make big bucks, right? And if you were the kind of journalist who wouldn't normally write advertorials, for example, well, you could stop holding your nose. Although the barrier between advertising and editorial gets more permeable every day, that barrier is still tougher to breach than the one between advertising and content. Because content isn't so much advertising or PR as it is just stuff that goes through a computer, the way everything does these days. So be content, like J., the junketeering journalist in Colson Whitehead's novel *John Henry Days.* A newly launched Web site asks J. to provide some "regional content." "Not stories," J. thinks, "not articles, but content. Like it is a mineral. It is so honest of them."

Interactive. *Interactive* was big well before everyone owned a PC. It usually referred to things we could do with video games or TV, like influencing a story's plot or voting during a televised community meeting. "What it is turning out to mean," Margaret Talbot, a fellow at the New America Foundation, has written, "is the 'opportunity,' as it's often called, to buy things."

Along the way from voting to buying, *interact* has also served to mean to talk, to meet, to be involved with, to play. A friend of mine was helping out in a kindergarten class when the substitute teacher told the children, "You have ten minutes of free time to interact with each other." "The kids looked at each other and had absolutely no idea what she was talking about," my friend says. *Interact* is a generic, distilled (and thus digital) version of ordinary talking, meeting, or playing. But *interact* has kept the gig because a silken flattery runs through it. The word implies that the interactor is a forward-thinking protagonist because—hold on—he's acting *with* someone or something else. *Interactive*'s reputation for brain-stimulating back-and-forth disguises what a meager condiment it usually is. As the art critic Dan Bischoff says, "Most 'interactive' exhibits in museums don't advance your knowledge or thinking about art that much, but what they *do* do is teach you how to use computers."

Much of what passes for interactive is really interpassive: One agent (mechanical or human) does what it has been programmed to do—display and/or sell something; the other agent (usually human) does what it has been programmed to do—press buttons and/or shop. Sounds inert, but compared to plotzing in front of the TV (the American baseline activity), interactors are practically action heroes. Out of the comparison to TV comes the dreamy suggestion of "the user in a utopian discourse of active agency in dialogue with technology," as Laetitia Wilson of the University of Western Australia wrote in an essay titled "Interactivity or Interpassivity: A Question of Agency in Digital Play." "But to what extent," she asked, "is there mutual reciprocity when we follow a pre-programmed direction, when we 'interact' according to a predetermined set of codes?"

LOL. "FOX LOL Sunday Season Finale!" read the heading on the May 2004 e-mail. This wasn't a typo for a joint FOX-AOL marketing scheme, which AFAIK (as far as I know) doesn't exist. *LOL* means "laughing out loud" and not only in e-mail, which generated *LOL* (to quickly convey that you think something is funny, whether or not it actually makes you laugh), and not only in teenagers' IM (instant messaging), where *LOL,* or *lol,* is indispensable. *LOL* is also said out loud, off line, in "face-to-face" interactions.

Like all pop, *LOL* has nuances. It can be detached, in the same way that many of us, when told a supposedly humorous anecdote, might say, That's funny, without cracking a smile. *LOL* can be sarcastic: Oh, yeah, I'm LOL. But the now common *LOL* isn't always enough. "My new favorite internet acronymic word is 'rotflmao,' which means 'rolling on the floor laughing my ass off,' " the mother of three teenagers e-mailed me. Her fourteen-year-old daughter "occasionally says this (the letters) sarcastically, mostly at dinner if my husband or I make a stupid remark about one of her friends. It used to be a deadpan, resentful 'ha ha.' "

Sometimes a spoken *LOL* supplements actual out-loud laughter. "I've seen people who've giggled and said 'LOL,' " Alicia, a fifteen-year-old girl, tells me. "I've also heard people say 'JKLOL' in real life with kind of a chuckle. It means 'Just kidding, laughing out loud.' It's to back up the idea that it's just a joke, instead of saying, 'I apologize, I'm just kidding.' " Alicia is not an *LOL* fan. "On IM I use *ha ha. LOL* seems less personal. You can't tell whether someone's really laughing or being sarcastic. But," she admits, "when I say *ha ha,* half the time I'm not actually laughing either."

It's probably not fair to say that people pronounce the letters LOL *instead* of letting rip unstoppable, audible bursts of sound, maybe with attendant stomach-jiggling and eye-watering. But I think it is fair to say, as Alicia did, that "*LOL* in real life is weird because it's giving the illusion of laughing." That is, at least around the edges, laughter itself is being digitally processed! 8-((An e-mail emoticon for "That makes me sad.")

What's also a bit sad is the redundancy of *laughing out loud.* By definition, laughter's usually not silent. It's as if the common response to humor in an age of irony were the wry smile and sotto voce chuckle—but that anything irrepressibly funny wins an "out loud" sticker.

Laughing out loud is not merely an accessory of youth. Adults, especially those in the media, will say or write a spelled-out *laugh out loud,* usually to modify *funny.* "Still laugh-out-loud funny after all these years," the *Detroit Free Press* wrote about Carol Burnett in a 2004 TV special. It's not clear whose stock rose first, the acronym's or the SOW's (spelled-out word; I made that up). But FWIW (for what it's worth), *laugh out loud* and *laughing out loud* between them get about 1.6 million Google hits; *LOL* and *lol,* about 7.8 million.

Although digital pop is hugely influenced by digital technology, most digital pop does not, in fact, derive directly from technical or online lingo. After all, people have been communicating digitally ever since they began counting on their digits. An internal human digital drive of sorts has always led people to slot things, time, space, and experience into distinguishable categories. "There is nothing more basic than categorization to our thought, perception, action, and speech," the linguist George Lakoff wrote in a book titled to illustrate just that *(Women, Fire, and Dangerous Things)*. "Every time we see something as a *kind* of thing, for example, a tree, we are categorizing."

And so there are categories of categories. The categories that are particularly rigid, I like to call units. I visualize them as steel or aluminum units, like those at a storage facility, their impermeable metal preventing one set of stuff from overlapping with or influencing another set of stuff. For other people, the better metaphor might be file cabinets, ziplock bags, or Al Gore's "iron-clad lock box."

Some of us try, for example, to put career or job in one unit that won't affect the home-life unit, or painful memories in a container that can't touch the good-memory container. Bill Clinton famously put impeachment and personal humiliation in a compartment separate from presidential duties. Others try to keep Iraqi deaths in a different class from American deaths, or disturbing news from Israel away from consciousness at all (my tendency).

You can also call this compartmentalizing, prioritizing, wearing blinders, or taking one thing at a time. Whatever you call it, our increasingly busy, technological world encourages us to live life, more frequently and fiercely, as units of experience, each discretely framed off from the previous transaction or task at hand.

In language, one way we put experience into units is by using "unit words" (a clunky phrase I made up for the sake of a neat categorization). Unit words and tech talk (both subcategories of the digital pop supercategory) overlap all over the place, totally discrete categories being an illusion to begin with. Let's just say, though, that the broader-based unit words are those that don't stem from technology but sound as if they do.

The top unit word is *unit*. Some schools teach subjects in "units," while "In today's system of corporatized medicine, patients are referred to as 'cost units,' " as Jim Hightower writes, "and the job of the doctor is that of an assembly-line worker who must hold down costs by rushing these 'units' through the system." The *unit* (and the *G*) of G-Unit, 50 Cent's hardcore rap group, refers to Gorilla Unit and not to the gang units of prison jargon. (In naming the group, 50 Cent said he was thinking of military *guerrilla* units.)

Unit words also emanate from form alone, as in the choppy, digital-beat injunctions popular in ads. "Find a place. Fill the space. Clean up . . . with Loot" (a New York City subway ad for a classified ads circular). "Go places. Come back. Gloat" (a 2000 Mitsubishi Montero Sport billboard showing a hulking SUV).

What the following unit words share with the harder tech words above is an ability to get you to Focus!, to sever one thing from the next thing in line with a verbal slash mark, to insinuate into communication a binary pulse.

Opt. The option of a new generation. *Opt* and *option* are a digitalized *choice*. *Choice* has an aspirational ring; *opt* sounds more like a deduction arrived at after you've done the math. The top option in can-do America when one must mention failure, for instance, is "Failure is not an option." This *option* gives an either/or heave-ho to any kind of failure, like taking a wrong turn. "LOST IS NOT AN OPTION," insists a 2004 ad for Nextel's GPS-enabled phones that "get you there with audible turn-by-turn directions." As the wireless communications company's clipped tagline goes, "Nextel. Done."

There are more opportunities than ever to *opt in* or *opt out* of things, often of online marketing lists. In fact, you may opt in or out of this hypothesis: We like the smart-rat-in-a-maze sound of *opt* and *option* because it flatters us by implying that we're decision-makers in control.

Or opt this: Corporations and politicians are getting away with more and more lies these days, because "when you're so informatized, truth is just another entertainment option," as Marc Maron, co-host of *Morning Sedition* on Air America Radio, says.

On the same page. In the spring of 2004, even contestants on different reality shows were on the same page. "Just want to make sure we're on the same page," Bill, the winner of the first *Apprentice,* told his team, who were struggling to pull off a Trump golf tournament. Meanwhile, on the finale of *Average Joe: Adam Returns,* Adam same-paged twice, once telling the finalist, good-girl Rachael, that he and she were "on the same page." That she mistook this common unit phrase (meaning to share a viewpoint or opinion, to align plans or schedules) for *romance* illustrates an overeagerness that probably explains why commitment-phobic Adam rejected her.

"This used to have a literal meaning," says the linguist Connie Eble. "Fifty years ago, the grammar school teacher said to the class, 'Let's make sure we're all on the same page.' It went on to mean, 'Let's make sure we're in agreement here.' " But over the last ten or fifteen years, the phrase has snowballed (and spawned the higher-tech *on the same screen*). Amid the myriad misunderstandings in BusyWorld, *on the same page* can help people orient themselves. But I think there's another reason for the phrase's utility: In a political culture where it can raise eyebrows not to agree, *on the same page* fleetingly provides the security of near-total accord.

A disconnect. If two parties really disagree, however, there might be more than pages or screens involved—there might be *a disconnect.* Used as a noun with the indefinite article, *a disconnect* is a more digital version of *He just doesn't get it* because it allows us to think of ourselves as plugs. A headline on CFO.com: "Rashomon in HR: Two new surveys reveal a disconnect between what employees want—and what employers think they want." The story went on: "That should be a wake-up call to executives and HR managers."

A wake-up call. *A wake-up call* often follows *a disconnect,* as it repeatedly did after the electrical blackout of the summer of 2003. Among the many officials who claimed to have been rudely awoken was President Bush. "It's a wake-up call," he said, though his proposed solution was his old call to drill in the Arctic National Wildlife Refuge. I'm wary of *wake-up call* when those in charge say it. The phrase diverts attention from anyone asleep at the wheel by implying that all of us together were in an innocent state of slumber. Only a screeching alarm shook us from ignorance to revelation, from off to on, from one walled-off unit of consciousness to another.

Stay on message. But Bush and others *stayed on message* by cawing "Wake-up call!" A battle cry of politics, *stay on message* is a way of reciting the catechism of the day, though it's based as much on the lessons of advertising as those of the Church. In advertising it's an article of faith that viewers must see an ad many times (some say a minimum of seven) for a message or brand name to even begin to register. *Stay on message* essentially says: Focus, repeat; focus, repeat; focus, repeat; and keep all other thoughts in a lock box. (If you need to throw someone off message, the following weaponlike digital options can be accessed: *It's a nonissue, It's a nonstarter, End of conversation, End of story.*)

DNA and **gene.** At the 2003 North American International Auto Show, Ford bragged that Mercury's "interior is the embodiment of Mercury's new DNA direction," while its "rear lights convey the DNA message." Nissan once hosted a "Nissan DNA Exhibition." In a TV commercial called "DNA," VW attributed its engineers' smarts to "some kind of weird DNA." For all the unique heritage that *DNA* is meant to imply, most marketers apparently have identical genes that predetermine their verbal choices.

Representing biological either/or codes themselves, *DNA* and *genes* are potent unit words. In the pop media mind, they stand for science at its most precise and lend a feel of scientific incontrovertibility to the ad claims they grace. A brand's purported specialness used to be called "the soul of a brand." But souls are boundary-blending analogue miasmas whose existence can't be proven; DNA is (relatively speaking) hard, testable—an indestructible unit of singularity. Plus, anyone can benefit from the hi-sci sell. A guy writes to his girlfriend on the Net, "I think that it's in my DNA, to go out with as many women as I can."

DIGITS WITH A HUMAN FACE

Problem: All the beep-beep-chop-chop of digit pop can accelerate the very anxiety it was hired to contain.

Solution: Hire facsimile analogue units as emotional care providers.

Result: Before the Caring Corporation cuts you off or drives you mad by making you interact with twenty-seven telephonic prompts, it plays an empathic, albeit prerecorded, female voice asking you to please hold because "your call is important to us."

Oh, God, a phone tree grows in my head. Trying to disconnect (in the verb sense) a telephone line recently, I spoke to a recording "who" couldn't understand me, so I yelled my numbers and yesses or nos into the phone. Endlessly patient, she replied, "Sorry, I didn't hear that," "I think you said 291," and "I'll read my list of eight possible situations." It drains the will to live out of you.

More pleasant but no less absurd was a phone call with a real person in customer service at a credit card company. At the end of my one-question call (Did they receive my check?), she asked, "Do you feel I treated you as a valued customer?"

But if I was feeling like a machine, her livelihood depended on acting like one. The reasons for digitalization go beyond computerization. They go to the heart of labor-management practices and the corporate processing of life's every moment into a marketing opportunity.

Like most companies, Verizon requires its service reps to talk from a script; those who fail to do so may lose performance points, reducing their chance of promotion. "Imagine if you're calling [the phone company] because you're getting harassing calls and you want a new phone number," Linda Kramer, a Verizon service rep and president of a local arm of the Communications Workers of America, told *The New York Times* during a 2000 strike. "The service rep is required to look at your account and see what features you have, and then try to sell you something. And not just one item, that's not good enough. I'm required to offer you voice mail if you don't have it, three-way calling if you don't have it. I'm required to do my best and sparkle and shine, and put you at ease so you say, 'Oh, all right, I'll take it for a month, just because you sound so nice.' "

Verizon and other corporations know that consumers won't reject the digital lifestyle (or as Verizon calls it, "the Broadband Lifestyle") as long as they forget what they gave up in exchange for it. And amnesia comes quicker if binary-care words like *your* and *family* are added to words like *content* and *DSL,* as in "your guide to Broadband Living & Content," Verizon's 2003 guide for new DSL users. It featured, hour by hour, "A Day in the Life of a DSL Family." The Hendersons, Verizon said, "are like any DSL family—power surfing at will"; checking the weather, stock portfolios, potential jobs; doing homework, banking, e-mail, virtual skateboarding; downloading recipes, the *Powerpuff Girls* movie trailer "for the 62nd time"; reserving tickets for said movie; planning a twenty-fifth anniversary with travelocity.com. (The gone-digit Hendersons are tripping on DSL as if it were spelled backward.)

THE CORPORATE CUBICLES OF OUR MINDS

At the end of the DSL day, digital pop, in all its varieties, is but a subsidiary of corporate America. Whether they produce technology or merely depend on it, corporations are the chief distributors of digital pop because money makes the world, and the word, go 'round.

This has been made transparent by Frank Lingua, "the nation's leading purveyor of buzzwords, catch phrases and clichés for people too busy to speak in plain English." An interview with Lingua, conducted by Dan Danbom, has been making the rounds on the Internet for years. An excerpt:

DANBOM: Is being a cliché expert a full-time job?
LINGUA: Bottom line is I have a full plate 24/7.
D: Is it hard to keep up with the seemingly endless supply of clichés that spew from business?
L: Some days, I don't have the bandwidth. It's like drinking from a fire hydrant.

D: So it's difficult?

L: Harder than nailing Jell-O to the wall.

D: Where do most clichés come from?

L: Stakeholders push the envelope until it's outside the box.

D: . . . Can you predict whether a phrase is going to become a cliché?

L: It's my job. I skate to where the puck's going to be. Because if you aren't the lead dog, you're not providing a customer-centric proactive solution.

Sure, that's just a spoof. But here, for real, is The Rock, telling MTV how deliciously busy his life has become as he transitions from WWE wrestler to major movie star: "Full plate, full plate is good. I can always make room." On his acting roles: "I'm not afraid to step out of the box. Bottom line is it's gotta be funny." (Though he wasn't trying to be when he said this.)

Now, hundreds of thousands of corporate employees realize that blather is flooding their plates. Variations of a game called Buzzword Bingo have long been played during meetings (you score every time you detect the boss or other speakers committing a cliché). And corporate-buzzword ridicule is rife in e-mail, as in the following exchange between a half-dozen marketing pros in the recording industry, some for a mainstream label, others for an independent. They're suggesting phrases to be added to their own list of clichés.

MARKETING PRO #1:   We all know what that list means: "ramp it up," "sidebar," "strap it on."

MP #2:   But wait! Surely there is: "looped in," "close the circle," and the unforgivable "tweak it," "It's Crunch Time," "It's In Our Sights," "Are you feeling it out there."

MP #3:   Alright you just made me think of a real offender: "massage the marketplace."

MP #4:   There really needs to be a collection box where if any of us are caught saying

one of the phrases on "the list," you
have to pay a dollar. After 6 months,
whoever has paid in the LEAST, wins
the pot. Think about it, it could be
VERY lucrative for someone out there,
especially me or [another MP], since us
"Indie Label" people don't use those
obnoxious phrases too often.

MP #5:   uh . . . hel-LO. don't go flattering
yourself. i've heard plenty of pro-speak
from you. you know how to run with the
big boys.

Big boy pro-speak has colonized the cubicles of all our minds. While thirty or forty years ago, people outside of the business sector rarely mentioned *bottom lines* or *business sectors,* today even artists and activists use such words to imply a getting-down-to-business sense of purpose—something we need more of lately, as work and the rest of life relentlessly blur together.

Biz pop also swelled with the ascent of entrepreneurs and the portrayal of them—and of once stodgy corporations—as leading-edge iconoclasts. The dot.com bubble may have burst, but the clichés that once inflated it continue to strive toward excellence.

It's all part and parcel of personal branding. Advertising oneself used to seem crass, but now you're a fool if you don't do it. Pundits derided the former California governor Jerry Brown during his 1992 presidential bid for announcing an 800 number; today politicians, or anyone with a business or a bio, are considered losers if they don't push a Web site. The right zeitgeist-adjusted biz buzz is, as companies like to cheer, a win-win. ("IT'S A WIN, WIN SITUATION," states a 2003 Volvo print ad. Check out "the Hyundai win-win year-end event," a 2003 Hyundai TV spot advises.)

When I say biz words are pop, I don't mean the utterly risible yup business jargon, like *massage the marketplace* or *eat your own dog food.* For the most part, I mean the basic, to the point of bland business words, the middle management that we rarely notice—even as their digitability helps us pop up our personal mission statements daily.

Manage. The hardest-working member of this team. We have *managed risk, managed care* (which has proved to be notably uncaring), *weight management, time management,* and "not just a ceiling fan but advanced air management," as a Grandin Road catalogue portrays a product. One of the many euphemisms for torture to come out of Abu Ghraib is "sleep management," aka severe sleep deprivation.

Now, *manage* isn't so bland that it escapes satire. The Jack Nicholson/Adam Sandler movie *Anger Management* and Tony Soprano's cover job in "waste management" suggest that the superego *manage* is the id's ideal fall guy. For the most part, though, society has faith that anything threatening to go wild—anger, eating, time, torture—can be contained in units and distributed in a businesslike manner.

Bottom line. This is still the current, if aging, CEO of biz pop. Barnhart and Metcalf write that at the end of the "anti-authoritarian 1960s," *bottom line* "became an established way of saying we were all business." The idea is that after you add up revenues and subtract expenses (again, after you *do the math*), the sum of all important stuff is at the bottom line. So while the phrase might refer to profits, or simply to money, it's also a way of saying *cut to the chase* or *when all is said and done.* But because *bottom line* so abruptly isolates the ends from the means, it cuts to the chase more digitally.

Bottom line has been training some of its snappier VPs, like *take-home message, take-away message, net net* and *leave-behind,* to take over one day. After the dot.com-ad-crazy Super Bowl of 2000, a brand consultant complained, "Meaningless names, meaningless messages and a serious lack of stature were the major leave-behinds." *Bottom line,* though, isn't going out quietly—it's verbing. "Bottom-line it for me: Which premium/priority submission options are the bare minimum for getting top rankings?" as a FAQ (frequently asked question) went on searchengineguide.com.

Product. Sometimes a digital quality is achieved by omitting certain parts of speech, so that the leave-behind is more unitlike.

To wit: the word *product* without an article preceding it and, as a plural, without an *s* ending it. "You are going to have a tremendous amount of product," a marketing executive said of the glut of 2001 holiday movies. On *Meet the Press,* Pat Roberts, chair of the Senate committee investigating intelligence failures that led to the war in Iraq, referred to intelligence as *product* seven times ("we can get a better intelligence product," "there was a lousy product," and so on).

So accepted is the commodification of everything that all products—high-end and low-, financial services and material "goods," films and fertility rates—share an underlying value as output, as entities of profit-making potential. And without distracting helpmeets like *a* or *s, product* stands prouder, a bolder— even more manly—soldier of capitalism. (Rising through the ranks is a word that formalizes the process of turning something not normally considered a product—ideas, expertise— into a sellable item: *productizing.*)

The lay-consumer word for *product* is *stuff.* If *product* is digital and masculine, *stuff* is analogue and feminine, and sometimes sexually so. But more significant, *stuff* is Teletubby infantile, full of fantasies of eternal suckling and rolling around in comfy clouds of cotton candy. Ten years ago, over just a few months' time, I counted some seventeen ads that turned on the word *stuff,* from the Snapple slogan "Made from the best stuff on earth" to the "anthem" TV spot of a $100 million Microsoft campaign. (Over a montage of "diverse" human faces, a druggy-sounding female voiceover oozed, "The stuff that we make . . . the stuff that we make, make trouble and good things will happen . . . stuff that we make is powerful.") Today, we're still unable to talk or think or put out a men's magazine (namely *Stuff*) without tufts of stuff love. Recently, Verizon helped sell itself with a line that could have been Microsoft's: "This is really powerful stuff"; a TV spot for Gold Bond medicated powder claimed, "This stuff really works"; Chef Boyardee said of itself, "Boy, this stuff is good!"; and a package of cupcakes beckoned with "Hostess: Now that's the stuff."

Midway between *product* and *stuff* on the digital/analogue spectrum is the clangy *thing.* Plowing down specific nouns with the general *thing* is a bad habit that, I recall, Norman Mailer railed against decades ago. *Thing* does live large as an independent pop player, as in *It's the right thing to do, It's a woman/guy/ black thing, Miss Thang*, and the Silver Ring Thing, the faith-based program in which teenagers buy a silver ring to symbolize their vow to abstain from premarital sex. But much more common is the self-effacing *thing*, a drab, East German–like place-holder for words we can't remember or be bothered with: "Hand me the thing," my husband says, meaning the remote control. But we also add *thing* to nouns we do remember: "Hand me the remote control thing," he also says. Adding a word to *remote control* would seem to fly in the face of the goal of speedy communication. But we have a thing for *thing*, as we have for *stuff*. It's not just that we want an endless supply of material things. We also want an endless supply of verbal rest stops, places along the sentences and the day where we don't have to be specific or struggle with words or ever be frustrated again.

Solution. *Product* may be better than *goods* but it's not always good enough. For that, there is a *solution*. In 1998, Scott Rosenberg wrote of *solution*'s "migration from the world of everyday English to that of high-tech marketing. Hardware and software companies now routinely describe what they sell—what we used to call their products—as 'solutions.'" Now in Net-found phrases from "consumer debt solutions" to "Practical anger solutions in a convenient format," the overpromising *solution* is no longer limited to technology product. Proactiv Solution is not a spyware blocker but, according to its Web site, "The Answer for Acne."

The jocks of biz buzz. Though used by all, the following words express a piquant sense of corporate vigor: *robust, churn, bundling, trump, crank up a notch, ramp up, ratchet up.* "Next: ratcheting up the violence and the rhetoric in the Middle East," Ted Koppel said before a commercial break. "Aggressive bundling underway to reduce customer churn"—subtitle in a 2004 Nortel Networks "e-seminar." Regarding the leader of this team, *proactive*, you could make the case that it really does hold a sliver of nuance over *active:* When you're *active*, you do something; when you're *proactive*, you do it before you have to. But people use *proactive* just as often to mean simply doing something but doing it bracingly, as if with a slap of aftershave.

Value-added. You might say the above phrases offer value-added energy. One of the few comprehensible definitions of *value-added* is "[of or relating to] the parts of the process that add worth from the perspective of the external customer." So popular has this business term become—because, I think, it is confused with getting something for free—that its MBA accent is turning up in the oddest places. In a sermon about loving Jesus, Wesley White writes (on wesleyspace.net), "We might ordinarily be jealous of someone loving someone or something beyond our self, but here it is this very extra-me love that brings a value-added love to me."

THE PAGE, THE SCREEN, THE ENVELOPE, AND THE BOX

Even some suits, however, feel that business values value-subtract them, as if they were interchangeable numbers on a spreadsheet. Not to worry: Periodically, the folks in marketing ship out verbal product and vocabulary solutions to help employees re-envision themselves as new-paradigm thinkers. If you want to fight the power and *not* be on the same freakin' page or screen for once, what are you going to say? You know: You're going to *think outside the box* or *push the envelope,* or be *cutting-edge* this or *forward-leaning* that. "Clive's the man. We're gonna think outside the box," the *American Idol* winner Ruben Studdard said after meeting with Clive Davis, the head of J Records.

Or maybe you'll undo the previously stultifying thing by going *unwired, unscripted, unfiltered, unmediated,* or *unfettered.* ("UNMODERATED. Uninterrupted. Unplugged," a Fox TV print ad brayed about the commercial-free half-hour each it provided for Gore and Bush in 2000.) The *un*'s are 7 Up's "Uncola" unreinvented.

The most dismaying aspect of trying to escape the limitations of "the box" is that, for the most part, we escape into more of the same—it's just labeled differently. There are good jokes to be made of this, like Taco Bell's slogan "Think Outside the Bun."

But almost all box-busting is contained within larger boxes—nationalist, religious, corporate, or media "mind-sets" that we see no better than fish see the water they swim in. (I can't think outside that metaphor.) In the movie *Traffic*, the Michael Douglas character asks the top illicit-drug fighting brass to think "outside of the box" for ideas on how to fight the drug war. No one does. Who can, when they grew up in it?

THE DISCRETE HARM OF DIGITALESE

I'm going to be unfiltered now: I am a Luddite. But only partly. In no way am I going to give up DSL, Google, or vitamin pills. I depend on them as much as I distrust them. In any case, I'm addicted. However, let's be grown-ups (as the pop persuasive goes) and acknowledge that every benefit has a cost and every advance a consequence. Here are some of them.

Dots 'n' Bots. As we internalize the rhythms of digital technology, we are transforming into human dots 'n' bots, fusing our messy human analogue emotions with the on-or-off beeps, buttons, blinking lights, and pixels around us.

Yeah, so what's the point? People as atomized dots or mechanized robots are just metaphors.

Well, yes, but metaphors metabolize the world. As Jaron Lanier, the writer, artist, and computer visionary who coined the term *virtual reality*, once wrote about computers and human identity: "As a consequence of unavoidable psychological algebra the person starts to think of himself as being like the computer. . . . The person starts to limit herself to the categories and procedures represented in the computer, without realizing what has been lost. Music becomes MIDI, art becomes Postscript." Logic, I'd add, becomes PowerPoint (coming up); doing more than one thing at a time becomes multitasking.

Lanier was writing in part about the effect of "smart agents," the computer programs that make decisions and act on behalf of humans. But, he added, "even without agents a person's creative output is compromised by identification with a computer. With agents, however, the person himself is compromised."

Or, as Andy Warhol and the eighties techno-pop band Ultra-vox more tightly put it: "I Want to Be a Machine."

MYALIENATION

Lanier has also said, "Information Is Alienated Experience."

That seems substantiated by a 2000 Stanford University study by the political scientist Norman Nie. He found that "the more hours people use the Internet, the less time they spend with real human beings." No surprise, but Nie's conclusion that "the Internet was creating a broad new wave of social isolation in the United States, raising the specter of an atomized world without human contact or emotion" has been fiercely disputed on the grounds that any isolation is more than offset by the new kinds of community made possible only because of the Internet. Maybe, but even granting that we're awash in e-community, human connections do take on a different nature when they are technologically chaperoned.

Again, don't worry: The digital diaspora will compensate us. In exchange for any ego loss, we're getting more *I*'s, *Me*'s, and *My*'s in the names of Web sites, companies, and products. Such ego-redistribution marketing includes the American Express slogan "My Life, My Card"; My Yahoo ("Free Personalized Content All in One Place!"); and Myway.com, an ad-free portal by the same folks who gave you the ad-heavy iWON.com.

By the (My)way, the *i* in iWON means "me," while presumably the *i* in iVillage.com., iPrint.com, and iParty.com stands for "Internet" or "interactive." Or maybe also "individual." It's not clear, but clarity isn't the point. Much as people are merging with computers, a print ad happily merged the ego *I* with the Internet *i* (and the individual with the crowd). "Who am i?" the ad asked over a photo of a punk-coifed young woman; "i am the internet generation. i am passionate. i am pushing the envelope. And i am waiting. . . . Snowball.com. We are i."

Snowball.com didn't snowball, but iPod certainly did. iPod's *i*, of course, is based on iMac's, one of the earliest individuality = technology *i*'s. iPod has advertised itself on TV and in street posters with silhouettes of individuals dancing while plugged in to product. For a day or two in 2004, some New York City posters were interrupted with graffiti that read: "The 'i' stands for isolated," "The 'i' stands for impolite," as well as "invisible," "insecure," "income," and "I want." The effect, Laura Conaway wrote in *The Village Voice,* was to turn "an ad campaign about being cool into a commentary on being alone."

POWERDUMB

Despite its nerdy-smart veneer, digital tech can speed up dumbing down. It's no mystery why: We believe that machines will think for us while we can just sit back and click. Take Christopher, the hotheaded young gangster on *The Sopranos* who very much wanted to write a screenplay about the mob. So he bought a computer and some software. But, as usual, he nearly came to violence—writing was *hard,* as he complained to the older Paulie:

CHRISTOPHER: I'm workin' my ass off on this movie script. You know how many pages I got? Nineteen.
PAULIE: Is that a lot or a little?
CHRISTOPHER: Books say a movie's supposed to be about 120 pages.
PAULIE: [whistles softly]
CHRISTOPHER: With this fucking computer, I thought it would do a lot of it. . . . I bought a scriptwritin' program and everything!

More dangerous than a frustrated writer/mobster is the real-life PowerPoint. Microsoft's enormously successful "slideware" program, several hundred million copies of which have served as the centerpiece of corporate, government, and educational presentations, was also used by NASA. When NASA's Columbia Accident Investigation Board reported on why the space shuttle had crashed, the board argued that NASA "had become too reliant on presenting complex information via PowerPoint, instead of by means of traditional ink-and-paper technical reports," Clive Thompson wrote in a *New York Times Magazine* piece called "PowerPoint Makes You Dumb." "When NASA engineers [had earlier] assessed possible wing damage during the mission, they presented the findings in a confusing PowerPoint slide—so crammed with nested bullet points and irregular short forms that it was nearly impossible to untangle. 'It is easy to understand how a senior manager might read this PowerPoint slide and not realize that it addresses a life-threatening situation,' the board sternly noted." And, as Thompson added, Colin Powell relied on PowerPoint in his now infamous presentation to the United Nations "proving" that Iraq had weapons of mass destruction.

PowerPoint confuses and bores us maybe, but does it make us dumb, too? That idea comes from the Yale information theorist Edward Tufte. The "popular PowerPoint templates (ready-made designs) usually weaken verbal and spatial reasoning, and almost always corrupt statistical analysis," he writes in his booklet *The Cognitive Style of PowerPoint,* which shows, simplistic bulleted line by simplistic bulleted line, how PowerPoint fosters stupidity. PowerPoint's bulleted lists may "create the appearance of hard-headed organized thought," but the technique is "faux-analytical."

As a "prankish conspiracy against substance and thought," PowerPoint is closer to advertising, Tufte writes. "Especially disturbing is the introduction of the PowerPoint cognitive style into schools. Instead of writing a report using sentences, children learn how to make client pitches and info-mercials."

PowerPointing is part of the seductive marketing promise that we can outsource our thinking. The relief of not having to think is pitched in the pop locution *smart [X]'s—smart cards, smart weapons, smart houses, smart toys, smart foods,* and (the exteriorized brain that Lanier discusses) *smart agents.*

But as much as I point my finger at PowerPointers, I cannot binarily bifurcate myself from them or from Christopher. Do I wish I could push a few buttons so that some software would write this book for me? Absolutely. And when I routinely take digital shortcuts (or ask rhetorical questions in a clichéd form like this), do I practically feel my brain cells leaking? You betcha!

For instance, I engage in digital reading. Instead of reading something on the computer screen, I'll do a search for the words I'm looking for, and thereby stay ignorant of the context. I do this even when the words I'm looking for are in the very paragraph in front of me. I could *read* the paragraph, but so habituated have I become to treating words as units on the monitor that focusing on larger units like paragraphs seems a waste of my pressurized time. Worse, I sometimes feel my eyes trying to do word searches in books and newspapers.

I also want to, but can't, listen digitally. That is, I want to make people talk faster, which I can do at will on my digital telephone answering machine—I just press a button to speed up (or slow down) a recorded message. So when speaking with in-the-flesh people (especially slow talkers, as Seinfeld called them), my index finger actually feels an impulse to push a button on them.

I sort of get my wish when I watch the news, especially with Fox News Channel anchor Shepard Smith, who says things like:

"Amazon.com celebrating a birthday! The Internet company ten years old."

"Texas! A school bus and two other vehicles colliding in Dallas. The bus rolling over on its side."

"We don't communicate in full sentences anyway," Smith told *The New York Times*, in a full sentence, juggling the interview with work on that day's script. "We don't need all those words. And it allows us to go faster."

But if the only concern of go-fast news were speed, Shepard might have said, "Internet company Amazon.com is celebrating its tenth birthday"—a full sentence, yet two syllables shorter. Dropping helping verbs like *to be* and putting tenseless participle verbs like *celebrating* in sole charge of the action is as likely to slow down as to speed up news reading.

But the problem with this style (and Smith is hardly its only practitioner—it's all over cable, network TV, and radio) isn't its speed or its lack of complete sentences. The more important effect of dropping tensed verbs is that the sense of time drops away. Had Smith said, "A school bus and two other vehicles collid*ed* in Dallas," he'd have the same number of syllables and a full sentence. But he wouldn't have unbound the event from time.

Michael Kinsley described the effect well: "Past, present, and future melting together as every newsworthy event taking place simultaneously in some dimension beyond the reach of time."

Tenseless news-reading (or what Geoffrey Nunberg calls Inglish) encourages us to suspend curiosity about *when* events happen, and it parallels other news-writing habits that encourage us to suspend curiosity, and therefore skepticism, about any biases the sources, reporters, or media owners may hold. In other words, go-fast news is another bit of dumbing down, another part of the vast media-wing unconspiracy.

As are all the malls and Web sites that are beyond the reach of time. Malls are devoid of clocks, so that you can swipe plastic in pleasant respite from guilt-inducing schedules. Just try finding a date on a Web site (most news sites and blogs excepted) other than a copyright date. Most Web pages could have been posted five years ago or this morning. Content, stuff, thing, product, always existing and available for purchase.

DICKHEAD DICHOTOMIES

Dickhead dichotomies, which I've alluded to throughout, are like everyday false dichotomies—only more pop, cocky, and obnoxious. Their drumbeat of either/or-ism contributes to an adolescent, contentious society that is unwilling to endure ambivalence, needs sandwich boards on its villains and victims, and breaks out in hives when asked to hold two seemingly contradictory thoughts at once. (The modern classic: O.J. murdered Nicole *and* he was framed.)

What's true and what's false about these journalistic and advertising dueling dualisms?: "Who Scored & Who Bored" (*Entertainment Weekly* cover line). "Hot (DSL) Not (dial up)" (Verizon Online DSL print mailer ad). "Either you are with us, or you are with the terrorists" (George W. Bush). "Red states and blue states" (most media).

What's true is that often you *do* have to reduce too much info to a yes-or-no decision: You either buy the movie ticket or you don't; you vote for A or for B. What's false is the drop-dead drama that says, "Here's the deal: black or white, on or off, ones or zeroes, winners or losers. Choose or die." Because, of course, you can score *and* bore; you can be lukewarm one minute, Cool Hand Luke the next. If you're not with "us," chances are actually rather high that you're not with the terrorists. Most states—even most people—are shades of purple, but that wouldn't help pundits pump their purple prose. And here I must remind myself: Things can be, and usually are, digital *and* analogue.

Some of What's Dichot & What's Not may reside in English itself. Despite our language's rich vocabulary, "we are strangely lacking in middling terms—words to describe with some precision the middle ground between hard and soft, near and far, big and little," Bill Bryson wrote in *The Mother Tongue*.

But mostly, our false-dichotomy habit comes from us, not from our lack of middling terms. Paul Fussell traces this "mode of gross dichotomy" back to World War I and "the modern *versus* habit: one thing opposed to another, not with some Hegelian hope of synthesis involving a dissolution of both extremes (that would suggest 'a negotiated peace,' which is anathema), but with a sense that one of the poles embodies so wicked a deficiency or flaw or perversion that its total submission is called for."

ALL BACKSLASH, NO BACKLASH

The last consequence of too much digital thought and speech is that we come to believe there are no consequences—especially not to anything we really, really want to do.

We're all bureaucrats now, and bureaucrats must compartmentalize experience and ignore nonpertinent info to such an extent that an anesthesia gradually sets in. Cutting up life into neat partitions can temporarily paralyze the delicate connective tissue necessary to appreciate context and continuity, not to mention history. Digital overdosing doesn't just obscure any middle ground between good and bad, it numbs us to a sense of relatedness at all—between now and later, action and reaction, cause and effect. We function more and more like our writing software, computer games, and digital cameras: Anything you don't like, you just redo.

In the Unit States, nothing can touch me. Digit-think enables the belief that—presto and poof—with enough back-slashes, there'll be no backlashes, that there is such a thing as a free (Halliburton-supplied) lunch: Topple Saddam\Install democracy\Exit cleanly\Collect oil bucks\War = a win-win.

I'm not blaming digital thinking for the war in Iraq (or, for that matter, for all consequence-blind thought). Digit-think is but a mite compared to other factors, such as George W. Bush's belief that God was directing him, the neocons' obsession, the press's shameful acquiescence. And forces on any side of any issue will shift into digital mode to convince themselves that nothing untoward could possibly result from their good intentions. But we are all a little more receptive to the no-consequences argument to begin with because it clicks right into our daily digital operations.

And we're a little less receptive to the more analogue notion that many technological solutions, necessary as they might be in alleviating problems, inevitably cause other problems. We might call them side effects, blowback, unintended consequences, or "revenge effects," as the historian of science Edward Tenner does in his book *Why Things Bite Back*. Wide-scale use of air-conditioning in some cities, he writes, has raised local outdoor temperatures by as much as ten degrees, and, as is better known, heavy use of antibiotics has created stronger strains of bacteria that don't respond to antibiotics. Or, I'd add, too much of a headache remedy can lead to worse "rebound" headaches, and a toxic chemical, PFOAs, used in a range of products from carpet stain protectors to nonstick frying pans, has been found sticking around in human bloodstreams.

Well, we'd love to cogitate on that, but wrapping our brains around product blowback is harder than nailing Jell-O to a wall.

In addition to being only part Luddite, I'm only part dickhead dichotomist. I don't see only the harms of digitalese—I also see poetry and loads of charm, albeit mostly in abbreviations.

We're talking, reading, and thinking in initialisms and acronyms: *AC, ATM, BYOB, OTC, DWI, DIY, IT, IPO, LBO, Y2K, WMD, IHOP, ICBIY, TCBY, TGIF, OMG, NIMBY, SUV, M.O., MOR, WYSIWYG;* and in "clippings" (apostrophes optional): *abs, Ab Fab, info, boho, pomo, J. Lo, burb, zine, toon, tude, hood, plex* (multiplex), *rents* (parents), *nads* (gonads, testicles), *coups* (coupons), *jects* (housing projects), *merch* (merchandise, as in "This seven-member artists' collective, which specializes in T-shirts, posters, stickers, and buttons, could set up one kick-ass merch table in the back of a bar somewhere"), and the clipping that describes all this, *phenom* (which isn't an eighties but a fifties creation, first applied to fast-rising baseball players). Not to mention numbers: *411, 911, 9/11, 24/7, 180, 360* (see chapter 3 on black-inspired pop).

And, whether they abbreviate or lengthen words, I'm a sucker for the *O*s, among them *Emo, Screamo, Coolio,* and *vio.* (Respectively: "the type of music you listen to when, try as you might, you cannot get laid . . . and cry about it"; "post hardcore emo punk with screaming and such"; the rap artist; *New York Post* shorthand, used in the 1990s, and possibly only once, for a game that ended in violence.)

O is important to all pop language, but it serves digit pop particularly well. As *Emo* and *vio* perhaps best illustrate, *O* compartmentalizes by encircling feelings that threaten to spread out of control and, in the process, makes them comic-book funny. I have a friend who says he's "depresso," which helps to cap his gloom. My son, influenced by superhero names, calls me Forgetto. The *O*-ed thing is more contained—and thus cuter—than the non-*O*-ed thing, as companies from Drāno to TiVo well know. And names aside, it's hard to find a corporation whose logo is not based on the circle.

O has childlike play written all over it, but to some extent most abbreviations have a kid and kidding quality. Generations X, Y, Z, and ABC are especially quick to appreciate the toon

POW-er of squeezed, encoded words. I recently heard a teenage boy in Rite Aid say to his friends, "By the way—BTW—ha ha ha!" For him, just saying the e-mail acronym after the words it replaces was a laff riot.

The number of abbreviations, whether initialisms, acronyms, or clippings, has soared in the last twenty or so years. Not to imply a causal relationship, but it does seem that as humans get fatter, the language gets skinnier. I mean, zero is sacred: Jesus Christ went digit pop a while ago, first with *WWJD?* (What would Jesus do? Or drive?), which spawned, among others, *WWJE?* (eat), *WWJVF?* (Who would Jesus vote for?), and *WWJB?* (Who would Jesus bomb?). And "We're all aware of what in some churches we call the 'C-and-E'ers,' " said the Reverend Karen Bockelman, the pastor of Our Savior Lutheran Church in Circle Pines, Minnesota, "people who attend only on Christmas Eve or Easter."

Of course, the rise of e-mail and text messaging has given abbreviations an enormous boost, with *GFUG* (Good for you, girl), *IMHO* (in my humble opinion), *e-business, e-commerce,* and *m-commerce* (mobile) already being old hat. Likewise, hip-hop wordplay amped the brevs, especially as every (Wall) street-cred-seeking corp stepped up to the plate. Reebok, for one, tattooed its stock ticker tag, RBK, onto a line of sneakers, as in the "G-Unit Collection by RBK."

But abbreviations didn't start with e-life or Jay-Z—people have been inventing them since B.C. The initials SPQR (*senatus populusque Romanus,* "the Senate and the People of Rome") were inscribed on public works throughout the Roman empire. "The impulse to shorten words is an ancient one," writes Bryson, adding that in the 1800s "syllabic amputations were the rage," and resulted in *mob* (short for the Latin *mobile vulgus,* a fickle crowd), *exam, gym,* and *lab.*

The primo abbrevo and one of the most-recognized words in the world originated in that century. Theories abound about *OK*'s etymology, but most linguists believe that Allen Walker Read of Columbia University, who spent years tracking down *OK,* nailed it. As Bryson writes, Read found that "a fashion developed among young wits of Boston and New York in 1838 of writing abbreviations based on intentional illiteracies. They thought it highly comical to write O.W. for 'oll wright,' O.K. for 'oll korrect,' K.Y. for 'know yuse,' and so on."

OK might have gone the way of *O.W.,* however, had it not become a rallying cry at the 1840 Democratic convention that renominated Martin Van Buren for president. Van Buren was known as Old Kinderhook, from his hometown in New York, and his supporters formed the "O.K. Club." "With great haste," Bryson writes, *OK* "established itself as a word throughout the country." The new word went much further than Van Buren, who lost the election to William Henry Harrison (whose own slogan, "Tippecanoe and Tyler Too," was catchy but no *OK*).

The word *acronym* itself gained currency during WWII as "wartime production of names using initials reached an all-time high," write Barnhart and Metcalf, who note the difference between initialisms like *USA, GI,* and *GOP* and "hard-core acronyms, which are initials pronounced as a separate word," like *WASP, AIDS,* and *radar* (radio detection and ranging). "In general use, however, these are all called acronyms."

ARS LONGA, LOGOS BREVIS

The need for speed and efficiency would seem to explain the popularity of abbreviations, and clearly it is a drag to say *electronic mail* or *sport utility vehicle.* But abbreviations are more than prosaic time-saving devices. In fact, they don't always save time. Compare the three syllables it takes to say *day and night* or *'round the clock* to 24/7's five. But, made of digits and a stick, 24/7 looks digital and speaks to dig's precision: Our store won't be closed for a single second. The emo msg: Time loves U unconditionally.

And the pop msg: Crack the code . . . if you can. Because WYSI*N*WYG (what you see is *not* what you get). Brevs' compression makes them pop out harder, and in the popping the shortened form becomes a less-is-more art form. I.e., abbreviations are cool. Concentrating more info into less space and getting on with it is cool. Abbreviations set off guessing games and offer dozens of chances daily to be an insider. To speak them is to suggest that you don't take too seriously the words they derive from. (Suburbs? Ha! Magazines? Gimme a break! Merchandise? That's for Willy Loman.)

Turning something large and unwieldy into something small and neat also speaks of magic: We control language—we can roll it into a ball, throw it where we want, make it disappear—rather than it controlling us.

And mostly, flashing dashing info-idea-word things begin to approximate their presumed nemesis, the image. The Japanese are already there, extensively using pictures instead of words for cell-phone e-mail. "Think of the happy face run wild," Howard French wrote in *The New York Times*. For instance, " 'Would you like to go out for a drink tonight?' has been radically shortened by the picture of an overflowing mug, followed by the verb ending used in invitations."

In the beginning was the word, the *logos*. The Next Big Thing was the logo—corporate shrines of design to improve brand image. Soon, each of God's children sought a brand image of her/his own. Now, the original *logos* requires a logo, a symbol for the symbol that is a word.

THE X-WORD FILES

As symbols, abbreviations put distance between themselves and the more analogue, spelled-out things they stand for. Such distancing tools can be important, even psychologically necessary. A friend told me that for more than a year after 9/11, her daughter and a friend, then both six, called the Twin Towers disaster "T" and anything about the war in Afghanistan "G." "It's too scary to say the words," my friend said, "so this way they can talk about it without getting upset."

A similar need to talk without getting upset is also behind formulations like *the F-word* and *the N-word*. Those two represent hardcore taboo words, and it's perfectly appropriate to give them the FLOTWOP (First Letter of the Taboo Word Only, Please) courtesy. But since we love to fetishize the forbidden, half of the *[X]-words* out there are wannabe taboo words, contorting themselves into mystery status.

In a sort of half-abbreviation, half-pig-Latin game, you just take the initial letter of a word and replace the rest with *-word*. The *[X]-word* formation has come to represent words that are taboo, words that someone wants to be regarded as taboo, or words that someone is avoiding for emotional, political, or legal reasons. Hence, *the M-word* for *mistake* ("You obviously don't want to use the M-word in here," Senator Bob Kerrey told Condoleezza Rice in questioning the administration's response to terrorism, during the 9/11 commission hearings) and *the I-word* for *intern* ("Post-Monica, Interns Prefer Any Title but the 'I-Word,' " read a *Wall Street Journal* subhead). Problem is, the letter game is used so liberally. *The I-word* also means, in other contexts, *interest rates, inflation,* and *impeachment.* And did you know that *the R-word,* often used for unspeakables like *retirement, recession, racism, retarded,* or *rape,* can also stand for *Republicans,* particularly those too stigmatized to speak the name of their party? *Rated R: Republicans in Hollywood,* a documentary about conservatives in Tinsel Town, was originally called *The R-Word.* Stigmatization pop quiz: Does *the L-word* = *liberal,* as in the *Salon* headline "Branding Kerry with the L-word," or does *the L-word* = *lesbian,* as in the Showtime series?

That ever-interesting wordsmith Donald Rumsfeld pulled a FLOTWOP double-inverse when he insisted that the treatment of Iraqi prisoners at Abu Ghraib was abuse but not torture. "I don't know if it is correct to say what you just said, that torture has taken place, or that there's been a conviction for torture," he told a reporter at a press conference. "And therefore, I'm not going to address the torture word."

It's unclear if, after having already uttered *torture* several times, Rumsfeld meant to say, "I'm not going to address the T-word" but mistakenly let slip the whole thing—or if he figured that, though the rest of the world thinks he can't bring himself to say the T-word because in their eyes he's guilty of inciting it, he can and, gosh darn, *will* say it, but he'll say it in taboo format to rub into the press's fat face that NOTHING TABOO HAPPENED!

In less tortuous words, *the torture word* might have been Rumsfeld's way to tell the press (to borrow from Dick Cheney), Go F-word yourself.

So when trying to draw attention *away* from a word, do not use the *[X]-word* format. To aid in forgetting, regular abbreviations work just fine. Which is one reason Kentucky Fried Chicken, coated with *fried*'s greasy rep, renamed itself KFC. And if the only connotation you need to escape is outdatedness, initials can spiff you up, as they have for International Business Machines, P. Diddy, and Mickey D's. Recently, the latter has even taken to calling itself "Mc." A magazine ad shows three attractive Gen Yers hangin' in a loft near the coffee-table-sized letters *M* and *c*. "What does Mc® mean to me?" the trademark-symbol-pocked copy reads. "Everything that I love. . . . To me, Mc means McDonald's®. So I'm cool with Mc and Mc is cool with me." While appealing to youth's appetite for abbreviations, McDonald's is also reminding other companies that Mc is *not* cool with them working those coveted letters into their names.

Whether used to disguise, to modernize, or to mark one's territory, the Initial Response System reflects the growing gap between the full, resonating word and the sportier, sometimes shallow progeny. In the gap, marketing opportunities are rife.

So, yes, brevs are busting out all over, and I adore their clever lil' hearts. But when *Republican* begins to cohabit *the R-Word* with *racism*, I sigh, OMG. Because even the freshest abbreviation can lose its charm and dry into a stale cracker of letters, with meaning N/A.

CLICKING TOWARD POLYMORPHOUS PERVERSITY

God dehydrated to *G,* laughing flattened to *L*—why would we put up with that or any of the other boxed-in consequences of living and talking digitally? Sure, we gain some efficiency (though many efficiencies create more work). But ultimately, we're digitalizing our lives for the same reason we do anything that might not be so good for us: It gives us pleasure.

Pulsating throughout digit tech—through all the e-mail, Web links, video games, remote controls, Palm Pilots, and other PDAs (personal digital assistants)—is the simple, sensual, quasi-sexual pleasure of the click. Tiny but palpable blips of pleasure: We press against a resistance, resistance gives way, a bit of energy transfers back to us (through our digits). And that small movement makes something BIG happen: Click to open. Click to see. Click to enlarge. Click to buy. Click to connect.

Repeated worldwide trillions of times a day, the click is the point of contact, the power point, between human and computer, computer and Internet, one's body and the global body politic.

Yet the more time we spend in disembodied digital busyness, the more we may need to feel a physical, "real time" body. We might not always be able to reach out and touch somebody—but we can usually direct any need for real sensation at the thing literally at hand: a mouse and/or a set of buttons. Now, the opposite reaction is just as possible, often within the same person: The more time we spend in disembodied busyness, the *less* we need to feel a physical body, even to the point of willing—and enjoying—our own atrophy. Hence, obesity, driving a car to go down the block, and so on.

But here's the beauty part. The desire to be in touch with physical sensation, and the desire to be numb to it, can both be satisfied by the same clicking motion.

Clicking contoured pieces of hard plastic might not be as pathetic a substitute for human bodily sensation as it seems. Although the clicking of keypads and mouses is emblematic of postmodern communication, some geneticists and biologists believe that clicking may have been instrumental to the beginnings of human speech itself. As Nicholas Wade wrote in *The New York Times*, "Geneticists reported in March [of 2003] that the earliest known split between any two human populations occurred between the !Kung of southern Africa and the Hadza of Tanzania. Since both of these very ancient populations speak click languages, clicks may have been used in the language of the ancestral human population. The clicks, made by sucking the tongue down from the roof of the mouth (and denoted by an exclamation point), serve the same role as consonants."

Ancient click languages may have evolved into the snap (to it), crackle, pop of today's corporate click dialects, into tribal sounds like *opt, interact, product, tech, link, tweak, ramp up, trump, net net.* That the business tongue clicks so often with plosive consonants is no coincidence: the *K, P,* and *T* "noise bursts," as they're called, are perfecto for punctuating points and packing them into distinct, easy-lock units. And as detailed earlier, those same plosives also kick butt on behalf of most of the "dirty" sex words and the various words for hitting, hard drugs, and sneaker brands.

Net net, clicking around for business purposes is a high-tech tweaking of a very primal urge.

To some, making money has always been as sexy as making love. But only relatively recently in human history has making money been taken over by electronic devices that transform efficiency into an interactive game with its own sensual rewards. We've learned to so closely associate a cue (a click) with a reward (a bargain found, a stock purchased) that—like lab mice rapidly pressing levers for food pellets—we've become conditioned to feel rewarded by the click itself. (Does pressing-for-pellets have anything to do with why the clicker is called a *mouse?*)

So the surge of satisfaction we get from clicking comes from two sources: the physical resistance/release sensation inherent in a click, and the emotional satisfaction we experience upon completing a task, any task. As they mingle, they enhance each other:

- a search successfully Googled: click.

- decoding an abbreviation: click.

- a door locked for the night: click.

- an in-group that, maybe cruelly, locks out others: clique (from the Old French for *latch,* and that from *cliquer,* for "to click").

- finding that right someone: click.

- finding that someone through Internet dating or porn:
  click to click.

Stationed at My Control Command Center, I am a wheeler-dealer, I get a player rush when I send off e-mail or find the right info. And I'm *so* not alone. According to a Reuters survey of a thousand Internet users in the United States, Europe, and Asia, "54% claim to get a 'high' when they find information they have been seeking." As the psychologist Michael G. Conner wrote in an online article called "Internet Addiction and Internet Sex": "Time begins to have no meaning when your next 'hit' is just a 'click' away."

As the click becomes more central to our nervous systems, our sensuality begins to merge with a corporate sensuality, and the seventies/eighties goal of multiple orgasms gives way to the nineties/twenty-first-century goal of orgasmic multitasking. We nouvelle player-transactors perform the lightest of touches and . . . Boom—our messages! Boom—a new link! Or, as Click-backamerica.org suggests, Boom—a new nation!

Click here! Now click here! Yes, right here! Don't stop!

EPILOGUE

It's Like, You Know, the End

On the other side of the binary divide are the extreme analogue words, words that shun either/or precision and the fidgety-digity beat. Thriving in the Big Muddy of blah blah, these words dismiss the busy, overcategorized world with a withering, passive-aggressive "Whatever."

The Slacker Seven—*Whatever, blah blah blah, yadda yadda yadda, go* (for *say*), *you know, like,* and *It's like, you know*—are at the end of this book, because, as they do in real life, they create the sense that they're tying up loose ends and expressing any as yet unexpressed thoughts. Other phrases may give bigger marketing buck for the pop, but the Seven specialize in one of pop language's most basic services: making a word's celebrity itself into the message. By vague-voguing their way through a sentence, they allow us to think we've communicated more than we have.

But while these words avoid communicating specifics, they do communicate all sorts of other things.

Whatever, for instance, vagues out in two directions: nice and mean. There's the agreeably laid-back, resigned *Whatever* that we say when a choice really doesn't matter much or when we don't know what else to say. And with just a shift of inflection, you have the dismissive put-down *Whatever* (as in the first paragraph above), used to say anything from "Don't overparse it, dude" to a permissible "Fuck you."

As for the earthy *blah blah blah* and the yuppie *yadda yadda yadda,* I believe (though I've no proof at all) that their function is an ancient one: Humans have probably always needed a set of repeated sounds to represent missing details or to suggest that the details are so unimportant as to not be worth specifying. But compared to the *so on and so on* or *et cetera et cetera* of a slightly more literary time, *blah blah blah* and *yadda yadda yadda* are teleready placeholders, evoking the blasé confidence of a Leno guest.

A LIKE/DISLIKE RELATIONSHIP

The lightning rod of this gangly gang is *like.* Critics, linguists, and I go back and forth between bewailing the prevalence of *like* and marveling at its versatility. My feelings about *like* are like *like* itself: protean, modern, and ticlike.

In defense of *like* (and, of course, we're not talking about the *like*'s meaning "similar to" and "feel favorable toward"), most linguists note that other languages have their equivalents. A twenty-seven-year-old teacher from Slovakia living in America tells me that in Slovak, for instance, *ako* or *akoze* (more or less meaning *like*) and *vies* (meaning *you know*) are used "like every other word, especially by young people."

In defense of those young people, who are tagged as idiots for saying *like* so much—well, we all know adults who are *like*-dependent, too. *It's Like, You Know* was, in fact, the title of a short-lived sitcom about some well-heeled L.A. residents, because "it's sort of emblematic of how people in L.A. speak," Peter Melman, the show's creator, told me. (Perhaps not coincidentally, Melman also wrote the famous *Seinfeld* "yadda yadda yadda" episode.) A really smart film critic I know was once raving about a movie she had seen. When I asked what she so liked about it, she struggled for a second and burst forth, "It's just like—you know?" She bubbled the words with such enthusiasm that I thought I *did* know. Has *It's like, you know* simply become a way to say "It's ineffable"—or do we say *It's like, you know* more now because our brains are less able to guide our thoughts toward the effable?

Either way, *like* is too complex to pin solely on adolescents or idiots. *Like* is indeed a "filler" (like *um* or *well,* filling time until you, maybe, find the right words), but it's much more. *Like* can also be a hedge, a form of *about,* when you're not sure whether what you're saying is quite accurate ("He was, like, fifty years old"); a "focuser" ("It's, like, come on already"); or a "quotative"—a replacement for *say* or *said* ("I was, like, I'll kill for this account"), which is related to the *goes* of "He goes, 'I'll be back.' " In this last function, *like* can "provide a stream-of-consciousness toggle switch between direct and indirect quotation, between thought and speech, between objective and subjective, and between real and perceived—the ultimate 20th century speech mechanism," Tom Dalzell writes.

Traveling the well-worn path from black jazz musicians to white beatniks and eventually to almost everyone else, *like* "contributed to the sense of a language that didn't actually mean anything so much as it evoked, the way a jazz riff does," Geoffrey Nunberg points out. "No other word embodies so many of the sensibilities that have been converging in the language since the hipsters first made their appearance—the ironizing, the mistrust of description, and particularly, the way we look to drama and simulation to do the work that used to be done by narrative."

Yet, I also mistrust the mistrust of description, and so I also agree with Dorothy Clark, a professor of English who told *The Los Angeles Times* that *like*'s prevalence among young people is a sign (that is, not a cause but a symptom) that "they're not involved in a language-rich environment, and they're so unsure of the words to use that 'like' eases them over the decision. . . . It's easy to get sucked into it yourself. It's comforting to feel you don't need to say what you mean, but can just rest on the assumption that your ideas are transmitted telepathically."

That jibes with what Jane Healy, an educational psychologist and the author of *Endangered Minds,* says about the effect of television and computers on children's brain development and their ability to reason with an "inner language." What was "behind the rise in filler words?" Healy was asked by *Stay Free!* magazine. She replied, ". . . visual skills—and in many cases, low-level visual skills—are being stressed heavily for children. The amount and quality of linguistic stimulation has declined. And this is happening during the period when brains are growing, when they are developing linguistic structures such as vocabulary and syntax. . . . Kids may have a thought floating around in their heads, but they cannot use the inner language to sort out what they're thinking." She speculates that this could "account for an increase in Attention Deficit Disorder. Because without the inner speech, you can't mediate your own thinking, and therefore you can't mediate your own behavior. You have trouble planning ahead, you have trouble saying to yourself, 'Look, I shouldn't be doing this, because, if I do . . .' Think of the complex language relationships going on with those sort of 'if/then' statements."

Maybe that's why too much *like* and *like, you know* are annoying: We sense that any internal discussion is even mushier. As is my inner speech about *like.* I appreciate how *like* surfs the ironic waves of language, but at the same time, I *want* to appreciate it— because predictably recoiling at *like* might make me seem uncool. But here's how uncool I really am: I'm appalled—yes, appalled—at how, if pop phrases drizzle over "grown-up" media, they storm over kids' media, the producers apparently terrified that if a single exchange fails to peak in a SuperFamiliar, Mega-Rockin' comeback, facial expression, or intonation, the littlest consumers will rule the content bor-ing! (To witness such slaves to pop, check out *Totally Spies, Teen Titans,* or *Teenage Mutant Ninja Turtles,* all hits with teen-talkin' first graders, of course.)

But now we're not just talking about *like* and the Slacker Seven—we're talking pop language in general. *Like* and *you know* may be more annoying (to some) than other big pop, but they're not at all more stupid-making.

Epilogue

BRAINS ON POP

What does make us stupid is the media's relentless promotion of any and all pop. Rather than encourage kids, or adults, to engage in "if/then" thinking (which could lead to bad thoughts, such as "If I look at screens all day, then my mind might become as flat as one"), professional cool-providers supply us with word/image plug-ins, like *Whatever, think outside the box, Yesss!, I don't* think *so,* and *Bring it on!* From sources high and low, media and marketing scrounge vivid, original language, glamour-shrink-wrap it, and retail it back to people, who pay for it by organizing their minds around it accordingly. The pop word becomes the password—to the group, to the beat, to the way out of struggling with words and thoughts.

Regardless of what a particular word means—or of whether it's ironic or sincere, digital or analogue, combative or community-oriented—once it has entered the pop pantheon, it acquires the power to win applause, build consensus, and close a deal. The pop word makes us an offer we can't refuse.

As I can't refuse now. I don't know how to end this book without a pop phrase. My only question is Which one? *End of story,* because in asserting (mock-rudely, of course) that my argument trumps all others, the phrase is as simple and finite as a click? Or should I go with something jazzier, more open-ended—something that puts the ball back in your court, you smart consumer, you—like, *It's like, you know?*

NOTES

PROLOGUE
Are We Having Fun Yet?

3   A little girl: She read my fortune in the late nineties.

4   Metamucil's Marine Corps: This ad appeared frequently on network news shows for several years until about 2002.

4   "What was he *thinking*?": "So universal was the desire to find some solace in the McVeigh verdict that practically no mention was made of the political culture that inspired his brutal truck-bombing. 'What was he thinking?' one survivor wondered on ABC, in a clip played over and over, as if there were no context for McVeigh's calculated violence." Editorial, "Getting McVeigh," *The Nation,* June 23, 1997, p. 3.

4   "Go for it!": "Oklahoma City bombing defendant Terry L. Nichols, crying during some of his ex-wife's testimony, today heard her recount how she discovered a letter in which he urged Timothy J. McVeigh to 'go for it' five months before the bombing." Tom Kenworthy, "Ex-Wife Describes Nichols's Letters; Defendant Moved to Tears," *The Washington Post,* November 20, 1997.

4   *Simple Life Reunion:* aired on Fox, January 13, 2004.

4   Albert Einstein: ad launched March 2000.

4   "Duh. Do I feel stupid, or what?": Carla Koehl, "Tragedy at the Prom (Infanticide Case)," *Newsweek,* June 23, 1997, p. 64.

5   "Yeah, right. It's about the money, dude. Hel-lo?": Alan Feuer, "Jungle, N.J., vs. Main Street, N.Y.; In Battle for Shoppers, Malls Emphasize Sense of Place," *The New York Times,* November 18, 1999.

5   Continental Airlines: print ad in *The New York Times,* November 25, 2003.

5   "You're history, man!": I saw this in 2001.

5   "You think I'm dissing you 24/7!": I saw this in 1999.

5   "Everyone is working 24/7": "Homeland Security Chief Holds First Press Conference," October 18, 2001, Fox News, www.foxnews.com/story/0,2933,36801,00.html.

5   "on crack": Daniel Eisenberg, "Ignorant & Poor," *Time,* February 11, 2002, p. 37.

5   "No way, José": "Helms, asked if Weld will get a hearing: 'No way, José.' " "National Briefing—Weld: Would Put Holdings in Blind Trust," *The Hotline* (National Journal, Inc.), August 6, 1997.

5   Roy Ratliff: Andrew Murr, "Sending Out an S.O.S.," *Newsweek,* August 12, 2002, p. 28.

5   NRA conventioneers yell, "Get a life!": Joe Mandak, "Columbine Father Challenges Cheney on Guns," Associated Press, April 17, 2004.

6   "Saddam is toast": Woodward, p. 266.

6   George Tenet's "slam dunk": ibid., p. 249. Tenet later said, "Those were the two dumbest words I ever said." Suzanne Goldberg, "Ex-CIA chief eats humble pie," *The Guardian,* April 29, 2005.

6   A videotape: The Fallujah bomb video is all over the Internet. Google "dude," "Fallujah," "video." The Freerepublic.com post is from July 14, 2004 (www.freerepublic.com/focus/f-news/1171674/posts). CNN ran the video October 11, 2004, and said about it: "Saturday, April 10, capped a bloody week in Fallujah. . . . U.S. Air Force F-16s dropped more bombs in support of the Marine offensive that Saturday than on any day that week. A cockpit video of one such engagement, never officially released, has circulated on the Internet for months. CNN has confirmed it's authentic." Jamie McIntyre, CNN senior Pentagon correspondent on *Anderson Cooper 360.*

6   Mac OS X ad: in twelve-page ad spread, *Time,* January 28, 2002.

6   "What is the dilio yo?": from August 20, 2003, www.graphx.net/sisters/2003_08_01_archive.html.

7   "If I ever want": "The Millennium (Quotations from the 1990s)," *Newsweek,* December 20, 1999, p. 81.

7   Star Jones: Col. Eileen Collins landed the *Columbia* shuttle July 28, 1999.

CHAPTER 1
Here's the Deal

10 "I'm outta here!": on *The Tonight Show,* December 1, 2003.

10 "Rock 'n' roll!": David M. Halbfinger, "For Helicopter Flight, Kerry Takes Controls," *The New York Times,* January 16, 2004.

10 Both Bush and Kerry say, "Bring 'em on!": Each has said it (or *Bring it on*) many times, including Bush on July 2, 2003; Kerry on November 25, 2003. See notes for chapter 4.

13 Postman on Orwell and Huxley: Postman, p. vii.

15 "It's so money": I saw this ad in 2000. Also: Michael McCarthy, "Ad Track: Founding Father Plugs Dollar Coin/Mint Capitalizes on First Image," *USA Today,* May 22, 2000.

15 Tenet and the Oval Office meeting: Woodward, p. 247.

16 "Joe Public": ibid., p. 249.

16 "it's a slam dunk!": ibid., p. 249.

16 "McLaughlin's presentation": ibid., p. 250.

16 "Saddam is toast": date and background, ibid., pp. 263–66; long quote: pp. 265–66.

18 "you are the real dilio": 27th Annual People's Choice Awards, aired January 7, 2001. *Dark Angel* was canceled in 2002.

19 Dictionaries and *Yadda, yadda, yadda:* Elin Schoen Brockman, "In the Dictionary Game, Yada Yada Yada Is Satisficing to Some, Not Others," *The New York Times,* August 22, 1999.

19 grunge slang: The *New York Times* piece on "grunge slang" ran November 15, 1992. *The Baffler* magazine revealed it as a hoax in its winter–spring 1993 issue. The whole story, including follow-ups, is recounted in "Harsh Realm, Mr. Sulzberger!," Frank and Weiland, eds., p. 203.

20 "Give me a break": *Newsweek,* May 31, 2004, p. 16.

20 it sheds the irony: Not all phrases follow the cycle of hot to ironic to tepid but indispensable. *Groovy,* which has gone in and out of fashion many times for decades, usually resurfaces on an irony life preserver.

21 "I'll write people off": quoted in Scotti and Young, p. ix.

21 "A lot of people": Alex Williams, "E-Dating Bubble Springs a Leak," *The New York Times,* December 12, 2004.

21 Bill Moyers set is "history": Chris Baker, "Expect a Newer Version of 'Now,' " *The Washington Times,* January 5, 2005.

21 "Cable is history": I saw the ad on September 13, 2003, on Starz.

CHAPTER 2
Pop Talk Is History

24 Charles Mackay: *Memoirs of Extraordinary Popular Delusions,* pp. 642–45; *flare up!:* pp. 645–47.

26 Jo-Ann Shelton quotes: from phone interview, 2000, and e-mail interview, December 2004.

26 Pompeii graffiti: Shelton, p. 99.

27 Cited some 33,000 times: Sarah Lyall, "Staid Know-It-All Goes Hip and Online; O.E.D. Enters the Dot-Com World," *The New York Times,* April 10, 2000.

28 "In Falstaff's seedy": Greenblatt, pp. 216–17.

28 Gross on Shakespeare: from phone and e-mail interviews in March 2005.

29 List of cant words: Claiborne, p. 268.

29 "Of all the trades": ibid., p. 266.

30 John McWhorter quotes: from phone interviews, 2000.

30 Yiddish words: from Leo Rosten's *The Joys of Yiddish.*

31 Paul Glasser on Yiddish: from phone interview, 2001.

31 David (the Slangman) Burke on French: from phone interview, 2001.

31 Marc Cooper on Cuban and Chilean Spanish: from phone interviews, 2001, and January 2005.

33 "Non-stop": from Barry Popik's posts to the American Dialect Society (americandialect.org) online discussion group.

33 In Germany: Suzanne Daley, "In Europe, Some Fear National Languages Are Endangered," *The New York Times,* April 16, 2001.

33 a sign in Nagasaki: from Popik's ADS posts.

33 Japlish: Nicholas D. Kristof, "Stateside Lingo Gives Japan Its Own Valley Girls," *The New York Times,* October 19, 1997.

33 "a list of 3,500": "Don't Say It," Periscope, *Newsweek,* February 3, 1997, p. 4.

33 OK soda: Leslie Savan, "Niked Lunch," *The Village Voice,* September 6, 1994, p. 51.

33 Arnold Zwicky on *Coca-Cola:* from his post to the ADS and an e-mail interview, April 2000.

34 Mexican soccer player: I saw this on TV in the late nineties, but I don't have the date or the name of the show.

34 "As all the peoples": *Roughing It,* p. 330.

35 Been There, Said That: All slang and history in this section come from Dalzell's book *Flappers 2 Rappers:* pre-flapper slang, pp. 1–7; 1920s flapper slang, pp. 8–23; 1930s phrases,

pp. 24–39; 1940s slang, pp. 41–63; "The Flapper movement was the first youth movement to generate": p. 7; *23 ski-doo*, p. 7. Last Dalzell quote in section: from phone interview, 2001.

36 *media* as we know it: Barnhart and Metcalf, p. 218.

37 superimposed titles; "There was more time": Leslie Savan, "Titular Head," *The Village Voice*, February 21, 1989. Reprinted in *The Sponsored Life*, pp. 40–43.

38 Personal Branding: I saw the site in 2000, but it's no longer up.

38 "Head Advertising": see www.Bodybillboardz.com.

38 "Viral marketing": see, for instance, Linda Stern, "Is It Buzz or Merely the Nosie of a Pest?," *Newsweek*, April 18, 2005, p. E4.

38 Pizza Hut logos: "The company reportedly paid about $1 million for the stunt and to emblazon a 30-foot-tall Pizza Hut logo on a Russian proton rocket in July 2000." ABC News, May 22, 2001, abcnews.go.com.

38 Men at urinals: "Alphabet flush with fall promotion plans: Get ready for 'Must Pee TV,' " Variety.com, July 17, 2000.

39 "Tagamet moments": John F. Dickerson, "In This Corner . . . The feisty McCain has been accused of losing control. But it's more complicated than that." *Time*, November 15, 1999, p. 40.

39 "alternative to Halcion": Matt Bai, "Bradley's Game: Peddling hoop dreams and hard work, he has built the campaign version of a Silicon Valley start-up. Will a public that's sick of slick pols buy in?" *Newsweek*, November 15, 1999, p. 37.

39 cartoony bounce: Some cartoons are creepy. A sixth-grade math book has worked product names and logos—Nike, Gatorade, Cocoa Frosted Flakes, Sony PlayStations, Burger King, McDonald's, Topps baseball cards, Barbie dolls—into the solving of math problems. These weren't paid-for product placements, as you might expect. Rather, brand names are so rooted in our collective brain that tossing them into a textbook apparently wasn't even a conscious decision. "Certainly we didn't discuss trying to use logos. It was more the examples that people came up with," one of the authors of *Mathematics: Applications and Connections* told *The New York Times*. Constance L. Hays, "Math Book Salted with Brand Names Raises New Alarm," *The New York Times*, March 21, 1999.

40 "Hello? Earth to liberals": "The Point," November 15, 2004, newscentral.tv/uploads/franchise/point/point-20041115.shtml.

41 Edmund Weiner: Sarah Lyall, "Staid Know-It-All Goes Hip and Online; O.E.D. Enters the Dot-Com World," *The New York Times,* April 10, 2000.

42 black-drag-queen-created: from Dalzell phone interview, November 2004.

42 "Slang is used": ibid.

43 Dalzell on *tight* and *sweet:* from phone interview, November 2004.

43 Dalzell compares slang and pop: from phone interview, 2001.

44 Charles Stone III: from phone interview, 2000.

CHAPTER 3
What's Black, Then White, and Said All Over?

45 "In the past": McCrum et al., p. 223.

45 "First, one cannot": Dalzell, p. xi.

46 "overwhelming": phone interview, 2001.

46 Here are just some: The list draws on various sources, including *Random House Historical Dictionary of American Slang,* vols. I and II; Smitherman, *Black Talk* and *Talkin' That Talk;* Lee, *American Speech* and in phone interview, 2002; and Dalzell, *Flappers 2 Rappers* and in phone interview, 2002.

48 Buick and NBA slogans: Geoff Edgers, "It's All Good and It's All over the Place," *Boston Globe,* November 2, 2002.

49 MTV wouldn't touch black music videos: Rose, p. 8.

49 "globally speaking": Greg Tate, "Hiphop Turns 30: Whatcha Celebratin' For?" *The Village Voice,* January 4, 2005, www.villagevoice.com/news/0501,tate,59766,2.html.

49 When Sprite realized: The Sprite ads with kids rapping about situations that aren't too sweet ran in 2001. The Sprite publicist also told me in a 2001 phone interview that the Sprite.com launch party occurred in "October or November of 2000."

50 fastest-growing: *Merchants of Cool,* which first aired February 27, 2001.

50 racial discrimination suit: "Coke settled the racial discrimination suit in late 2000 for an estimated $192.5 million." Scott Leith, "Key Figure in Bias Pact Quits Coke," *Atlanta Journal-Constitution,* February 10, 2004.

50 The company denied: "The deal eclipses the previous record $176.1 million settlement in a racial discrimination suit against oil giant Texaco. Coke, which has denied the allegations, said it planned to take a $188 million charge in the fourth quarter related to the agreement." "Coke Settles Dis-

crimination Suit for Record $192.5M," *Brandweek,* November 20, 2000.

51 "it still suggests . . . hardly likely": Trudgill, *Sociolinguistics,* p. 49.

51 "define black language from a black perspective": Smitherman, *Black Talk,* p. 123.

52 "In homes, schools, and churches": Rickfords, pp. 3–4.

52 "these are risky propositions": Smitherman, *Black Talk,* p. xiii.

52 "The approach Smitherman takes": Margaret Lee, phone interview, 2002.

53 "Get the 411": I saw the ad in *GQ,* November 2004, p. 161.

53 "Its origins are": *America in So Many Words,* p. 98.

53 "so good that it's bad": Smitherman, *Black Talk,* p. 20.

53 "from black to white": Rickfords, p. 97.

53 On *cat* and *fly,* see Dalzell, pp. 96–97, 212.

54 *Wannabe:* various sources, including Smitherman, *Black Talk,* p. 293.

54 "podcaster wannabes": "the Whole Wheat Radio Blog, which now houses a growing number of excellent WWR podcasts, as well as some tips for podcaster wannabes," j-walkblog.com/blog/index/P17025/ from October 8, 2004.

54 "artist wannabes": in a TV ad for UPN's "Road to Stardom with Missy Elliot," December 12, 2004.

54 "geek wannabes": said by Tavis Smiley on his NPR show, December 15, 2004.

54 "wannabe homeland security chief": said by Mark Reilly on *Morning Sedition,* Air America Radio, December 17, 2004, referring to Bernard Kerik, who withdrew his nomination for the Homeland Security cabinet position.

55 "serious as a heart attack": Smitherman, *Black Talk,* p. 3.

55 "Chill, Orrin": *Time,* July 27, 1998, p. 13.

55 signs throughout Virgin Records: I saw them in February 2001.

56 "Everybody give it up": quoted in *Random House Historical Dictionary of American Slang,* vol. I, p. 899.

56 As mocking bloggers: http://andrewteman.org/blog/index.php?p=39.

56 Dan Rather: Lee, *American Speech,* p. 369.

56 "In an effort": Phyllis Furman, "Headline News Hot for Hip-hop Phrases: CNN Headline News Wants to Get Jiggy with It," New York *Daily News,* October 2, 2002.

56 "You Go, Girl!" in *Today's Christian Woman:* Annette Smith, "You Go, Girl! How to find some can-do friends to give you the support you need," January/February 2004, www.christianitytoday.com/tcw/2004/001/5.36.html.

56 " 'You go, Teresa' ": Deborah Sontag, "The 2004 Campaign: The Democratic Nominee; Rock Stars Are Highlight, but Kerry Is the Headliner," *The New York Times,* October 31, 2004.

57 "Women to Heinz Kerry: You Go, Girl: Nominee's Wife Finds Support for Her Outspoken Ways," Associated Press, MSNBC. com, August 5, 2004.

57 "You're the man!": James Carney and John F. Dickerson, "W. and the 'Boy Genius,' " *Time,* November 18, 2002, p. 40.

57 "golf tournaments": "Wistful Day: Before We Give Thanks, Let's Fondly Remember What We Don't Have," sportsillustrated.com, November 24, 2004, sportsillustrated.cnn.com/2004/writers/ frank_deford/11/24/wistful.day/.

58 Colonel Sanders: The *This American Life* episode, including audio from the ad, originally ran November 26, 1999, from Public Radio International.

58 "Breathing While Conservative": www.rightwingnews.com/ comments.php?id=1232, August 20, 2003. On Abrams: "Elliott Abrams, who pleaded guilty in 1991 to withholding informa- tion from Congress in the Iran-contra affair, was promoted to deputy national security adviser to President Bush . . . [and] will be responsible for pushing Bush's strategy for advancing democracy." News services, "Iran-Contra Figure to Lead Democracy Efforts Abroad," *The Washington Post,* Febru- ary 3, 2005.

58 *Breathing while Republican:* freerepublic.com/focus/news/ 726159/posts, August 1, 2002.

59 *Beanz Meanz Heinz* and Kwik Save: Crystal, 1995, p. 275; EZLern, p. 400.

59 Phunny Phellows: Kevin Mac Donnell, "Collecting Mark Twain: A History and Three New Paths," *Firsts* magazine, 1998; found on www.abaa.org/pages/collectors/bctwain2. html. Mac Donnell is a rare-book dealer.

59 In the 1920s: Dalzell, pp. 215–16.

60 "trend in comic . . . the impact": Crystal, 1995, pp. 84–85.

61 "BestLoanz.com": I received its spam June 1, 2003. The site is no longer up.

61 Snoop Dogg's izzle: " 'Izzle' is dizzle," *Chicago Tribune RedEye,* June 1, 2004.

62 Jell-O sales declined: "To counter this loss, Kraft will stray from targeting moms to introduce a new line of X-TREME Jell-O Gel Sticks and Gel Cups directly to children." "Kraft Losing Market Share in Nation's Supermarkets," *The Food Institute Report,* November 26, 2001, p. 3. I saw the Jell-O ad on February 23, 2003.

62   *Maximum EXposure:* As of late 2004, Spike TV was syndicating reruns of the show on local channels.

63   "AS NOT SEEN": I saw it in 2001.

63   *X* crosses the chrome: Phil Patton, "Attention Shoppers: Vehicle X-ing Ahead," *The New York Times,* January 14, 2001. Also phone interview with Patton on December 10, 2004.

63   "World Reax": I saw it April 10, 2003.

63   ESPN's X Games . . . Bagel Bites: Kim Cleland, "Action Sports Form Fabric of Generation," *Advertising Age,* April 16, 2001, p. S22.

64   "a positive term": Smitherman, *Black Talk,* pp. 58, 72.

64   "to help marketing": December 2, 2004, home.businesswire. com/portal/site/google/index.jsp?ndmViewId=news_view &newsId=20041202005565&newsLang=en.

64   Verizon Wireless and Burger King commercials: I saw them both sometime between 2000 and 2002.

65   "have favorable attitudes": Margaret Lee, phone interview, 2001.

65   "A large number": Trudgill, *Sociolinguistics,* pp. 72–79.

65   "Slavery made its own traditions": McCrum et al., p. 200; "into the mainstream": ibid., p. 201.

66   "but minstrel shows": Metcalf, *How We Talk,* p. 159.

66   For the list of jive words from Calloway's dictionary, see McCrum et al., p. 213.

66   Dan Burley's *The Original Handbook of Harlem Jive* is quoted in Dalzell, p. 61.

66   "Hiya cat": ibid., p. 42.

66   Lou Shelly: ibid., p. 43.

67   "The end of the jive generation": ibid., p. 42.

67   Kerouac is quoted in ibid., p. 89.

67   For Dalzell on jive, and the list of jive words, see ibid., p. 43.

67   ". . . perhaps the richest period": Smitherman, *Black Talk,* p. 4; "The 1960s was a defining moment": p. 28.

68   Gerald Boyd is quoted in Sam Roberts, "Round Table; Writing About Race (And Trying to Talk About It)," *The New York Times Magazine,* July 16, 2000, p. 11; the quotation appears on p. 22.

68   "Unlike the hippie movement": Dalzell, p. 200.

69   *Whassup?!:* This discussion is based on research, including interviews with Stone and a Budweiser publicist, that I did for a piece, "Hip Hops," *ArtByte* magazine, July–August 2000, p. 14.

69   Lighter says *What's up?* goes back at least to 1838: " 'What's up?' has presumably been around for as long as there's been the phrase 'What's up?' (at least since 1838: OED)," American Dialect Society online post, October 19, 2004.

70 long-haired white dudes: Dalzell, p. 185.

70 trademarked the term: In his bio as a jurist for 2005 Andy Awards, Bob Scarpelli, Chairman, DDB Chicago, DDB's U.S. "Chief Creative Officer," wrote, "He is such a passionate believer in 'Talk Value (r)' that he trademarked the term," http://www.andyawards.com/jurors/ScarpelliBob.php.

72 "Most black people are not delighted": from phone interview with John Russell Rickford, 2000.

73 "It's something to see": "The Sound of Our Young World," *Time,* February 8, 1999, p. 66.

73 "Razom Nas Bahato": www.orangeukraine.squarespace.com/ journal/2004/11/29/razom-nas-bahato.html.

73 "Well, *girl* is just used": Connie Eble interview, 2001.

74 "bargain-basement prices" and "They don't have to PAY NO DUES": Smitherman, *Black Talk,* p. 32.

74 "Cool is all about": Donnell Alexander, "Are Black People Cooler Than White People?" from *Step into a World,* p. 16.

75 "A wooden-faced model": These quotes come from Margaret Visser's appearance in *Cool,* a 1995 documentary by TVOntario.

76 "about completing the task": Alexander, ibid., p. 17.

76 "*Square,* a vital word": Dalzell, p. 112.

76 John Leland: "A Cool Dozen Questions for John Leland," www.harpercollins.com/global_scripts/product_catalog/book _xml.asp?isbn=0060528176&tc=ai.

76 *Cool's* opposite number: I saw this ad in *The New York Times,* March 7, 2005, p. C9.

77 "tricked out" cars and quote from *Dub* publisher: Keith Naughton, "Cars: What's In? Tricked Out," *Newsweek,* January 17, 2005, p. 11.

77 "Capitalism's original commodity fetish": Greg Tate, "Nigs R Us, Or How Blackfolk Became Fetish Objects," introduction to *Everything But the Burden,* p. 4.

77 "in a market-driven world": ibid., p. 14.

78 "Most think cool is": Alexander, ibid., p. 17.

78 The history of the Ebonics controversy comes from the Rickfords' excellent section "The Ebonics Firestorm," in their *Spoken Soul,* pp. 163–218. "The Night Before Christmas" parody: p. 212. "Since the recent decision": p. 213. "The Ebonics controversy confirmed that linguists": p. 175.

80 "One of those dialects": McWhorter, *Losing the Race,* p. 187.

81 McWhorter reminds us: He reminded me, in a phone interview in 2000.

81   "The variously named vernacular": Rickfords, p. 67.
81   "During the Harlem Renaissance": ibid., p. 9.
82   He said his reticence: Bruce Shapiro, "Thomas Speaks!" *The Nation,* March 12, 2001.
82   "Americans of all types": Rickfords, p. 74.
82   "Appreciating sung soul": ibid., pp. 75–76.
82   "The part of black language": John Russell Rickford in phone interview, 2001.
83   Khephra Burns: in "Yakkity Yak, Don't Talk Black!" *Essence,* March 1997, p. 150. Quoted by the Rickfords, p. 199.

CHAPTER 4
Don't Even *Think* About Telling Me "I Don't *Think* So":
The Media, Meanness, and Me

84   The *Fresh Air* episode ran April 9, 2001.
86   Teed off: Peter Chandler, "Melanie in Love: At Home with Antonio Banderas, Melanie Griffith Sheds Her Wild-Child Skin, Steadied by a New Self-image, the Love of Her Life and Baby on the Way," *InStyle,* March 1996, p. 80.
86   at a supermarket: I witnessed this in 2002.
86   *North Shore:* I saw this episode on September 20, 2004.
86   JetBlue: I saw the ad in March 2002.
86   "Puffy is *sooo* two years ago": Michael Specter, "I Am Fashion: Guess Who Puff Daddy Wants to Be?" *The New Yorker,* September 9, 2002, p. 117.
86   Donald Trump: *Newsweek,* October 18, 1999.
87   "let's not go there": Powell said this, and I saw it, on the *NBC Nightly News,* February 11, 2004.
87   "Sex with a minor. Don't go there": Corrie Pikul, " 'Isn't she a little young?' " *Salon.com,* July 26, 2004.
87   "I thought you were sexy—you suck": *American Idol,* February 2003.
87   Hyundai Santa Fe: I saw the ad in September 2002.
87   "The principal laughed": The incident happened in September 1996; I saw the mother repeat the principal's remark soon afterward on a local Los Angeles TV news station.
87   Canon Canada: Solange De Santis, "Kid Says Darndest Things in Ad, and Canadians Say, 'Spare Us!' " *The Wall Street Journal,* March 25, 1998.
89   "Yo momma": Smitherman, *Black Talk,* pp. 115–16; on snappin, p. 265.
89   "The slang of the 1970s and 1980s": Dalzell, p. 166.

90   "What's ya worst nightmare?": from "Queens Is" on the 2000 album *G.O.A.T.*

90   "Project Worst Nightmare": "Donald Beauregard, a Pinellas County militia leader, called the plan of destruction 'Project Worst Nightmare,' federal agents say," Ace Atkins and Michael Fechter, "Pinellas Militia Leader Arrested," *Tampa Tribune*, December 9, 1999.

91   The *Apprentice* quotes all come from the show that first aired November 18, 2004.

93   "do" Syria or Iran: "And now, in the language of Beltway strutting, are we really to 'do' Syria or Iran?" David Remnick, "War Without End?" *The New Yorker*, April 21 and 28, 2003, p. 61.

93   "I don't do quagmires": Rumsfeld said this during a Department of Defense news briefing, July 24, 2003, http://www.defenselink.mil/transcripts/2003/tr20030724-secdef0452.html.

93   "I don't do nuance": Bush said this to Senator Joe Biden. In an interview with Joshua Micah Marshall in late March 2004, Biden recalled, "You know the president always brags with me. And what he said to me not long ago was, 'Joe, I don't do nuance' as if that was a real cool thing, right?" The interview was published July 2, 2004, on www.talkingpointsmemo.com/archives/003118.php.

93   "I know how to do mud": "When an Iowan asked if he had the fortitude to endure a nasty campaign, Kerry responded: 'Listen, man, I fought in Vietnam and I know how to do mud. I'm ready for them.' " Adam Nagourney, "As Campaign Tightens, Kerry Sharpens Message," *The New York Times*, August 10, 2003.

93   John Ellis: The quotations come from Jane Mayer, "George W.'s Cousin," *The New Yorker*, November 20, 2000, p. 36.

95   Clotaire Rapaille: Keith Bradsher, "Was Freud a Minivan or S.U.V. Kind of Guy?" *The New York Times*, July 17, 2000.

95   Bill Maher on SUVs: from his stand-up special, *Victory Begins at Home*, HBO, July 17, 2003.

95   "a pervasive warlike": Tannen, p. 3.

96   "programmed contentiousness": ibid., p. 8.

96   "a crystal": ibid., p. 10.

97   "Many attorneys feel": ibid., p. 165.

97   Richard Sherwin: He made these remarks in an interview with Julie Scelfo. "When Law Goes Pop: Interview with Richard Sherwin," *Stay Free!*, no. 18, May 1, 2001, pp. 40–42.

97   "Instead of becoming more divergent": Bryson, p. 169.

100 *The Family Guy:* I'm quoting from an episode of a few years ago. Fox canceled the show in 2002, but after reruns proved

to be a hit on the Cartoon Network, Fox began airing new episodes in 2005.

100 Genesys: I saw the ad in *The New York Times,* June 5, 2000.

102 *Show me the money:* Susan Wloszczyna, " 'Maguire' Shows How a Film's Impact Can Turn on a Phrase," *USA Today,* January 24, 1997.

103 Some say that Jim Carrey invented: for instance, Armstrong and Wagner, p. 68.

103 *Gooood!:* "*Bruce Almighty* also boasts a new crop of Carrey catchphrases, like 'It's good' and 'B-E-A-U-tiful,' that might not read on paper but will be repeated ad nauseam as audiences exit theaters. 'That's all Jim,' says [*Almighty* director Tom] Shadyac. 'He's very conscious of what he's doing with those phrases. . . . You know it's got a chance when the crew starts repeating it. You'll see your [director of photography] on day 20 and ask, "How's work?" And he goes, "It's good, it's gooood." ' " Nancy Miller, "The God Couple," *Entertainment Weekly,* April 25, 2003, p. 32.

105 "That sort of confrontational banter": Most of Jones's remarks in this chapter come from several phone and e-mail interviews, primarily in the spring of 2002.

107 Fonzie's "Aaaaay": Jones, p. 242.

108 $1 million an episode: Samantha Miller, "Earn, Baby, Earn," *People,* March 17, 2003. Kelsey Grammer's salary: Lynette Rice, "On the Air: The Latest News from the TV Beat," *Entertainment Weekly,* October 25, 2002.

108 More important: Claire Atkinson, " 'Idol' Tops TV Price Chart," *Advertising Age,* September 27, 2004, cover.

110 Jack Burditt's remarks are quoted from my phone interview with him, October 2001.

111 Peter Tolan's remarks are quoted from my phone and e-mail interviews with him, October 2001.

116 *S* is one of the most frequently used: Crystal, 1997, p. 86. ("The average rank order [of all letters in American English], based on a description of 15 categories of text totalling over a million words, is" e, t, a, o, i, n, s, h, r.

117 "always detaching themselves": Geoffrey Nunberg, "Yadda Dabba Do," *Fresh Air,* NPR, May 8, 1998. The actual line from *The Treasure of the Sierra Madre* is "Badges? We ain't got no badges! We don't need no badges. I don't have to show you any stinkin' badges!" (Internet Movie Database: www.imdb.com/title/tt0040897/quotes).

119 Reese's Pieces in *E.T.:* Reese's didn't pay for the plug. "0: Amount paid by Hershey's to have its Reese's Pieces appear in

the film. The candy makers, who were approached after the M&M's people passed, were at first reluctant to have their product associated with a 'monster' movie." Brian M. Raftery, "E.T. by the Numbers," *Entertainment Weekly*, March 29, 2002.

119 "The newborn talkies": DiBattista, p. 40. For the list of Hollywood writers, see p. 41.

119 "Wisecracks still ricochet": ibid., p. xi.

120 "We gravitate": from phone interview with DiBattista, 2002.

120 "Invention of": H. L. Mencken quoted in DiBattista, pp. 48–49.

121 *Privatize This!:* Blogs, for instance, "talkingpointsmemo.com's 'Privatize This!' Shop," www.cafepress.com/privatizethis. In headlines, Lenore Skenazy, "Hey George, Privatize This," *Daily News*, March 13, 2005.

121 "Outsource This: The Dems Smell Blood": Paul Magnusson with Alexandra Starr, *Business Week*, March 1, 2004, p. 47.

121 HIGHJACK THIS, FAGS: David Talbot, "Andrew Sullivan's Jihad," *Salon*, October 20, 2001. Photo can be seen by typing in "highjack this fags" on Google under "Images."

121 "Scan This!": Rob Turner, "Faceprinting: Perps Beware: Your Cheekbones Are a Dead Giveaway," *The New York Times Magazine*, August 12, 2001, p. 18.

121 Hey ARNOLD: GROPE THIS: photo in *The New York Times*, "Week in Review," October 5, 2003.

121 "to a particular constituency": Dalzell, phone interview in 2003.

122 Wherever it came from: No one I asked—Margaret Lee, Jesse Sheidlower, Tom Dalzell, Evan Morris of worddetective.com, or the ADS group at large—could say with certainty where the phrase comes from.

123 Shiny writerly objects: For more on media clichés *(urban, diva, trial balloon)*, see *On the Media*'s "Word Watch," through www.NPR.org.

123 These may be the only people: I exaggerate. Laura Bush "characterized Karl Rove, her husband's chief political adviser, as not as powerful as 'the chattering class' believes." Elisabeth Bumiller, "A First Lady Fiercely Loyal and Quietly Effective," *The New York Times*, February 7, 2004.

124 *The Simpsons:* For Marge and Homer watching TV, see "Wild Barts Can't Be Broken," original air date January 17, 1999.

124 For Apu chilling his loins, see "Eight Misbehavin'," original air date November 21, 1999.

124 phrases that Bart popularized: "While Bart (or his writers)

coined none of them, he has certainly popularized them."
Dalzell, p. 226.

124 church sermons: Sam Smith, "Sitcom Spirituals," *The New York Times Magazine,* August 12, 2001, p. 18. Harry Potter in churches: Nadya Labi, "The New Funday School," *Time,* December 16, 2002, p. 60.

125 *Seinfeld:* An unnamed writer recalled a sleep-inducing sermon at a United Church in Vancouver, in which the minister suddenly changed tack. " 'Jerry Seinfeld said, "Life is like a rollercoaster," ' the minister said. ' "It takes your money, from time to time it makes your hair stand up, and the best you can hope for in the end is that you didn't puke." ' Big laughs. He now had everyone's attention. . . ." *Adbusters,* vol. 19, no. 6 (November/December 2001), unpaged.

126 *Merchants of Cool* aired as a *Frontline* series February 27, 2001.

126 P-O-P trade show: The P-O-P Show/New York, September 4–5, 2002; the catalogue was produced by P/O/P Times and P.O.P. Design.

127 Protect Our Privacy: Jim Hightower, "Going Down the Road," *The Nation,* July 22–29, 2002, p. 8.

127 Plosives are consonants: Crystal, 1997, p. 159; on "voiceless plosives": p. 137.

128 My thesaurus: It is *Roget's 21st Century Thesaurus in Dictionary Form* (New York: Delta, 1992, 1993).

129 *New York Post* headline: Lisa Marsh, March 27, 2002.

129 sneaker names: Some sneakers have no plosive *K* sounds: New Balance, Fila, Avia, Puma. On sneakers and dirty words, I drew heavily from my column "Sneakers and Nothingness," *The Village Voice,* April 2, 1991.

129 "Plosives are much more likely": Crystal, 1995, p. 153.

129 Leanne Hinton made these remarks in a phone interview with me in 2002. She co-edited the anthology *Sound Symbolism* (Cambridge, England: Cambridge University Press, 1995) with Johanna Nichols and John J. Ohala.

131 Martha Stewart: I saw the promo on February 19, 1996.

131 "The problem with 7 Up": from a 1999 phone interview with an executive on the campaign.

131 "The brand was repositioned": phone interview with a 7 Up spokesperson February 2005.

131 *The West Wing:* "Two Cathedrals" episode, originally aired May 16, 2001.

131 *Chicago Hope:* Jim Rutenberg, " 'South Park' Takes Gross to New Frontier," *The New York Times,* June 25, 2001.

131   *NYPD Blue:* James Poniewozik, "Turf War," *Time*, January 27, 2003, p. 56.

131   "first all-out barrage": Bill Carter and Lawrie Mifflin, "Mainstream TV Bets on 'Gross-Out' Humor," *The New York Times*, July 19, 1999.

131   *South Park:* Rutenberg, " 'South Park' Takes Gross to New Frontier."

132   *"Fuck* probably reached": Bryson, pp. 216–17.

132   Jesse Sheidlower's remarks: "the word's impact has been diminishing" is from an interview in 1999; "is still going in that direction" is from a follow-up interview in January 2005.

132   in-house marketing video: I saw this.

132   FCUK magazine ads: Jeffrey Goldfarb, "Ad Regulators Tell FCUK Off," Reuters, January 12, 2005, www.reuters.co.uk/ newsArticle.jhtml?type=topNews&storyID=65288.

133   blamed its clothing: "But French Connection operations director Neil Williams said the group believed its problems lay in the appeal of its clothing, rather than its branding." "FCUK problems lie with clothes, not branding," *Northern Business Daily, The Journal* (Newcastle), November 17, 2004, icnewcastle.icnetwork.co.uk/0500business/0100local/ tm_ objectid=14880754&method=full&siteid=50081&.

134   "If these media outlets": "Bono's New Casualty: 'Private Ryan,' " *The New York Times*, November 21, 2004. That's just one of Rich's columns on politics and the culture war. This entire section, and much of this book, is informed by Rich's powerful work in this area.

134   "Swearing . . . has always": Geoffrey Nunberg, "Revenge of the Comfit-Makers' Wives," commentary on *Fresh Air*, NPR, March 16, 2004.

134   *Desperate Housewives:* Bill Carter, "Many Who Voted for 'Values' Still Like Their Television Sin," *The New York Times*, November 22, 2004.

134   grandma Barbara Bush: I saw her smiling on the news. David Shuster, "A Day of Unity and Rain in Little Rock," MSNBC, November 19, 2004, www.msnbc.msn.com/id/ 6526487/ - 34k.

134   PHUK sweatshirts: "Planet Hollywood said the sweatshirt sales were 'very strong,' " Richard Wilner, "Planet's Tacky T-Shirts," *New York Post*, November 30, 2004.

134   *Meet the Fockers:* "While not a weekend record, the film did set a record for Christmas Day, earning $19.1 million." " 'Fock-

ers' sets holiday record at box office," Associated Press, *Seattle Times*, December 28, 2004.

135 told Senator Patrick Leahy: Charles Krauthammer, "In Defense of the F-Word," *The Washington Post*, July 2, 2004.

135 therapeutic effects: "Cheney Unapologetic for Curse at Senator," Fox News, June 27, 2004, www.foxnews.com/story/ 0,2933,123810,00.html.

135 "I do not deny": from "Ron Butters' Comments on Blanche Poubelle's 'Homophobia Sucks' " photocopied (by Butters) onto copies of "Loose Lips: Homophobia Sucks: But What Does It Suck?" *The Guide: Gay Travel, Entertainment, Politics and Sex*, March 2000, p. 8. Butters's other comments are from Ronald R. Butters, " 'We didn't realize that lite beer was supposed to suck!' The Putative Vulgarity of 'X sucks' in American English," *Dictionaries: Journal of the Dictionary Society of North America* 22 (2001). (Revision of a paper read at the meeting of the American Dialect Society, January 6, 2000.) In it, he discusses the Teresa Labov study ("Social and Language Boundaries Among Adolescents," *American Speech*, 67, pp. 339–66) and the T-shirt court case *(Broussard v. School Board of the City of Norfolk, Virginia)*. Butters also replied to my questions in an e-mail, June 21, 2002.

136 *CBS Evening News:* January 7, 2002.

136 Mike's Hard Lemonade: I saw the ad and did phone interviews, fall 2002.

136 The AMA's warning and the industry's insistence that alcopops are marketed only to adults: " 'We're alarmed and concerned with these findings,' said the AMA's president-elect, J. Edward Hill, a family doctor in Tupelo, Miss." "Jeff Becker, president of the Beer Institute, which represents the industry, said the marketing of 'flavored alcohol beverages is directed at adults.' " Jamie Talan (of *Newsday*), "Fruit-Flavored Alcohol Pulls in Teens," *The Kansas City Star*, December 17, 2004.

137 "Shut. Up": from the first *Shrek* movie.

137 "Big whoop": Alex Kuczynski, "She's Out of the Closet. Now What?" *The New York Times*, March 3, 2002.

138 Indignant because: *Friends*, aired March 13, 2003.

138 "Subways and Manners? Hell-o-o!": Clyde Haberman, *The New York Times*, November 15, 1996.

138 "Hel-lo: School Shootings": Tanya Gallagher, *People Who Matter* ("America's Collegiate News Source"), www.peoplewhomatter. org/lifemyway/shootings, March 22, 2001.

138 *Just Shoot Me!:* the "Hello, Goodbye" episode, originally aired

November 16, 1999. In syndication, the show is no longer mentioned on the NBC Web site.

139 "Chaim Yankel": Rosten, p. 66.

139 "Rock Hudson as iconic": Peter Ranier, "Sex in the Suburbs," *New York*, November 11, 2002.

139 "You reviewed": *Now Toronto*, online edition, December 5–11, 2002.

139 Apolo Anton Ohno ad: part of Partnership campaign that launched February 2002.

139 impeachment "psychopathic": Conyers said this on *Meet the Press*, December 6, 1998. "This thing is clinical now. It's psychopathic."

140 Joy Behar: I saw this September 9, 1999.

140 Ford Focus: I saw the ad in January 2004.

140 "Mr. Clinton drawled": Francix X. Clines, "Reporters No Match for 2 Press Conference Pros," *The New York Times*, February 7, 1998.

141 ESPN promo: I saw it on June 13, 2002.

141 "Talk Is Good": *Advertising Age*, March 17, 2003, p. 1.

142 Martha Stewart: The May 2003 sweepstakes was tied into Stewart's TV show *Martha Stewart Living Television*.

142 *1066 and All That* quotes: from Amazon.com excerpts.

143 "might have called a messy bedroom": Emily Wax, "In Times of Terror, Teens Talk the Talk, Boys Are 'Firefighter Cute,' Messy Room Is 'Ground Zero' in September 11 Slang," *The Washington Post*, March 19, 2002.

143 "Regime change begins at home": for instance, from MoveOnpac.org.

143 "Axle of Evil": by Gregg Easterbrook, *The New Republic*, January 20, 2003.

143 "One of Bush's worst faults": Norman Mailer, "Only in America," *The New York Review of Books*, March 27, 2003, p. 49.

143 a favorite of Nazi propagandists: For instance, during the German occupation of the Netherlands, Dutch radio broadcasters were ordered to air German shows like *Gruss aus der Heimat* ("Greetings from the Homeland"). Theatrical Productions: German Radio Trends (http://histclo.hispeed.com/the/radio/cou/rc-ger.html).

144 crops up among neo-Nazis: "The Deutsche Liga für Volk und Heimat (German League for People and Homeland—DLVH), which was founded on the date of German reunification, October 3, 1991, was dissolved as a party in October 1996 in order to become an association, thus enabling members to join other right-wing parties." From the Stephen Roth

Institute for the Study of Contemporary Anti-Semitism and Racism at Tel Aviv University (http://www.tau.ac.il/Anti-Semitism/asw97-8/germany.html).

144   homeland security: While the word *homeland* itself is quite ancient, *homeland security* has been used in *our* homeland only since the late nineties and primarily in military circles. Mark DeMier, editor-in-chief of the online *Journal of Homeland Security,* believes the phrase first appeared in a 1997 report by the National Defense Panel. *Homeland security* quickly entered the lexicon of subsequent commissions, like the U.S. Commission on National Security, headed by former senators Gary Hart and Warren Rudman, who called for a National Homeland Security Agency. (I interviewed DeMier by phone in September 2001 for a piece on *homeland security* that ran in *Salon,* October 1, 2001.)

144   *Heartland with John Kasich:* Fox has also called the show, which debuted in 2002, *From the Heartland.*

144   "The home to the heartland tour": "Bush's vacation and the trips he took to some states during the month were promoted as the 'Home to the Heartland Tour.' " Siobhan McDonough, "Bush on Aug. 6, 2001: Work, Play and a Forewarning," Associated Press, April 11, 2004.

144   "know Secretary Rumsfeld's heart": At a December 20, 2004, press conference, a reporter asked why Rumsfeld didn't sign condolence letters to the families of troops killed in Iraq. Bush replied, "Listen, I know how—I know Secretary Rumsfeld's heart. I know how much he cares for the troops." Transcript from CNN (www.cnn.com/2004/ALLPOLITICS/12/20/bush.transcript.ap/).

144   Bush sees Putin's heart: "The more I get to know President Putin," he said, "the more I get to see his heart and soul . . . the more I know we can work together in a positive way." "Bush and Putin 'best of buddies,' " BBC News, November 15, 2001 (news.bbc.co.uk/1/hi/world/americas/1659048.stm).

144   Monica Crowley: on *Real Time with Bill Maher,* March 2003.

144   Peggy Noonan: Peggy Noonan, "Homeland Ain't No American Word," WSJ.com, Friday, June 14, 2002.

145   William Safire: "On Language: Roll's Roles," *The New York Times Magazine,* December 23, 2001, p. 16.

145   "Are you guys ready?": Richard Sisk, " 'Let's Roll' Flight's Last Seconds: The Hijackers Give Up," New York *Daily News,* July 23, 2004.

146   "My fellow Americans, let's roll": CNN, Jeff Greenfield,

"President Bush Seeks to Reassure Americans; Defines Stakes in the War," November 9, 2001.

146 "When Bush said": November 16, 2001.

146 State of the Union address: "State of the Union: Excerpts from the Address," *Newsday* (Long Island), January 30, 2002.

146 "We're ready": *CBS Evening News,* November 6, 2002.

146 later got Lott fired: Lott initially explained that he was only toasting Strom Thurmond's long political career during a "lighthearted affair" when he told the birthday party crowd, "When Strom Thurmond ran for president, we voted for him. We're proud of it. And if the rest of the country had followed our lead, we wouldn't have had all these problems over the years, either." Jill Zuckman, "Lott Calls Segregation 'Stain' on U.S.," *Chicago Tribune,* December 14, 2002, p. 1. Lott later apologized and said that his "choice of words were totally unacceptable and insensitive." "Lott: Segregation and Racism Are Immoral," CNN.com, December 13, 2002.

146 filing applications: "Let's Roll Trademark and Service Mark Applications," www.cursor.org/backhome/letsroll2.htm.

146 Wal-Mart's . . . football team: Nick Gillespie, "Logocentrism," *Reason,* November 1, 2002, p. 51.

147 "in Molly's bar": Ed Vulliamy, "Battle for Iraq: The Home Front: America—Mood of a Nation—Passions Stirred As Intensity Rises," *The Observer* (London), March 23, 2003, p. 14.

147 Bill Steigerwald: "*Newsweek,* Nation Ponder Pros, Cons of Gulf War II," *Pittsburgh Tribune-Review,* January 30, 2003, www. livesite.pittsburghlive.com/x/tribune-review/columnists/ steigerwald/s_115440.html.

147 pro-war rallies: Justin Pritchard, "Anti-war Demonstrations Cause Mayhem, Spur Counterprotests," Associated Press, March 21, 2003.

147 Gary Bauer: Gary Bauer, "Commentary: Choosing Sides," Cross-walk.com, http://new.crosswalk.com/news/1190666.html.

147 "Way to go!": Jarrod Aldom, "Local Woman Calls for Rally," on WHSV (Harrisonburg, Va.), no date, www.whsv.com (the story is no longer available online).

147 The blogger: www.l8r.blogspot.com/2003_02_09_l8r_archive. html.

147 Northrop Grumman: I saw the ad in January 2003.

147 did indeed escalate: "Three months after Bush declared 'Bring 'em on,' attacks on Americans have increased from 20 to 25 or 30 a day, according to Gen. Ricardo Sanchez, the U.S. military commander for Iraq." Rod Nordland and

Michael Hirsh, "The \$87 Billion Money Pit," *Newsweek*, November 3, 2003, p. 26 (quote on p. 29).

148   dates back further: *Charlie's Angels: Full Throttle* opened June 27, 2003; Bush said "Bring 'em on" July 2, 2003; Davis spokesman said "Bring them on" July 8, 2003. (On the latter: John M. Broder, "Foes of California's Governor Say Recall Vote Is a Certainty," *The New York Times*, July 9, 2003.) "Bush said he regretted the words": "One of the things I've learned is that sometimes words have consequences you don't intend them to. 'Bring 'em on' is a classic example." "Notebook," *Time*, January 24, 2005, p. 15.

148   John Edwards defended: He said "Bring it on" at a Democratic National Committee meeting. Dan Balz, "Democratic Hopefuls Score Bush, Trio of Candidates Assails Economy, Foreign Affairs," *The Washington Post*, February 23, 2003.

148   "If George Bush": *NewsHour*, PBS, November 25, 2003, www.pbs.org/newshour/bb/politics/july-dec03/newhamp_11-25.html.

148   The story of how Kerry found: Evan Thomas and *Newsweek*'s Special Project Team, "The Inside Story: How Bush Did It," *Newsweek*, November 15, 2004, p. 50.

150   *Wayne's World:* Barnhart and Metcalf, p. 286.

150   *Not!* may seem: *RHHDAS*, vol. II, p. 682.

150   "Every war is ironic . . . the Idea of Progress": Fussell, pp. 7–8.

151   Philip Gibbs: Fussell quotes him at ibid., p. 8.

151   "a collision between innocence and awareness": ibid., p. 5.

151   "Irony is the attendant of hope": ibid., p. 18.

151   "index of the prevailing innocence": ibid., p. 23.

151   "I am saying": ibid., p. 35.

152   "you go to war with": "Troops Put Thorny Questions to Rumsfeld," CNN.com, December 9, 2004.

152   "First we tell you": Barbara E. Martinez, "On the Web, a Network of Television Viewers," *The Washington Post*, November 12, 2002.

153   "hipness unto death": Miller, p. 15.

153   David Foster Wallace: See his essay "E Unibus Pluram: Television and U.S. Fiction," *The Review of Contemporary Fiction* (1993), which was reprinted in *A Supposedly Fun Thing I'll Never Do Again*. The page numbers are those from the book: "enfeebling" and "tyrannizes," p. 67; "agents," p. 49; "new junta," p. 68.

In criticizing irony, Miller and Wallace both distinguish between the smarmy irony and the sharp kind, and did so long before September 11. As Miller wrote in *Boxed In* (footnote, p. 15), "Irony can be an invaluable rhetorical means toward real enlightenment: the televisual irony is a sort of commercial antibody against just such a possibility."

153 "an era enervated": Richard Schickel, "Can Irony Kill Comedy?" *Time*, March 6, 2000, p. 72.

154 "Her new show": The *Newsweek* cover story appeared on July 15, 1996.

154 "The bitch": Rosie is "going on a celeb-trashing spree, throwing nasty jabs at Bill Clinton, Michael Jackson, Sharon Stone, Anne Heche and Oprah Winfrey.

"Or, in her own words: 'I'm no longer a TV talk-show host. The bitch ain't so nice anymore.' " Mark Armstrong, "From Queen of Nice to Royal Bitch?" E! Online News, June 25, 2002. www.eonline.com/News/Items/Pf/0,1527,10153,00. html.

154 "The ironic individual": Purdy, p. xi.

154 "Anyone with the heretical": Wallace, p. 68.

155 "dead on the page": ibid., p. 68.

155 "Purdy-pounding": Yvonne Zipp, "Able to Leap Cynicism in a Single Bound," *The Christian Science Monitor,* October 7, 1999, p. 17.

155 "One good thing": Roger Rosenblatt, "The Age of Irony Comes to an End," *Time*, September 24, 2001, p. 79.

155 "end of the age of irony": Seth Mnookin, "In Disaster's Aftermath, Once-Cocky Media Culture Disses the Age of Irony," Inside.com, September 18, 2001.

156 David Beers called: "Irony Is Dead! Long Live Irony!" *Salon*, September 25, 2001.

156 "In peaceful and prosperous times": Purdy quote from David D. Kirkpatrick, "A NATION CHALLENGED: THE COMMENTATORS: Pronouncements on Irony Draw a Line in the Sand," *The New York Times*, September 24, 2001.

157 "Greeting-card sentimentality": Michiko Kakutani, "The Idea Was Not to Have a New One," *The New York Times*, December 9, 2002.

157 fired writers and cartoonists: Matthew Rothschild, "The New McCarthyism," *The Progressive,* January 1, 2002, p. 18.

157 shoppers arrested: Winnie Hu, "A Message of Peace on 2 Shirts Touches Off Hostilities at a Mall," *The New York Times*, March 6, 2003.

158 "like the cool clique": RJ Smith, "The Wonk Who Blogged Me: Liberal iconoclast Mickey Kaus suits up, hunkers down,

and leaps into the mosh pit," *Los Angeles* magazine, August 2003 (online through www.findarticles.com).

158 "Winners & Losers": *Time,* June 12, 2000, p. 21.

158 Richard Zoglin quote: phone interview, March 18, 2003.

158 "Conventional Wisdom" column: on Eminem, September 9, 2002, p. 6; on Dean, February 9, 2004, p. 6; Another column: November 11, 2002, p. 6; on Koran, May 30, 2005, p. 8.

159 World Health Organization: Mary Carmichael, "Chips: Eat Just One," *Newsweek,* July 8, 2002, p. 58.

159 "HELLO, 2004 was her year": www.whatevs.org, December 23, 2004.

159 online fan forum: November 27, 2002.

161 upside-down clown: The ad ran during the Super Bowl, 2003.

161 Donald Rumsfeld: *NewsHour,* September 10, 2003.

161 "Don't even think of parking here": sermon at Pennsylvania church is dated June 17, 2001 (www.nsrchurch.org/ Sermons/2001/s_06172001.htm); at Georgia church: November 5, 2000 (www.apibs.org/sermon/s02006.htm).

161 Mohegan Sun: I saw the ad in the late 1990s.

162 Richard Karn: tvplex.go.com/touchstone/homeimprovement/ bios/karn.

163 " 'I'm a moron' ": Barnhart and Metcalf, p. 260.

163 "Did you know": I saw the ad on the Comedy Channel, March 28, 2002.

163 Microsoft Office ads: "Duh": *Newsweek,* April 25, 2005, p. 13; "no-brainer": *Newsweek,* May 9, 2005, p. 17.

163 "News flash": The dialogue was reprinted in "Sound Bites," *Entertainment Weekly,* May 2, 2003, p. 1.

163 Donkey notices: from the first *Shrek.*

164 "Would you say": *The Daily Show,* December 9, 2002.

164 "rhetoric of irritation": David Remnick, "Comment: Making a Case," *The New Yorker,* February 3, 2003, p. 31. "I am sick and tired of games and deception": Bush quote from CNN, January 15, 2003.

164 Cheney has praised: "So the notion that the president is a cowboy—I don't know, is a Westerner, I think that's not necessarily a bad idea. I think the fact of the matter is he cuts to the chase." *Meet the Press,* March 16, 2003.

164 Bush has said: quoted in Susan Faludi, "An American Myth Rides into the Sunset," *The New York Times,* March 30, 2003.

164 Bush, who has also been known to say *fabulous:* "Bush says 'fabulous' at least as much as any interior decorator." Jay Nordlinger, "A Voice for Our Time," *National Review,* Septem-

ber 16, 2003, http://www.nationalreview.com/nordlinger/
nordlinger091603.asp.

164 first two words: "The phrase, or at least the first two words of
it, were written by David Frum": Susan Page, " 'Axis of Evil'
Often Repeated, but Not by Bush; Still, White House Defends
Phrase on Which Much of the President's Year Has Turned,"
USA Today, January 27, 2003.

164 "He can be very sarcastic": Frum on *Hardball,* MSNBC, January 8, 2003.

165 "television commercials can be": Kirk Johnson, "Today's Kids
Are, Like, Killing the English Language. Yeah, Right," *The
New York Times,* August 9, 1998.

165 "When the more passé terms": Pinker, p. 400.

166 "If someone cuts off": Pinker e-mail to me, March 2000.

166 "Our language puts blinders on us": Robin Lakoff said this on
The Leonard Lopate Show, WNYC-AM, New York, July 13, 2000.

166 *mean:* And in slang, *mean* means the opposite: excellent, as in
"dances a mean tango," writes *Webster's Third.*

167 "Duh and yeah right are matchless tools": Johnson, "Today's
Kids Are, Like."

167 "We're so reducing language": phone interview with DiBattista, 2002.

168 "Rethink TV": "The new commercial, part of DirecTV's
'rethink' campaign, had its premiere during the Super Bowl,"
Josh Ozersky, "A Life in Reruns: Watch Out, the Ending Goes
Quickly," *The New York Times,* March 20, 2005.

168 "Rethink 50+": "The tagline of the campaign, which includes
a sweepstakes and a guerrilla marketing team featuring 40+
models standing in front of agencies handing out AARP-
branded flip-flops and key chains, 'Rethink 50.' " Matt Kins-
man, "Forever Young," *Promo,* October 1, 2003, p. 22.

168 Boston Market: I saw the ad on April 19, 2004.

168 "I would gladly pay": *Entertainment Weekly,* February 7, 2003,
p. 4.

168 "If I could talk": Steve Schurr, "The Exiled Foster Winans Has
a Message for Jayson Blair," *The Black Table,* blacktable.com,
May 20, 2003. (On Winans's conviction: "financial columnist
R. Foster Winans was convicted on 59 counts of conspiracy
and fraud in 1985 for using his articles to make money in the
stock market," Nancy Gibbs, "Reading Between the Lies,"
Time, May 19, 2003, p. 56.)

168 "Real easy": *The Splendid Table,* February 28, 1998, on WNYC-
AM, New York.

169 identity thief: *CBS Evening News,* March 12, 2002.

169   Halle Berry: quoted by Richard Corliss, "Top Performances," *Time,* January 21, 2002, p. 125.

CHAPTER 5
The Great American *Yesss!*

170   bid on a house: My friend said this to me in September 2003.

170   Michael Douglas: on *The Barbara Walters Special,* March 20, 2000.

170   promo for *Millionaire:* I saw it May 29, 2003.

170   *Will & Grace:* March 13, 2003.

172   Celebrex: I saw the Santa ad during the 2001 Thanksgiving Day parade. "One rival painkiller, Pfizer's (PFE) Celebrex, was also thought to be safer—until two weeks ago, when a new study suggested that it also posed a greater risk of cardio-vascular events than other pain pills," Ron Insana, "Pfizer Leader Steps Up to Plate for Celebrex," *USA Today,* January 4, 2005.

174   "As the huge debt": Frank Pierson, "Up Close and Personal," AlterNet.org (www.alternet.org/mediaculture/16569/), August 8, 2003.

174   an editor who worked: My sources for *Yesss!* in movie trailers were my interviews with *Tin Cup*'s trailer editor, Kevin Wagner, and Peter Adee in 1997. Follow-up interview with Adee: August 1, 2003.

176   "story of American pluck": Traci Hukill, "Seabiscuit's Joyride," Alternet.org (www.alternet.org/movies/16514/), July 31, 2003.

177   promo for *Lucky:* I saw the promo on June 14, 2003.

177   "While some people": www.americangaming.org/casino_entertainment/aga_facts/facts.cfm.

177   press-release-writing.com: "Make Every Word Count in Press Release Headings," *PRW Newsletter* (www.press-release-writing.com/newsletters/make-word-count.htm), April 19, 2000.

178   "There was an official": Pete McEntegart, "Q&A with Marv Albert," sportsillustrated.com. (www.cnnsi.com/si_online/QandA/2003/0428/), April 24, 2003.

179   "Good to see you" . . . "and disconnected": Peter de Jonge, "Man's Best Friend: Who Cares About the Game? How Sports-casters Evolved from Experts to Baby Sitters for a Nation of Lonely Guys," *The New York Times Magazine,* July 21, 2002, p. 26.

181   her ad agency convened a focus group; the inspiration of Meg Ryan's famously fake orgasm: Kaplan Thaler discussed this at

a panel discussion, "She's Got the Urge: Women in Advertising and Advertising to Women," at the New-York Historical Society on April 24, 2003. I was another panelist.

181 Jeff Z. Klein: phone interview, October 2003.

181 The material from Morris et al.'s *Gestures* is taken from pp. 80–86.

183 "fist beat": Morris, *Bodytalk*, p. 70.

184 "YES, IKON!": The ad ran in *Time*, September 17, 2001.

CHAPTER 6
Populist Pop and the Regular Guy

186 Pabst Blue Ribbon: Pabst, for instance, "has sustained a sales resurgence based on working-man brand values, scarcity and price," Jonah Bloom, "High Life, Timberland Give Lesson on Cultivating 'Cool,' " *Advertising Age,* January 5, 2004, p. 14.

186 In my paraphrasing of Robin Lakoff on "unmarked," I draw on Robin Tolmach Lakoff, p. 44.

187 the great unmarked: By calling guys unmarked, I'm sure I'm stretching the meaning of unmarked far beyond what linguists intend. They might argue, in particular, that the word *guy* is not unmarked because it has no marked variations—no guyess, guyette, or lady guy. *Gal* is available, and it does say "normal female." But unlike *guy, gal* hails from Hokeyville and is often said with irony. Personally, though, I love it and feel as much a gal as a woman.

187 Dave Barry: Barry, 1995, p. xxiv.

188 "Can you guys": "The Testing of a President: Lewinsky's Testimony on Love, Friend and Family," *The New York Times,* September 22, 1998.

188 jjoan ttaber: "Dysenyouguysing American English: Now Back to You Guys in the Studio," *The Vocabula Review,* April 2003, www.vocabula.com.

188 "She is a 'real guy' ": from *Selected Letters*, p. 263, as cited by Lighter, *RHHDAS*, vol. I, p. 1003.

189 Art Guys, etc.: from Google.

189 kidnapperguy: Hendrik Hertzberg, "Kidnapped," *The New Yorker,* February 18 and 25, 2002, p. 57.

189 William Safire: "Aggie Awards," *The New York Times Magazine,* October 12, 2003, p. 56.

190 "The time has come": *Maxim*'s "Guy Pride" manifesto was published April 1997.

190 pubic hair waxing: *Cargo,* March 2004 (premier issue), p. 75; on Botox, p. 76.

190 "That's a real anxiety": Jon Fine, "Who Is 'Cargo' Man?" *Advertising Age,* March 1, 2004, p. 4 (the quoted material is on p. 35).

190 "Honey, does this embroidered shirt": *Cargo,* March 2004, p. 64.

191 print ad for the Territory Ahead: It appeared in a 1997 issue of *The New Yorker;* "a somewhat upscale" and other Pitchford quotes are from my phone interview with him, January 8, 2004. "Guy Stuff Gear Bag" and "Guy Stuff Gym Bag" are from 2003 and 2004 catalogues.

191 "empire unto himself" . . . "everymen in the middle": Peter de Jonge, "Man's Best Friend," *The New York Times Magazine,* July 21, 2002, p. 26 (the quoted material is on p. 29).

192 "Working-class speech": Trudgill, *Sociolinguistics,* pp. 72–76.

192 "If Governor Bush wants": Larry Copeland, "Anger at Bushes as Time Grows Short for Schiavo," *USA Today,* March 27, 2005.

193 An editor of mine: Yo, Marty Gottlieb.

193 "to call attention": *Webster's Third New International Dictionary of the English Language Unabridged,* 1993.

193 "We talked about": Maureen Dowd, "Tiger's Double Bogey," *The New York Times,* April 19, 1997.

194 On HEY!hats: www.meshhat.com.

194 First they were: On the mesh hat trend cycle, see Adam Sternbergh, "The Instantly Passé Trend," *The New York Times Magazine,* December 14, 2003, p. 75.

194 "Companies have no choice": *ABC World News Tonight,* March 4, 1998.

194 Bubba the Love Sponge: Jennifer Barrs, "DJ Cleared in Hog Slaughtering," *Tampa Tribune,* March 1, 2002.

194 Clear Channel fired him: "Clear Channel Head Says Bubba Fired for 'Inappropriate' Show," Associated Press, *Naples Daily News*/Naplesnews.com, February 25, 2004. (Clear Channel's president John Hogan said in a statement, "This type of content is inappropriate.")

195 "Piling On Rush": larrythecableguy.com, October 8, 2003.

195 *Big-time* quotes: On Julia Roberts: FoxNews.com, December 20, 2003; Pete Rose: Clyde Haberman, *International Herald Tribune,* IHT.online, January 10, 2004; Drudge: Michelangelo Signorile, "Drudge Report: The Cyberhack Jumps the Gun," *New York Press,* February 18, 2004; Cheney: Jake Tapper, *Salon,* "A 'major league asshole,' " September 4, 2000.

195 *Zip* and *nada:* I saw the Jell-O ad on January 24, 2004; Countrywide recording was running as of November 2002.

196 "walked the walk": "Last night's Republican presidential

debate in New Hampshire," *Morning Edition*, NPR, January 7, 2000.

196 Nita Lowey: BBC News online, November 17, 2003.

196 "Janus walks": I saw the ad on CNBC, September 15, 2004.

197 "There's an endemic paranoia": phone interview with DiBattista, 2002.

197 The Yo of Joe: John Adams's remark appears in *RHHDAS*, vol. II, p. 299, which also describes how *Joe* overtook *John* to represent a specified quality or identity.

198 "Joe-mentum": CNN, January 26, 2004.

198 FTC had to kill him: Associated Press Newswires, "FTC Drops Complaint Against R. J. Reynolds Mascot Joe Camel," January 28, 1999. ("The FTC's action Wednesday, promised after last year's $206 billion tobacco settlement, officially ends litigation the agency first launched in May 1997. R. J. Reynolds dropped Joe Camel more than a year ago, nearly 10 years after introducing the mascot.")

198 Ragu Rich & Meaty: I saw the ad on January 16, 2004.

198 John Madden promoting: Bob Tedeschi, "E-Commerce Report: Consumer Products Companies Use Web Sites to Strengthen Ties with Customers," *The New York Times*, August 25, 2003. (Steve Savino, vice president and general manager for Unilever's Ragu, said that Ragu's promotion with Madden calls "on customers to rate the best of seven Ragu recipes and [to enter] a contest to win a trip to the NFL All-Pro game in Hawaii.")

199 Nissan Sentra: Leslie Savan, "Stuff Love," *The Village Voice*, May 30, 1996, p. 44.

199 "Bobfest": Penny Parker, "Lights, Camera, Bob!" *Denver Post*, November 7, 1997.

199 Microsoft once named: Savan, "Stuff Love," p. 44.

199 Breathe Right: 1997 Super Bowl ad.

199 "I found my Bob": *The New York Times*, July 3, 2001.

200 *See Bob Run:* at Rattlestick Theatre, listed in *The New Yorker*, May 28, 2001.

200 *God, the Devil and Bob:* "NBC cancels 'God' in wake of low ratings, complaints," *Atlanta Constitution*, March 31, 2000, p. E6.

200 Leni Riefenstahl: The CNN headline about her hundredth birthday (August 22, 2002) ran earlier, I believe in July.

201 " 'Don't send' ": quoted in Barnhart and Metcalf, p. 174.

202 Public Defender Dude, etc.: from Google.

202 "Neither has any pretension": Jason Lynch, "Happy Drew Year," *People*, April 25, 2005, p. 92.

202 Ron Rosenbaum points out: in "Dude, Where's My Dude?

Dudelicious Dissection, from Sontag to Spicoli," *New York Observer,* July 7, 2003, p. 1.

203 "If you don't have": Faludi was quoted in Gina Bellafante, "Catering to Cable Guys," *Time,* June 7, 1999, p. 72.

204 "Yes, I have behaved badly": Editorial, "They're All So Sorry," *San Francisco Chronicle,* October 17, 2003.

205 "I'm just like": Patrick E. Cole, "An Exclusive Interview with Timothy McVeigh," *Time,* April 15, 1996, p. 56.

205 "faux populism": Frank Rich, "Love That Bill," *The New York Times,* March 7, 1998.

205 *Cold Pizza:* Andrew Grossman, "ESPN2 Delivers 'Pizza' for New Morning Talker: Offbeat Show Targets 18–34 Males," *Hollywood Reporter,* October 16, 2003, p. 1.

206 "French-looking" . . . "reputed Vietnam veteran": I heard this on Limbaugh's show August 13, 2003. The following longer quote is from "Would you have any Grey Poupon, Monsieur Kerry?" RushLimbaugh.com, the same day, and is a shorter version of what he said on the show.

206 "There are two ways": from the October 10, 2003, Democratic primary debate.

206 favorite Bordeaux: Limbaugh told *Cigar Aficionado* magazine, "And from France, there's the 1961 Château Haut-Brion. And the 1982. I have learned that any time you find a bottle of Bordeaux from 1961, no matter what the label says, buy it." Mervyn Rothstein, "Rush's Judgment: Media Phenomenon Rush Limbaugh Is Winning Bigger and Bigger Audiences with His No-Holds-Barred Brand of Commentary," *Cigar Aficionado,* Spring 1994, www.cigaraficionado.com (www.cigaraficionado.com/Cigar/CA_Profiles/People_Profile/0,2540,18,00.html).

206 $75 haircuts: This was in the same rant as the line about Cheez Whiz.

207 Clinton asked: "Vox Pop," *Time,* May 20, 1996, p. 19.

207 "have a namby-pamby": Moore, p. 192.

207 "Talk is cheap": Haiman, p. 106. The "flamethrower" quote is from the movie *Torch Song Trilogy.*

208 "is today triumphant": Frank, "The Elitism Myth," www.tompaine.com, March 8, 2004 (originally appeared in the February 2004 issue of *Le Monde diplomatique*).

208 "If you lived here": *Morning Edition,* NPR, November 3, 2003.

209 "have spent the past several months": Sheryl Gay Stolberg, "Seeking the Words That Will Win Back the House," *The New York Times,* September 10, 2003.

209 "regular people": William Saletan, "Wise Counsel: Edwards

Copies Clinton's Message—in Invisible Ink," *Slate,* January 2, 2003.

209 "We ought to cut these lobbyists off": Jonathan Alter, "The Democrats' New Red Meat," *Newsweek,* January 26, 2004, p. 39.

209 "a total perceptual split": Peggy Noonan, "A Bum Ride," *The New York Times,* October 15, 1991. (I quote Noonan's piece from Robin Tolmach Lakoff, p. 140. That chapter, "Mad, Bad, and Had," provides a good discussion on the manipulations of "normal" in the Hill/Thomas case.)

CHAPTER 7
The Community of Commitment-Centered Words

210 "ORANGE NIGHT OUT" sign: I last saw the sign in July 2002.

211 "It's an idiom": Rosen, p. 11.

211 "One of these days": Kate Zernike, "Conservatives Are Differing over Role in Controversy," *The New York Times,* December 18, 2002.

212 "It's a big": *NewsHour,* PBS, November 18, 2003.

212 "Thank you for sharing": Jake Tapper, "Judging W's heart," *Salon,* November 1, 2000.

212 "The aide said": Ron Suskind, "Without a Doubt," *The New York Times Magazine,* October 17, 2004, p. 44 (quote on p. 64).

213 "Conservatives use": Geoffrey Nunberg, "Using the Other Guy's Vitriol to Win Votes," *The New York Times,* Week in Review, December 28, 2003.

213 "to measure on a second by second basis": *The News with Brian Williams,* MSNBC, July 27, 2000.

213 "I do not subscribe": Deborah Tannen, "Let Them Eat Words," *The American Prospect,* September 1, 2003. Luntz, a PC thesaurus unto himself, has also advised Republicans to avoid the word *privatization* when talking about Social Security and to rename the *estate tax* the *death tax,* because the latter sounds scarier. (Fred Barnes, "Negotiating with Himself," *The Weekly Standard,* January 3, 2005.) Less successfully, during the 2004 election, Luntz tried to get the GOP to dub John Edwards a "personal-injury lawyer" rather than a "trial lawyer," because the former says "ambulance chaser," while the latter evokes *Law & Order* heroes. (Alex Williams, "The Alchemy of a Political Slogan," *The New York Times,* August 22, 2004, Section 9, p. 1.)

213 *multicultural* . . . has been around: Barnhart and Metcalf, p. 236.

213 "the nine years of Vietnam": Ken Ringle, "Them's Fightin' Words: War Lingo Rushes to the Front," *The Washington Post,* November 10, 2001.

214 "After many years": Joel Bleifuss, "Food Flacks Say: Skip the Science," *PR Watch,* Fourth Quarter, 1996.

215 Blimpie using Devo song: "Blimpie Has Plans to Raise the Sub," *Mediaweek,* March 21, 2005, http://www.mediaweek. com/mw/search/article_display.jsp?schema=&vnu_content_ id=1000846549.

217 "put the humidity": Glenn Collins, "Don't Touch, Don't Push, Don't Delay: Tombs Closing," *The New York Times,* February 18, 2004.

217 *appropriate*s: from Google, March 2004.

217 The definition of *agere* (as the root of *agenda* and *agitate*): *Webster's Third New International Dictionary.*

217 Evans assured: March 5, 2003. www.commerce.gov/opa/ speeches/Evans/2003/March_05_Evans_NAM.htm.

217 John Edwards told: *The Washington Post,* July 29, 2004.

218 "God has graciously": Maureen Dowd, "Slapping the Other Cheek," *The New York Times,* November 14, 2004.

218 "Evolving artist": The *People* magazine ad ran in *Advertising Age,* September 8, 2003, p. 5.

218 "Celebrate Capitalism": celebratecapitalism.org.

218 *Community center:* Barnhart and Metcalf, p. viii.

219 "When Wal-Mart determines": Ann Woolner, "Let Me Count the Ways People Don't Love Wal-Mart," Bloomberg.com, February 13, 2004.

219 *God-centered*s: from Google, February 2004.

219 "contribute at whatever level is comfortable": WNYC-AM public radio fund drive, February 21, 2004.

219 "comfortable with new management": Douglas Jehl, "Two Top Officials Are Reported to Quit C.I.A.," *The New York Times,* November 25, 2004.

220 "If consumers feel comfortable": Lyn Chitow Oakes, "Editor's Cut: Measuring success beyond the click," www.adbanter. com/editors_cut/editors_cut_012.shtml-13k (no date).

220 "It's not an ad, it's a": I last saw the ad February 6, 2005; personals.laweekly.com/.

220 "The communities that have some importance": *Metropolis,* November 1996.

221 "You can support": heritage.org/About/Community.

221 "The talk of the town": Robert Novak, *Inside Politics,* CNN, January 27, 2003.

221 conflict of interest: " 'It's a sad commentary on politics in

Washington that a member of Congress who pushed through a major piece of legislation benefiting the drug industry gets the job leading that industry,' said Public Citizen President Joan Claybrook." William M. Welch, "Tauzin Switches Sides from Drug Industry Overseer to Lobbyist," *USA Today,* December 16, 2004.

221 took the legal heat: "If [Judith] Miller has any regrets about taking the heat for Novak, she isn't airing them." Charles Duhigg, "Robert Novak: How Does He Stay Out of Jail?" editorial, *The Los Angeles Times,* December 12, 2004.

221 "commercial real estate community": 12,800 hits on Google in April 2005.

221 "Commercial developers": William L. Hamilton, "Five Rooms, Gucci View," *The New York Times,* February 21, 2002.

222 "The word . . . has become": I interviewed Putnam for a piece I wrote about *community:* "Community Disservice," *New York,* January 27, 1997, p. 20. Most of the material on *community* comes from research I did for that piece (unless otherwise noted).

223 "One of the animating": "Fashioning the Future," *Fast Company,* February 2003, p. 16.

223 "The American Conversation": "The subtitle 'The American Conversation'—which had adorned early prototypes of the magazine—has been dropped from the cover." Alex Kuczynski, "Editor Who Thrives on Celebrity Is Pleased with Latest Sensation," *The New York Times,* July 26, 1999.

223 "Play into": American Society on Aging, www.asaging.org/networks/lgain/outword-Fall 2003.

223 Omarosa: She said it on *The Apprentice,* April 8, 2004.

224 As James Traub wrote: James Traub, "Forget Diversity," *The New York Times Magazine,* February 2, 2003, p. 15.

224 "a bit more diversity": Bob Herbert, "The Wrong Message," *The New York Times,* September 21, 2000.

224 "If you're going to keep making them": Warren St. John, "Parties Where an ID Is the Least of What You Show," *The New York Times,* January 11, 2004.

224 "empowerment" campaign: I covered this in my *Voice* columns in the 1990s. Also, as Bob Herbert wrote: "Hardly anyone found it peculiar that a company could ride a so-called women's empowerment campaign to new heights of wealth while at the same time insisting that most of its products be made by grossly underpaid women stuck in utterly powerless and often abusive circumstances." "From Sweatshops to Aerobics," *The New York Times,* June 24, 1996.

224   began on the left: "A lot of the language that we now associate with conservatism had its origin in left or liberal discourse— cf. 'bias,' 'color-blind,' 'political correctness,' 'empowerment,' and more recently 'hate speech.'" Geoffrey Nunberg in a March 11, 2004, online post to the American Dialect Society.

224   "Dana Frydman": Associated Press, "Workers Bond, Then Are Treated," *The New York Times,* October 8, 2001.

225   Some companies even spend: Dan Bischoff, "Consuming Passions," *Ms.,* December/January 2000–2001, pp. 60–65.

225   "cares little": Frank Rich, "Trump Is Firing as Fast as He Can," *The New York Times,* March 14, 2004.

225   "It's all about": first season of *The Apprentice,* February 12, 2004.

225   "Wal-Mart has been": Ashley Harrell, "Wal-Mart Donates Necessities to Soup Kitchen," BocaRatonNews.com, February 12, 2004.

225   "One of the biggest": Norm Narvaja and Calvin Jefferson, "Wal-Mart Sparks Love, Hate," *Mansfield* [Ohio] *News Journal,* February 8, 2004 (online).

225   striking grocery workers: "[The new contract] requires employees to pay for health benefits for the first time." Alex Veiga, "SoCal Grocery Workers Ratify Tentative Agreement, End Strike," MercuryNews.com, March 1, 2004.

225   "We recognize": http://www.philipmorrisinternational.com/pages/eng/ourbus/What_we_do.asp.

226   "ExxonMobil strives": www.synergos.org/globalphilanthropy/organizations/exxon.htm.

226   "Bill Jones is": Jerry Bier, "Race for Boxer's U.S. Senate seat subdued," *Fresno Bee,* February 20, 2004, p. A1.

226   *This is what [blank] looks like:* examples from Google.

226   "This is what $1,594,649.21 looks like!": www.guide2casino.com/asp/news.asp.

226   Gloria Steinem wrote: "Gloria Steinem: First Feminist," *New York,* April 6, 1998, p. 89.

226   "I Am Ann Taylor" . . . fictitious: Mercedes M. Cardona, "Largest Ever Ad Outlay: Ann Taylor Gets Back to Business," *Advertising Age,* August 9, 2004, p. 3.

226   held signs and wore T-shirts . . . "a charge that the firm": Kurt Eichenwald, "Andersen Wins an Early Trial as Date Is Set for May 6," *The New York Times,* March 21, 2002. The signs and T-shirts appear in an accompanying photo.

227   "I am Arthur Andersen": David Turnley, "Andersen 'Protesters' Exposed!" AlterNet, March 21, 2002, www.alternet.org/story/12670/.

227 "I think the issue": I was there, in March 2004.

227 Lifestyle Store: lifestylestore.com.

227 Life Style Movement: lifestyle-movement.org.uk.

227 "Candy Bites": Kate Zernike and Marian Burros, "Low-Carb Boom Isn't Just for Dieters Anymore," *The New York Times,* February 19, 2004. The package appears in an accompanying photo.

227 the LifeStyle Company: thelifestylecompany.com.

228 "counts herself": Warren St. John, "Parties Where an ID Is the Least of What You Show," *The New York Times,* January 11, 2004.

228 Redwaterlily: Redwaterlily.com, July 27, 2002.

228 "Because it's a life": cafeshops.com/lesworlds.

228 *the life* and *in the life:* See entry for *life, RHHDAS,* vol. II, p. 429.

228 Georg Simmel: Arnold Zwicky told this to William Safire, "General, No," *The New York Times Magazine,* July 20, 2003, p. 20.

228 "Community von Body-Lifestyle!": body-lifestyle.com/forum/phpBB.

228 *TalkBack Live:* I saw this sometime in the late 1990s.

229 "I am really sorry": CNN, February 4, 2004.

229 "It was not our intention": "MBNA Drops 9/11 Card," CNNfn, Money.CNN.com, March 5, 2004.

229 "The Catalina . . . philosophy": marinesource.com/builders/Catalina_Yachts/.

229 "Home Depot has": homedepot.com.

230 "God is a verb": from an untitled poem in *No More Secondhand God* (Carbondale: Southern Illinois University Press, 1963), p. 28.

230 Calvin and Hobbes: reproduced in Pinker, *Words and Rules,* p. 157.

230 "easy conversion of nouns": Pinker, *The Language Instinct,* p. 379.

230 Pinker pointed me: I think it was Pinker who suggested this, but I don't have a citation.

230 Anderson Cooper . . . "efforting": CNN, April 26, 2003.

231 Hamlet on Olde Oyster Bay: Nadine Brozan, "The High-Stakes Game of the Name," *The New York Times,* July 27, 2003, and Cara S. Trager, "Good Gates, Good Neighbors," *Newsday* (Long Island), September 20, 2002.

231 "Verb. It's what you do": information confirmed in phone interview with CDC, March 4, 2004.

231 "the campaign's corporate sponsors": Stephanie Mencimer, "A Sluggish War on Indolence: Why the Bush Ad-

ministration's Anti-obesity Campaign Is Doomed," *Slate,* August 22, 2002.

CHAPTER 8
Digit Talk in the Unit States of America

234 A man looks out: I last saw this January 22, 2004.

236 "Digital systems are based": Meyrowitz, p. 97.

237 "so honest of them": Whitehead, p. 21.

237 "What it is": Margaret Talbot, "Turned On, Tuned Out," *The New York Times Magazine,* February 16, 2003, p. 9.

238 Bischoff on *interactive*: Bischoff is the art critic for the *Star-Ledger* of New Jersey and my husband. (If you'd like to a experience a museum without a computer screen, or a corporate sponsor, in sight, go to the amazing City Museum in St. Louis; info: www.citymuseum.org.)

238 "the user in a utopian discourse": Laetitia Wilson, "Interactivity or Interpassivity: A Question of Agency in Digital Play," fineartforum.org, August 2003, http.//www.fineartforum. org/Backissues/Vol_17/faf_v17_no8/reviews/wilson.html.

239 "I've seen people": phone interview, July 2004.

239 "Still laugh-out-loud funny": "TV Best Bets," May 12, 2004, www.freep.com.

239 Numbers of Google hits for *LOL* and *lol* vs. *laugh out loud* and *laughing out loud* are as of July 2005.

240 "There is nothing more basic": George Lakoff, pp. 5–6.

241 "In today's system": Jim Hightower, "HMO Honchos Take Hypocrite's Oath," AlterNet, April 26, 2000, www.alternet. org/columnists/story/13394/.

241 "when you're so informatized": I heard Maron say this on a *Morning Sedition* rerun on October 30, 2004; the program originally aired earlier that week.

242 On the same page: on *The Apprentice,* April 18, 2004; on *Average Joe: Adam Returns,* April 5, 2004.

242 "a literal meaning": Eble phone interview, 2001.

242 "Rashomon": Lisa Yoon, CFO.com, December 5, 2002.

242 "It's a wake-up call": "Bush: Blackouts a 'Wake-Up Call,'" CBSNews.com, August 15, 2003.

243 DNA and gene: The information here is based on my research for a piece I wrote, "The New Soul," *Seed,* March/April 2003, p. 64.

244 "Imagine if you're calling": Mary Williams Walsh, "When 'May I Help You' Is a Labor Issue," *The New York Times,* August 12, 2000.

245 "A Day in the Life of a DSL Family": I received this in the spring of 2003.

245 Frank Lingua: Variants of the interview appear on several Web sites.

246 The Rock, telling MTV: May 31, 2001.

248 "advanced air management": July 2003 Grandin Road catalogue.

248 "sleep management": Adam Hochschild, "What's in a Word? Torture," *The New York Times*, Week in Review, May 23, 2004.

248 Barnhart and Metcalf write: p. 266.

248 brand consultant complained: Stuart Elliott, "Advertising: Big Plays, Surprise Heroes, Shocking Defeats and Other Super Bowl XXXIV Marketing Memories," *The New York Times*, February 1, 2000.

249 "a tremendous amount of product": "Preholiday Rush Causes Bottlenecks at Box Office," *Advertising Age*, October 8, 2001, p. 59.

249 Pat Roberts: on *Meet the Press*, July 11, 2004.

249 Ten years ago: Savan, "Stuff Love," *The Village Voice*, May 30, 1995, p. 44. As for more recent *stuffs*, I saw the Verizon line in an ad in 2003; the Gold Bond TV spot, January 20, 2005; Chef Boyardee, February 2005; the Hostess cupcake package in 2004.

250 Scott Rosenberg: in "Technospeak, Part 2: A Turnkey Solution in Every Pot," *Salon* Table Talk, February 5, 1998.

250 Ted Koppel: *Nightline*, October 18, 2001.

250 "Aggressive bundling": Kevin Drury, "Delivering Optical Ethernet Services," nortelnetworks.com, March 18, 2004.

251 "the parts of the process": American Society for Quality Web site, www.asq.org/info/glossary.

251 "value-added love": http://www.wesleyspace.net/sermons/sermon,_2004/may_2004/051604prep.html, May 16, 2004.

251 "Clive's the man": Jessica Shaw, "Idol'ing the Hours Away," *Entertainment Weekly*, June 6, 2003, p. 43.

252 "As a consequence" and "Information Is Alienated Experience": Jaron Lanier, "Agents of Alienation," *Journal of Consciousness Studies*, 2, 1995, pp. 76–81; www.cs.ucsd.edu/users/goguen/courses/171sp02/lanier.agents.html.

253 Norman Nie: See John Markoff, "A Newer, Lonelier Crowd Emerges in Internet Study," *The New York Times*, February 16, 2000.

253 Snowball.com: The ad ran in *The New York Times*, 1999.

254 interrupted with graffiti: Laura Conaway, "New York Scene,"

The Village Voice, www.villagevoice.com/issues/0422/conaway. php.

254 *The Sopranos:* from the first season, episode VIII.

254 "had become too reliant": Clive Thompson, "The 3rd Annual Year in Ideas: PowerPoint Makes You Dumb," *The New York Times Magazine,* December 14, 2003, p. 88.

255 Edward Tufte: Tufte, *The Cognitive Style of PowerPoint* (Cheshire, Conn.: Graphics Press, September 2003), pp. 3, 5, 25, and 13.

256 Shepard Smith: Warren St. John, "News Reports for Ultra-Short Attentions," *The New York Times,* March 28, 2004.

257 "Past, present, and future": Michael Kinsley, "Is Disappearing: What TV News Doing to Our Precious Verbs," *Slate,* November 1, 2001.

257 Inglish: Nunberg, p. 188.

257 "Who Scored": *Entertainment Weekly,* June 7, 1998.

257 Verizon: I received the undated mailer in 2002 or 2003.

257 "Either you are": Address to a Joint Session of Congress and the American People, September 20, 2001.

258 "we are strangely lacking": Bryson, p. 68.

258 "mode of gross dichotomy": Fussell, p. 75.

258 "the modern *versus* habit": ibid., p. 79.

259 PFOAs: Much has been written on PFOAs; see, for instance, "EPA Seeking Review on Potential Health Risks of Chemical Used in Teflon," *Life Science Weekly,* February 1, 2005, p. 598, and Environmental Working Group: www.ewg.org.

260 "This seven-member": Gina Kaufmann, "Pabst Cheer: Here's a Toast to the Blue Ribbon Press," June 3, 2004, www.pitch. com/issues/2004-06-03/ culture/seesaw_print.html.

260 *Emo, Screamo:* definitions are from Urbandictionary.com.

260 *New York Post:* This is from my memory and a torn clip from the *Post* I had for years and have since lost.

261 "We're all aware": Gustav Niebuhr, "Predicament in the Pulpit: The Christmas Eve Crowd," *The New York Times,* December 24, 1996.

261 "The impulse to shorten words": Bryson, p. 82.

261 "a fashion developed": ibid., pp. 165–66.

262 "wartime production": Barnhart and Metcalf, p. 238.

263 "Think of the happy face": Howard W. French, "Tokyo Journal: In E-Mail Wrinkle, Cell Phones Are Chatterboxes," *The New York Times,* June 8, 2000.

264 "You obviously": "You obviously don't want to use the M-word in here. And I would say fine, it's game, set, match. I understand that." From Fox News Channel transcript of Condo-

leezza Rice's testimony before the National Commission on Terrorist Attacks on April 8, 2004.

264 "Post-Monica": Edward Felsenthal and Christina Duff, "My Summer Job? Uh, Well, Ma, I Run Rackets for the Mob: Post-Monica, Interns Prefer Any Title but the 'I-Word'; Short-Skirting the Issue," *The Wall Street Journal,* June 3, 1998.

264 *Rated R: Republicans in Hollywood:* Alessandra Stanley, "In Search of Hollywood's Anti-Republican Conspiracy," *The New York Times,* September 14, 2004.

264 originally called *The R-Word:* "Also Coming This Fall: 'The R Word,' Described as 'a Democrat's Investigation into Hollywood Republican Life.' " John Carroll, "Moore Is Less," Campaign Journal, *Greater Boston,* July 2, 2004, greaterboston.tv/features/cj_20040702.html.

264 *Salon* headline: March 2, 2004.

264 "the torture word": Pentagon Press Briefing, CNN, May 4, 2004.

265 Which is one reason Kentucky Fried Chicken: Believing that emphasizing its Southern roots could boost sales, KFC announced in 2005 that it would unabbreviate its name for select stores. Some fifty remodeled restaurants would be re-renamed Kentucky Fried Chicken and would offer items like collard greens and sweet potato pies. Reuters, "Kentucky Fried Chicken reclaims its name," MSNBC.MSN.com, April 21, 2005.

265 A magazine ad: I saw the ad in *Newsweek,* Dec. 6, 2004.

266 click languages: Nicholas Wade, "Early Voices: The Leap to Language," *The New York Times,* July 15, 2003.

268 According to a Reuters survey: "Glued to the Screen: An Investigation into Information Addiction Worldwide" came out in 1997. Paul Taylor, "Dataholics Find PCs Addictive," *Financial Times,* December 10, 1997, p. 6.

268 The Michael G. Conner article is on www.crisiscounseling.com/Articles/InternetAddiction.htm. The Web page is not dated; as Conner writes, on the Internet "time begins to have no meaning."

EPILOGUE
It's Like, You Know, the End

271 "provide a stream-of-consciousness toggle switch": Dalzell, pp. 190–91.

271 "contributed to the sense of a language": Nunberg, p. 266.

271 "they're not involved": S. J. Diamond, "Like It or Not, 'Like' Is

Probably Here to Stay," *The Los Angeles Times,* August 21, 2000.

271 Jane Healy: quoted in Carrie McLaren, "Endangered Minds: An Interview with Jane Healy," *Stay Free!,* no. 18 (Spring 2001), pp. 38–39. See also article citing Healy: Jane E. Brody, "TV's Toll on Young Minds and Bodies," *The New York Times,* August 3, 2004.

BIBLIOGRAPHY

Armstrong, Nancy, and Melissa Wagner. *Field Guide to Gestures: How to Identify and Interpret Virtually Every Gesture Known to Man.* Philadelphia: Quirk Books, 2003.

Barnhart, David K., and Allan A. Metcalf. *America in So Many Words: Words That Have Shaped America.* Boston and New York: Houghton Mifflin, 1997.

Barry, Dave. *Dave Barry's Complete Guide to Guys.* New York: Random House, 1995.

Baugh, John. *Beyond Ebonics: Linguistic Pride and Racial Prejudice.* New York and Oxford: Oxford University Press, 2000.

Brasch, Walter M. *Black English and the Mass Media.* Lanham, N.Y., and London: University Press of America, 1981.

Bryson, Bill. *The Mother Tongue: English and How It Got That Way.* New York: Avon Books, 1990.

Claiborne, Robert. *Our Marvelous Native Tongue: The Life and Times of the English Language.* New York: Times Books, 1983.

Crystal, David. *The Cambridge Encyclopedia of the English Language.* Cambridge, England: Cambridge University Press, 1995.

———. *The Cambridge Encyclopedia of Language* (2nd ed.). Cambridge, England: Cambridge University Press, 1997.

Dalzell, Tom. *Flappers 2 Rappers: American Youth Slang.* Springfield, Mass.: Merriam-Webster, 1996.

DiBattista, Maria. *Fast-Talking Dames.* New Haven and London: Yale University Press, 2001.

Dillard, J. L. *All-American English.* New York: Random House, 1975.

———. *Black English: Its History and Usage in the United States.* New York: Vintage Books, 1973.

Folb, Edith A. *Runnin' Down Some Lines: The Language and Culture of*

Black Teenagers. Cambridge, Mass.: Harvard University Press, 1980.

Frank, Thomas. *The Conquest of Cool: Business Culture, Counterculture, and the Rise of Hip Consumerism.* Chicago: University of Chicago Press, 1997.

———— and Matt Weiland, eds. *Commodify Your Dissent: Salvos from The Baffler.* New York: W. W. Norton & Company, 1997.

Fussell, Paul. *The Great War and Modern Memory.* New York and Oxford: Oxford University Press, 1975, 2000.

Greenblatt, Stephen. *Will in the World: How Shakespeare Became Shakespeare.* New York: W. W. Norton, 2004.

Gross, Kenneth. *Shakespeare's Noise.* Chicago: University of Chicago Press, 2001.

Haiman, John. *Talk Is Cheap: Sarcasm, Alienation, and the Evolution of Language.* New York and Oxford: Oxford University Press, 1998.

Healy, Jane M. *Endangered Minds: Why Children Don't Think—and What We Can Do About It.* New York: Touchstone, 1990.

Jones, Gerard. *Honey, I'm Home!: Sitcoms: Selling the American Dream.* New York: Grove Weidenfeld, 1992.

Lakoff, George. *Women, Fire and Dangerous Things.* Chicago: University of Chicago Press, 1987.

Lakoff, Robin Tolmach. *The Language War.* Berkeley, Calif.: University of California Press, 2001.

Lee, Margaret. "Out of the Hood and into the News: Borrowed Black Verbal Expressions in a Mainstream Newspaper." *American Speech,* vol. 74, no. 4 (1999).

Lighter, J. E., ed., vol. I (1994), vol. II (1997) of *Random House Historical Dictionary of American Slang.* New York: Random House.

Mackay, Charles. *Memoirs of Extraordinary Popular Delusions.* London: Richard Bentley, New Burlington Street, 1841; reprinted as *Extraordinary Popular Delusions & the Madness of Crowds.* New York: Crown, 1980.

McCrum, Robert, William Cran, and Robert MacNeil. *The Story of English* (revised ed.). New York: Penguin Books, 1987.

McWhorter, John H. *Losing the Race: Self-Sabotage in Black America.* New York: The Free Press, 2000.

Metcalf, Allan. *How We Talk: American Regional English Today.* Boston and New York: Houghton Mifflin, 2000.

Meyrowitz, Joshua. *No Sense of Place: The Impact of Electronic Media on Social Behavior.* New York and Oxford: Oxford University Press, 1985.

Miller, Mark Crispin. *Boxed In: The Culture of TV.* Evanston, Ill.: Northwestern University Press, 1988.

Bibliography

Moore, Michael. *Dude, Where's My Country?* New York: Warner Books, 2003.

Morris, Desmond. *Bodytalk: The Meaning of Human Gestures.* New York: Crown, 1994.

———, Peter Collett, Peter Marsh, and Marie O'Shaughnessy. *Gestures: Their Origins and Distribution.* New York: Stein & Day, 1979.

Nunberg, Geoffrey. *Going Nucular: Language, Politics, and Culture in Confrontational Times.* New York: PublicAffairs, 2004.

Pinker, Steven. *The Language Instinct: How the Mind Creates Language.* New York: HarperPerennial, 1994, 1995.

———. *Words and Rules: The Ingredients of Language.* New York: Basic Books, 1999.

Postman, Neil. *Amusing Ourselves to Death: Public Discourse in the Age of Show Business.* New York: Viking Penguin, 1985.

Powell, Kevin, ed. *Step into a World: A Global Anthology of the New Black Literature.* New York: John Wiley & Sons, 2000.

Purdy, Jedediah. *For Common Things: Irony, Trust, and Commitment in America Today.* New York: Alfred A. Knopf, 1999.

Putnam, Robert D. *Bowling Alone: The Collapse and Revival of American Community.* New York: Simon & Schuster, 2000.

Rickford, John Russell, and Russell John Rickford. *Spoken Soul: The Story of Black English.* New York: John Wiley & Sons, 2000.

Rose, Tricia. *Black Noise: Rap Music and Black Culture in Contemporary America.* Hanover, N.H.: Wesleyan University Press/University Press of New England, 1994.

Rosen, R. D. *Psychobabble: Fast Talk and Quick Cure in the Era of Feeling.* New York: Atheneum, 1977.

Rosten, Leo. *The Joys of Yiddish.* New York: Pocket Books, 1970.

Savan, Leslie. *The Sponsored Life: Ads, TV, and American Culture.* Philadelphia: Temple University Press, 1994.

Scotti, Anna, and Paul Young. *Buzzwords: L.A. Freshspeak.* New York: St. Martin's Press, 1997.

Sheidlower, Jesse. *The F-Word* (2nd ed.). New York: Random House Reference, 1999.

Shelton, Jo-Ann. *As the Romans Did: A Sourcebook in Roman Social History.* New York and Oxford: Oxford University Press, 1997.

Sherwin, Richard K. *When Law Goes Pop: The Vanishing Line Between Law and Popular Culture.* Chicago: University of Chicago Press, 2000.

Shorris, Earl. *A Nation of Salesmen: The Tyranny of the Market and the Subversion of Culture.* New York: W. W. Norton & Company, 1994.

Smitherman, Geneva. *Black Talk: Words and Phrases from the Hood to the Amen Corner* (revised ed.). Boston and New York: Houghton Mifflin, 2000.

————. *Talkin That Talk: Language, Culture, and Education in African America.* London and New York: Routledge, 2000.

Tannen, Deborah. *The Argument Culture: Moving from Debate to Dialogue.* New York: Random House, 1998.

Tate, Greg, ed. *Everything But the Burden: What White People Are Taking from Black Culture.* New York: Broadway Books, 2003.

Tenner, Edward. *Why Things Bite Back: Technology and the Revenge of Unintended Consequences.* New York: Alfred A. Knopf, 1996.

Trudgill, Peter. *On Dialect: Social and Geographical Perspectives.* New York and London: New York University Press, 1983.

————. *Sociolinguistics: An Introduction to Language and Society* (revised ed.). New York: Penguin Books, 1995.

Twain, Mark. *Roughing It* (1872). New York and Oxford: Oxford University Press, 1996.

Wallace, David Foster. *A Supposedly Fun Thing I'll Never Do Again: Essays and Arguments.* Boston: Little, Brown, 1997.

Whitehead, Colson. *John Henry Days.* New York: Anchor Books, 2001.

Woodward, Bob. *Plan of Attack.* New York: Simon & Schuster, 2004.

ACKNOWLEDGMENTS

I went into this project with no special knowledge or academic background in language or linguistics. Always there to guide me was Tom Dalzell. In addition to bringing me up to speed on slang and its history, relating it to pop, and graciously reading this book, Tom became my friend. I'm also very grateful to another friend, Carrie McLaren, writer, activist, and publisher of the kick-ass magazine *Stay Free!*, which unmasks marketing in all its forms. Our many discussions about commercialism and language—and her frequent pop-word alerts—were instrumental to this book.

Taking me through the history of sitcoms, Gerard Jones was generous with his time and ideas, even while working on books of his own. Though they surely don't know how much they've helped me, I want to also thank everyone on the American Dialect Society online discussion group, where I lurked, learned, and occasionally asked questions. One ADS guy who should know how much he helped me is Jesse Sheidlower, editor-at-large of the *Oxford English Dictionary*. Early on in this project, Jesse deftly sketched in the large language picture and helped me to put pop in perspective.

Whether for their word tips or jokes, for reading parts of the book, or for showing interest when I went on about it, I want to thank Allen Barra, Nancy Cardozo, Marc Cooper, Sheenah Hankin, Emily Hubley, Mark Jacobson, Jeff Z. Klein, Kevin Jon Klein, Stephen Kolozsvary, Barbara O'Dair, Kathy Rich, Will Rosenthal, Sadie, Ilena Silverman, Pate Skene, and the gals in my Jersey writing group. I'm especially grateful to Lisa Jones, for helping me through self-doubts, and to Darlene Vander Hoop, my oldest (in the good sense) best friend, for all the times we spoke and I said, "Wait. Let me write that down," regarding some pop distillation of a complexity. To all of you: I owe you, man.

Parts of this book appeared earlier in a number of publications, but two deserve special mention. Writing about advertising for *The Village Voice* woke me up to the power of commercialized language. Most of my *Voice* columns that focused on favored phrases in ads were made immeasurably better by two friends and former editors there, Andy Hsiao and Jeff Salamon. When I pulled some ideas on pop language together and knocked on *Time* magazine's door, Mark Alan Stamaty and Bruce Handy opened it for me; when I said to Jim Kelly, "Trust me," he said, in effect, "Go for it." The resulting essay, "Yadda, Yadda, Yadda," is the core of this book.

I never would have written a book were it not for my friend and agent, Susan Ramer, who educated me on proposal writing, nursed me through the process, and helped me move from kicking and screaming about writing a book to actually doing it. Jon Segal, my editor, immediately got it, no translation needed. Jon has made my writing sharper, prodded me to go deeper, and, from the beginning, gave me one of the best gifts a writer could have: the encouragement to use my full range, including the crazy part. Jon's patience has been extraordinary, and every time we spoke, I felt calmer. Ida Giragossian and Lydia Buechler at Knopf have been a pleasure to work with.

My family has shaped this book in untold ways. As my stepmother, Barbara Savan, read bits and pieces over the years, her enthusiasm helped my confidence enormously. My father, Sid Savan, has always been completely supportive. His pride and belief in my brother and me taught us that we could do much more than we expected. We both became writers; Glenn was a novelist. I don't have words for how much I miss him. Even while Parkinson's disease was destroying his body, Glenn's humor and intelligence never left him. Once, after spending twenty minutes looking for the right metaphor, I called him; he thought for a second and supplied it. A true lover of words and the life of the mind, Glenn took immense pleasure in my writing a book about language. This book is a tribute to him.

My son, Boone, has lived his entire life with me working on this project. As he began to discover language, I saw the extra excitement with which he'd repeat a phrase from a TV show or commercial. I felt a mixture of pride and dismay when I overheard him at five years old correct a four-year-old friend: "It's not 'Don't think about it.' It's 'Don't *even* think about it.'" He eventually learned that I was writing about exactly such phrases, and he has delighted in teasing me with them ever since.

Above all, I want to acknowledge the massive contributions of my husband, Dan Bischoff. Dan read every word, often many times,

Acknowledgments

and saved me from innumerable embarrassments. More important, we think together, especially about politics, both national and individual. To Dan I owe the concept of the transactional "Person Nouvelle." I put it in French, but it was Dan who stepped up, thought outside the box, and realized that there was a new kind of person who needed a new kind of language. And so when I write that my loved ones are nouvelles, these are the people I mean.

INDEX

Index

Index

Index

Index

Index

Index

Index

PERMISSIONS ACKNOWLEDGMENTS

Grateful acknowledgment is made to the following for permission to reprint previously published material:

Clear Channel Communications, Inc.: Excerpt from "Would you have any Grey Poupon, Monsieur Kerry?" by Rush Limbaugh from www. rushlimbaugh.com (August 13, 2003).

The Conde Nast Publications, Inc.: Excerpts from John Ellis from "George W.'s Cousin" by Jane Mayer from *The New Yorker* (November 20, 2000). Reprinted courtesy of *The New Yorker* and The Conde Nast Publications, Inc.

Copyright Clearance Center: Excerpts from "Kids Say the Darndest Things in . . ." by Solange De Santis from *The Wall Street Journal Eastern Edition* (March 25, 1998). Copyright © 1998 by Dow Jones & Co. Inc. Reprinted by permission of Dow Jones & Co. Inc. in the format trade book via Copyright Clearance Center.

Tom Dalzell: Excerpts from *Flappers 2 Rappers* by Tom Dalzell. Reprinted by permission of the author.

Dan Danbom: Excerpt from "Interview with Frank Lingua" by Dan Danbom. Copyright © by Dan Danbom. Reprinted by permission of the author.

The Estate of R. Buckminster Fuller: Excerpt from the poem "God Is a Verb" from *I Seem to Be a Verb* by R. Buckminster Fuller. Copyright © The Estate of R. Buckminster Fuller. Reprinted by permission of The Estate of R. Buckminster Fuller.

Houghton Mifflin Company: Excerpts from *Black Talk: Words and Phrases from the Hood to Amen Corner* revised edition by Geneva Smitherman. Copyright © 1994, 2000 by Geneva Smitherman. All rights reserved. Reprinted by permission of Houghton Mifflin Company.

John Wiley & Sons, Inc.: Excerpts from *The Spoken Soul* by John Russell Rickford and Russell John Rickford. Copyright © 2000 by John Russell

Rickford and Russell John Rickford. Reprinted by permission of John Wiley & Sons, Inc.

Journal of Consciousness Studies: Excerpt from "Agents of Alienation" by Jaron Lanier from *Journal of Consciousness Studies* 2 (1995). Reprinted by permission of the *Journal of Consciousness Studies.*

Carrie McLaren: Excerpts from "Endangered Minds" by Carrie McLaren from *Stay Free! Magazine* (Spring 2001, #18). Reprinted by permission of the author.

The New York Times Agency: Excerpts from "When 'May I Help You' Is a Labor Issue" by Mary Walsh from *The New York Times* (August 12, 2000). Excerpts from "Was Freud a Minivan or S.U.V. Kind of Guy?" by Keith V. Bradsher from *The New York Times* (July 17, 2000). Copyright © 2000 by The New York Times Co. Excerpts from "Early Voices: The Leap to Language" by Nicholas M. Wade from *The New York Times* (July 15, 2003). Copyright © 2003 by The New York Times Co. Excerpts from "Today's Kids Are, Like, Killing the English Language" by Kirk L. Johnson from *The New York Times* (August 9, 1998). Copyright © 1998 by The New York Times Co. Reprinted by permission of The New York Times Agency.

The New York Times Magazine: Excerpts from "Man's Best Friend" by Peter De Jonge from *The New York Times Magazine* (July 21, 2002). Copyright © 2002 by Peter De Jonge. Reprinted by permission of *The New York Times Magazine.*

Newsweek: Excerpt from "How Bush Did It" by Evan Thomas from *Newsweek* (November 15, 2004). Copyright © 2004 by Newsweek, Inc. Excerpts from "Don't Say It" by Periscope from *Newsweek* (February 3, 1997). Copyright © 1997 by Newsweek, Inc. All rights reserved. Reprinted by permission of *Newsweek.*

Geoffrey Nunberg: Excerpt from listserve response dated March 11, 2004, by Geoffrey Nunberg. Reprinted by permission of the author.

Oxford University Press, Inc.: Excerpts from *The Great War and Modern Memory* by Paul Fussell. Copyright © 1975 by Oxford University Press, Inc.

PR Watch: Excerpt from "Food Flacks Say" by Joel Bleifuss from *PR Watch* (Fourth Quarter, 1996). Reprinted by permission of *PR Watch.*

The PRW Newsletter: Excerpt from "Make Every Word Count in Press Release Headings" from *The PRW Newsletter* (April 19, 2000). Reprinted by permission of *The PRW Newsletter,* Press-release-writing.com, www.press-release-writing.com.

Salon.com: Excerpts from "Irony is Dead! Long Live Irony!" by David Beers from Salon.com (September 25, 2001). Reprinted by permission of Salon.com.

The Village Voice: Excerpts from articles by Leslie Savan. Copyright © 1985–1997 by Village Voice Media, Inc. Reprinted by permission of *The Village Voice.*

The Vocabula Review: Excerpt from "DisenYOUGUYSingAmerican English," by jjoan ttaber from *The Vocabula Review* (April 2003). Reprinted by permission of *The Vocabula Review* (www.vocabulareview.com), an on-line journal dedicated to the correct and elegant use of the English language.

A NOTE ABOUT THE AUTHOR

Leslie Savan wrote a column about advertising for *The Village Voice* for thirteen years and was a finalist for the Pulitzer Prize in criticism three times. Her columns are collected in her first book, *The Sponsored Life: Ads, TV, and American Culture.* Her work has also appeared in *Time, The New Yorker, New York, The New York Times,* and other publications. She lives in New Jersey with her husband and son.

A NOTE ON THE TYPE

This book was set in a type called Baskerville. The face itself is a facsimile reproduction of types cast from the molds made for John Baskerville (1706–75) from his designs. Baskerville's original face was one of the forerunners of the type style known to printers as "modern face"—a "modern" of the period A.D. 1800.

Composed by Creative Graphics,
Allentown, Pennsylvania

Printed and bound by Berryville Graphics,
Berryville, Virginia

Designed by Soonyoung Kwon